*Peerless among Princes*

# Peerless Among Princes

## The Life and Times of Sultan Süleyman

KAYA ŞAHİN

OXFORD
UNIVERSITY PRESS

# OXFORD
## UNIVERSITY PRESS

Oxford University Press is a department of the University of Oxford. It furthers
the University's objective of excellence in research, scholarship, and education
by publishing worldwide. Oxford is a registered trade mark of Oxford University
Press in the UK and certain other countries.

Published in the United States of America by Oxford University Press
198 Madison Avenue, New York, NY 10016, United States of America.

© Oxford University Press 2023

CIP data is on file at the Library of Congress
ISBN 978–0–19–753163–1

DOI: 10.1093/oso/9780197531631.001.0001

1 3 5 7 9 8 6 4 2
Printed by Sheridan Books, Inc., United States of America

# Contents

Acknowledgments                                                          vii

Note on Usage                                                            xi

Introduction                                                             1

1. The Family Story: The Ottomans before Süleyman                        8

2. Childhood and Adolescence: Raising a Prince, 1494/5–1509             36

3. Apprenticeship: Service as District Governor, 1509–20                63

4. Ascent: The First Years on the Throne, 1520–25                       97

5. Growth: A New Imperial Vision, 1525–33                               133

6. Maturation: The Middle Years, 1533–53                                177

7. Old Age: The Final Years, 1553–66                                    228

Conclusion: Legacies                                                    272

Notes                                                                   279

Bibliography                                                            331

Index                                                                   357

# *Acknowledgments*

THE JOURNEY OF this book began with a phone call from Bonnie Smith more than six years ago. Having read my first book, which dealt with empire-building during the reign of Süleyman, Bonnie wanted me to write a biography of the sultan. I was initially cautious about writing the biography of a "great man," and I also wondered about whether there was an audience for such a project. Bonnie's reassurance was comforting and convincing, and I slowly started working on a first version under her guidance. That first version was supposed to be a short book, with a minimum of notes, geared toward a student audience. I was done after three years, working during breaks and summer holidays. However, due to the vicissitudes of the publishing world, there came a point when it felt like the short book I wrote would be doomed to a desk drawer, or rather a corner of a computer hard drive.

Susan Ferber, my editor at Oxford University Press, entered the picture at that critical point. She took on the project and immediately came up with the idea of expanding the short book into a much larger one. Thanks to her guidance, and the two wonderfully detailed anonymous review reports she obtained, I started working on a new version. Susan was kind enough to read and profusely comment on everything I wrote; her suggestions, and the generous comments of another anonymous reviewer, helped me finalize the book you now have in your hands or on the screen of your electronic device.

I could not have written this book in a vacuum. I was fortunate to rely on the help and support of a group of fellow historians and good friends, whose scholarship and collegiality were instrumental in improving the book. They read and commented upon various versions, helped me obtain research materials that were hard to locate, discussed some general and some very arcane matters pertaining to Ottoman history, and unanimously offered their encouragement. I mention their names in alphabetical order of their surnames here, aware that this does not come even remotely close to thanking them appropriately: Gabor Ágoston, Nikolay Antov, Ahmet Arslantürk, Hall Bjørnstad, Günhan Börekçi, Erdem Çıpa, Sinem Eryılmaz, Emine Fetvacı, Vural Genç, Christopher Markiewicz, Kevin Meskill, Nedim Nomer, Burak Onaran, Kahraman Şakul, Murat Şiviloğlu, Ralph Walter, Zeynep Yelçe. Halil Dilek, the late Saltuk Dönmez, Işıl Ertüzün, Murat Arayıcı, Müge Gürsoy, and Semih Sökmen lent their expertise in medicine, psychology, and publishing. Defne Halman kindly gave permission to use translations of Süleyman's poetry by the late Talât Sait Halman.

Talking about encouragement, I want to particularly mention two senior colleagues whose exemplary work has been a guiding light for so many Ottomanists and scholars of Islamic societies. At a critical turning point in the writing process, Gülru Necipoğlu offered extremely useful insights on the task of writing a biography of Süleyman. Feridun Emecen generously shared a copy of his own biography of Süleyman before its publication and commented on my manuscript. I am very grateful to both for their support.

Even in a research-focused institution, like my current home, Indiana University Bloomington, teaching and administrative service occupy the bulk of an academic's time. Research and writing almost always require additional support. I conducted extensive research and began writing the final draft in 2019–20, thanks to a New Frontiers of Creativity and Scholarship Grant and a sabbatical semester. A new office provided by the Hamilton Lugar School of Global and International Studies allowed me to work particularly productively. I finished the final draft during the academic year 2020–21 as a fellow of the Swedish Collegium for Advanced Study in Uppsala, a true refuge for scholars. Wendy Gamber, then chair of the Department of History at Indiana University, was my advocate and guide in navigating the bureaucratic details of these leaves, and the Office of the Vice Provost for Research offered additional financial help. I began the final stage of my writing in December 2021–January 2022 as a senior fellow at the Leibniz Institute for European History (IEG) in Mainz. While working on revisions in 2022, I was helped by a course release provided to me as the director of the Islamic Studies Program. The book's production has been supported by grants from the College Arts and Humanities Institute, the Office of the Vice Provost for Research, and the Indiana University Presidential Arts and Humanities program. Michael McGerr, who has been a mentor and a friend since I came to Bloomington, constantly offered valuable advice on how to deal with the challenges of academic life

Staff at many research institutions, from directors to librarians, archivists, and others, helped me access their collections, locate manuscripts, and obtain high-quality images, among other things. I am particularly grateful to staff at the Ottoman State Archives, the Süleymaniye Library, and the Topkapı Museum Archive and Library in Istanbul, the Herman B Wells Library and the Lilly Library in Bloomington, the Austrian National Library in Vienna, the Uppsala University Library, the Chester Beatty Library in Dublin, and the British Museum.

As I kept working on this book over the years, it became clearer at every turn that I could not have written it without the work of generations of colleagues, who helped elevate the study of the Ottoman Empire from a pursuit deter-mined by Orientalist and Eurocentric cliches to a multilingual, multidiscipli-nary field. I was lucky to study with one those transformational figures as a graduate student at the University of Chicago, Cornell H. Fleischer, whose unsurpassable knowledge in all things Süleymanic has been a source of inspi-ration and learning for over two decades.

Any work of history owes a debt to the record keepers and history writers of the past. We do not admit enough, however, that the mighty empires on which we write were built on the labor of millions of peasants, artisans, shopkeepers, merchants, and slaves, without whom figures like Süleyman would not and could not have existed.

My last thank you note is addressed to Rita Koryan. Ever since Bonnie's phone call, Rita enthusiastically espoused the idea of having this biography written, even though it meant that we had to sacrifice almost all our free time to do it. From the first page on, she read and commented upon everything I wrote, traveled with me to Uppsala and Mainz in the middle of a pandemic, and suffered the dark moods and the moments of despair that accompany the writing process. She is the toughest travel companion, the most meticulous copy editor, and the most supportive partner I could ever hope to encounter. I cannot repay her, which she knows, but she does not mind.

# *Note on Usage*

DURING SÜLEYMAN'S LIFETIME, the Ottomans wrote in the Arabic alphabet and used the Hijri calendar, which is based on the lunar year and whose beginning corresponds to July 16, 622 CE. A book of Ottoman history written in English needs to make multiple accommodations, and these are explained below.

The Hijri dates of the Ottoman sources are provided in their Common Era equivalents throughout the book. Wherever Hijri dates are also given, as in the section about Süleyman's date of birth, these are necessary for clarity in the discussion.

For personal names, place names, and other words in Ottoman, I use the post-1928 modern Turkish spelling with Latin characters. I refrain from special characters such as â and î unless they are needed to distinguish between two words that would otherwise look like homonyms. For Arabic and Persian, from Quranic passages to personal and place names, I similarly use a simplified transliteration into Latin characters, without any diacritical marks.

It is difficult to find perfect English equivalents for many Ottoman words. In order to emphasize their specificity, certain terms, like *tımar* or *sipahi*, are used as is. They are italicized to mark their difference from the surrounding English text. Their meaning is provided the first time they are mentioned in the book. Many other Ottoman and Arabic words that have Anglicized forms, such as dervish, Sharia, Quran, and vizier, are used in that form.

Place names follow similar conventions. For cities and towns within the boundaries of the Republic of Turkey today, I use their modern Turkish spellings. Place names in the Middle East and Europe, such as Aleppo, Belgrade, Sofia, or Baghdad, are used in their Anglicized form. When it is necessary to distinguish between an Ottoman place name and, for instance, a Hungarian name for the same location, both are provided the first time that particular place is mentioned.

Careful readers will realize that there are slightly different spellings for certain authors or certain works in the notes and the bibliography. This is because I follow the original spelling of editors and publishers. For published and manuscript works written with Arabic characters, I use a simplified Latinization in the notes. In the bibliography, I provide a full transliteration with diacritical marks of the author's name and the work's title.

I prefer Constantinople to Istanbul for a specific reason. Ottomans from different linguistic communities and social classes referred to the city with various names. The City of Constantine, *Kostantiniyye*, was one that was commonly used in everyday language as well as official usage. Constantinople is the word that best matches that multi-lingual, multi-cultural consensus and the historical usage.

While discussing matters of finance, pay, and revenue, I use the *akçe* of the original Ottoman sources as a currency. During Süleyman's lifetime, an *akçe* corresponded approximately to 0.7 grams of silver.

*Peerless among Princes*

# Introduction

STARTING WITH THE early 1540s, everything around Süleyman reminded him that he was entering old age. There were grey flecks in his beard and hair. He got gout, whose debilitating pain affected him more and more despite his physicians' aggressive treatments. There were persistent, ever-growing rumors about him being replaced by one of his sons. He felt increasingly lonely. His tutor Hayreddin, his constant companion since adolescence, died. His favorite son Mehmed succumbed to a contagious disease at the tender age of twenty-one.

His political life was filled with frustrations as well. In his early years on the throne, he had dreamed of subjugating all his enemies, and ruling over east and west with justice. After many long and costly campaigns, what he had was a stalemate on both fronts, as his Habsburg and Safavid rivals initially retreated then regrouped. As for his allies, such as the anti-Habsburg Hungarians and the French, he thought they were weak, uncommitted, unreliable.

Süleyman became an angry man. He openly scolded foreign envoys during audiences, abandoning his usually austere demeanor. He more and more consulted a geomancer to find out whether his health would improve, he would be able to remain on the throne, and he could conduct his armies to victory. His life became even more complicated in the 1550s. He ordered the execution of a son on the suspicion of rebellion. A few years later, another son rebelled, was defeated, escaped to Iran, and was executed there on his instructions. All along, Süleyman's health continued to worsen. Then his beloved wife Hürrem died. The empire he had expanded and the bureaucratic machinery he had helped build suffered from over-extension. Social and economic problems persisted, becoming increasingly more difficult to ignore as casual or haphazard occurrences.

Süleyman created a self-curated legacy in this environment. He ordered the building of a major charitable complex centered around a mosque in Constantinople. He dotted the entire realm with signs of his charity and wealth, from bridges to waystations for pilgrims, from aqueducts to city walls, and from prayer houses large and small to soup kitchens. As a lifelong reader and composer of poetry, he gathered his compositions together to leave behind his voice, perhaps the most intimate part of his legacy. He also decided to have the story of his reign written from his own perspective. The result was a lavishly illustrated history in versified Persian, called *Sulaymannama* ("The Book of Süleyman"). It described three and a half decades of Süleyman's sultanate, from his accession in 1520 to the mid-1550s.[1] The work was composed by a court historian, calligraphed by a scribe, and decorated by artists.

The *Sulaymannama* remains the most comprehensive political and cultural statement produced by an Ottoman sultan under his personal supervision, even though it stops short of covering the events of Süleyman's last decade in power. It monumentalizes the period between 1520 and 1555 as an exceptional time in Ottoman, indeed human, history. Throughout its pages, Süleyman receives the submission of foreign rulers, rides to war, hunts, captures cities and regions, and is entertained by servants and musicians. His enemies ineptly conspire against him and eventually bring about their own ruin. He barely grows old from painting to painting, and his glory never wanes. This is the image he wanted to leave to posterity.

For scholars working on Süleyman's life and reign, his multifaceted legacy offers a unique opportunity. Very few pre-modern rulers, Ottoman or other, left behind such a detailed, sophisticated body of evidence to make sure they would be remembered in a particular way. At the same time, this legacy is a challenge. How do we surmount its obvious biases, its willful ignorance of certain individuals and events, its re-writing of the historical record?

Thankfully, there is answer to this question. Süleyman's ambitious imperial agenda inspired many, within and beyond the Ottoman domains, to write and comment on his actions in a variety of languages, from Ottoman, Arabic, and Persian to Italian, French, German, and more. We have works of history that extend from campaign narratives to regnal, dynastic, and universal chronicles. We have pieces of official correspondence among rulers, diplomatic reports, poems, propaganda tracts, newsletters, woodcuts, broadsheets, and religious treatises that broadcast Süleyman's activities, image, and voice from western Europe to central and southeast Asia. We have documents produced by the Ottoman bureaucracy, from expense registers and records of the imperial council's proceedings to land surveys and law codes. Correspondence

FIG. 1.1 Süleyman receives a Safavid envoy. The panel above his head reads, in Arabic, "The sultan is the Shadow of God [on Earth]." Detail from *Sulaymannama*, 332a. Courtesy of the T.C. Cumhurbaşkanlığı Milli Saraylar İdaresi Başkanlığı.

between Süleyman and members of his family, and the extensive body of poetry he wrote, give glimpses of his personal life. Thus, there is sufficient documentation, in terms of both volume and variety, that allows us to tell a broader story than the one Süleyman meant to leave behind and that previous biographers have been able to tell.[2]

Why write another biography of Süleyman? That question has a long, but hopefully comprehensive and convincing, answer. Revisiting Süleyman's life by bringing together the rich body of evidence mentioned above and the methods and approaches of modern historical scholarship produces an intriguing story of empire-building and institutionalization at the time of the Renaissance, a critical turning point in European and global history. During his reign, the Ottoman realm expanded significantly beyond the Ottomans' power base in Anatolia and the Balkans. Süleyman received dispatches from rulers stretching from France to southeast Asia. He personally traveled long distances throughout southeastern and central Europe, Anatolia, and the Middle East. His fleets sailed across the Mediterranean and into the Indian Ocean, and his armies marched into the Caucasus, Yemen, Hungary, and Austria. *Kanun*, Ottoman dynastic law, was promoted as the best instrument for the equitable management of a multireligious, multilinguistic empire. Ottoman bureaucracy grew from a small group of scribes into a sizeable institution with separate branches that dealt with administrative and financial matters. The promotion of Sunni Muslim orthodoxy against the Christians in Europe and the Shiites in the Middle East became both a doctrinal and a political and cultural concern for the Ottoman elite.

Moreover, the story of Süleyman not only contributes to our understanding of Ottoman history, but also to European, Middle Eastern, Eurasian, and world history. Süleyman was contemporaries with figures similar to him, who either inherited dynastic enterprises that they subsequently expanded or built them themselves. These included Charles V, Francis I and Henry VIII in Europe, Shah Ismail and Shah Tahmasb in Iran, Ivan IV in Russia, and Babur and Akbar in India. Like Süleyman, these figures resorted to warfare as an instrument of empire building, while they sought to establish control over their own elites and aristocracies, with whom they competed over available resources. They all paid particular attention to creating and maintaining a multilayered reputation as ruler, patron, soldier, statesman, etc. They all sought to establish central control over religious matters during a time of intense theological debates and spiritual anxieties. They were also acutely aware of each other, and they openly competed among themselves for control of land and resources and for prestige.

In the coming centuries, the global perspectives of sixteenth-century rulers were increasingly erased. Especially in the age of the nation-state and European political and economic domination, from the early decades of the nineteenth century onward, non-Western figures like Süleyman have been pushed into irrelevance. For instance, two recent and extremely accomplished biographies of Charles V barely mention Süleyman, even though Charles' own historians and bureaucrats left behind ample evidence to show that the Holy Roman Emperor was intensely preoccupied with Süleyman's actions.[3] As a result, another task of this biography is to restore Süleyman's place among the major figures of the sixteenth century. This is not a simple matter of doing justice to Süleyman and his legacy. Rather, it is about advocating for a more complete story of modernity, from the rise of a new form of commercial capitalism to the emergence of new kinds of states and bureaucracies, which cannot be fully told without including non-Western actors.

In the midst of it all, there is also an individual who has to be rescued from underneath the weight of history, as much as that is possible. This is the reason why Süleyman's early life, including his education and political formation, are given considerable coverage in this book. He spent a difficult childhood and adolescence under the supervision of an overbearing father. He witnessed violent succession struggles in his late teens. He lived under the shadow of near-certain death because Ottoman dynastic practice justified fratricide in order to preserve the unity of the realm. The tensions and challenges of his early years are typically erased from the story of his life. Even after he came to the throne, seemingly all powerful, he had to surmount his image as an inexperienced prince, establish a martial reputation, and attend to family matters.

Süleyman's biography is an opportunity to highlight the fact that, even in strong monarchical regimes, the exercise of political power required considerable personal effort, which rendered it open to scrutiny and criticism. Süleyman had to make decisions that pertained to the empire's management, in the company of his viziers and high officials. As the ultimate decision-maker about appointments, he had to find skilled people to assist him in his efforts. He had to keep himself informed about everyday affairs, proceedings of the imperial council, tensions within the ruling elite, and myriad other tidbits of knowledge and gossip. As the largest landowner and the wealthiest individual in the empire, he had to ensure that his properties were well managed, and fulfill his duties toward the public in the form of charity. He had to carefully choreograph his relationship with everyone from his palace servants to the members of the civilian population he encountered on all occasions, from

Friday prayer processions to military campaigns. The personal dimension of sovereignty preoccupied him constantly, to the point of wearing him down in his later years. In old age, devastated by gout and digestive issues, he still had to personally lead his army to besiege a minor castle, to prove that he was healthy enough, powerful enough, sultan enough, to remain on the throne.

Süleyman's personality had many traits that are recognizable in the present day. Like many men of his time as well as ours, having grown up in a patriarchal culture, he was buoyant, ambitious, and hopeful in youth, sober and a tad depressed in middle age, and pious and cautious in old age. He ensured good educations for his children, especially his sons. He kept an eye on them as they grew up in the palace, as well as later, when they served as district governors. He had a close relationship with his mother and his tutor, both of whom were constant presences during the first half of his life. He had an affectionate relationship with his wife Hürrem. He sought friendships with individuals in whom he saw a particular spark, from personal charm to profound learning. At times, he looks like someone who sought the small comforts of the life of a paterfamilias in the midst of a tumultuous, unpredictable, violent world.

This is where it becomes possible, indeed tempting, to romanticize him and to humanize political and economic power through his example. Many popularizing narratives, which have existed since the late sixteenth century, have adopted this approach. Similar narratives continue to be produced today, in the form of television shows and journalistic accounts. The lure to normalize Süleyman is strong. As a work of historical biography, however, this book must stress that that he did live five centuries earlier and that we cannot always assume emotional commensurability. He will remain at least partly unknown to us, a familiar stranger.

Indeed, there are other aspects of his life that render him and his experience significantly different from ours, which should caution us against a strong identification or sympathy. It is true, for instance, that he led an affectionate relationship with his wife Hürrem. However, he met her as a slave, as part of his duty to produce heirs for the perpetuation of the dynasty. The fact that the two were able to establish a family life of sorts within a palace household and a political system that traditionally did not leave room for such a possibility is remarkable. At the same time, he was unable to shield his sons from the fate that awaited the men of the Ottoman dynasty: civil war and death, until only one heir survived. This gave his life, particularly his last decades, the quality of a Shakespearean tragedy.

Süleyman lived in a world full of violence, which he experienced firsthand, especially during his military campaigns: men dying of combat as well as various illnesses, enemy soldiers executed en masse, civilians starving, villages looted and burning. In addition, Süleyman's world was very much characterized by slavery. In his case, this took the form of service slavery, not of plantation slavery. Many, indeed most, people around him were legally his slaves. Purchased in slave markets or obtained through the levy of children from the empire's Christian subjects and converted to Islam, these slaves served him as concubines, members of his household troops, palace servants, janissaries, governors, and viziers. Süleyman used the institution of slavery with particular effect, to expand the service class around him and enhance his political and military power.

While the Ottoman political establishment advanced toward the bureaucratization of its everyday activities, auguries and prophecies played an important role in the ways in which Süleyman saw and interpreted the world around him. He keenly solicited the help of astrologers and geomancers for all his critical decisions. He and the society around him were also attuned to signs from nature. The quick flight of a flock of blackbirds, a sudden rainstorm, a fight between two herds of pigs could easily point out all sorts of ominous developments. Theirs was a world that was at the mercy of plagues, natural disasters, rural rebellions, and urban unrest. Despite all attempts at institution-building, moments of optimism could easily yield to a profound fatalism.

*Peerless among Princes* aims to bring together these disparate threads by telling the story of Süleyman's life from beginning to end. Themes and issues, such as cultural and institutional developments, or regional and global transformations, are discussed within their historical contexts. Given the variety and volume of contemporary testimonies and sources, it is possible to write about Süleyman in some detail. However, gaps in sources necessarily exist. The tension between the availability and the unavailability of specific information constitutes perhaps the biggest challenge to writing the biography of Süleyman. It presents an opportunity as well: to invite the readers into the story and leave certain things open to their judgment and interpretation, rather than resorting to forced, indeed ahistorical, speculations. After all, our understanding of history is very much based on the dialogue between text and audience, as Süleyman himself knew well.

# *I*

# *The Family Story: The Ottomans before Süleyman*

SÜLEYMAN'S ANCESTORS WERE Turkish-speaking nomads who had converted to Islam during their journey from Inner Asia toward the Middle East. Pushed westward by the Mongol invasions, they entered the Anatolian peninsula around the middle of the thirteenth century. They proceeded farther west, until they found suitable summer and winter pastures for their livestock. There, in a small corner of northwest Anatolia, 80 miles southeast of Constantinople as the crow flies, they adopted a semi-sedentary existence and established a symbiotic relationship with town dwellers, farmers, and other pastoralists. The area they chose to settle was situated on the edges of the Anatolian Seljuk Sultanate and the Byzantine Empire.

The Seljuks and the Byzantines were a shadow of their former selves around the time Süleyman's ancestors arrived in the region. A rebellion in 1240, started by a charismatic religious leader and supported by large numbers of nomads, had weakened Seljuk authority considerably. A crushing defeat at the hand of the Mongols in 1243 was the coup de grace that turned the Seljuks into vassals of their victors. As for the Byzantines, they had lost their capital Constantinople and most of their territories to the armies of the Fourth Crusade on and after 1204. They were able to recover Constantinople in 1261, but that meant that most of their limited energies were devoted to the western borders of their domain, leaving their eastern frontier largely unattended. As a result, Süleyman's ancestors lived mostly unfettered by the control mechanisms of larger political entities. Then, in the last years of the thirteenth century, they transformed themselves into a military movement and a political community. Their substantial skills in horse riding and archery were of critical importance in this transition. They also found a leading figure in their midst: Osman (d. 1324).[1] The Ottoman dynasty is named after him: *Âl-i Osman* (the family of Osman), or simply *Osmanlı* (of Osman, Ottoman).

Osman was able to survive and then thrive in a challenging environment in which many others like him competed for resources and sought to establish their authority. First, he consolidated his power over his own tribe by eliminating internal threats, including a paternal uncle whom he reputedly murdered. Then, he proceeded to obtain the support of allies and associates beyond the tribe. His new followers included nomads from a background similar to his, as well as members of the Byzantine frontier forces, with whom he shared a martial outlook. Initially, while Osman was recognized as leader, he was a first among equals. His authority grew as he was able to guide his men into successful ventures. Those ventures laid a path to enrichment through predatory attacks against surrounding communities.

The actions of Osman and his followers were legitimized by a frontier version of the Muslim duty to wage holy war (*cihad, gaza*).[2] Some interpreted that duty as a personal struggle against temptation; others, like Osman and his men, used it to present themselves as Muslim holy raiders, *gazis*, who fought against infidels. That gave them a group identity and a mission. It is true that Osman had many Christian followers, and that he fought against Christian as well as Muslim rivals. Moreover, his relationship with settled communities and agriculturalists in his vicinity did not solely consist of pillaging their resources. Still, the *gazi* identity formed the dynamic core of the movement and community he established and expanded. Another crucial factor in the survival of the whole enterprise, and a concrete step toward the establishment of an Ottoman dynasty, was the apparently seamless transfer of leadership from Osman to his son Orhan (d. 1362) upon Osman's death in 1324.[3]

In 1326, after a multi-year blockade, the Ottomans captured the large Byzantine town of Prousa (modern-day Bursa). They had taken small towns and fortresses before, but Bursa, a regional commercial center, marked an important moment in the transition of a group of militarized nomads toward a sedentary principality.[4] It is no coincidence that some of the first Ottoman documents extant today, in the form of endowment deeds and inscriptions, date from this time. The growing economic and political power of the Ottoman dynasty, and its deepening relationship with Muslim scholars and preachers, are also reflected in the buildings Orhan sponsored: a mint and a mosque in Bursa, madrasas in several towns, and dervish lodges in the countryside.

In the following decades, the Ottomans continued to expand west and north on the coastal plain alongside the shores of the Sea of Marmara, and east and south toward the Anatolian interior, at the expense of the Byzantines and the neighboring Turko-Muslim principalities. Another turning point was reached when they established a foothold on the other side of the Dardanelles in 1352, which gave the Ottomans a new zone of expansion beyond their relatively small corner in northwest Anatolia. Shortly thereafter, around 1361, they captured Adrianopolis (modern-day Edirne), a major Byzantine urban center, and began to entrench themselves in the Balkans.[5]

From the mid-fourteenth century onward, the Ottoman enterprise expanded, and sometimes contracted, on two distinct fronts: the Balkans and Anatolia. In the Balkans, Ottoman progress was aided by multiple factors. Ottoman forces initially consisted of light infantry and horse archers, which gave them the advantage of speed over the heavy armor of their rivals. Religiously sanctioned *gaza* against non-Muslims and the pursuit of wealth in the form of booty continued to motivate Ottoman military men and to serve as a tool of recruitment into their ranks. Rather than proceeding as random waves of invasion, Ottoman expansion was relatively planned. Prominent commanders, some of whom were descendants of Osman's initial followers, had designated zones of expansion where they established themselves as frontier lords.

The Ottomans entered the Balkans at a time when many of their potential opponents were affected by major troubles. Eurasia and northern Africa were ravaged by a bubonic plague pandemic, later called the Black Death. The papacy, a unifying force behind projects of crusade, spent the entire fourteenth century and the first decades of the fifteenth in a state of disarray. Under political pressure, it relocated to Avignon in southeastern France for nearly seven decades. Then, between 1378 and 1417, there were two, and eventually three popes, residing in different cities, with their own College of Cardinals and chancery. Secular rulers were not faring much better either. With the Golden Bull of 1356, the Holy Roman Empire was transformed into a quasi-constitutional entity within which ecclesiastical and lay prince-electors enjoyed legal immunity and political independence. Further west, the Hundred Years' War (1338–1453) continued to rage between the French and the English.

The fractured political world of the Balkans, in which Serbs, Bulgarians, Bosnians, Hungarians, Italians, and others frequently fought for supremacy, facilitated Ottoman expansion. Thanks to ongoing religious and economic tensions, such as the one between Italian Catholic nobles and Orthodox Christian peasants, or feudal lords and serfs, the Ottomans were able to present themselves as better rulers to local communities. Born in an environ-ment where different religious and linguistic identities coexisted and mingled, they knew how to strategically utilize accommodation and adaptation. For instance, instead of seeking direct control after initial contact, they often adopted a loose relationship of vassalage with the local elites they vanquished, turning them into their allies and associates. Full-fledged conquest occurred only after several generations. An important component of it was the transfer of Muslim communities from Anatolia to the Balkans. Farmers, wandering preachers, and military men with land assignments were settled in areas where no Muslims had lived before.[6]

European Christian powers rallied against Ottoman expansion only after the final years of the fourteenth century, which gave the Ottomans four decades to establish themselves in the Balkans, during which their main rivals were local and regional entities. Anti-Ottoman crusades in 1396, 1443–44, and 1448 registered some initial successes, but were eventually defeated. In the second half of the fifteenth century, as smaller powers such as the Serbian Despotate and the Kingdom of Bosnia collapsed under the weight of regional competition, the Ottomans and the Kingdom of Hungary emerged as the two most influential political actors in southeastern Europe. Venice, a mari-time empire spread across the eastern Mediterranean, preserved its trade net-work and naval presence, but it did not have the military capabilities of either land-based kingdom.[7]

The second front of expansion for the Ottomans was Anatolia, where they faced a different set of challenges. To their east and south, they were surrounded by several Turko-Muslim principalities whose founders and rulers similarly came from a background of militarized nomadism and adopted the *gazi* mission and identity. The political and military skills of the Ottomans had a greater impact in the Balkans, where they were relative newcomers, but they were a known quantity in Anatolia. Moreover, many of their rival Turko-Muslim dynasties had genealogies and histories much more illustrious than theirs, and were larger, more powerful, and wealthier during the first decades of the fourteenth century. Their subjects and allies had no pressing reasons to change sides and support the budding Ottoman enterprise. Furthermore, Sharia law prohibited attacking one's fellow Muslims. While that did not stop wars among Muslims, it made it difficult to legitimize violence.

The Ottomans developed a complex argument as an answer: they claimed that, by keeping them occupied on the Anatolian front, their fellow Turko-Muslim principalities prevented them from waging holy war against Christians in the Balkans. Thus, Ottoman military action against these *gaza*-hindering

Muslims was legitimate according to the Sharia. The wealth the Ottomans garnered in the Balkans, the allies they recruited, and the military tactics they sharpened were deployed relentlessly against their Turko-Muslim rivals in Anatolia. Finally, Ottoman deftness at exploiting succession struggles within rival dynasties, and their skill in arranging marriages of alliance, helped them expand on both the Anatolian and the Balkan fronts.[8]

Perhaps the biggest challenge to Ottoman expansion to the east came at the very beginning of the fifteenth century. It took the form of the last great nomadic empire-builder in Eurasian history, Timur (d. 1405). In a field battle near Ankara in the summer of 1402, Timur routed the Ottoman forces and captured Bayezid I (r. 1389–1402), who died in captivity seven months later. For the next decade, the Ottoman realm was divided. Some of the Turko-Muslim principalities taken over by the Ottomans were re-established, while Bayezid's sons vied for control over the remnants of their father's domain. Ironically, this near-collapse also showed that, by the early fifteenth century, the Ottoman enterprise had passed a significant threshold and had become deeply rooted in Anatolia and the Balkans. Despite fragmentation, the dynasty had enough political capital to command loyalty and gather resources. It successfully maintained a network of allies and associates across the region, and its administrative and fiscal structures remained relatively strong. As a result, an Ottoman prince was able to eliminate his brothers and re-establish control over most of Bayezid I's domain after 1413.

The ensuing period was a time of reconstruction and further expansion on the Anatolian front. Like in the Balkans, the Ottomans were helped by external circumstances. Timur died shortly after his victory at Ankara. His son and successor Shahrukh (r. 1405–1447) ruled from Herat, located today in western Afghanistan. While he kept a close eye on the western borders of his domain in Azerbaijan and eastern Anatolia, Shahrukh did not disrupt the Ottoman reconstruction. Consequently, by the last decades of the fifteenth century, most of the Turko-Muslim principalities in Anatolia were taken over by the Ottomans. These included Karaman, the largest and strongest of them, which had held the old Seljuk capital of Konya and resisted Ottoman expansion successfully for more than a century. The Byzantine Empire was no more, after losing its capital Constantinople to the Ottomans in 1453. Ottoman territories extended into eastern and southeastern Anatolia, where they abutted the lands of the Akkoyunlu tribal confederation to the east and the Mamluk Sultanate to the south. Farther north, incursions into the Black Sea brought the Ottomans into contact with the Crimean Khanate, which was ruled by descendants of Genghis Khan, the founding figure of the Mongol Empire.[9]

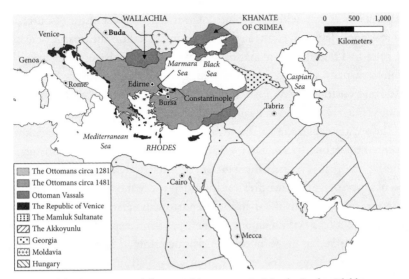

**FIG. 1.1** The Ottomans and their neighbors, ca. 1481. Map by Jordan Blekking.

By the time Süleyman's grandfather Bayezid II came to the throne in 1481, the enterprise that was started in the last years of the thirteenth century by a motley crew of nomads and soldiers of fortune had become a relatively well-managed dynastic sultanate. The key to this transformation was institutionalization.

## Managing the Realm

Compared to their rivals and competitors in Anatolia and the Balkans, the Ottomans were more adept at building institutions. During the two centuries preceding the birth of Süleyman, the dynasty and its growing body of servants developed critical skills for governing a predominantly agrarian society that was populated by members of different ethno-linguistic and religious communities. Ottoman administration had specific objectives, such as taxing all forms of economic production and activity and creating and maintaining a military-political elite, which in turn assisted the dynasty in waging war and managing the realm. Another aim was to prevent anyone other than the ruler from becoming too powerful and independent, and to ensure that resources were not over-exploited.[10]

Sources of revenue for the dynasty included taxes on land, crops, and animals; levies from artisans and merchants; the poll tax collected from the non-Muslims; tax farms (*mukataa*); and taxes and other revenues in cash from mines, customs, salt fields, and mints.[11] Control over most of the resources of the realm was legitimized through a reasoning based on the Sharia, whereby the ruler had the right to manage the land and its resources on behalf of the public treasury, and thus the public itself. In conjunction with the Sharia, dynastic and customary law, *kanun*, was utilized to determine and implement various forms of taxation and land tenure.[12]

The steady expansion of the realm, and the predominantly agricultural nature of the economy, created logistical challenges for the collection and accumulation of tax revenue. One solution, adopted quite early, was the application of a type of land tenure previously used by the Seljuks and the Byzantines. In return for service to the dynasty, the Ottoman ruler granted individuals the right to draw a certain amount of revenue from a specific area. The total amount, collected in the form of taxes, was determined by the grantee's rank, seniority, and function. The revenue grant was called a *timar*.

The overwhelming majority of the grantees were cavalrymen, called *sipahi*s, who joined the ruler's army during campaigns. Their lack of ownership rights prevented them from passing on their *timar*s to their male children. However, the sons could inherit their father's status as *timar* recipient and obtain one in a different area. This allowed the Ottomans to recruit and maintain a large military force. Moreover, through small and large *timar*s, Ottoman rulers could manage locations farther from the center since most of the grantees resided in their assigned areas and helped maintain law and order locally.[13] *Timar*s thus helped the Ottomans incorporate the lands they conquered and create a degree of order and stability that lasted even when the dynasty's power weakened, as it did during the turmoil that followed the defeat of Bayezid I by Timur in 1402.[14]

As the ruler's power grew, often at the expense of members of the military-political elite, Ottoman territorial administration became more complex. Regular surveys of new and existing territories, compiled in registers, gave the central authorities a sense of the economic and demographic attributes of specific areas. In the first half of the fourteenth century, districts (*sancak*) were established, managed by centrally appointed district governors (*sancakbeyi*). In the following decades, even larger units called *eyalet*, provinces, were instituted under a *beylerbeyi*, a governor-general. A district typically consisted of a large town and its hinterland, which often included a few towns and many villages. Most of a district's territory was divided into a few hundred *timar*s, granted to cavalrymen and others who served the Ottoman dynasty. Together with agriculture, sources of economic activity and taxable revenue in a district might include small manufacturing, mining, and animal husbandry as well as local and regional commerce.[15]

Obviously, a district's geographic location and the available human and natural resources affected its wealth, which varied significantly across the realm. The central town of a district served as its administrative, economic, and cultural hub. Mosques, one of which was designated as the main location for the Friday prayer, served as places of worship and received local and dynastic patronage. Quran schools and madrasas, often attached to mosques, offered education to Muslim boys. Endowments (*vakf*, pl. *evkaf*) by notables past and present fulfilled charitable functions, from hosting travelers to distributing food to the poor. Lodges of Sufi confraternities served as venues for religiosity as well as socialization. In areas with Christian populations, churches and monasteries also dotted the urban and rural landscape.

A district governor was typically someone with a history of service to the dynasty. One of his chief responsibilities was to command the *tımar*-grantees of his *sancak* in times of war. He also supervised the collection of taxes, a portion of which was kept locally while another portion was sent away to the capital. The pursuit of criminals and the preservation of peace and security were part of his duties. Another major task was the management of the men drawing revenue from *tımars*, in order to prevent them from overexploiting available resources and mistreating the local population. Governors were aided by judges (*kadı*) appointed by the central administration, who were present in almost all townships to hear cases and register transactions.

The ruler and his high officials provided guidance to the districts on administrative matters, exercised legislative control through law codes, and ordered investigations when necessary. Ottoman princes also served as district governors. By the time of Süleyman's birth at the end of the fifteenth century, such service had become a form of advanced training for princes, all of whom were recognized as potential heirs to the throne. Since princes were appointed at a relatively young age (Süleyman was around fifteen years old), they were assisted in their governorships by their *lala*, a powerful overseer assigned by their father. Their tutors and their mothers also moved with them to their posting and offered support and advice.[16]

In addition to and in conjunction with territorial administration, military power was vital for the management, defense, and expansion of the realm, and the Ottomans constantly developed their military capabilities. For instance, their adoption of gunpowder weapons (muskets and artillery) around the mid-fifteenth century, coupled with their ability to fiscally sustain the use of costlier materials, gave them a critical advantage over most of their

rivals.[17] The Ottomans paid particular attention to recruitment. In addition
to *timars*, they enrolled salaried infantrymen and cavalrymen and recruited
auxiliary troops in return for tax privileges.[18] A more consequential form of
recruitment was conducted through enslavement.

The enslavement of non-Muslim enemies captured in battle, legal according to the Sharia, was the basis for the establishment of the janissary
(*yeni çeri*, meaning new soldier) corps around the mid-fourteenth century.
The janissaries, initially the personal guard of the ruler, were the first permanent military unit in Eurasian history. Their numbers expanded steadily, and
they came to constitute the most effective component of the Ottoman army.
That transformation was helped by another form of enslavement that became widespread by the last decades of the fourteenth century: the uniquely
Ottoman practice of selectively enslaving the male children of their Christian
subjects and taking them into Ottoman service.

This form of enslavement was not legal according to the Sharia, since
non-Muslims living under Muslim rule were meant to be protected from
such treatment.[19] However, convenience trumped legality as the practice of
*devşirme* (collection) expanded. Boys between the ages of twelve and fourteen were selected for their physical strength, mental acuity, and social background by agents sent to the countryside. They were then transported to the
capital, converted to Islam, and socialized in Muslim environments. Some
were given under the tutelage of Muslim farmers, while others were raised in
the ruler's palace. As they came of age, most of them served in a military capacity in the janissary corps or in the palace household troops, another component of the Ottoman standing army that emerged after the janissaries.

The *devşirme* practice was not solely directed at the recruitment of soldiers,
however. Many of the enslaved, converted children eventually worked in
the palace household in various capacities. Those who distinguished themselves through service and initiative continued to move upward within the
palace and the military-political hierarchy. The most successful received
appointments as district governors. A very small group among them became
governors-general. Even fewer were able to reach the positions of vizier and
grand vizier, the most senior military-administrative ranks in Ottoman government.[20] To the end of their lives, regardless of rank, their legal status was
that of a slave, and the ruler was their master.

As the ruler and his slaves increased their power, other groups lost theirs.
Among them were descendants of Osman's first companions, who had been
active in the Balkans as frontier commanders. Members of Anatolian Muslim
families, who had served the Ottoman dynasty in various administrative

**FIG. 1.2** Boys selected as *devşirme* are being taken in as parents and community members look on. Detail from *Sulaymannama*, 31b. Courtesy of the T.C. Cumhurbaşkanlığı Milli Saraylar İdaresi Başkanlığı.

capacities, also became less prominent. The military-political elite initially had included some Christian members, especially individuals with ties to old aristocracies in the Balkans, but those also vanished over time. Especially after the mid-fifteenth century, high officials and viziers from a slave background became more dominant in the administration. The use of slaves afforded rulers more control over their own officials and servants, since the slaves theoretically owed allegiance to their master and to no one else, which would ideally prevent them from establishing independent political relationships.

By the time of Süleyman, many, indeed most, of the men around him were enslaved converts: the servants who surrounded him in his everyday activities, the administrators who helped him govern the empire, and the thousands of janissaries and palace household troops who accompanied him to war.

However, the military-political elite was never entirely dominated by slave-origin individuals. Freeborn Muslims served, and fought for, the dynasty as *sipahis*. Those with a madrasa education worked in Ottoman service as judges, teachers, and scribes. From the perspective of the Ottoman ruler, all members of the elite, called *askerî* (military), were the sultan's servants (*kul*), be they slaves or freeborn Muslims.[21] In return for their services, those who belonged to the *askerî* elite enjoyed economic and legal privileges that were not available to the commoners, called the *reaya* (flock).

Another dividing line in Ottoman society was the one that separated the Muslims from the non-Muslims. While *kanun*, Ottoman dynastic law, promised protection and justice to all tax-paying subjects, the Sharia conferred legal superiority to Muslims and imposed restrictions on non-Muslims.[22] Sharia law had begun to be developed during the early centuries of Islam, in a demographic environment in which large Christian communities and significant Jewish communities existed under the minority rule of a Muslim upper class. The Sharia separated the Muslims from the Peoples of the Book (*ahl al-kitab*), mainly the Christians and the Jews, who were described as having received a genuine form of revelation that was subsequently corrupted. Members of these communities were recognized as parties to a pact (*dhimma* in Arabic, *zimmet* in Turkish) between them and their Muslim rulers. In return for a poll tax and their acceptance of a series of rules that rendered them legally, socially, and culturally inferior to the Muslims, those recipients of ancient revelation could continue to live under Muslim rule. They could worship according to their faith, manage their communal affairs according to their own rules, and expect to be protected from mistreatment and oppression.[23]

This was the foundation of the relationship between the Ottoman ruler and his non-Muslim subjects, classified as *zimmi*s, that is, parties to the pact. The issue at hand was not solely the application the Sharia, however, but also the establishment of a form of accommodation that allowed the Ottoman authorities to present themselves to non-Muslim communities under a positive light. This accommodation was necessary throughout the life of the Ottoman enterprise, as non-Muslim subjects constituted a majority, or at least a very large minority, in many parts of the realm.

Still, restrictions emphasized the inferior status of non-Muslims vis-à-vis Muslims, particularly in settings where they lived together with Muslims. Those restrictions extended from a ban on exhibiting signs of their religion (such as ringing bells and carrying crosses and icons for Christians) to riding horses, bearing arms, dressing up ostentatiously, wearing clothes associated with Muslims, and constructing houses overlooking those of their Muslim neighbors. These were not only policies ideally enforced by officials of the dynasty, but also components of a social hierarchy that was demanded and maintained by Muslim individuals and communities. Indeed, at times, the authorities' preference for accommodation might clash with the stricter demands of pious Muslims.[24]

As a result of these administrative and legal transformations, Osman's relatively non-hierarchical, simpler world of *gazi*s and dervishes had vanished almost completely before Süleyman's birth. Writing in the last decades of the fifteenth century, the dervish and chronicler Âşıkpaşazade Ahmed described Osman with a profound nostalgia. Upon capturing a town, his first such conquest, Osman was said to have been baffled when he was told he should impose and collect marketplace taxes. He reluctantly agreed; he then instructed those around him to impose low taxes, never take away *tımar*s without cause, and transfer them from father to son upon death. On another occasion, a dervish asked Osman for a written title for three villages he had received as property. Osman told him he could do no such thing since he was illiterate, and instead gave him a sword and a cup as proof of the transaction.[25] Rulers like Süleyman's grandfather Bayezid II, in contrast, presided over an administrative-fiscal system whose main task was to assign and collect taxes. Bayezid II and his officials did take away and redistribute *tımar*s, sometimes in disregard of a *sipahi*'s condition, in contravention of Osman's instructions as well as the nostalgic vision of those like Âşıkpaşazade Ahmed.

Indeed, by the last decades of the fifteenth century, the main tenets of the Ottoman administrative system were in place. The ruler, residing in the capital city, was assisted by an imperial council (*divan*). A grand vizier (*vezir-i azam*) and a few other viziers, two chief treasurers, the chancellor, and two chief judges who oversaw the *askerî* elite were the main figures in the council. The council supervised the affairs of the realm, from the collection of taxes and decisions to go to war to the adjudication of cases that made their way from the provinces to the capital. A specialized military force, consisting of the janissaries and the palace household troops, was stationed in the capital. *Sipahi*s spread across the realm, helping to keep the peace and ready to join the ruler on his military campaigns. Madrasa teachers taught the next generation of instructors, jurists, and literati while judges sent to all corners of the land dispensed justice.

The administration of justice was conducted through judges' decisions and scholars' legal opinions, local and general law codes issued in the name of the ruler, and the decisions of the ruler and the imperial council. As such, it

FIG. 1.3 The imperial council in session. Detail from *Sulaymannama*, 37b. Courtesy of the T.C. Cumhurbaşkanlığı Milli Saraylar İdaresi Başkanlığı.

was one of the dynasty's main tools for control, conflict resolution, and legitimization.[26] Dynastic law (*kanun*) increasingly came to the fore to manage the interactions between rulers and subjects, from fiscal affairs to criminal law. Its inherent promise of peace and security for all subjects was a crucial component of the Ottoman dynasty's claim to legitimacy. Indeed, Süleyman's image, both during his lifetime and later, relied heavily on the argument that he ruled efficiently and justly through *kanun*.

Any account of Ottoman administrative practices risks creating the impression of a smooth progression from a small group of militarized nomads to an empire. In fact, adaptation to local practices, experimentation, and transformation were the predominant characteristics of Ottoman institution-building. Despite the ruler's growing authority and control, other actors with political and military power existed, such as the frontier commanders in the Balkans who survived well into the first decades of the sixteenth century. The dynasty's attempts at controlling all the resources of the realm notwithstanding, private ownership persisted, and some properties were placed under endowments with a charitable purpose that made them legally inalienable. The administration of justice, or the collection of taxes, often depended on negotiations among the political center, its representatives in the provinces, and the local communities. Moreover, succession from one ruler to another could be very violent and destabilizing, and it often shook the Ottoman polity to its core. It should be mentioned as well that natural events, geographical distances, simple inefficiency and corruption, and a bevy of other reasons further complicated the work of government.[27]

There were also varieties of political discontent that sometimes expressed themselves through violence. In kingdoms and empires like that of the Ottomans, whose internal stability depended on the loyalty of military men, the successful management of a large agrarian economy and population, and even the vicissitudes of the climate, rebellions large and small were inescapable.[28] They were initiated and supported by groups and individuals whose grievances were not always properly addressed by the Ottoman administration: nomads whom the central authorities wanted to settle on land and turn into taxpaying agriculturalists, townspeople who resented Ottoman economic and legal control, old Anatolian families who had lost their privileges after the Ottoman conquest, *sipahi*s who had been dismissed from their *timar*s, and low-level scholars, dervishes, and pious believers who viewed social change as unsavory and immoral. Urban revolts were another source of concern for the dynasty, especially as Constantinople grew into a large city that housed a wide variety of social and political divisions.[29]

Despite these impediments, the Ottoman dynasty was able to impose most of its priorities, at times through violence, and at times through negotiation and persuasion. Its ability to secure wide-ranging support partially depended on the creation and propagation of specific justifications and narratives about its right to rule. In this regard as well, Süleyman was going to distinguish himself as the scion who took the family legacy further than ever imagined before him.

## Legitimacy and Dynastic Identity

In the period between Osman, the founder of the enterprise, and Bayezid II, Süleyman's grandfather, the head of the Ottoman dynasty was transformed from a charismatic chieftain who rode to war with his companions to a monarch who lived behind palace walls, surrounded by hundreds and then thousands of servants.

Initially, the dynasty's legitimacy depended on its successful redistribution of resources to its supporters, and its protection of the communities under its rule from violence and over-exploitation. Waging war against the "infidels" in the Balkans enhanced its reputation and brought prestige. Then, especially from the first quarter of the fifteenth century onward, Ottoman claims to rule were supported through a new set of justifications, which were based on genealogy and history.[30] These were to a large extent motivated by Bayezid I's defeat in 1402 in front of Timur, and the subsequent revival of the Anatolian Turko-Muslim polities previously conquered by the Ottomans. The defeat resoundingly reminded all and sundry of the weakness of the Ottoman family pedigree. This weakness became particularly obvious vis-à-vis rivals like Timur, who was closely connected to the family and legacy of Genghis Khan (d. 1227), one of the most prestigious figures in the Turko-Muslim political universe.[31]

The justifications formulated by the Ottomans and their allies are found in historical and literary works that were composed in the decades following 1402. The wide variety of arguments that are encountered in these works helped create what has been called an "Ottoman dynastic myth."[32] Some stories connected the Ottoman family to Japheth, son of Noah, anchoring them in deep prophetic history. Others claimed that the Ottomans were related to the mythical leader of the Turkic tribes Oğuz Han through a senior line, which was meant to give them supremacy over all tribal polities of Turkic origin. Another set of stories told of a dream Osman supposedly had, in which he and his descendants were made the founders and rulers of a great empire. For those keen on legality, there were stories that informed their readers and listeners that the last Anatolian Seljuk ruler had designated the Ottomans as his heirs.

Yet another notion that entered circulation around this time asserted that the Ottoman polity was culturally different from both its Christian rivals and its Turko-Muslim competitors. The Ottomans had a "Rumi" (Roman, referring to the lands of Byzantium) identity, which promoted the Ottoman realm to the level of the two major regions of Islamic civilization: the lands of the Arabs and the lands of the Persians. As a cultural construct, the Rumi identity had the advantage of appealing to all current and future Ottoman subjects. It also had the advantage of eschewing any genealogical speculations, except the idea that the Ottomans were worthy successors of the Byzantine/ Eastern Roman Empire, an argument that was political and cultural rather than biological.[33]

Another way to observe the growing authority of the Ottoman rulers during the first two centuries of the enterprise is to look at the titles they adopted and others ascribed to them. Osman and Orhan are typically presented in the Ottoman historical tradition as *bey*. This is an undistinguished honorific that may be applied to the commander of a small force, the ruler of a district, or a strongman with a retinue. However, epigraphical evidence in Arabic from the late 1330s shows that Orhan and those around him had a higher opinion, since he is referred to as *amir al-kabir* (great prince) and *sultan al-mujahidin* (sultan of the holy warriors).[34] With Murad I (r. 1362–89) and his successor Bayezid I (r. 1389–1402), whose reigns saw further territorial expansion as well as administrative development, the Ottoman ruler became worthy of a variety of titles. *Padişah, sultan,* and *hünkar,* from the Arabo-Persian and Islamic traditions, denoted a king-like figure ruling over large territories, while *han* (and its variants like *kağan* and *hakan*), meaning ruler of the steppe, tied the Ottomans to the Turko-Mongol tradition. Bayezid I added *sultan-ı Rum* (king of [Eastern] Rome) to this expanding vocabulary of titles, underlining the Ottoman claim to rule in Anatolia and the Balkans.

The defeat to Timur in 1402 interrupted these aspirations to greatness for a while but did not undermine the most prominent and widely used title in the dynasty's arsenal: that of *gazi*. Warfare in the Balkans, a constant in Ottoman history after 1352, became even more intense under Murad II (r. 1421–44, 1446–51), who faced two significant crusades against the Ottomans.[35] His son Mehmed II (r. 1444–46, 1451–81), the conqueror of Constantinople in 1453, contributed to Ottoman dynastic political imagination with new titles that ranged from *kayser-i Rum* (emperor of Byzantium/Rome), which presented the Ottomans as the inheritors of the Eastern Roman Empire, to *sultanü'l-berreyn ve hakanü'l-bahreyn* (sultan of the two lands [Anatolia and the Balkans] and sovereign of the two seas [the eastern Mediterranean and the Black Sea].[36]

Indeed, the shift to a monarch with regional and eventually universal claims to rule became particularly obvious under Mehmed II. Following his conquest of Constantinople, he established a sophisticated court life. When the first palace he had built was deemed insufficient for the needs of his growing household and heightened ceremonialism, he ordered a second residence, called the New Palace, to be built on a location overlooking the Golden Horn and the Bosphorus. Most of the building was completed by the late 1460s. Several hundred servants worked there in the stables, kitchens, and gardens, or as gatekeepers and artisans. The ruler's household, centered at the palace, steadily grew to include a few thousand individuals in the first decades of the sixteenth century.[37]

Mehmed II's palace was renowned for its focus on learning across different linguistic and intellectual traditions, from Arabic and Persian to Greek and Latin, both in translations as well as in original texts. These cultural interests were fostered as part of his universalist imperial agenda, and they eventually formed the foundation of a new Ottoman dynastic identity and culture.[38] Another transformation instigated by Mehmed II was the creation of a strong legal basis for the elevation of the ruler over his servants and subjects. This was realized through a *kanun* code issued in the last years of his reign. It not only limited and regulated access to the ruler, but also introduced a new level of organization into the upper ranks of the *askerî* elite by laying down specific rules on hierarchy, promotion, and pay.[39]

Süleyman learned an epic, dramatic version of this family past from anecdotes that circulated orally, and from Ottoman works of history that were penned in the fifteenth and early sixteenth centuries.[40] As the son of a prince and the grandson of a reigning sultan, he was an inheritor of the dynasty's cultural and institutional legacies. He spent his life under their weight, mindful of the benefits of tradition yet eager to instigate change. Moreover, he needed to deal with the consequences of major changes that had just started, or were about to start, around the time he was born.

## The Wider World around Süleyman

Süleyman's birth coincided with upheavals that began transforming Ottoman, European, Eurasian, and indeed global history. In 1492, Christopher Columbus reached what was later called the New World. In 1497, Vasco da Gama began his first voyage to India, following in the footsteps of Bartolomeu Dias, who in 1488 had circumnavigated what is known today as the Cape of Good Hope. These "voyages of discovery" have typically been viewed as the first stages of European expansion to and mastery over the rest of the globe. The Ottomans have been assigned at best a passive role in this process. They are reputed to have blocked the shorter and quicker access routes to India, thus forcing the Europeans (at first primarily the Portuguese and the Spanish, assisted by Genoese capital and know-how) to look for alternative routes. The absence of Ottoman fleets in the oceans in coming centuries, with the exception of a brief appearance in the Indian Ocean, is interpreted as a major political and economic failure caused by misjudgment, incuriosity, and cultural conservatism.[41]

These traditional explanations fail to convey a complete panorama of a critical era in world history, often called the early modern period. Between ca. 1450 and 1750, non-European polities, from the Ottomans to Muscovy, and from the Ming and Qing in China to the Mughals in India, expanded in size, developed better administrative structures, and became part of regional and global commercial networks.[42] From the last decades of the fifteenth century on, the impact of the global political and commercial expansion was deeply felt by the Ottomans, in everything from changes in their diet to monetary inflation. Ottoman markets were connected to the rest of the world by land and sea. Diplomatic relations with Muslim and Christian rivals turned into intense cultural and political exchanges. In Ottoman historical works and diplomatic documents, Ottoman rulers were increasingly presented as imperial figures with a universalist claim to rule over east and west.

The main concerns of Süleyman on the European front were going to be the control of Hungary, and the competition with the Habsburgs across east-central Europe and the Mediterranean. His rivalry with the Habsburgs also included a strong ideological dimension around claims to universal sovereignty. The foundations of these struggles were laid in the 1490s, a few decades before Süleyman's arrival to the throne. After the death of the Hungarian king Matthias Corvinus in 1490, the political and fiscal power of the Hungarian nobles increased at the expense of the crown, while the tensions between the peasantry and the nobility intensified. As a result, the Hungarian kingdom's ability to defend itself against both Habsburg and Ottoman advances diminished significantly. Other events set the stage for the emergence of the Habsburgs as the most powerful European dynasty in the first decades of the sixteenth century.

Maximilian of Habsburg had succeeded his father Frederick as King of the Romans and *de facto* Holy Roman Emperor in 1493, further strengthening the dynasty's political clout. His son Philip married Joanna, the daughter of Queen Isabella of Castile and King Ferdinand II of Aragon, who had completed the centuries-long Reconquista in 1492 and ruled over a dynastically and territorially unified Spain. Columbus' voyages, which took place under their auspices, gave them a foothold in the New World. Together with other lands and titles collected by the Habsburgs over the previous few centuries across Europe, this constituted the inheritance of Joanna and Philip's son Charles, born in 1500, and future rival of Süleyman. Another critical development was the invasion of Italy by the French king Charles VIII in October 1494. When the Ottomans received news of the French advance into Italy, they were at first concerned that the French might lead a joint attack against their territories in

the Balkans. In fact, the invasion led to an intense military and political competition that ensnared the Italian peninsula, the French, the Habsburgs, and
their various allies for decades to come.[43]

Other events, taking place farther east, were to have equally critical
repercussions for the Ottomans in the coming decades, indeed centuries. In
1494, around the time Süleyman was born, a seven-year-old child escaped almost certain death at the hands of his family's enemies and took refuge with
the local ruler of Gilan, a region on the southwestern shore of the Caspian
Sea. His name was Ismail. He descended from a family whose members had
come to prominence as religious leaders in western Iran and eastern Anatolia
in the first years of the fourteenth century. Eventually, they had established
a Sufi religious confraternity named after their ancestor Safiyyuddin of
Ardabil (d. 1334): the Safaviyya. By the second half of the fifteenth century,
the Safavid confraternity was mobilizing its followers, many of them Turkish-
and Kurdish-speaking nomads, to fight a holy war against the "infidels" in the
Caucasus.

The rise of the Safavids is reminiscent of the rise of the Ottomans to a
certain extent. Both families presented themselves and their followers as
*gazis* and initially relied on a dynamic force of nomadic raiders. While they
claimed to fight against non-Muslims, both had powerful Muslim rivals
against whom they waged war. The Safavids had certain advantages compared
to the Ottomans, however. First, through the Safavid confraternity, Ismail's
forefathers were able to exercise a form of spiritual leadership that Osman
and his immediate descendants could not claim. In addition, the Safavids
had married into the Akkoyunlu dynasty (Ismail was the grandson of the
Akkoyunlu ruler Uzun Hasan), which gave them a political pedigree that the
first Ottoman generations lacked.[44] On the other hand, without the strategic
advantages enjoyed by the Ottomans, such as the relative weakness of the
neighboring polities, or the opportunity for expansion created by the passage into the Balkans, the two generations before Ismail struggled to establish
their rule in eastern Anatolia and western Iran.

Ismail's eventual rise to power was facilitated by the dissolution of the
Akkoyunlus. By the last years of the fifteenth century, the Akkoyunlu domain,
the largest political entity in western Asia at that point, was on the brink of
implosion under the weight of intra-dynastic competition.[45] Meanwhile,
upon the death of his eldest brother and the withdrawal of his middle brother
from the family's affairs, Ismail had become the leader of the Safavid confraternity. Following the example of his ancestors, he started gathering troops
around 1499; in 1501, he conquered the Akkoyunlu capital of Tabriz, the seat

of his late grandfather Uzun Hasan. In the following years, he continued to expand his domain and his spiritual authority. His message was conveyed across the Middle East by agents dispatched specifically for that purpose as well as his Turkish poetry. It resonated strongly with both nomadic and sedentary communities, including many who lived in areas under Ottoman control.[46]

Ismail was particularly successful in constructing a sovereign image that presented him as an invincible warrior, indeed a claimant to the glory of ancient Iranian kings whose imperial title of shah he adopted. Additionally, "Shah" Ismail claimed to be the representative of the twelfth imam and the Messiah of the Imami Shii tradition. He is also reputed to have maintained that he was the incarnation of the Messiah; the incarnation of Ali (d. 661), who was Muhammad's cousin and son-in-law and foundational figure of Shiite Islam; and indeed the embodiment of Divinity itself.[47] These claims stemmed from a deep political and spiritual crisis that was widespread throughout most of the Islamic world in the period that followed the Mongol invasions of the thirteenth century. Ismail was thus able to capitalize on ongoing debates regarding the right to rule, the nature of divinity, the meaning of the relationship between spiritual master and disciple, and the impending arrival of the Last Judgment.[48]

In the Ottoman lands too, many viewed the radical transformations of the time through the lens of eschatology. For instance, Mehmed II's capture of Constantinople in 1453 pushed to the fore Muslim and Byzantine prophecies about the fall of the city as a sign of the end times.[49] Rivalries with the Christian kingdoms in Europe, especially with Hungary, were increasingly interpreted as part of a cosmic struggle that preceded the apocalypse. Aware of Islamic and Byzantine prophecies that foretold the attack of the *Benî Asfer* (Blond Peoples) during the final tribulations, the Ottomans associated the Hungarians and other European Christians with them.[50] On the European side as well, Ottoman incursions were read through an eschatological perspective.[51] Many anti-Ottoman prophecies enthusiastically discussed the Christian recovery of Constantinople and Jerusalem from the Muslims and the establishment of the Last World Empire. Another component of these apocalyptic anxieties was the expectation of radical religious renewal and new religio-political leadership.[52]

The date of Süleyman's birth itself could potentially be interpreted as a significant turning point. Süleyman was born near the beginning of the tenth century of the lunar Hijri calendar used by Muslims. This was the century that led up to the Hijri year 1000, which ran from October 1591 to October 1592 CE. Many believed that this was the last century on Earth, and that the year 1000 marked the end.[53] During Süleyman's reign, the intense rivalry with the Habsburgs and the Safavids deepened these speculations about the imminence of the end times. The heightened fears and anxieties of the period also enabled Süleyman to develop the claim that he was a leader specifically chosen to fulfill a mission at a time of tribulations.

## The Grandfather's Reign

Süleyman's grandfather, Bayezid II, was the first Ottoman ruler to face the major transformations that underscored the passage from the ninth into the tenth Hijri century, and from the fifteenth to the sixteenth century of the Common Era. Bayezid II's image has been tarnished, in the Ottoman historical tradition, by the cataclysmic last years of his reign, which saw rebellions in Anatolia and a civil war among his sons. He is thus mostly remembered as a pious old man who lost control of his domain. The officials around him in the last years of his reign are typically described as irresponsible courtiers who spent more time drinking wine and hunting than attending to the affairs of government.[54] However, a closer look at Bayezid II's long reign reveals a different picture, that of a ruler whose policies relied on caution and careful calculation. Moreover, Bayezid II was quite adept at creating and circulating a new image of the Ottoman sultan as patron, poet, devoted mystic, book collector, and gentleman. Süleyman inherited and eventually emulated this particular image.

The first decade and a half of Bayezid II's reign was spent under the shadow of his younger brother Cem. Their father Mehmed II died in the spring of 1481, leaving behind two sons serving as district governors, Bayezid in Amasya and Cem in Konya. With the support of his allies among the high officials, Bayezid reached the capital city of Constantinople first and acceded to the throne in May 1481. He rebuffed Cem's offer to divide the realm. He then defeated his brother and his forces of light cavalry and infantry, thanks to the superior firepower of the central troops under his command.

Cem fled to Cairo to seek help from the Mamluk Sultanate. He returned to Anatolia in early 1482, but he and his allies could not prevail. Isolated in Anatolia, Cem crossed to the nearby island of Rhodes, which was controlled by the Order of the Knights of St. John of Jerusalem. Established in Jerusalem after the First Crusade, the Order of St. John had relocated to Rhodes in the 1290s, after the Mamluks recovered the last bastions of what had been the Outremer of the Crusaders, a determined yet somewhat tenuous presence established in the Levant after 1099. Reaching an understanding with Bayezid

II, the Order dispatched Cem to France, denying his request of passage to the Balkans.

Members of the Ottoman family had always been in touch, politically and culturally, with neighboring dynasties, but this was the first time an Ottoman prince was travelling this far, geographically and culturally, in search of power. During his years in France, Cem became the center of attention for various powers who wanted to use him in their anti-Ottoman activities, from the Mamluks to the Hungarians. Pope Innocent VIII eventually prevailed and had him moved to Rome in 1489. When the French invaded Italy they took the Ottoman prince into their army camp, ostensibly to benefit from his presence in a crusade against the Ottomans. Cem died soon after, in February 1495, without having to serve as a figurehead in an anti-Ottoman campaign.[55]

Managing the Cem affair was the foremost preoccupation for Bayezid II in the first decade and a half of his reign. He paid significant sums to the Order of St. John and to the papacy for Cem's continued virtual incarceration in France and then in Rome. Ottoman diplomatic relations with various European actors increased significantly in this period, both formally through treaties and agreements, and informally through information gathering and secret negotiations. Venice strengthened its role as the chief information provider of the Ottomans about inter-European affairs, a role that was going to become even more prominent during the reign of Süleyman, despite occasional wars between the two sides.

Bayezid II had other objectives on the European front. In 1484, he took the strategic cities of Kilia (in present-day Ukraine) and Akkerman (today Bilhorod-Dnistrovskyi in Ukraine) from the Moldavians. These critical conquests helped strengthen Ottoman control on the Black Sea and the lower Danube basin, and over the regional grain trade. A few years after Cem's death, Ottoman forces attacked Venetian possessions in the eastern Mediterranean, touching off a war that lasted from 1499 to 1503. It ended in a stalemate, despite papal, French, and Hungarian support for the Venetians, demonstrating the growing naval presence of the Ottomans in the eastern Mediterranean. Finally, while Bayezid II's cautious foreign policy precluded a large-scale military campaign against the major rival of the Ottomans in Europe, Hungary, the Ottoman-Hungarian frontier, extending from east-central Europe to the Dalmatian coast, continued to witness violence in the form of skirmishes and small wars.[56]

Bayezid II similarly kept a close eye on the eastern borders of the Ottoman realm. Ottoman expansion eastward in the previous decades had brought them head-to-head with the Akkoyunlus to the east and the Mamluks to the south. Ottoman forces also had taken over, but not yet subdued, areas with significant populations of Turkish-speaking nomads. The Ottoman dynasty's evolution over the previous two centuries had rendered it increasingly alien to the nomads' mobile and seasonal life and their fondness for political and military autonomy. Existing fault lines erupted into war when Bayezid II supported his ally and father-in-law Alaüddevle, ruler of the Dulkadir principality on the Ottoman-Mamluk border, in besieging a Mamluk city. Between 1485 and 1491, the Ottomans fought against both the well-trained Mamluk heavy cavalry and rebellious nomads in southeastern Anatolia. The usually invincible Ottoman forces, buoyed by their gunpowder weapons, suffered major setbacks before the Mamluks. The conflict ended in a stalemate.[57] Cautiousness and pragmatism determined the tone of Bayezid II's later relationship with the Mamluks. A decade and a half after the hostilities, when the Mamluks asked for help against Portuguese encroachments in the Red Sea, he sent them captains, sailors, and gunpowder weapons.

Keen to manage difficult situations through diplomacy, Bayezid II likewise observed the first stages of Ismail's rise to power from a safe distance and exchanged envoys with him. Ismail was cautious as well. While he sent his spiritual messengers deep into Ottoman territory to spread his message, he refrained from any major military campaigns against the Ottomans. Bayezid II was later blamed for his shortsightedness by his son Selim, Süleyman's father, who emerged as the advocate of an aggressive policy against Ismail. In fact, Bayezid II was no stranger to the risks posed by the intersection of radical religious ideas and political action. In 1492, he had survived an assassination attempt by a dervish, who had attacked him sword in hand while shouting "I am the Messiah!" He had ordered investigations of Sufi communities in the Balkans and had some of them relocated to Anatolia to dilute their influences.[58] Similarly, he had ordered the removal of some groups from Anatolia to the Balkans.[59] He and his officials were aware of the popularity of Ismail's propaganda among Ottoman subjects. However, they mostly thought that Ismail was taking over the Akkoyunlu realm, and that the threat he posed to the Ottomans could be managed through passive measures.

While handling these challenges from east and west, Bayezid II enhanced the Ottoman establishment, and thus Süleyman's inheritance, in significant ways. The workload and reach of the imperial council continued to expand, as seen in a register from 1501 that recorded orders (*hükm*) sent to various administrators in Anatolia and the Balkans.[60] In addition, Bayezid II's officials issued codes of dynastic law to be used in the management of districts, which covered matters extending from taxation to criminal law. A general code, from

1499, formalized the non-tax-paying status of the *askerî* elite and stipulated the conditions for becoming and staying a member.[61] While the imperial council thus increased its control over the military-political elite, wealthy subjects were appeased through the restitution of endowed properties and freeholds confiscated under Mehmed II.

Concomitantly, Bayezid II expanded his father's urbanization agenda in Constantinople, which aimed at creating an Ottoman presence within the overwhelmingly Byzantine cityscape. A significant outcome was a mosque complex he had built, intentionally situated on Constantinople's main artery.[62] The capital's strategic importance and cultural status as the home of the Ottoman dynasty continued to grow in this period. However, outbreaks of the plague in the early 1490s and 1502 and a massive earthquake in 1509 (later called the Little Apocalypse) ominously brought to the fore the challenges of living in Constantinople, a large port city built near a major fault line.

Bayezid II was a patron of literate culture as well. He wrote classical *divan* poetry under the pen name *Adlî* (the one who abides by justice), although his output of around 125 poems pales in comparison with the corpus his grandson Süleyman later produced. His interest in history led Bayezid II to support the composition of works that narrated the story of the Ottoman dynasty from the days of Osman to his time.[63] Upon his request, a catalogue of the palace library was prepared circa 1502–1504.[64] This unique catalogue offers precious information about the cultural interests of upper class Ottomans at the end of the fifteenth century. One could use the books in the palace library to divine the hidden meaning of past and future events; to learn lessons from the rise and fall of Arab, Persian, Mongol, and Roman/Byzantine dynasties and rulers; and to find respite or seek inspiration in Arabic, Persian, Eastern Turkish/Chaghatay, and Western/Anatolian Turkish poetry. The catalogue also lists works on Quranic exegesis and the sayings of Muhammad (*hadis*), Sufism, theology and jurisprudence, cosmology and geography, the art of war, mathematics and optics, medicine and agriculture, and philosophy and logic.

By the early sixteenth century, as the palace library catalogue attests, the Ottoman dynasty and the scholars associated with it had studied and accumulated the learning of the Arabo-Persian Islamic culture, conveyed to them in large part through works produced in the Anatolian Seljuk, Ilkhanid, Timurid, and Mamluk lands.[65] This learning is reflected in the inclusion of more than five thousand works in Arabic and Persian in the catalogue, compared to around two hundred in Turkish, a strong indication of the trilingual character of Ottoman literary culture. The promotion of Turkish as the main idiom of literary and intellectual production as well as statecraft, a development observed under Süleyman, was thus still a work in progress during his grandfather's reign.[66]

As for the new dynastic identity that emerged after the conquest of Constantinople in 1453 and intensified under Bayezid II, its ramifications can be observed in a Register of Donations (*Defter-i İnamat*).[67] Spanning the period from 1503 to 1527, the bulk of the register's contents are from Bayezid II's reign. They record disbursements from the central treasury in cash and kind, the latter mostly in the form of precious textiles and clothing items. The meticulous listing of the gifts given by the sultan, together with gifts sent to him, shows the emergence of a new relationship between the ruler and his subjects, whereby loyalty was secured and maintained through regular rewards to the military-political elite. Servants working in the palace household, high-ranking officials, and district governors received payments and gifts on important events such as the two major Muslim holidays, appointments to new posts, weddings, and circumcisions, as well as in recognition of various services rendered. Poets, dervishes, foreign envoys, and others also benefitted from the sultan's munificence.

Members of the Ottoman dynasty are often encountered in the register as recipients of sultanic generosity. Bayezid II had eight sons and at least a dozen daughters.[68] Many of his daughters were married to high-ranking members of the military-political elite even before he became sultan in 1481, and the support of his sons-in-law had been instrumental in his succession to the throne. That support extended well into his reign, as his sons-in-law occupied increasingly important positions in the Ottoman administration. Moreover, his eight sons all received appointments as district governors in their adolescence, as had become the Ottoman custom, and seven of them are mentioned in the register, one having died before the register's beginning date. Bayezid II's sons, their children, their concubines, and their servants and officials established households in the districts where they served, spreading the Ottoman ethos, learning how to manage the affairs of government, and deeply anchoring themselves and the dynasty in the life of the realm. Süleyman was born into one of these princely households.

## A Prince Is Born

Like his father, uncles, and male cousins, Süleyman was born with the right to become sultan. Compared to their rivals east and west, the Ottomans had a peculiar approach to dynastic succession in the first centuries of their history. They abided by two interrelated and seemingly contradictory principles.

First, every prince had an equal right to come to the throne. This was common practice among Turkic and Mongol dynasties. Second, only one Ottoman prince could become sultan. In this, the Ottomans differed from the Turko-Mongol practice. The realm, seen as the common property of the dynasty, could not be partitioned among princes.[69] In cases where more than one heir existed at the time of a sultan's death or incapacitation, the princes and their respective supporters fought for the throne. The prince who prevailed killed his brothers and their sons, eradicating any potential heirs to the throne, apart from his own male children.[70]

Fratricide gave the Ottoman dynasty a tremendous advantage in the fragmented political world of Anatolia and the Balkans. Unlike many of its rivals, the dynasty was able to preserve and bequeath its territories undivided from one generation to the other. Besides, victory over dynastic rivals was seen as a sign of the victorious prince's personal aptitude and his good fortune. Fratricide was seen as such a fundamental component of Ottoman dynastic practice that, in the second half of the fifteenth century, it was written into dynastic law. The justification was the preservation of *nizam-ı âlem* (the order of the world), that is, political stability.[71]

All of this meant that Süleyman was born with a conditional mandate to become sultan. That mandate, however, was accompanied by the overwhelming likelihood of violent death at the hands of an executioner. In his case, that likelihood was enhanced by the existence of many paternal uncles who, like his father Selim, served as district governors in different parts of the Anatolian peninsula. Upon the death of Bayezid II, Selim would have to fight with his brothers in a life-or-death struggle. The outcome would determine Süleyman's fate: either death, or survival and continued training as a potential heir until Selim's death, after which he would have to compete with his own brothers, if any, to come to the throne. The Ottoman practice of succession thus hurled the princes into a competitive world upon birth. The psychological burden imposed by the inescapability of these struggles and the near certainty of death is almost never discussed in contemporary sources, yet it must have been considerable. For instance, Süleyman's father Selim's rashness and restlessness, personality traits that are often mentioned by contemporary observers, surely can be partially attributed to that burden.

Around the time Süleyman was born, the household of a prince serving as district governor, such as the one presided over by his father Selim, looked like a smaller replica of the sultan's household in Constantinople.[72] Access to the prince was controlled by gatekeepers. Scribes and treasurers managed his correspondence, collected taxes, and controlled expenses. Grooms looked after stables stocked with horses and pack animals; others kept birds of prey and dogs used for hunting. Kitchen staff cooked and served elaborate meals, artisans made and repaired clothes and other objects for everyday use, and servants catered to the prince's needs day and night. Well-trained officers formed a company of guards protecting the prince. Courtiers, companions, and scholars offered distraction and advice. An overseer (*lala*), appointed by the sultan, helped the prince in managing the district and the household and kept an eye on his affairs on behalf of his father.[73]

A boy growing up in this environment was particularly cared for since he had a chance to become sultan one day. The father's household provided a milieu for education, socialization, and political alliances, some of which lasted for decades. There, the young prince received martial training, learned how to read and write, and studied under the supervision of tutors. He became accustomed to, and knowledgeable about, the rituals and hierarchies of the life of the *askerî* elite. He was turned into a carrier of the Ottoman dynastic ethos.

In Ottoman dynastic culture, princes developed strong ties with their fathers and mothers, both of whom were responsible for properly training their son as a well-rounded courtier and future sultan. Süleyman was a product of concubinage, born to a slave woman named Hafsa.[74] In the early stages of the Ottoman enterprise, Ottoman princes and princesses wed people of equivalent rank from neighboring dynasties. These were marriages that were meant to create or enforce political alliances, and they had become increasingly rare by the time of Süleyman's birth. The dynasty's sexual reproduction was mostly, and eventually solely, secured through concubinage.[75] Süleyman's mother, like other female slaves, had been either purchased by Selim's household or received as a gift, probably from Bayezid II, who was actively engaged in finding suitable sexual partners for his sons.[76]

The legality of concubinage in the Sharia provided a convenient instrument to the Ottoman dynasty. Islamic law stipulated that men and women who lived in areas not under the rule of Islam could be enslaved; women could further be used as concubines. While the number of legal wives was restricted to four, the number of concubines was not limited. Concubines did not have to be Muslims, but children born to them by a Muslim father were free and Muslim.[77] In the Ottoman case, concubines in the harem were Muslims, likely converted shortly after purchase or upon entry into the harem. They were also given a specifically Ottoman training that prepared them as potential sexual partners and companions as well as mothers. Like the Christian children of the sultan's subjects taken in through the *devşirme* and raised as soldiers, servants, and officials, the women of the harem played a crucial role, albeit one that they did not initially choose for themselves, in Ottoman politics and administration.

As the protected/forbidden interior of the household, the Ottoman harem has been the subject of much discussion, from the observations of European travelers in the fifteenth and sixteenth centuries to the present. Some viewed it mainly as a space of debauchery, yet another peculiarity of an "Orient" that existed in contradistinction to the "West."[78] Some scholars of Ottoman history, eager to attribute a level of rationality and institutionalization to the harem, have portrayed it as a palace school for women.[79] The Ottoman harem and the practice of concubinage were indeed dynastic institutions, the likes of which were encountered in other societies throughout history. Their main function was to carefully manage the relations between concubines and princes and secure viable heirs to the throne. Unlike princess brides from neighboring dynasties, concubines did not have any external political attachments. Their children belonged solely and entirely to the Ottoman dynasty.

Hafsa was around fifteen years of age as she gave birth to Süleyman. When a concubine gave birth to a boy, her life changed radically, as happened to Hafsa. Legally speaking, she remained a slave, but her standing was elevated over that of the other women, as was her stipend. Her sexual relationship with Selim quite likely ended. Her new role, with the help of others inside the harem, was to care for the baby's health and wellbeing. If a prince survived childhood diseases and epidemics and lived long enough to receive his own appointment as district governor, his mother traveled with him and helped him establish his own household, including his own harem.[80] If the son ended up becoming sultan, his mother's status grew into that of the most senior female member of the ruler's household. That was a rare eventuality, however. Upon her son's death, whether from natural or political causes, the mother could be relegated to a life of relative poverty and oblivion on the margins of the Ottoman dynasty, her livelihood depending on the charity of the ruling sultan. These were the prospects awaiting Hafsa as Süleyman's mother.

Besides concubines, the harem also included physicians, midwives, wet nurses, various female servants, and eunuchs who assisted Hafsa during and after Süleyman's birth. In a world full of germs and viruses for which no cure existed, and in a culture in which belief in the lethal powers of curses and magic was nearly universal, the harem and its women provided shelter and relief for all sorts of ills. There the newborn was bathed, swaddled, fed, and placed in his cradle. He was then given a name.

## 2

---

# *Childhood and Adolescence: Raising a Prince, 1494/5–1509*

THE CHILD WHO was to become the longest-reigning Ottoman sultan was born in Trabzon, on the Black Sea coast, in northeast Anatolia. His father Selim served there as district governor. His mother Hafsa was one of Selim's many concubines.

There are two sets of dates provided for Süleyman's birth. The first is the night of Safer 6, 900, of the Hijri calendar, which corresponds to November 5/6, 1494. It is from a work written a few decades after Süleyman's death, and its author claims that he consulted a horoscope. It is impossible to either prove or refute his information since the horoscope is not available today. As he had access to the Ottoman palace, it is not unlikely for him to have seen a record that may have been kept there.[1] The second date for Süleyman's birth comes from sources compiled during his lifetime, such as the illustrated history he commissioned during the later decades of his reign. Accordingly, Süleyman was born at the beginning of the Hijri year 901, that is, at a date that falls within the few months following September 21, 1495.[2]

The existence of two separate birth dates for Süleyman is not necessarily about faulty record-keeping. Rather, it is representative of the anxieties and expectations of the time, the exigencies of politics, and the constant search for legitimacy. In Süleyman's case, the seemingly small difference of a year signified the closing of an era and the opening of a new one. The tenth Hijri century, believed by many to be the last century on earth before the Last Judgment, was meant to be a time of religious renewal and political transformation in the Islamic world and beyond. If Süleyman were to be born at its beginning, he could, for instance, be presented as the Renewer (*müceddid*) said to be sent to the community of Muslims by God at the beginning of every century. It is possible that the horoscope was erroneous or the recollection of that first author was faulty, and that Süleyman was indeed born at the beginning of the tenth Hijri century. Even if he were not, however, it would have been convenient to claim that he did. At times, indeed oftentimes, being sultan required a constant rewriting of one's life story.

## *The Naming of a Child*

For a patrilineal dynasty like the Ottomans, the naming of sons was a sensitive act that was subject to careful consideration.[3] Members of the dynasty shared, together with Muslims living under their rule and beyond, specific cultural traditions that determined the naming of children. One of those traditions was Persian high culture, particularly literature and history, which was common to a variety of political and linguistic communities across the Islamic world. For instance, Firdavsi's (d. 1020) Persian *Shahnama* (*"The Book of Kings"*), an epic work on ancient Iranian kings, was widely used as a source for literary and historical references and models.[4] Islamic history, which includes Old Testament prophets as well as Jesus among its chief actors, was another source of inspiration. In fact, names of Old Testament prophets in their Turkicized/Arabicized form were frequently used by Muslims, Jews, and Christians alike.

For the Ottomans, the mythical Turkic/nomadic past and its heroes, and the history of the Ottoman dynasty itself, provided other examples and models. Turkish names could cut across religious boundaries as well, as seen in the case of common names encountered among Turkish-speaking Christians and Turkish-speaking Muslims. Moreover, patronymics and family names, professional titles, references to geographic origin, nicknames, or pen names were often used to distinguish individuals from one another. Class, status, and cultural milieu determined the ways in which a particular individual's given name evolved during their life by the addition of these other markers.

These different yet interrelated cultural traditions are reflected in the names of Ottoman princes around the time of Süleyman's birth. Süleyman's great uncle Cem was named after Jamshid, one of the heroes in the *Shahnama*. One of Cem's sons, murdered during the struggle for the throne in 1482, was called Oğuz, after the mythical ancestor of Turkic-speaking tribes of the same name in western Eurasia. One of Süleyman's uncles was called Korkud, a name he shared with Dede (ancestor/elder) Korkud, who figured in many stories about Turkic tribes as narrator and a source of ancestral wisdom.[5]

Other uncles had names associated with Muhammad: Mehmed, a Turkish colloquialization of Muhammad; and Mahmud and Ahmed, names that stem from the same Arabic root as Muhammad.[6]

Two of Süleyman's uncles had particularly memorable names. One was called Âlemşah, an Arabic-Persian compound meaning king of the world, and another Şehinşah, both a Persian name and a title in the Persian political tradition that meant king of kings or emperor. The names of Muslim women came from the same cultural universe. Süleyman's paternal grandmother was Gülbahar, a Turkicized Persian compound meaning spring rose. His mother Hafsa was named after a figure in early Islam, a wife of Muhammad and the daughter of one of his closest companions.

As for Süleyman, there are different stories about why he received that particular name. According to one, Selim was in the company of scholars when news of his son's birth reached him. There was a discussion among those present about the baby's name. Then, as it was customary to consult the Quran for divine signs, Selim's imam opened a random page. The verse, on top of the righthand page, was "*Innahu min Suleimana wa innahu bismi Allahi ar-rahmani ar-rahimi.*" This is a passage in which the Queen of Sheba receives a letter from Prophet Solomon. "Verily it is from Suleiman," she says, "and verily it is, 'In the Name of God, the Compassionate, the Merciful.'"[7] The tutor thus proposed Süleyman, the Turkicized Arabic form of Solomon, as the newborn's name.[8]

There are other anecdotes that give Süleyman's father, and his name, Selim, center stage in the naming of the newborn. An Arabic-origin name, Selim means safe, secure, undamaged. However, this literal meaning seems not to have played a role in the naming of the child. According to one story, when Selim heard his teacher call the newborn after Solomon, he felt humbled. He stated that only God's will could make his son a new Solomon. He then proposed to preserve the name given by his teacher but find a different origin for it. That origin was the Arabic diminutive of his name, *Süleym*. Using the Persian rule of word combination, Selim then came up with *Süleym-i ân*, "this little Selim," which by contraction became Süleyman.[9]

Another story offers a more straightforward explanation. Rather than consulting any books to look for inspirations and signs, Selim simply chose to name his son after himself. He used his literary skills to invent *Süleym-i ân*, this little Selim.[10] According to his near-contemporaries, Selim was headstrong, proud, arrogant.[11] It is thus not difficult to imagine him naming his son little Selim or, to chance a more elaborate translation, the little one from Selim.

Selim had another son, probably born soon after Süleyman, who died as a child in 1499. He was named Salih, after an ancient prophet mentioned in the Quran, whose name meant righteous, pious. Selim had at least six daughters, with different concubines, who survived beyond childhood, but Süleyman remained his only surviving son and heir.[12] There were rumors that another concubine bore Selim a son after she was released from his harem and wedded to an Ottoman official. This putative son, called Üveys, was born around 1512 but was never recognized as legitimate.[13] He later served as a high-ranking Ottoman official and died in 1545 as governor-general of Yemen. Thus, the little Selim, who entered the world as Süleyman, remained the only son, inextricably tied to his father in name and everything else.

Across Ottoman society, however, almost everyone, both around 1494/ 5 and later, associated the name of Süleyman with the biblical and Quranic Solomon rather than Selim. The Quran describes Solomon as a prophet-king who descended from another prophet-king, David. Solomon is portrayed as a true believer in the one God, to whose glory he builds his temple. He is also depicted as a supreme ruler who reigns over humans, animals, and genies. He does so with knowledge and wisdom, which are bestowed upon him by God.[14]

In the Ottoman lands, the legend of Solomon was further developed to include elements of Persian and Turkic history and myth, as seen in a compilation of Anatolian lore around the turn of the fifteenth century.[15] This particular Solomon, presented in an accessible language, is a prophet, a divinely sanctioned ruler, a wise man, and a hero whose peregrinations encompass the entire Old World. Not all Solomonic lore was positive, however. For instance, there were stories, passed down from Byzantine apocalypticism into Ottoman culture, that portrayed Solomon's building of the temple, and by extension the Ottoman imperial project itself, as an act of vanity. However, those critical views remained underground, like other elements of political opposition at the time, only flaring up during crises.

Süleyman, after he became sultan, was keen to emphasize the profound historical and cultural connotations of his name. He felt that it granted him precious political and cultural capital, as well as a sense of destiny to be fulfilled: to become a Second Solomon (*Süleyman-ı Sanî*), or the Solomon of the Age (*Süleyman-ı Zaman*), to rule wisely, justly, over the realms both seen and unseen. Thus, throughout his reign, he addressed his interlocutors as the Solomon of the Age in a variety of places, from his own poetry to diplomatic letters and inscriptions. In his and his wife's extensive patronage works in Jerusalem, a city with strong Solomonic associations, the ancient legacy of Solomon found a contemporary resonance.

Another telling sign of the value Süleyman attributed to his name and its cultural and religious associations is found in the *Sulaymannama* he commissioned. The manuscript displays, as an ornament at the top of the first two pages of the narrative, the Quranic verse after which he was supposedly named: "Verily it is from Suleiman, and verily it is, 'In the Name of God, the Compassionate, the Merciful.'"[16] In the ensuing prologue, and throughout the text, multiple Solomonic references are used to promote the greatness of Süleyman's power and achievements. Additionally, many other poetic and historical works from his reign often addressed him as a Second Solomon whose exploits reputedly equaled those of the first.

Selim and Süleyman were not alone in laying a claim to the Solomonic legacy, however. There were others who aspired to the same legacy, including Selim's brothers Ahmed and Mahmud, each of whom had a son also named Süleyman. Thus, in the 1490s and 1500s, the name Süleyman merely implied a potential that had to be realized in the face of great challenges, in competition with rivals within the dynasty.

## Growing Up in Trabzon

Süleyman spent his childhood and adolescence in Trabzon. The town's natural and built environment and its demography formed his first impressions on everything from food and nature to religious and linguistic difference and a sense of history.[17]

Trabzon and its vicinity were acquired by the Ottomans in 1461, following a military expedition personally commanded by Mehmed II. The Ottoman conquest signaled the end of the Empire of Trebizond, a Greek Orthodox entity ruled by members of the Komnenos family. The family had an illustrious past, its members having served as Byzantine emperors in Constantinople between 1081 and 1185. They had fled to Trabzon as Constantinople fell to the armies of the Fourth Crusade in 1204.[18] There, they continued to use imperial titles that underscored their claims to the Byzantine Empire. They intermarried with other Byzantine dynasties as well as the Akkoyunlu, the regional Turko-Muslim rivals of the Ottomans.[19] By 1461, however, the Empire of Trebizond merely consisted of the town of Trabzon and the surrounding areas, and the Komnenos could not resist the Ottoman advance.

For Mehmed II, who sought to establish better control over the Black Sea and the eastern frontiers of the Ottoman lands, Trabzon was an attractive target. Many traders used the town as a way station between Tabriz and Caffa (today Theodosia in the Crimea), two major centers of Eurasian trade. Others

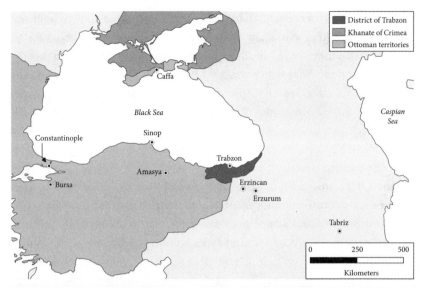

FIG. 2.1 The district of Trabzon, ca. 1500. Map by Jordan Blekking.

from the east stopped by Trabzon before traveling to Constantinople or Bursa. Genoese and Venetian merchants connected the town to the Mediterranean, and Georgian and Abkhazian merchants to the Caucasus.[20]

An Ottoman survey of the area's resources and population, completed around 1486, provides clues about the town's economic life. Around that time, Trabzon had 177 shops, seven storage houses, and a small yet active harbor. Various businesses catered to the needs of the town and the traveling merchants. They included an herbalist, grocers, drapers, dyers, tanners, a shoemaker, saddlers, a planer, a carpenter, butchers, an ironsmith, bakers, a jeweler, candlemakers, cotton fluffers, a box maker, and a rope maker.[21] Large quantities of grain flowed to the town, where nearly forty mills dotted the landscape. Slaves, wheat, and caviar came from over the sea, and silk, clothes, and candle wax over land.

Trabzon was built on a narrow strip between the Black Sea and the Pontic Mountains. The Ottoman district of the same name, established shortly after the conquest, extended 100 miles east from Trabzon and 80 miles west, covering the seashore as well as land on both slopes of the mountains. For Trabzon's inhabitants, access to the wide expanse of the central Anatolian plateau required arduous journeys over difficult terrain. For instance, in the early spring of 1404, a Castilian diplomat on his way to visit Timur in Samarkand spent three days to go from Trabzon to a mountain pass 50 miles south, at a height of 6,600 feet. He and his party traveled on narrow paths, across a sloping and snowy terrain, often having to ford rapid streams, not to mention needing to negotiate passage with local armed groups. From the mountain pass at Zigana, they needed another four days to reach Erzincan, a further 100 miles south on the Anatolian plateau.[22] On the way back, they followed a different route for safety reasons. Approaching Trabzon from the southeast, they crossed the Pontic Mountains during four difficult days, on paths so narrow that loaded animals could not pass, forcing travelers to carry their packs on their backs. In places, the road merely consisted of wooden bridges stretched from one rocky promontory to another.[23]

The Ottomans had faced the same obstacles to reach Trabzon in 1461. A bureaucrat and historian, quite likely present during the campaign, later described how soldiers armed with axes and picks went ahead of the army to open a path, assisted by auxiliary units working night and day.[24] Another Ottoman historian, writing a few decades later, compared the Pontic Mountains to the legendary Wall of Alexander, built to contain Gog and Magog. The sinuous, rock-strewn mountain paths, sloping upward then descending into valleys and ravines, were too narrow for mounted men. Even Mehmed II himself, the commander of the campaign, had to dismount and march on foot.[25]

The sea did not provide much respite either. There was no unbroken access on the coast from one end of the district to the other. The southern shore of the Black Sea has no natural ports other than Sinop, and Trabzon and other shore settlements had to rely on small man-made harbors. The unpredictable winds and the rough waves often upset travel via the sea. The Castilian diplomat and his party, for instance, sailed from Constantinople to Trabzon in twenty days in March 1404, their voyage often delayed due to foul weather. The return was even longer: twenty-five days.[26] Still, the sea offered a precious link that tied Trabzon to the wider world.

Despite being seen as nearly impenetrable by travelers and invaders alike, the Pontic Mountains were a boon to Trabzon and its vicinity thanks to the unique ecosystem they helped create. In contrast to the barren scenery of the central Anatolian plateau to the south, the northern side of the mountain range is covered with trees (spruce, pine, oak, and maple in the mountains; alder, ash, and poplar in the valleys) and a vivid undergrowth that extends from azaleas to rhododendrons. This flora is accompanied by an equally rich fauna that includes multiple species of birds of prey, wolves, jackals, foxes, brown bears, boars, ibex, and deer. Northern and northeastern winds hit the steep slopes and help produce thirty-five inches of rain per year, a level commensurate with that of Seattle. Eastern winds chase the rain clouds, clear the air and allow the sun to shine over the town. The warm southern wind makes for a temperate climate during winters. The median temperatures are seventy-five Fahrenheit during summer and forty-five in winter.[27]

The inhabitants of the area, which had been settled nearly two millennia before Süleyman was born, knew how to use this specific ecosystem to their advantage. According to Ottoman records produced shortly after the takeover, they raised sheep and other livestock and engaged in small-scale agriculture and horticulture. The local diet included wheat and millet, olives and olive oil, walnuts, chestnuts, pears, apples, cherries, and grapes, the latter of which were used for wine as well as a slightly fermented, non-alcoholic grape juice called *şıra*. Animal proteins were available from sheep, goats, and cows, and local Christians kept pigs. An Ottoman traveler who visited in 1640 added to the list figs, bitter oranges, and Oriental persimmons, which are named in Turkish after the town (*Trabzon hurması*). The fish, as the traveler remarked, were plentiful and various: perch, gray mullet, turbot, red mullet, and mackerel. He particularly noted the locals' love for the bountiful anchovy, which they used in soups, stews, kebabs, and pies.[28]

At the end of the fifteenth century, Trabzon's center was a fortified hilltop and a walled low-lying area between the hill and the sea. Outside the walls, there were houses, a lively marketplace, artisans' workshops, fields, and orchards. The hill gently rose from the sea to reach an elevation of 225 feet at its highest point. It felt like a natural fortress, surrounded by two valleys crossed by streams east and west, and a ravine in the south. The hilltop was divided into two sections, separated by a wall: the site of the ancient settlement, at the highest and narrowest one-third, called *Yukarı Hisar* (Upper Fortress) or *Kule* (the Tower); and the remaining two-thirds, lower and wider, called *Orta Hisar* (Middle Fortress). Two bridges stretching over the valleys east and west, and a gate in the north, were the only access points into the Middle Fortress from the rest of the town.

Süleyman lived in the Upper-Middle Fortress neighborhood. The neighborhood looked over the Lower Fortress (*Aşağı Hisar*) and the settlements outside the walls.[29] The Komnenos dynasty's palace was located at the very top of the Upper Fortress section. While such a structure may have been an obvious choice for the new rulers of the town, it is impossible to ascertain the exact location of Selim and Süleyman's living quarters.[30]

Süleyman grew up in a town that had seen significant demographic changes in the decades before his birth. Around a third of Trabzon's pre-conquest population, a group of nearly two thousand individuals, had been removed by the Ottoman authorities. As one of the major concerns of Mehmed II was the

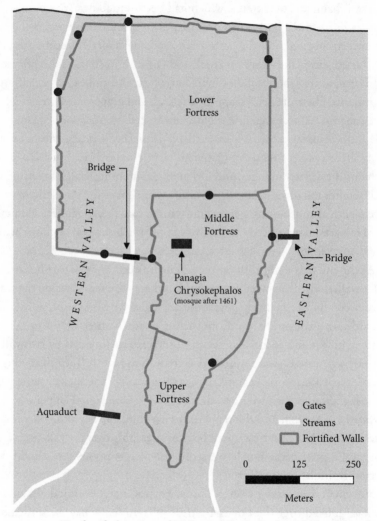

**FIG. 2.2** The fortified section of Trabzon. Map by Jordan Blekking, based on H. F. B. Lynch, *Armenia: Travels and Studies*, vol. 1, *The Russian Provinces* (London: Longmans, Green, and Co., 1901), facing page 13.

repopulation of Constantinople after he took the city in 1453, most of those removed from Trabzon were resettled in the new Ottoman capital. In addition, some of Trabzon's youth were forcibly recruited into Ottoman service through the *devşirme* practice.[31] Moreover, in newly captured areas without

Muslim populations, Ottoman authorities often settled Muslim communities to change the demographic balance, and this policy was applied in Trabzon as well.

Conversion to Islam was another reason behind the expansion of the number of Muslims living in the district. In general, conversion happened under the weight of various factors, such as economic pressures and the promise of upward mobility upon conversion, socialization with Muslim settlers, the impact of religious syncretism, or the failure of the local clergy to motivate and sustain their congregations.[32] A mixture of these factors could have contributed to the adoption of Islam by local Orthodox Christians in Trabzon. However, during Süleyman's childhood, Christians continued to constitute the bulk of the population both in the town and in the district. Muslims who were recently relocated to Trabzon mostly lived within the fortified sections, while Christian neighborhoods were located to the east and west of the walls.[33] The self-isolation of the Muslims may be attributed to their sense of cultural difference from and superiority to the Christians, as well as their real or imagined security concerns in a town with a Christian majority.

The Muslim inhabitants of the area, among whom Süleyman grew up, reflected a broad spectrum. There were artisans and shopkeepers living in Trabzon, nomads and agriculturalists scattered across the district, and members of the *askerî* elite serving in various capacities, from *tımar* holders and fortress guards to members of Selim's household. Ottoman records also mention dozens of individuals who had titles and occupations related to the teaching and preaching of Islam. These included *hacı* (someone who completed a pilgrimage to Mecca), *pir* (elder, perhaps referring to elders of confraternities), *şeyh* (sheikh of a confraternity), imam, *hatib* (preacher), *müezzin* (reciter), and most notably *fakih* (religious scholar).[34] In addition, seventy individuals were listed as mosque helpers, probably fulfilling everyday tasks in places of worship. Twenty-two *hacı*s, eight *pir*s, one *fakih*, and six *hoca*s (a title that could refer both to a merchant and a religious scholar) were recorded as living in Trabzon. A number of them were given *tımar*s by the authorities; indeed, many of them must have relocated for the prospect of land and property.

These men with religious affiliations and duties were in Trabzon as members of a Muslim upper class that supported the Ottoman administration, from changing the demographic balance to boosting the morale of the recent Muslim settlers. For a district that had few Muslims before 1461, and a town that had none, their numbers are significant. By comparison, Ottoman records from 1486 listed sixty-six priests (*papas*), twenty-one Christian elders (*papa,* perhaps a different spelling for priest by Ottoman scribes), and two monks, who served a Christian population that was more than ten times larger than the Muslim one across the district, and four times larger within Trabzon. Consequently, Süleyman grew up in an environment in which being an Ottoman Muslim preserved that old frontier flair, with its mixture of combativeness and pragmatism.

Indeed, very much like in the early days of the Ottoman enterprise, Süleyman, Selim, their servants, and their fellow Muslims lived as a minority in the midst of a large Christian population. In 1486, the district's population consisted of 123,500 Christians, nearly 92 percent of the total population, and 9,650 Muslims.[35] Within the town of Trabzon, those percentages slightly improved to the advantage of the Muslims. In 1486, the town's population was around seventy-five hundred.[36] Muslims, including both civilians and those with *askerî* status, totaled around two thousand, 27 percent of the urban population. More than half of them were recent settlers who had been forcefully relocated there from central Anatolia.[37] Among the Christian majority, the Greek Orthodox were the largest group, followed by a sizeable Armenian community and a small cluster of Venetian and Genoese inhabitants.[38] Most of the Christians were *zimmi*s, tax-paying non-Muslim Ottoman subjects. The Venetians and the Genoese, on the other hand, had a separate legal status that would have been determined through agreements with the Ottoman authorities, unless some of them declared themselves to be tax-paying resident subjects of the Ottomans.

As a result, Süleyman lived in a town whose residents spoke Pontic Greek, Eastern/classical Armenian, the Venetian and Genoese dialects of Italian, and Anatolian Turkish. Merchants and travelers from the Caucasus, the Eurasian steppe, and western Asia added Slavic dialects, Georgian, Abkhaz, Persian, and other languages to the town's soundscape. A simple stroll would have exposed Süleyman to the sights and sounds of a multi-lingual, multi-religious population. At the same time, as a Muslim, and a member of the Ottoman dynasty, he would never forget, and never be allowed to forget, that he belonged to the highest stratum of the society he lived in.

Trabzon's built environment similarly displayed the influence of multiple cultural and religious traditions. Süleyman grew up exposed to a variety of influences from the town's ancient and recent, pre-Ottoman and Ottoman, history. As they did in cities conquered from non-Muslims, the Ottomans tried to put their imprint on the townscape. Charity and patronage played important roles in creating markers of Ottoman and Muslim presence. One such patron was Şirin Hatun (d. 1500), mother of Prince Abdullah, an older brother of Selim. She accompanied Abdullah during his time as district governor of Trabzon, from 1469–70 to the early 1480s, and she provided funds for a small mosque to be built in the Upper Fortress around 1470. Signs of the town's brief Ottoman past included two inscriptions, one by a previous governor and the other by Selim, which commemorated repair works done on the fortified walls in 1468–69 and 1491–92. Other Ottoman works included fountains in the Middle Fortress, a new bridge connecting the Middle Fortress to the eastern suburbs, and bathhouses, both refurbished and new.

Despite the recent Ottoman additions, however, the built environment had not changed radically since the conquest. Near the shore stood two small fortresses that had originally belonged to the Genoese and the Venetians. Among the largest churches in the town before 1461, the Church of the Golden-Headed Virgin (Panagia Chrysokephalos in Greek) and the Church of Agios Eugenios had been turned into mosques after the Ottoman conquest. These conversions mostly consisted of the addition of a minaret and the placement of a pulpit. Sometimes, interior walls were whitewashed to hide the Orthodox Christian imagery. Otherwise, these buildings continued to reflect much of their original architectural and ornamental features, which included reliefs of crosses, eagles, doves, grapes, and vines on the outside walls of Agios Eugenios. The ancient walls of the Upper Fortress, inscriptions in Greek, and stone reliefs of the Byzantine double-eagle scattered around the town were constant reminders of Trabzon's past under the Komnenos dynasty.[39]

While it fell into disuse sometime after the Ottoman conquest, the palace of the Komnenos emperors must have been visited by Selim and Süleyman, even though they may not have lived there. A Trabzon native, who became a prominent Orthodox clergyman and then a Catholic bishop, left a description of it from around 1426–27. He was in his native town on a diplomatic mission from Byzantine Constantinople, and he was admitted into the palace. He mentions multiple rooms and halls, floors paved with white marble, and ceilings gleaming with gold. He also talks about painted walls that depicted past emperors and major historical events. The palace included a variety of ceremonial spaces used by the Komnenos rulers to distance themselves from their subjects, conduct domestic and diplomatic activities, and organize feasts and banquets.[40] While it is likely that the buildings were not kept up in the years following the conquest, what remained of them, together with the rest of the town, constituted an impressive legacy to which the Ottoman dynasty, always self-conscious about its genealogy and its place in history, would not have been oblivious.

There may have been additional reasons to feel connected to the Komnenos past. According to one anecdote, Mehmed II, Süleyman's great-grandfather, had claimed that the Ottomans were related to the Komnenos dynasty. He apparently believed that Osman, the founder of the Ottoman dynasty, was the descendant of a Komnenos family member who had converted to Islam and married the daughter of an Anatolian Seljuk sultan.[41] Selim and Süleyman may not have heard of it. Regardless, serving as governor and living in the capital of an old empire, one that had represented an important part of the Byzantine legacy, must have boosted their self-image and enhanced their belief in their ultimate goal: to become sultans.

## Friends, Family, and Rites of Passage

In the days and months that followed his birth, Süleyman's wellbeing must have been a major preoccupation in the harem, particularly since he lived in a society with high levels of infant and early childhood mortality. To make matters worse, a commercial way station like Trabzon was regularly exposed to contagious diseases. Thus, a nursing mother was sought, and a woman named Afife was found. Afife's husband served as an Ottoman judge (kadı) in Trabzon, and they had a son named Yahya (d. 1571), born shortly before Süleyman. Thus, according to tradition, Süleyman and Yahya were connected through the milk they were fed, becoming brothers by nursing. Local lore claimed that, as they grew up, the two trained as apprentices with a goldsmith in Trabzon, a Greek Orthodox man named Constantine.[42] Moreover, it has been suggested that Yahya and Süleyman must have studied together and that their love of poetry, for which both became known later in their lives, must have started during their Trabzon years.[43] Yahya and members of his family were probably the first individuals outside Selim's household with whom Süleyman became closely acquainted.

Following one of the paths available to the son of a judge, Yahya attended a madrasa in Trabzon. He moved to Constantinople shortly after Süleyman became sultan, continued his education in upper-level madrasas, trained with a prominent scholar, and eventually became a madrasa teacher himself. Despite his affinity with the sultan, he did not rise in the Ottoman learned hierarchy to become a high-level official with a visible political role in the management of the realm. In fact, he spent his last decades in relative isolation, as a Sufi living in a lodge he built on the shores of the Bosphorus. There are many anecdotes about the sultan and the Sufi friend, particularly during the later years of their relationship.[44] Regardless of whether these stories reflect the whole truth, they sent powerful messages to their readers and listeners. The figure of a mighty sultan who nevertheless maintained a childhood friendship, and the figure of a mystic who served as an example of humility vis-à-vis the sultan's occasional vanity, resonated strongly with multiple audiences.

Important aspects of Süleyman's early years remain in darkness. Did he, for instance, live in a separate house with his mother, since the concubine mothers of boys were usually elevated above the rest of the harem? Did they have their own rooms within a larger structure? Similarly, the nature of the relationship between Süleyman and his several half-sisters, as well as his mother and grandmother, is impossible to fathom. Given his close relationship with female members of his family later in his life, it is possible to assume that he had a close relationship with them. There were traumatic events in the life of the family that would have been equally formative for Süleyman. For instance, when he was around four years of age, his half-brother Salih died. There are no documents about the death, but Salih's sarcophagus, with an inscription on it, is still in Trabzon today.

There were other losses in the family as Süleyman grew older. He was around eight at the time of his half-sister Kamerşah's death in 1503 and ten at his grandmother Gülbahar's death in 1505. The causes of these deaths are unknown. Kamerşah's death may have been due to a serious illness or a contagious disease that may have threatened the entire family. Indeed, Selim wrote in haste to Constantinople to ask for a physician a few months before his daughter's death, and one was quickly dispatched to Trabzon.[45] In another sign of the particularly strong inter-dynastic ties established by Süleyman's grandfather Bayezid II, the palace in Constantinople was informed of Kamerşah and Gülbahar's deaths, in response to which the sultan sent condolence presents to Trabzon.[46] Soon after Gülbahar's death, Selim had a small mosque and a tomb built in her memory.[47]

Not every major event in the life of the family was grim. In spring–summer 1509, following the Ottoman custom of matching daughters of princes and sultans with members of the *askerî* elite, one of Süleyman's half-sisters was wedded to a district governor. Süleyman was around fifteen years of age then. Selim sent news of the wedding to Constantinople in both his name and his son's, underlining Süleyman's status as his sole heir as well as one of the two grown men in the family.[48] It is possible to imagine that Süleyman played a visible role during the wedding festivities, seated next to his father.

Perhaps the most significant event in Süleyman's early life was his circumcision, which occurred a few months before the death of his grandmother in 1505, when he was around the age of ten. Male circumcision was and is a crucial rite of passage for pre-pubescent males in many societies: Muslims, Jews, and Copts, as well as African and Polynesian cultures. For Muslims, the act symbolizes, from a historical and communal perspective, the adherence of the boy and his parents to the traditions of Muhammad.[49] It also often marks a transition from boyhood into adolescence, with its expectations of maturity. In Süleyman's case, circumcision was a rite of passage that additionally symbolized his advancement into a stage of his life where he would soon become eligible for a district governorship. Circumcision thus had biological and cultural as well as political implications for him and his family.

Starting in the mid-fifteenth century, circumcisions prevailed over weddings as major events in the life of the Ottoman dynasty. Süleyman thus found himself at the center of lavish celebrations.[50] His grandfather Bayezid II, informed of his grandson's impending circumcision, sent generous gifts to Trabzon.[51] These included a one-time disbursement of 300,000 akçes to Selim, a sum close to his annual revenue as district governor. This was quite possibly sent to offset the considerable expenses associated with circumcision celebrations, such as special banquets for the officials, the distribution of food to the entire town, and various entertainments that included musicians, jugglers, and other performers. Bayezid did not forget to send the customary gift of valuable clothes to the child's closest relatives: his father Selim, mother Hafsa, grandmother Gülbahar, and one of his half-sisters and her mother.

The gifts Süleyman received were much more numerous and elaborate. More importantly, they underscored his passage into adolescence. They came in three groups. First were clothes, which included two overcoats of heavy gilded velvet of "Frankish" (probably Venetian) make. One was red, the other green, and they came with matching pieces of muslin to be worn as turbans. Such pieces were meant to be worn outside the home, and Süleyman would use them in public settings, as a prince on his way to embark into his political career. Other pieces added variety to his wardrobe: five house dresses of different colors and fabrics and three hats. Two of those were *üsküfs*, high hats meant for formal use, and one was a *börk*, a low hat of softer material suited for everyday use.

Süleyman's passage into adolescence also implied that he would soon begin to establish his own household, and his grandfather and his officials, aware of this eventuality, sent him many household items. These could be used to refurbish Süleyman's chamber during and after circumcision, and they would then become his property: a box for spoons, a salt pot, and four knives, ornamented or plated with gold; a tray, an ewer, a basin, and two candleholders, made of silver; two mattresses, two quilts, four cushions/

pillows, one mattress sheet and two duvet covers, two Menemen carpets, and a green rug.

These consumer goods, as their meticulous descriptions in a palace register of donations attest, were made of high-quality materials produced in Europe and the Anatolian peninsula. A third group of gifts completed the generous package from the grandfather: a sword ornamented with gold, a gold-plated armor, a bow, and a quiver with gold ornaments that contained forty arrows specially made in palace ateliers. The piece de resistance, however, was a horse, accompanied by a saddle of walnut wood with silver hooks, a bridle with silver reins, and a saddle blanket of red velvet and green plain Frankish cloth.[52] As a boy growing up in a patriarchal dynastic environment that promoted refinement in dress and material culture, as well as martial values and combative masculinity, Süleyman must have received these gifts with great excitement. This was truly a milestone in his life.

## *A Prince's Education*

While Süleyman's life thus underwent a major transition around the age of ten, his formal education must have started several years before his circumcision. The scarcity of specific information about the early years of his life is true for his education as well. However, it is possible to shed light on its nature, progression, and contents by drawing parallels with other, better-documented cases. Thus, it is likely that he began his studies between the ages of five and seven.[53] A typical elementary school ran five days a week, from early morning to the afternoon prayer, which amounted to around thirty hours per week. Children first learned how to write the individual letters of the Arabic alphabet, then how to spell them. Next, they learned to write and read words and sentences. Elementary education included arithmetic, Islamic rituals and basic theology, and manners.

The texts the children might encounter at this stage included popular stories of an epic nature, which narrated the life of Muhammad, the biographies of Sufi saints, and the daring exploits of heroes and warriors. Despite the growing weight of texts in children's education, orality—from rote learning and recitation to storytelling as an instructional method—played a crucial role. Finally, elementary education often included the reading of the Quran. The correct reading and recitation of what was accepted by Muslims as the direct, unchanged, and unmediated word of God was a significant act of piety. Since quotations from the Quran often appeared in texts produced in Islamic societies, from religious sciences to history, literature, and political/moral writings, the reading of the Quran also marked a child's entry into a wider literate culture.

What distinguished Süleyman's education was its elite character. Throughout his studies, he probably did not have to huddle with other boys in a small building adjoining one of the newly built or recently converted mosques in Trabzon. His friend Yahya may have accompanied him, but it is quite likely that he studied mostly by himself, under the care of a special instructor, in a well-furnished room. As a member of the Ottoman dynasty, he would not be subject to frequent corporal punishment, a major pedagogical instrument in many premodern societies. Moreover, he would have plenty of access to materials that could be expensive, such as paper (a precious commodity that was often re-used), high-quality inks, well-made quills, sturdy inkwells, and ornate bookstands. His first completion of the reading of the Quran, no doubt helped by the diacritical marks provided in many versions, and under the close attention of an instructor, would have been celebrated in the family as a significant achievement on his part.

The passage into adolescence in the years following his circumcision had various implications for Süleyman. For one, he was expected to behave as a mature individual vis-à-vis his parents and the wider community around him. This transition was already announced by the gifts he received from his grandfather, such as the clothes that were meant to be worn publicly and to impress the onlookers, and the weapons and the horse that signaled the true beginnings of his martial training. Another component of his passage into adolescence was related to his religious duties. Pubescent adolescents are required to fulfill Muslim rituals, from praying five times a day to attending the Friday prayer, fasting during the month of Ramadan, and generally respecting the rules of ritual purity. These would have been taught to Süleyman as part of his elementary education, through a Sunni Hanafi interpretation followed by the Ottoman dynasty and its servants and officials. As he left childhood behind, Süleyman was obliged to follow the precepts of Islam fully.

In terms of his education, the most visible development after its elementary phase was the appointment of a tutor, probably shortly before or soon after his circumcision. While Trabzon was far away from the palace library in Constantinople, and even from major regional cultural centers like Amasya, suitable candidates for the job were available. Migrant scholars from Arabic- and Persian-speaking lands, Anatolian-born scholars who had studied in Iran and the Mamluk territories, and graduates of Ottoman madrasas offered their services to the Ottoman dynasty. Many of them served as madrasa teachers and magistrates, and some were available to tutor princes.[54]

Süleyman's tutor was a man named Hayreddin.[55] Why he in particular was chosen is not known. Selim's imam and advisor Abdülhalim was from Kastamonu,[56] and Hayreddin was from a nearby town. In a society in which micro-solidarities played an important role in social relationships, that connection may have led to Hayreddin's appointment. One of Hayreddin's madrasa teachers had served previously as tutor to Bayezid II's son Ahmed, and it is possible that he recommended his pupil. In addition, there may have been Sufi affinities between Hayreddin and members of Selim's household. What is known is that, like Süleyman's mother Hafsa, his tutor eventually became a lifelong presence in his life. Hayreddin remained in Süleyman's company until his death in 1543 as a revered tutor and advisor, and the intensity of the connection between them was often remarked upon by contemporary observers.

Following a madrasa education Hayreddin had worked as judge and madrasa teacher before joining Selim's household. His madrasa education would have included the "rational sciences" (geometry, arithmetic, astronomy/astrology, logic, philosophy, medicine), the "transmitted sciences" (Quranic exegesis, Muhammad's sayings, theology, jurisprudence), and a hefty dose of Sufism, which permeated everything from ontology to cosmology.[57] While Hayreddin and Süleyman communicated in their native tongue, Anatolian/ Western Turkish, many of the reference works they used would have been in Persian and Arabic, reflecting the pronounced trilingual character of Ottoman elite learning.

Thus, Süleyman depended on Hayreddin, and probably a few others, for language instruction as well as the selection of works to be studied. The tutor and his pupil clearly had a productive time together. Süleyman eventually developed considerable skills in Persian, to the point of producing a body of poetry in that language, next to his larger output in Ottoman Turkish.[58] He was presented with a variety of poems and histories in Arabic during his reign, and he had the required skills to read, understand, and appreciate them.

Other elements of Süleyman's studies under Hayreddin may be guessed based on his lifelong interests, such as history, which he read and asked others to write, and Sufism, whose sensibilities are often found in his poetry. The tutor and the pupil must have read works on Ottoman and Islamic history (including elements of world history), geography and cosmography (including pre-Islamic history since Creation), and hagiographies of prominent Sufis. Popular stories, from legends of Alexander to the feats of ancient Turkish heroes, were mainstays of Ottoman culture. For a potential heir to the Ottoman throne, readings in political/moralistic literature would have been part of the agenda as well. Finally, since Hayreddin was a madrasa-educated scholar whose main expertise was in religious matters, it is likely that he discussed the interpretation of the Quran, the analysis of the sayings of Muhammad, and the fundamentals of Islamic law and theology.[59]

Another lifelong interest of Süleyman was reading and writing poetry. Hayreddin was not known as a poet, but Selim's household was frequented by many of them, the most prominent of whom was Abdülhalim, who wrote under the pen name Halimî.[60] Halimî's poetry was seen by his contemporaries as more technical than sentimental, a veiled criticism that underlined the dryness of his tone. However, having studied in Arab- and Persian-speaking lands, his knowledge in Arabo-Persian poetry was vast, and he was known for his skills in deciphering and explaining difficult passages and poetic enigmas. Süleyman could not have found a better teacher.

His poetry education would have been, on the one hand, highly technical. He would learn the meter system, *aruz*, which was based on the alternation of long and short syllables, and which also included a series of pre-composed, line-long meter patterns that had to be followed. Another component would be the careful reading of the literary canon. Here too, many reference works and respected authors belonged to Arabo-Persian literature, while Chaghatay/Eastern Turkish offered a thin layer and Ottoman/Anatolian/Western Turkish a mere sprinkling. Even a comprehensive collection such as Bayezid II's palace library in Constantinople included only eighty-six entries for Turkish poetry, some of them in Eastern Turkish, compared to nearly six hundred entries for Persian poetry.[61]

As a result, Süleyman, who eventually became one of the most prolific and original poets in Ottoman Turkish, received most of his poetry education in Persian and Arabic. A strong poetic tradition in Ottoman Turkish, with its own idiom and its cultural identity, was emerging in the early years of Süleyman's life, but it would become truly dominant only under his reign.[62] However, the notion of a larger body of literature in several languages remained relevant for him as well as other Ottoman poets. His Ottoman Turkish poetry thus includes many references to the main figures of the Persian poetic tradition, such as Hafiz (d. 1390), whose profound lyricism he emulated; and Nizami (d. 1209), Feriduddin Attar (d. 1221), Sadi (d. 1292), and Jami (d. 1492), whose synthesis of philosophical wisdom and mystical search permeates Süleyman's own literary work. It is also likely that he read the poetry of Ali Shir Nevai (d. 1499), who strove to produce a Chaghatay/Eastern Turkish counterpart of the Persianate poetic legacy, and whose efforts at producing a Turkic poetic voice resonated strongly among the Ottomans.[63] These are poets he would have studied and admired during his years of instruction under Hayreddin and Abdülhalim.

As in language learning, reading aloud and listening played a crucial role in becoming acquainted with poetic rhythm, rhyming, and vocabulary. Socialization had a role to play as well. Poetry was often recited in the company of other poets, patrons, and literature lovers. It was indeed the most distinguished pathway into Ottoman literary culture. For instance, during his years as sultan, his poetic skills helped Süleyman converse and communicate with other poets and foster a literary atmosphere based on patronage and poetic dialogue. In addition to structure, vocabulary, composition, and recitation, poetry was an instrument through which a poetic persona and a genteel sensibility were developed and performed.[64] This is particularly true of the most popular short form in the Islamic traditions, the *ghazal* (*gazel* in Ottoman Turkish), a lyric poem that typically includes several couplets.

All poets chose a pen name to use in their poetic output, and Süleyman's reflects his understanding of poetry as a space where he developed an alternately lyric and mystical voice that ran parallel to his image as sultan and warrior. It is Muhibbî, "the one who loves." Here, love refers both to worldly, physical, romantic affection, as well as the individual's love for God, and the Sufi's yearning for divine love. It is quite likely that the emotional and devotional modes of his poetry offered him a respite from the tensions of a competitive elite culture and the burdens of politics and war. Reading and composing poetry was a lifelong endeavor, and this is very much true of Süleyman. During his education, however, even if he may have penned a few verses, it is unlikely that he wrote poetry regularly. While studying under his tutor, his role was that of a careful listener.

Even though his formal education thus provided Süleyman with a strong foundation in Arabo-Persian and Ottoman Turkish literary cultures, it was clear that he was not meant to become a scholar. Literary skills were seen as important components of Ottoman dynastic culture and identity, but the ultimate task of a prince was to manage the *askerî* elite and the realm, after surviving the seemingly inevitable succession struggles. He needed a different sort of training in this regard. There, at least initially, the main responsibility belonged to his father.

## In His Father's Company

Selim, who served as district governor of Trabzon since 1487, contributed to Süleyman's education and training in various ways. He was involved in the selection and appointment of Hayreddin as tutor, and it is quite likely that he demanded to be informed regularly about his son's progress. Selim was a reader of history and poetry, and he must have suggested authors, titles, and subjects to be studied. His own book collection, the contents of which are unknown, was obviously available to Süleyman. Composing poems in Persian under the pen name Selimî, he also must have served as a literary model. Some of his favorite tropes, such as the suffering of the all-powerful monarch who is rejected by a ruthless beloved, seeped into Süleyman's poetry as well.[65] Equally importantly, Selim's household was the locale where Süleyman experienced the social and public aspects of poetry for the first time. A number of poets had congregated in Trabzon around Selim, and presumably there were gatherings, attended by Süleyman as he came of age, where poems and pleasantries were exchanged.

Selim was also Süleyman's personal guide into the history, customs, and traditions of the Ottoman dynasty that may not have been widely known or recorded. For instance, he told those around him anecdotes about his meetings with his illustrious grandfather Mehmed II, the conqueror of Constantinople. On one occasion, he narrated how he traveled to Constantinople from Amasya together with his brothers, when he was around ten years of age, for his circumcision. The entire city was turned into a festive space, and celebrations lasted for a month. The young princes, potential heirs to the throne, had an opportunity to converse with their grandfather. The sultan teased them, asking them whether they liked him or their father best. However, he was displeased when Prince Ahmed, Selim's future rival, bluntly told the sultan he loved his father more than him.[66]

On another occasion, during his years as sultan, Selim was presented with the draft of a portrait of Mehmed II. After studying it carefully, he stated that he fondly remembered his grandfather, who had made him sit on his knees as a sign of affection, and that the painter did not render his facial features well.[67] He probably told many other stories to his son, both publicly and in confidence. Selim's brothers were rivals on the way to the throne, and he must have offered his son anecdotes on them, including comments about their present and future actions, inter-family tensions, and the struggles that awaited Selim and Süleyman.

Martial training was another important component of Süleyman's upbringing. Selim's household included many military men with different specializations, and they must have served as Süleyman's instructors in the use of weapons and horseback riding. There was a designated space for military exercises to the west of the town walls, and it is possible to imagine the young prince training there in the company of others. The skills he gained would be further displayed and developed during hunts, a regular occurrence in the everyday lives of the men of the dynasty. The vicinity of Trabzon was particularly suitable for these excursions since the Pontic Mountains offered both a difficult terrain to be mastered and a rich array of animals to be hunted.

Using weapons to shed the blood of animals, riding horses well, and socializing with other men during pursuits and at barbecues were important components of upper class male identity. Moreover, hunting was seen, in Ottoman as well as other contemporary dynastic cultures, as both a form of training for war and a much-needed distraction, indeed a form of leisure.[68] Like poetry, where he found a refuge for his innermost feelings, hunting became a lifelong passion for Süleyman, offering him a respite from the everyday burdens of the sultanate and the complications of his personal life.

Another form of training he received in his father's household was to become acquainted with different classes of soldiers and servants. The fortress of Trabzon was garrisoned by artillerymen, janissaries, and foot soldiers.[69] Selim's officials included the chief of the stables, the chief standard bearer, the chief attendant, the chief gatekeeper, sea captains, and the chief infantry and cavalry officers, who presided over the servants and soldiers of the household. Selim's overseer (*lala*), scribes, treasurer, physicians, and legal officials appointed to Trabzon were constant presences whose advice and services were often sought. Cooks, drink-pourers, tent-pitchers, musicians, keepers of the menagerie, valets, and others were constant presences around Selim and Süleyman. Moreover, the household was staffed with and frequented by many individuals from a variety of backgrounds.

As a result, Süleyman was exposed to different markers of identity among the *askerî* elite, from dress and accent to religion and physical features. For instance, the district was inhabited by members of the Turkic Çepni tribe, whose leaders frequented Selim's retinue. They would have been dressed as tribal riders, speaking a form of Turkish that would have sounded simple and unrefined to the educated. Albanian tribal leaders, exiled from their native land to the easternmost edge of the Ottoman realm, who probably spoke a broken Turkish with a heavy accent, were also found in Selim's company. Soldiers of Kurdish origin served in Selim's forces, and some Akkoyunlu noblemen had taken refuge from the Safavids by moving to Trabzon and its vicinity. One of the sons of the last Komnenos emperor of Trabzon, having converted to Islam and adopted the name of Hüseyin, was recorded as the commander of Selim's cavalry in September 1506. One of Selim's physicians, Yosef, was Jewish.[70]

Süleyman began to develop his post-childhood self in this environment, adapting his dress and his speech to the requirements of elite culture, learning how to conduct himself in the presence of others, and discovering the complex web of macro- and micro-hierarchies that dominated the public life of a prince. He must have been treated well by those around him, but he would also be expected to find ways to inspire respect. The royal persona he began to build during this time, although constantly in need of honing and readjusting, stayed with him throughout his life.

On a more practical level, while spending more time in the company of his father and the members of his household, Süleyman had many occasions to observe the ways in which the Ottoman administration worked, from the collection of taxes to the application of the law. The district governor of Trabzon drew revenues from properties that belonged to the dynasty, such as mills, pastures, vineyards, and olive orchards.[71] Other sources of revenue for the governor, various Ottoman officials, and the sultan himself included taxes from the use of farms and pastures, produce (grains, fruit, olive oil), animals (livestock, beehives, fisheries), the bridal tax, fines for criminal infractions, fees for recording transactions, taxes from sales, and road tolls.[72] While Süleyman would not yet be introduced to the finer details of Ottoman fiscal administration, he must have witnessed the comings and goings of tax collectors, treasurers, and scribes, and the storing of goods and money.

FIG. 2.3  The walls of Trabzon. Zeytun Travel Images/Alamy Stock Photo.

Selim's activities included repairs to the walls of Trabzon in 1491–92, and the construction of a mosque and the refurbishment of the port in the small, fortified town of Giresun. He endeavored to shore up the district's defenses by sending contingents to unoccupied fortresses. He oversaw the construction of small ships and the opening of mines, to fully utilize the available resources. In constant communication with Constantinople, he spent a considerable time on *tımar* assignments and the *sipahi*. For instance, he appointed a janissary to head a group of *sipahi* in the southwest of the district and negotiated the continuation of *tımar* assignments for descendants of Çepni tribal leaders. These attempts were directed at establishing control over the *askerî* elite and securing the loyalty of the tribes. Moreover, like any other governor, Selim was keen on having members of his own household rewarded, through either the allocation of *tımar*s or the increase of their assigned revenues.[73]

Despite his considerable administrative work, however, Selim's tenure as district governor is mostly remembered for his military activities. Given Trabzon's location in northeast Anatolia, Selim was in a suitable position to observe the decline of the Akkoyunlu and the rise of Ismail. Already in 1501, he had dispatched reports to Constantinople on the movements of the Safavids.[74] In an order he received, he was encouraged to keep the Ottoman palace informed about future developments in the region. However, his request for ships and funds for the repair of some fortresses were denied. Not heeding the palace's advice for caution, Selim chose to adopt an active stance. He raided and briefly controlled strategic towns on the other side of the Pontic Mountains. He welcomed into his entourage Akkoyunlu officials, who had been defeated and chased from their lands. He also relocated Akkoyunlu subjects, seeking refuge from Ismail, in his district.

Selim's actions were serious enough to irritate Ismail. In the summer of 1505, a Safavid envoy to Constantinople complained about him, but Selim did not back down. In 1507, in retaliation against the dispatch of several thousand Safavid men to the vicinity of his governorate, he attacked Erzincan and then defeated a much larger Safavid force sent against him. The following year, he directed his attention east and organized an expedition against neighboring Georgian Christian princes, from which he reputedly returned with ten thousand captives.[75]

Did Selim engage in these activities to build a reputation for himself and to gather more supporters? By the first years of the 1500s, he already knew that succession struggles with his brothers were approaching. A strong martial reputation and a loyal group of followers both had their uses. It is also true that his actions were partly meant to ensure his district's security. The

small towns he raided, such as Bayburd and İspir, were important for controlling access to the mountain passes leading to Trabzon. His raids against
the neighboring Georgians may be interpreted as attempts to shore up his
district's frontiers and to prevent raids and marauding activities from the east.

Selim's plans notwithstanding, his military activities must have left a strong
mark on Süleyman, who was in his early teens. He regularly witnessed Selim
leave for expeditions and return with slaves and booty. He must have felt anxious. On the likelihood of his father's death during one of his campaigns, he
would lose his only protector. His chances of ever acceding to the Ottoman
throne would decrease significantly. It is unclear whether he accompanied his
father on any of his military activities, but it is more likely that, as the only
son, he would have been left behind in the safety of Trabzon. Still, he grew
up within a military ethos from an early age. He must have heard countless
anecdotes about the rise of the Safavids and the threat posed by Ismail and his
followers. Those anecdotes would have included strong religious elements as
well, from the supposed errors of the Safavids' unorthodox religious message
to the duty to wage holy war against Georgian Christians.

There were other issues that must have added to Süleyman's fears and
anxieties, and many of these stemmed from the checkered relationship
between Selim and Bayezid II. Indeed, Selim is often depicted in near-
contemporary works of history as a lonely figure fighting against impossible
odds.[76] He thought that Bayezid II and his officials were oblivious to the
Safavid threat. He was almost always dissatisfied with the overseers (*lala*) sent
by his father, asking for them to be replaced. He thought his revenues as district governor were too low. His increasing expenses were probably related to
his military activities in the early 1500s. Typically impatient, he took steps to
solve his financial difficulties. In 1507, he sent some men to Bursa to borrow
money from the city's merchants. In 1508, he asked the palace for advance
payments from his assigned revenues.[77]

Bayezid II tried to appease his son. For instance, in August 1507, he sent
160,000 *akçe*s in cash to Trabzon, nearly half the amount of Selim's annual
revenues.[78] Moreover, even though he refrained from open military confrontation with the Safavids, a position that Selim supported, he did not leave
Selim and others alone in front of the Safavid onslaught. Already in June 1501,
around the time Ismail entered Tabriz, Bayezid wrote to his four sons serving
as governors, including Selim, and ordered them to execute those associated
with the Safavid movement.[79] In 1505, he had extensive military measures
taken against a potential Safavid attack. In 1507, large Ottoman contingents
commanded by high officials were sent to east-central Anatolia to dissuade

the Safavids from any incursions, and Selim's brother Ahmed was present there at the head of his own forces.[80] Regardless, Süleyman must have been exposed to Selim's perspective, and he grew up feeling that he and his father had been relegated to a remote corner of the realm without much support from Constantinople.

Another set of challenges stemmed from the ecology of the region around Trabzon. The humid climate of the district and its mountainous terrain did not allow for intensive agriculture. The town and its vicinity could not sustainably feed more than five or six thousand, the pre-1461 population. Even then, Trabzon had relied on importing grain, via the sea and over land, to feed its inhabitants.[81] After the Ottoman conquest, some of the productive classes were displaced while new migrants arrived, putting pressure on the area's delicate ecological balance. Some of the new arrivals were civilians, unaccustomed as yet to the region, and others were military men, whose subsistence depended on local resources and who did not contribute directly to agricultural production. Selim drafted additional forces for his campaigns, and they too had to be supported through the district's limited resources. Ismail's rise was another negative factor. Many producers in the area left to join him, lured by his message of solidarity and salvation. In return, some of those displaced by Ismail and his supporters moved to Trabzon, placing yet another strain on the regional economy.[82]

Selim's correspondence with his father often included concerns related to these difficulties. In one letter, appealing strongly to Bayezid II's compassion, he bitterly complained about the scarcity and high price of wheat and barley in the district.[83] His complaints are supported by Ottoman sources, according to which prices for grains and pulses in Trabzon increased by 100 percent between 1486 and 1515.[84] In the same letter, Selim voiced other fears. If an epidemic broke out, he wrote, there were no other suitable towns or villages to which he could relocate with his household. In other words, Trabzon, well protected from the outside by the sea and the mountains, also felt like a trap. Selim's solution was to ask for additional resources. Thus, in another letter, he requested the district of Karahisar, on the other side of the Pontic Mountains, to be added to his governorate. Karahisar would supply Selim with more resources, financial and agricultural, as well as give him a foothold on the Anatolian plateau.[85] His request was denied.

Süleyman spent his childhood and the first years of his adolescence in this environment, strolling in the streets and among the landmarks of Trabzon, receiving a literary education, going through martial training, listening to his parents' advice, interacting with his father's officials, learning how to become an upper class Ottoman and a member of the dynasty, and living the life of a Sunni Muslim adult. His mind was filled with the legends of Alexander the Great, the feats of the Turkic Oğuz tribes, the deeds of his Ottoman ancestors, the teachings of the great Sufis, the contours of the inhabited world, the mysteries of Creation, and the enigmas of the stars. He was exposed to the difficulties and intricacies of a trilingual elite culture and the excitements of poetry.

Thus, by the time he was considered for a district governorship when he was around fifteen years old, Süleyman had completed the first steps of his formation as an Ottoman prince. He had established a lifelong, intense, indeed intimate relationship with his father, whom he both emulated and later tried to surpass; with his mother, who supervised the private aspects of his life; and with his tutor, who continued to advise him on intellectual and spiritual matters in the later years of his life. Behind it all, however, lingered the anxieties of the approaching, inescapable succession struggles that were going to change the course of his life.

# 3

# Apprenticeship: Service as District Governor, 1509–20

SÜLEYMAN'S FORMAL EDUCATION, together with his socialization and training in his father Selim's household, constituted the first stage of his development as a prince. The second stage was to serve as district governor (*sancakbeyi*). When Süleyman was around fifteen, Selim contacted the palace and asked for his son to be considered for an appointment.

The ruling sultan and the high officials usually determined the location where a prince was appointed, and their decision could have a significant impact on the princes' subsequent careers. Serving closer to Constantinople, with unfettered access to communication with the capital, especially during troubled times, was of vital importance. Receiving news of the sultan's death early could allow a prince to rush to Constantinople or to the sultan's last location, negotiate the succession with high officials and soldiers, and control the palace and the treasury. Alternatively, an unpopular or unfavored prince and his offspring could be sent or relocated to a remote location, thus limiting their chances of reaching the capital first. Governing a district with considerable resources was another advantage. A prince serving in a wealthy district could create and sustain networks of patronage that were useful in establishing a reputation and preparing for the eventual succession struggles.

Selim, who often complained about the economic situation in Trabzon, was well aware of the relationship between wealth and political and military power. He was further motivated by the fact that sons could act as allies of their fathers in succession struggles. This is why he was very much interested in obtaining for Süleyman a resource-rich, strategically important district, possibly not too far from Trabzon. Even though he must have discussed the situation with Süleyman, the young prince was at best an informed observer of his father's attempts at building a future for both. Indeed, Süleyman's appointment was inextricably linked with Selim's plans to survive the impending succession struggles, prevail over his father and brothers, and come to the throne.

## In Search of a Suitable Appointment for Süleyman

Discussions between Selim and the palace on Süleyman's first appointment as district governor occurred in a particularly tense political environment. Selim's unsanctioned military activities had been criticized by his father on many occasions. His constant complaints about his financial and logistical difficulties in Trabzon further strained his relationship with his father and the high officials. Additionally, if we are to believe pro-Selim histories written after his enthronement, Selim was certain that his older brother Ahmed, the district governor of Amasya, would use his clout to prevent Süleyman from receiving a strategically important, wealthy district.[1] Rumors about Bayezid II's declining health and his intention to abdicate, which circulated widely across the Ottoman realm and beyond, added to Selim's worries.[2] There were other rumors about how Bayezid II's high officials favored Ahmed as Bayezid II's successor.[3] Still, however intense Selim's fears and expectations of unfair treatment may have been, he had to contact the palace to start the appointment process. First of all, he had to write a letter and make a formal request.

The date and contents of Selim's first letter are not known, but it must have been sent after mid-1508. Either with his letter, or separately, he also dispatched a high-ranking officer of his household, his chief beverage-server (şarabdar başı), to plead his case in Constantinople. His second letter to the palace, which is available today, establishes that the chief beverage-server was in the capital talking to high officials.[4] From an entry in a register of donations kept at the palace, it is possible to ascertain that Selim's man was in the capital in mid-January 1509.[5] Negotiations on Süleyman's appointment were concluded around the middle of summer 1509, and his appointment was formalized on August 5.[6]

The length of the negotiations around Süleyman's first appointment may be explained only partially by the slow pace of communications in the early sixteenth century. While Selim's initial letter and the answer he received are lost, his second letter, his reply to the palace, clearly establishes the stakes involved as well as the reasons behind the year-long deliberations. It appears that the palace initially suggested two locations for Süleyman. The first one was Sultanönü, nearly 600 miles to the west of Trabzon. The second was a small area near Trabzon to be newly instituted as a district. It extended from

Giresun on the Black Sea southeast to Kürtün, in a mountainous area, and farther south to Şiran, on the other side of the Pontic Mountains.

As soon as he saw those two locations on the written page, Selim must have felt his worst fears were coming true. The first, Sultanönü, would have meant complete isolation for Süleyman, far away from his father, doomed to certain death as succession struggles turned into open warfare among the princes. The second offer, a district that would cover the Giresun-Kürtün-Şiran area, was almost insulting. The area itself was not economically or demographically suitable to support a new princely household. Moreover, since it was already part of the Trabzon district, its institution as a separate governorship would take resources away from Selim.

Selim's reply, written in an emotional tone, oscillated between pleading and remonstrating. Considering that he was writing in response to a sultanic decree, his refusal to abide by it is particularly significant. Selim first of all registered his dissatisfaction with both locations offered to Süleyman, whom he called Süleyman Şah, in one of the first instances a regal title is officially used for his son. After pointing out the distance between Trabzon and the proposed Sultanönü, Selim complained about the lack of resources in Giresun-Kürtün-Şiran, the rugged terrain of the region, and the fact that many inhabitants of the area had run away to join Ismail. At times respectful, and at times rebellious, Selim argued that the offer of these two unsuitable locations constituted an unfair treatment that went both against the Sharia and courtly etiquette.

Selim may have dictated his letter to one of his scribes since the letter follows the flow of his thoughts rather than offering a structured counterargument. Thus, in the remaining part of his reply, Selim first offered to withdraw from politics and cancel his request for a governorship for his son. This was a strong statement of protest, but his interlocutors would also find it disingenuous since Ottoman princes did not and could not take their names out of the succession struggles and retire. Selim's next step was to confess to his own errors, an uncharacteristic move on his part. His intention must have been both to ask for his father's forgiveness and to imply that Süleyman was being unduly punished because of Selim. He thus explained that his military campaigns, which he undertook against his father's instructions, were meant to protect the lands of Islam. He emphasized that his intention had not been to gain land and riches on his own behalf. He even went so far as to commit himself to desist from any further action against Ismail.

Finally, toward the end of his long missive, Selim reversed his earlier dramatic pronouncements about withdrawing his request for Süleyman's governorship and suggested two other districts. His first choice was Karahisar (today Şebinkarahisar), 150 miles southwest of Trabzon, in north-central Anatolia. Selim was familiar with this location, which adjoined the district of Trabzon. Previously, he had asked for it to be given to him in addition to Trabzon, but his request had not been fulfilled. Having Süleyman there was another way of benefitting from the region's resources while keeping his son close enough that they would be able to support each other. Selim's second choice was Caffa (today Feodosia in Crimea), 400 nautical miles to the north. This was a city that was considerably far from Trabzon, yet one closely connected to it through commerce.

Selim was not the only prince seeking a favorable appointment for his son around this time. His rival and brother Ahmed was likewise in communication with the palace, since he had four sons at or near the age of appointment. Later sources claim that Ahmed, using his favorite status with his father and the high officials, intervened to make sure that his nephew Süleyman would not receive Karahisar, Selim's first choice in his reply to the palace. Ahmed served in Amasya and he apparently found Karahisar, 160 miles east, uncomfortably close to his own territory. This is the reason why the palace supposedly accepted Selim's second suggestion, Caffa.

Bayezid II was in a difficult position during these negotiations. Ottoman dynastic culture as well as elite and popular opinion required the equal treatment of princes. To give that impression, Süleyman and Ahmed's eldest son Murad were appointed on the same day, August 5, 1509, and they were given the exact same gift of appointment offered to all *sancakbeyi*: a copper finial to be used atop a flagpole, a ceremonial object (*sancak* meaning both banner/ flag and district); and 15 yards of plain silk cloth, an ordinary piece of textile.[7] Still, the preference accorded to Ahmed over Selim around the palace manifested itself in between the lines. In the record of appointment of their sons, Ahmed was called "*Sultan Ahmed*," with a regal title, while Selim was mentioned as "*Selim Beg*," a lesser title that meant lord.

What were Süleyman's thoughts during this critical time in his life? Was he apprehensive about leaving his father's company and starting his own household? Or was he excited about his first formal posting? Selim must have relayed the details of the negotiations to his son, including his frustration with his father and the high officials. As for Caffa, why had Selim picked that particular location? It is possible that, as an experienced administrator, he had calculated for several contingencies.

In a unique account that brings together Selim's life and reign and Süleyman's early years on the throne, a contemporary historian argues that

Selim had planned all along to have Süleyman posted to Caffa. His suggestion of Karahisar was a ruse, since he knew in advance that his father and Ahmed would reject it because of its relative proximity to Amasya. It is true that, if Süleyman had been granted Karahisar instead of Caffa, Selim and Süleyman would have been isolated in northeast Anatolia, without an easily accessible and wealthy hinterland, surrounded by Safavid supporters to their south, Georgian princes to their east, and Ottoman districts to their west. Caffa, however, was located on the other side of the Black Sea, out of the reach of rivals, with plenty of opportunities for a prince preparing for coming battles. The move to Caffa helped Selim and Süleyman circumvent both their natural as well as military and political isolation in Trabzon.[8]

Indeed, at the time of Süleyman's appointment, many Ottoman princes served as district governors in Anatolia. They and their supporters in the *askerî* elite posed a significant barrier in front of anyone, be they Ismail or Selim, planning a move from east to west, toward the wealthy Ottoman districts in central and western Anatolia, and toward Constantinople itself. Around 1509, only four of Bayezid's eight sons were still alive. Ahmed had been in Amasya since 1481. Şehinşah had been in Konya, the center of the Karaman district, since 1483. (He would die in the summer of 1511, in the midst of a rebellion, under suspicious circumstances.) Korkud had been in-itially posted to Manisa, the center of the Saruhan district, in 1483. In 1502, possibly in order to establish better control in an area filled with Safavid supporters, he was moved to the district of Teke, with the city of Antalya at its center.

Süleyman's appointment came at a time when many other princes had just been or were being appointed district governors. Just before Süleyman's appointment, Osman, son of Selim's deceased brother Âlemşah, was sent in March 1507 to Kangırı in north-central Anatolia. Musa, the son of Selim's deceased brother Mahmud, was appointed in September 1508 to Kastamonu, also in north-central Anatolia. Musa's brother Osman was in Sinop, on the Black Sea coast, already in November 1508.[9] Şehinşah's son Mehmed was in Niğde. Of Ahmed's four sons, Murad, initially appointed to Bolu, was moved to Çorum, and his brother Alaeddin took over Bolu. Süleyman was in Koca Kayası, and Osman was in Osmancık, close to their father.[10]

Rather than engaging in a game of strategic checkerboard against his brothers and nephews, Selim must have decided to find a new playing field. Caffa gave him that unique opportunity. That he engaged in the appoint-ment negotiations on his own behalf, using Süleyman as a legitimate excuse

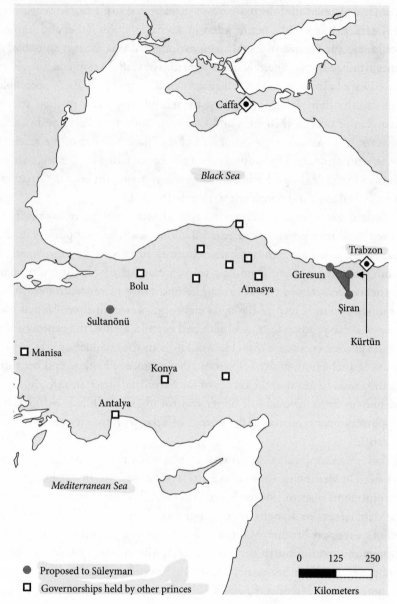

**FIG. 3.1** Locations where Ottoman princes served as district governors, ca. 1509. Map by Jordan Blekking.

to obtain an advantage, is clear from his actions following his son's appointment in August 1509. First of all, he kept Süleyman in Trabzon for more than a year. He spent that time observing developments in and around the Ottoman realm, and quite likely accumulating resources and supporters.

Then, in yet another unprecedented act, he traveled alone to Caffa at the end of September 1510. He claimed he wanted to inspect the district before sending his only son there. He must have told Süleyman that, beyond a simple inspection visit, this was the beginning of something much bigger for both of them.[11]

## Süleyman's First Years in the Ottoman Administration

Süleyman remained behind in Trabzon as his father's unofficial substitute. This was a perilous time, and not only because of the impending succession struggles. Even a sympathetic observer recognized that Selim's departure for Caffa had created a vacuum around Trabzon and encouraged Safavid sympathizes nearby. [12] Soon after he left, forces allied with the Safavids attacked and pillaged the region around Torul and Şiran. These were areas that had been initially offered to Süleyman as a location for his district governorship, and he must have realized, once again, how vulnerable he would have been there. Even Trabzon did not provide much safety, however, as Süleyman was soon informed that the attackers planned to besiege the seat of the district. In what may have been his first act of command, he sent out a contingent. His men prevailed and defeated the enemy and severed heads of the Safavid dead were sent to Caffa, to Selim. Safavid forces attacked one more time, and they were repulsed.

Probably instructed by his father to inform the palace, Süleyman then wrote a detailed report about these events as well as some recent developments in Safavid territories. This is quite likely the first item of official correspondence he signed with his own stamp.[13] Either together with or shortly after his letter, he also dispatched to Constantinople severed heads of enemy fighters with his chief treasurer and three of his men, who received cash disbursements and textiles as a reward from the palace.[14] The letter and the entry in the register of donations show that Süleyman was in Trabzon in early 1511, still waiting for his father's signal to move to Caffa. In the register he is called *"Emir Süleyman,"* a respectful yet simple appellation for someone of his status.

The next mention of Süleyman in the palace records is related to a death in the dynasty. After his uncle Şehinşah died, Süleyman received a notification from Constantinople as well as the customary gifts sent to members of the dynasty on such occasions. In the record, he is addressed as *"Hazret-i Süleyman Şah bin Sultan Selim,"* a proper honorific for a prince. More importantly, the record establishes that he was in Caffa in July–August 1511.[15] Indeed, he had been invited there by Selim, who was about to launch the next phase of his plan to accede to the throne, namely, a confrontation with Bayezid II. For that, he needed to move with his men to a location near Constantinople and he did not want to leave Caffa vacant.

Thus, Süleyman finally sailed from Trabzon to Caffa, in what was the first long sea voyage of his life, around May 1511. The nearly two-year delay between his appointment and his arrival, a mostly undocumented gap in Süleyman's life, must have been spent with instruction under the supervision of his tutors and his mother Hafsa, in military training (riding, hunting, the use of weapons), and in the throes of anxious thoughts about the future as the tensions between his father and the rest of the Ottoman dynasty continued to rise. With his departure from Trabzon, Süleyman was leaving behind the tombs of his brother, sister, and grandmother; his oldest friend Yahya; and the familiar sights and sounds of the town where he had spent his childhood and adolescence. He must have had one last glimpse from the deck of his ship: the fortifications, the central hill smoothly rising from the sea, the orchards outside the walls, and the green mass of the Pontic Mountains in the background.

By the time of Süleyman's arrival, Caffa had been under Ottoman control for only a few decades. The city was captured from the Genoese in 1475, as part of the Ottoman policy to control the commercial networks around the Black Sea, which had become particularly relevant for the Ottoman economy following the conquest of Constantinople in 1453.[16] Caffa was not as politically prestigious as Amasya or Saruhan, two locations where Ottoman princes typically served as district governors, nor as strategically critical as Bolu or another district on the road to Constantinople. Still, it was seen important enough by the Ottoman palace to appoint a prince there before Süleyman: one of Bayezid II's sons, Prince Mehmed, had served as district governor of Caffa from the last years of the 1400s until his death in 1504.[17]

Compared to Trabzon, Caffa had a significantly larger population. According to an Ottoman survey prepared a decade after Süleyman's arrival, the city itself had around twenty-five thousand residents, with Muslims making up one fourth of it. The largest group among the non-Muslim population was the Armenians (around 70 percent), followed by Greeks, Jews (both Karaites and "European-origin" communities), and Russians. As for the district, its population around 1520 was approximately thirty-eight thousand, 23 percent of which was Muslim.[18] Like Trabzon, Muslims were concentrated in urban areas, while non-Muslims constituted a majority in urban areas and particularly in the countryside. Süleyman most likely resided in Caffa's citadel, called *Frenk Hisarı* (the Frankish Castle), a name that referred to the city's previous Genoese rulers.

Caffa's large port, its agricultural hinterland, and its position as a major center of the Eurasian and Black Sea trade created tremendous potential for tax revenue.[19] Food from around the Black Sea (grains, meat, dairy products) helped provision Ottoman cities, particularly Constantinople. Caffa was also a major center of the Eurasian slave trade.[20] It served as a marketplace for the zone of contact between the Crimean Khanate and the Slavic speaking populations of an area that stretched from Poland and Lithuania to Muscovy and the northern shores of the Caspian Sea. Hürrem, the future concubine and later wife of Süleyman, was one of the slaves captured there, although it is difficult to establish whether she ended up in the Ottoman territories through Caffa or another route. Beyond concubinage, many of the slaves transported from that zone of contact to the Ottoman lands fulfilled various roles in economic life as free labor, extending from domestic and farm work to serving as artisans, shop assistants, and even commercial travelers on behalf of their masters.[21]

In addition to its commercial importance, the capture of Caffa and its vicinity had allowed the Ottomans to establish a close relationship with the Crimean Khanate. Nomadic tribes of Mongol and Turkic origin had been present on the northern shores of the Black Sea for several centuries by then, and the Crimean Khanate as a separate entity had been established around the mid-fifteenth century. The Khanate enjoyed tremendous political prestige due to its descent from Genghis Khan, the Mongol conqueror of the thirteenth century, and its allies and associates constituted a strong cavalry force. However, like many Turko-Mongol entities from a nomadic origin, the ruling dynasty was vulnerable to succession struggles, which gave the Ottomans the opportunity to intervene in the affairs of the Khanate.

Thus, following their first incursions into Crimea around the mid-fifteenth century, the Ottomans were able to establish an increasingly dominant relationship with their northern neighbors. They also supplied gunpowder weapons and skilled military personnel and acted as ally and protector of the Khanate against its competitors on the Eurasian steppe. In return, the Khanate lent military support to the Ottomans during campaigns, patrolled the Eurasian steppe on their behalf, and kept the north-south and east-west trade routes open. For Selim, around 1510, the immediate value of the Khanate was as a supplier of military assistance during his march to the throne. It is ironic that the Crimeans, whose succession struggles gave the Ottomans

cause to meddle in their internal affairs, found themselves in a position to
return the favor by helping Selim.[22]

The uncertainties and ambiguities of Süleyman's transition into adulthood
and a political career continued in Caffa. On the one hand, he became district governor of an area that was significantly wealthier and more populated
than his father's. His newly elevated status is apparent in his correspondence
with the palace in Constantinople as well as with the Khan of Crimea, Mengli
Giray (d. 1515). For instance, when he arrived in Caffa, Süleyman sent his overseer (*lala*) and treasurer Kasım to inform the Khan and pay his respects. In
his reply, written in a flowery chancery idiom, Mengli Giray called Süleyman
"my son Süleyman Şah." He then reaffirmed that the "gate of communication" between them was open and that they should soon meet in person.[23]
Still, Selim's unofficial yet prominent presence in Caffa, where he was busy
with preparations for the eventual succession struggles, curtailed the young
prince's authority. Indeed, in a letter from Constantinople written in June
1511, the Venetian resident envoy in the city called Selim governor/ruler ("*si-
gnor*") of Caffa without even mentioning Süleyman.[24]

Both Süleyman's elevated status, and his position as a subordinate of his
father, are further reflected in a register that was prepared in September–
October 1511. The register lists those who worked for Süleyman, his
*vazifehoran*. He is addressed on the first page as "*Hazret-i Mir*" (exalted lord),
and his name is followed by the usual formula of respect that accompanies
the names of princes: "*tale bekahu*" (May his existence be long-lived.)[25] This
is the first document concerning the household Süleyman began to establish
with the help of his parents, his tutor, and his *lala*. Together with the prince,
there are 152 individuals in the register. This number may not be exhaustive.
For instance, his *lala* and treasurer Kasım is not there since he probably drew
revenue from an assigned source or through Selim's own household. Despite
some exceptions, however, it is likely that the register represents the bulk of
Süleyman's household. Apart from the prince's concubines, it provides every
household member's name, mentions their functions and duties, and gives
the amount of their daily stipends; for some, it also mentions ethnic origins
in addition to names.

Süleyman is recorded first. He is grouped together with his mother Hafsa
and "*daye hatun*," a wet nurse or child carer who may have been tasked with
catering to the needs of the harem. Significantly, Hafsa's monthly stipend is
higher than Süleyman's, a thousand *akçe*s compared to his six hundred. This
is a clear sign that she had multiple responsibilities in the harem and con-
comitant expenses. The innermost part of the household also includes ten

concubines and five eunuchs, who typically served in and around the harem.[26] The fact that none of the concubines are mentioned by name suggests that they were either recent purchases or recent transfers from Selim's household into Süleyman's. The presence of concubines and eunuchs suggests that Süleyman's active sexual life within the confines of the harem was about to start or had just started, in conjunction with the other major transitions in his life.

The register proceeds from the private core of Süleyman's household outward. After him, his mother, and the concubines come the servants of the "interior" (*enderun*), twenty-four in total. These include the chief officials responsible for the larder, for his clothes, and for his chambers, as well as many pages (*gulam*). The pages, youths of slave origin, fulfilled various menial tasks; they were also educated, and assigned to specific household units as they grew up. Ethnic origins are provided for some of them: Russian, Georgian, Albanian, and Circassian. The use of these specific references probably stemmed from the belief that ethnic/racial origin determined character and skills and had to be taken into account during education and subsequent employment. These ethnic markers also show that, with the exception of the Albanians, many of Süleyman's household slaves had been obtained from the vicinity of Trabzon and Caffa.

With the next group, which includes nine individuals, the register advances from the interior to the "exterior" (*birun*), the more formal, indeed political component of the household. Süleyman's tutor Hayreddin and high officials such as the chief gatekeeper, the head of the stables, the chief food taster, the officers of separate military units, and a chief falconer are listed there. On the same page are also the "notables," a group of six, such as Süleyman's imam Sıdkı, his call to prayer announcer Hüsam, an accountant to supervise food purchases, two scribes (one tasked with recording purchases of animal fodder), and a castle warden, who would take charge of the citadel in Caffa.[27]

Süleyman's first household looks like the embryo of a much larger unit, a household-in-making, rather than a complete entity. For instance, the number of military men in it is strikingly low: thirty-seven in total, divided among armorers, personal guards, and cavalrymen. Of pursuivants (*çavuş*), important servants of the household whose tasks extended from carrying messages to providing security and keeping order, there are only six. The household includes five tent-pitchers, six gatekeepers, fourteen cooks and kitchen helpers, five bakers, six artisans (including two tailors), and twelve stable boys. There is only a single falconer, which further underlines the in-progress nature of this avid hunter's first household.[28]

The state of the household may be related to the fact that Süleyman was still relatively young at the time, just at the beginning of his political life. Another reason may be that his father, who was getting ready for a major succession struggle, did not want to spare more men or spend more resources. Bayezid II, careful to maintain a semblance of equal treatment toward his sons and grandsons, must have provided some financial support but nothing extraordinary. This is where Süleyman was in the final months of 1511, anxiously waiting for the outcome of his father's actions. He knew that their move to Caffa was a necessary condition for Selim to become sultan, and for Süleyman to succeed him one day as his only son. He was also aware that there were seemingly insurmountable obstacles to overcome for that to happen.

## Selim's Arduous Road to the Throne

Ever since he was appointed as district governor to Trabzon in 1487, Selim had lived in anticipation of the day when he would face his brothers in battle. Living far from wealthy Anatolian cities where his brothers served fueled his sense of indignation while his high self-regard sustained his dream of coming to the throne. He was bold, with a knack for turning disadvantage into advantage, and a flair for strategy. Thus, while his military actions against the Georgians and Ismail attracted the ire of Bayezid II and the high officials, the same actions helped him establish a martial reputation that resonated throughout the Ottoman realm, and especially among the low-ranking members of the *askerî* elite. Nevertheless, his brother Ahmed was at a more advantageous position compared to him. He was wealthier, and he enjoyed the support of the high officials who saw him as a better candidate to the sultanate than the uncouth, tempestuous Selim.

Selim's sheer persistence and hard work were not enough to overcome the coalition of forces against him. As it turned out, he was not only the boldest of Bayezid II's sons, but the most fortunate as well. Unpredictable developments created a volatile political situation within the Ottoman realm and prepared the ground for Selim to excel. He was the only prince who at that juncture was able to manage a major crisis with skill and ruthlessness. That crisis was triggered by two events: a sudden move by Selim's brother Korkud that irreversibly announced the beginning of succession struggles, and a major rebellion in Anatolia that threatened the very foundations of Ottoman power.

Korkud believed that his relocation from Saruhan to Teke in 1502 had placed him at a disadvantage, pushing him farther away from Constantinople. When Saruhan's governorship became vacant in 1507, he unsuccessfully pleaded with the palace to be returned there. Then, out of frustration, he left his seat in May 1509 without the sultan's permission, in gross contravention of Ottoman princely etiquette. He traveled to Cairo, the capital of the Mamluk Sultanate, claiming that he would go from there to Mecca for the annual pilgrimage. He also declared, around this time, that he had withdrawn his claim to the throne. It is more likely that he harbored other plans, such as obtaining the help of the Mamluks in an eventual succession struggle.[29]

Korkud returned from Egypt in July 1510, without having gone on pilgrimage or secured a concrete support from the Mamluk sultan against his father and brothers. His abandonment of his governorate and his journey to Egypt had heightened the rumors about an impending war among the Ottoman princes. He had also created a power vacuum in southwestern Anatolia that was exploited by rebellious elements. Heedless of these issues, he once again left his governorship in Teke in March 1511. This time, he traveled to Saruhan to take up its district governorship, without permission from the palace. Korkud's departure from Teke was soon followed by the outbreak of a rebellion, which rendered the overall situation even more volatile.

Selim and Süleyman observed these developments from their relative isolation in the north. Korkud's journey to Egypt coincided with Süleyman's appointment to Caffa, and one reason behind Selim's decision to keep Süleyman in Trabzon may have been to wait for the outcome of Korkud's actions and the reaction of the palace. Shortly after Korkud returned from Egypt, at the end of September 1510, Selim followed the example of his brother by leaving Trabzon without permission from the palace and traveling to Caffa. Selim's move was as brazen as Korkud's journey to Egypt, and a further sign that the succession struggles were becoming more and more impossible to manage for Bayezid II.

In Caffa, where he stayed from October 1510 to May 1511, Selim first established a respectful relationship with the Khan of Crimea to ensure his support and to prevent him from siding with Bayezid II. Having arrived from Trabzon with six hundred men, Selim possessed a military strength that paled in comparison with that of the Khan. During his stay, Selim also contacted potential supporters among the Ottoman military serving in the Balkan frontier, many of whom must have had a high opinion of Selim thanks to his martial reputation. Finally, to explain his actions and his current situation, he pursued an intense correspondence with his father (who also sent an envoy for face-to-face discussions), his sisters, and various high-ranking Ottoman officials.

In his correspondence and in his remarks to the envoy sent by his father, Selim first and foremost insisted that he would not return to Trabzon. As an excuse, he stated his desire to wage war against the "infidels" (i.e., Christians, mostly Muscovites) near Crimea, and asked for a district governorship in the Balkans. His request was denied based on dynastic custom: no Ottoman prince had ever served there in that capacity. Selim also suggested that he might be amenable to a district in Anatolia, but that he would only accept one as wealthy as that of his brother Ahmed. Indeed, the rivalry between the two brothers is palpable during these discussions, as Selim often complained about the favorable treatment enjoyed by Ahmed.

Throughout this period, Selim appears to have been biding his time. Süleyman, utterly dependent on his father, is in the background, almost invisible. In the end, the change Selim hoped for and needed came from an unexpected direction: not from Bayezid II and his officials, but from a rebellion in southwestern Anatolia that broke out in the spring of 1511.[30]

The rebellion had been brewing for a long time. Ismail's fusion of already existing messianic and apocalyptic sensibilities under his political leadership, and the movement he was subsequently able to create and expand, constituted a serious alternative to Ottoman rule in the first decade of the sixteenth century. There were significant internal factors as well. The mismatch between available *tımar*s and the number of those eligible, and the monetization of the process of *tımar* assignments, had led to a growing number of disgruntled ex-*sipahi* in the Anatolian districts during the reign of Bayezid II. Moreover, recently acquired parts of Anatolia, such as the lands of the Turko-Muslim Karaman principality, had been incorporated into the Ottoman realm with great difficulty, and anti-Ottoman sentiments were widespread. Ottoman attempts at taxing and supervising nomadic tribes created further discontent. The coexistence of disgruntled military men ready to lend their martial skills to a rebellion and an overtaxed population exposed to a message of redemption and salvation rendered the situation particularly explosive.

The loss of trust in the Ottoman establishment's ability to respond to the social and spiritual anxieties of the time was deepened by the failure to manage a smooth transition from Bayezid II to one of his sons. It seems that news about Bayezid II's illness and the reckless behavior of the princes had convinced many in Anatolia that the Ottoman house might be in irreversible decline, very much like the Akkoyunlu just a few decades earlier. As for near-contemporary Ottoman sources, they prefer to blame Ismail and his proselytizing as the main reasons behind the rebellion in 1511, which allows them to portray the event as an externally induced crisis and condemn its participants' actions in moral and religious terms.

The spiritual leader of the rebellion was a man called Şahkulu in Ottoman sources, which means a slave/servant of the shah. This direct reference to Ismail seems to prove the point of the Ottoman side. On the other hand, while it is true that the leaders of the rebellion were influenced by Ismail's example, it is fairly certain that, rather than doing his bidding, they acted in their own name.[31] Şahkulu claimed to be a man of messianic abilities, and his followers devastated town and country from southwestern to western Anatolia in subsequent months. They defeated the increasingly larger forces sent against them and killed many Ottoman officials, including those at the rank of district governor and governor-general.

Ottoman princes living in areas close to the center of the rebellion were drawn into the turmoil. There were serious suspicions that Şehinşah as well as Ahmed's son Murad communicated with the rebels.[32] While Şehinşah died in Konya under dubious circumstances, Korkud escaped from the rebels and took refuge in the fortress of Manisa. Ahmed, whose forces were supported by a large contingent sent from Constantinople with the grand vizier Ali, did not fare much better. His attempt to obtain an oath of allegiance from the forces sent from Constantinople was rebuffed by the soldiers as improper, since receiving an oath was a sultan's prerogative. His failure to provide appropriate support to the forces of the grand vizier Ali, who died during the final battle with the rebels in July 1511, ruined any military reputation Ahmed had, even though the rebellion finally fizzled out. Moreover, Ali's death robbed Ahmed of a powerful ally in Constantinople. Finally, the shock of the rebellion and the need to mobilize large forces prevented both Ahmed and Bayezid II from concentrating all their energies against Selim.

While the rebellion raged, Selim left Caffa in May 1511 and landed on the northwestern shore of the Black Sea on the first day of June. His small contingent was expanded through the participation of commanders and their troops from the Ottoman territories in the Balkans. As he continued his correspondence with Bayezid II and his officials, Selim kept on marching toward Edirne, where his father often resided after a major earthquake in 1509 had wreaked havoc in Constantinople. The palace, eager to stop Selim, offered to move his governorship from Trabzon to Caffa, in an indication that Süleyman, still officially district governor there, was seen as completely subordinate to his father. However, Selim insisted on his demand for a district governorship in the Balkans and continued his march. His intention was, on the surface, to have a personal audience with the sultan where he would explain himself. Selim and Bayezid II initially seemed conciliatory in their letters and actions, and Selim's wish to have a district governorship in the Balkans was finally granted.

Still, Selim did not rush to his new governorship, mindful of his father's movements and the situation in Anatolia. When Bayezid II decided to leave Edirne for Constantinople, his move precipitated fears in Selim's camp that he might abdicate in favor of Ahmed after reaching the capital. Rushing after Bayezid II, Selim met his father's forces in late July 1511 in Çorlu, midway between Constantinople and Edirne. Selim's men were no match for Bayezid II's troops. While Ottoman historians almost universally equivocate about the details of the military encounter between father and son, it is generally recognized that Selim barely escaped with his life. When he returned to Caffa in August, his forces were decimated, and his military and political support seemingly eroded. Süleyman, who awaited his father in Caffa, must have listened to Selim's narration of the events of the past months, during which a rebel prince had engaged in battle with a reigning sultan, a rare occurrence even in the stormy history of the Ottoman dynasty. For Selim and Süleyman, the situation looked dire.

After defeating Selim's forces and arriving in Constantinople, Bayezid II indeed invited his son Ahmed to the capital in preparation for his eventual abdication. Once again, however, Selim proved fortunate. The janissaries, the core of the Ottoman standing army, openly rejected Ahmed as the next Ottoman sultan. According to some interpretations, the janissaries had come to an understanding with Selim, although it is unclear how he would have communicated with them. According to others, the janissaries favored the warrior-like Selim and resented Ahmed and the high officials who, they believed, condescended to the janissaries and dictated their political choices to them without deliberation. Ahmed's inability to quickly subdue the Şahkulu rebellion was apparently another argument against his sultanate. In other words, apprehensions about the survival of the Ottoman polity moved first the janissaries and then a number of high officials to Selim's side.

In late September 1511, while Ahmed waited in Üsküdar, on the other side of the Bosphorus from Constantinople, to enter the city and succeed his father, the janissaries made their position known in a meeting, after which they rioted and plundered the houses of pro-Ahmed officials. Receiving the news within sight of Constantinople and realizing the risk of entering the city under the circumstances, Ahmed returned to his governorate in Amasya. He immediately began consolidating his base by occupying towns, gathering forces, and appointing his allies to important positions, actions for which he was soon labelled as rebellious by the palace. Under pressure, in late March 1512, Bayezid appointed Selim as commander of the troops. In early April, he sent a dispatch to Caffa, ordering Selim to move with the army against Ahmed in Anatolia.

Selim soon arrived in Constantinople where he found his brother Korkud, who had entered the city secretly to make a final bid for his own sultanate, to no avail. Korkud was sent away. Next, following negotiations with officials, janissaries, and his father, Selim was finally able to impose himself as the new sultan, rather than merely becoming commander of the troops. He thus acceded to the Ottoman throne on April 24, 1512, as his father abdicated. Sent to reside in Dimetoka (today Didymoteicho in Greece) shortly after, Bayezid died on the road in late May, 75 miles east of Constantinople, quite likely as the result of a poisoning orchestrated by Selim. This was the first time an Ottoman sultan was forced to leave the throne by one of his sons, and the first time when he was most probably murdered by one of his offspring.

While Bayezid's death removed one challenge to Selim's authority, his brothers Korkud and Ahmed and many nephews were still alive as potential heirs to the throne. Reports from Anatolia informed Selim about the activities of Ahmed, his sons, and their allies. Ahmed clearly acted as sultan in the territories under his control, and the general opinion was that he would eventually march to take over Constantinople. Selim's first step was to send word to Caffa and ask for Süleyman to be dispatched to Constantinople. It is quite likely that Selim wanted to ensure that his son succeeded him in case he failed to defeat his brothers and perished. Since it would take considerable time for news of Selim's potential demise to reach Caffa and for Süleyman to travel from there to the capital, it was safer to bring over Süleyman before Selim moved out against his rivals.

Süleyman traveled to Constantinople as the only son of a reigning sultan. His first sea journey had taken him from Trabzon to Caffa, toward an uncertain future. His second travel on water, despite the existence of rivals in Anatolia, carried him toward an entirely different prospect. Süleyman's reaction to their unlikely survival, the sudden change of fortune, and his father's meteoric rise to the throne following a humiliating defeat remains unknown. Clearly, he must have been relieved. It is also possible that these developments made him and his father believe in their extraordinary *kut*, an intangible mixture of political charisma, good fortune, and felicity. However, he could not rest, like his father Selim, until all their rivals were eliminated.

Süleyman arrived in Constantinople in late June or early July 1512. Two near-contemporary sources offer details on the prince's reception in the capital.[33] While these sources, completed during the reign of Süleyman, may have embellished the event, Süleyman would certainly have been welcomed formally. After presiding over a small household in Caffa, the young prince experienced the full extent of Ottoman ceremonialism in Constantinople. Thus, as soon as the ship that brought him was sighted, vessels large and small were sent out to greet the arrival of the prince, and cannons were fired in a celebratory announcement of this happy occasion.

This was the first time Süleyman was traveling to the famed city of Constantinople. As he came from the direction of the Black Sea, on a north-south approach, he would first see the New Palace overlooking the Bosphorus, on a hill rising up above the sea walls. A few viziers and high officials came out to meet him on his boat. As a sign of submission, they kissed the prince's hand. Süleyman, who had traveled on a light, fast ship, was then transferred to a large galleon and taken to Constantinople. There, palace servants and household troops waited on the shore. Mounting a horse, Süleyman trotted through throngs of cheering city dwellers to a residence appointed for him.

The following morning, he joined his father at an imperial council meeting, where he was formally met by all the high officials and a hand-kissing ceremony was held. While the further details of the ceremony are not known, it is possible that Süleyman also kissed his father's hand. Then, he was quite likely given instructions on what to do following his father's impending departure for Anatolia at the head of an army. The prince was obviously needed for administrative as well as strategical reasons. The presence of Selim's son as a viable heir to the throne and as a healthy young man (contemporary sources remarked upon Süleyman's handsomeness and impressive stature) also symbolized the continuity of the Ottoman house through Selim's bloodline.[34]

Still, as long as other princes were alive, Selim's authority was not absolute. At the end of July, roughly two months after his accession, and shortly after Süleyman's arrival, Selim left for Anatolia, where his brothers and nephews held governorships. Initially, Ahmed, like Selim in his correspondence with Bayezid II nearly two years earlier, bided his time by communicating with Selim. He asked to be given the governorship of a large province in central Anatolia and promised to maintain a peaceful presence during Selim's reign if he were allowed to survive. As the corresponding parties themselves knew well, this semi-polite correspondence was a ploy in a ruthless struggle for survival. During these months, while exchanging letters, Selim and Ahmed intensified their military preparations and strategic planning, which included communicating with members of the *askerî* elite in Anatolia and drafting them as allies. Korkud, on the other hand, was stuck within a succession struggle without the military resources and political charisma of his two brothers. He adopted a peaceful stance, emphasizing his scholarly activities and his desire to abstain from political strife.

The diplomatic phase of the succession struggle ended after a few months as Selim passed into action around December 1512/January 1513. He first ordered the execution of his grand vizier Mustafa, who was suspected of being allied with Ahmed. This was soon followed by the execution of five Ottoman princes, sons of his previously deceased brothers, who had been sent to Bursa and were captured there. Selim next moved against his brother Korkud and besieged him in the town of Manisa. Korkud escaped but was found while hiding in southwest Anatolia, possibly trying to escape to Egypt. He was executed by strangling in March 1513. The execution of the five princes residing in Bursa and of Korkud meant that Ahmed and his sons were now the only remaining legitimate claimants to the throne in addition to Süleyman.

The biggest battle was going to be the last. Selim's sense of urgency is seen in a dispatch he sent to Süleyman in early April. Süleyman had been in Vize, 100 miles northwest of Constantinople. Selim informed him of his plans to meet Ahmed in battle and ordered his son to set up camp in the vicinity of the capital.[35] The letter does not state the reason behind this order, but its reasoning must have been similar to the one inviting Süleyman from Caffa to Constantinople. Selim likely wanted his son to be in a position to enter the capital and sit on the throne if something were to happen to him during battle. Thus, even though Selim had the bulk of the Ottoman imperial forces under his command, anxieties never abated, and death's shadow never disappeared as long as rivals to the throne were alive.

Selim and Ahmed's forces finally met on April 15 in a place called Yenişehir, near Bursa. Ahmed's forces were defeated; he was captured shortly after the battle and strangled. Ahmed's son Osman, left behind to defend Amasya, was captured in mid-May and killed, together with his brother Murad's son Mustafa. Out of the four remaining sons of Ahmed, Murad escaped to Iran, and Alaeddin, Süleyman, and Kasım to Egypt, disappearing from Ottoman political life. Murad's fate is unknown. Alaeddin and Süleyman died in Cairo of the plague in 1513. Kasım survived, but he was captured after the Ottoman conquest of Egypt and killed in January 1518.[36] Thus, Selim, and by extension Süleyman, finally prevailed as the sole victors of another violent and drawn-out Ottoman succession. Their victory meant that Süleyman could now begin the next stage of his training and career: a new district governorship.

## *Waiting for the Throne*

Many historians past and present have claimed that Süleyman had an un-
complicated princehood since he was Selim's only heir.[37] That argument
ignores the fact that Selim engaged in a violent and unpredictable succession
struggle in the name of both himself and his son. That struggle, whose impact on Süleyman is not recorded anywhere, very likely imposed a significant
psychological burden on the adolescent prince. Even though he was raised
with stories of the House of Osman and was thus familiar with the dynasty's
history and customs, watching his father leave for what could be his ultimate
fight and waiting for news from the Anatolian front must not have been easy.

Then, soon after his father returned victorious, he had to relocate to a new
district governorship. He had stayed in Caffa for a relatively short period,
from around mid-1511 to around mid-1512. During that time, his father had
other priorities than supervising his training. His next posting was going to
be different. This was a time in his life when Süleyman began siring children,
presided over a large household, cultivated a group of close associates, and
acted as a surrogate for his father during the latter's military campaigns. He
had to achieve all this under the distant yet constant supervision of Selim.

In mid-1513, after all the other claimants to the throne had been either
exterminated or forced to flee, Selim appointed Süleyman district governor
of Saruhan, with the town of Manisa at its center. The long association of
the Ottoman dynasty with Saruhan and the wealth of the district may explain why Selim chose it for his son. There may have been more immediate
considerations as well. The area around Manisa had been the scene of much
violence during the rebellion in 1511, and then briefly when Selim laid siege to
his brother Korkud there in 1513. The presence of Süleyman, at the head of a
large household, might help rejuvenate the area.

The district had once been controlled by the House of Saruhan, a Turko-
Muslim principality that was annexed by the Ottomans in the last decade
of the fourteenth century.[38] It was one of the most desirable locations for
Ottoman princes serving as governors. A town with a long history, Manisa
had a number of remains from classical antiquity, an old fortress from the
late Byzantine period later refurbished and used by Muslim occupants, and a
central mosque built by the House of Saruhan in 1366–67 with an adjoining
madrasa. The tomb of Saruhan Bey (d. 1346) stood there as well, another rem-
nant of the city's pre-Ottoman past.

Ottoman officials added several mosques to the townscape from the first
decades of the fifteenth century onward. A royal residence was constructed

by Murad II in 1445, after his abdication and relocation to Manisa. A mausoleum nearby was the resting place for children of Ottoman princes who had
died there. One of the larger mosques in the town, supported by an endowment, had been built by Hüsnişah, the mother of Prince Şehinşah, in 1490.
These buildings established a strong connection between the town and the
Ottoman dynasty. There were smaller dwellings for the governors' use in two
plateaus near the city, where one could take refuge from the summer heat
and indulge in hunting. With its fortress, inns and marketplaces, artisans'
workshops, a Friday mosque and smaller places of worship, and dervish lodges
and madrasas, this was a well-built, wealthy town.

Manisa's population was around sixty-five hundred in 1531, a decade or
so after Süleyman moved to Constantinople to become sultan. It was possibly higher during his governorship, given his large household. The town
was overwhelmingly Muslim, with the exception of a few hundred Jews and
some Orthodox Christians. The total population of the Saruhan district itself
was slightly above thirty thousand in 1531. Urban dwellers constituted one-
fifth, and agriculturalists one-third. Nomads, who traveled between summer
pastures in the mountains and winter quarters on the plains, made up nearly
half the district's population, a significant percentage, especially given the fact
that Ottoman authorities preferred sedentary communities over nomadic
ones for purposes of taxation.

Manisa was on the north-south trade route that connected Antalya
to Bursa. Another branch of the same route went through Manisa north
to Karesi, and from there to Gallipoli and into the Balkans. Besides commerce, agriculture, textiles, and leather work were important components
of the region's economy. The land of the district yielded large quantities of
crops common in western Anatolia and the eastern Mediterranean: wheat
and barley as the main grains; chickpeas, lentils, onions; grapes, pears,
pomegranates, figs, almonds, olives, walnuts, chestnuts, and all sorts of garden
vegetables and fruits from orchards. Meat came from sheep and cows, but also
from camels, used by the nomads in the area. Extensive beekeeping produced
plenty of honey.[39] Compared to Trabzon and Caffa, Süleyman had moved to
a region with a richer diet and a warmer climate.

For Süleyman, after the tensions and uncertainties of the past few years,
his new appointment signified a much-altered status. Of course, the patriarchal and sultan-centered nature of Ottoman political culture demanded respect and deference. It curtailed the autonomy of the prince and his officials,
who needed approval and guidance from Constantinople.[40] Still, even though
Ottoman dynastic practice at the time did not allow for any formal status

such as heir apparent or crown prince, Süleyman was, functionally speaking, a sultan-in-waiting and a sultan-in-making as the son of a ruling monarch and the only heir to the throne.

The first tangible sign of Süleyman's elevated status was a group of gifts he received from his father on the occasion of his appointment. Just as his circumcision gifts had represented a transition from childhood to adolescence, this new set heralded the next stage of his life: one caftan of Frankish green velvet, with a Frankish red silk lining, adorned with golden buttons with a lattice pattern; another caftan of Frankish green velvet, with a simple red lining and plain gold buttons; a sword with a gold chain, a gilded dagger studded with precious stones, and a gold-plated knife. When worn, these ceremonial objects would clearly reflect his identity as a prince during his public appearances.

Süleyman also received velvet, silk, and plain fabrics of Frankish and Ottoman make to dress him and members of his household, and a cash disbursement of one million *akçes*, a sum that could pay the salaries of his entire household for more than half a year. His gifts included ten pages (*gulam*) and fifteen horses. The list ended with two golden signet rings, one ornamented with rubies and another with diamonds. The signet rings were both practical and ceremonial objects, meant to dazzle the onlookers and to be used by the prince for stamping documents. His closest helpers were not forgotten either. His mother Hafsa, who kept him constant company, received thirty thousand *akçes* as well as a large quantity of fabrics. His tutor Hayreddin was given five thousand *akçes* and a robe made of woolen cloth.[41]

Another testimony to Süleyman's elevated status at the time comes from an undated salary (*mevacibat*) register, which offers important clues about his new household. The register is probably from the early years of his governorship, and it lists the names, titles and functions, and daily stipends of his associates and servants.[42] These stipends were paid from Süleyman's assigned revenues as district governor. The contrast between his status in Caffa, as the son of a prince fighting against all odds to become sultan, and his status in Saruhan, as the sole heir, is very stark. His household expanded from 152 individuals to 759. His monthly stipend went from six hundred to two thousand *akçes*. His mother Hafsa, supervisor and manager of the inner household and of Süleyman's personal life, received two hundred *akçes* per day, compared to a thousand per month in Caffa.[43] The annual salary cost of the household was a staggering 1,673,872 *akçes*, especially considering that a mid-ranking district governor usually received around three to four hundred thousand *akçes* in annual revenue.

Süleyman's household was, first of all, an abode. He lived there with his mother Hafsa, and an unnamed sister who had traveled with him, with whom he must have maintained a close relationship. His harem included a wet nurse (*daye hatun*, perhaps the same one who had traveled with him to Caffa), six eunuchs, and fifteen concubines. In conjunction with the segregation of the sexes and the cultural norms of propriety, a female physician and two laundrywomen were assigned solely to the service of the women and children of the household.[44] The next group around Süleyman included twelve household officials and pages who dressed him, supervised his larder, and managed his expenses. He was entertained by an experienced instrument-player, two singers, and a jester, a dwarf named Hızır. A large group of nearly sixty pages handled menial jobs in the inner household and received training for further tasks. Nine individuals supervised food service, and twenty-two pursuivants kept order and acted as messengers and intermediaries.

Two physicians catered to Süleyman's health. A *müezzin* chanted the call to prayer five times a day and an imam led the congregation, with the exception of the Friday midday prayer, when the prince would travel to the town's main mosque with his retinue. The kitchens, which fed Süleyman and the entire household and on occasion served food to the poor in Manisa, employed sixty-three: cooks and their helpers, bakers, keepers of the larder, and those who prepared drinks. Four pages kept the gardens tidy, while five workers handled repairs to the residence, maintained the plumbing, and prepared the bath. One hatter, two furriers, one cobbler, one goldsmith, two laundrymen, and thirteen tailors sewed, repaired, adorned, and cleaned the clothes of the household, the appearance of whose members from the prince down to the simplest servant was supposed to be refined. Süleyman's mother Hafsa had her own tailor and an apprentice, who must have worked on the kinds of precious clothes she received before her departure for Manisa. As a charitable act, two orphans, quite likely taken in in Manisa, lived in the household. Finally, there were fifty-one gatekeepers who regulated access to the palace, as well as movement between its separated, segregated spaces.[45]

Süleyman's household was also a seat of government, the chief representative of Ottoman power in the area. In addition to those tasked with the management of his domestic life, his household included twenty-two chief officials who presided over the different groups working in it, from the chief standard-bearer and chief gatekeepers to the commanders of different military companies. Süleyman's tutor Hayreddin, as a sign of the elevated status he also began to enjoy, is listed in the register before all others. Two treasury scribes, and two others assigned to the prince's *divan*, his administrative council, supervised the collection of taxes, conducted his correspondence, and helped him manage the affairs of the district. Many supervisors and scribes handled the expenses of the household units such as the kitchens and the stables.

Local officials are represented in the register through *zaim*s, high-ranking *tımar* assignees who presided over the *sipahi*, helped collect taxes, went to war, and oversaw peace and security. While they lived across the district and drew the bulk of their revenues through their *tımar* assignments, their inclusion in Süleyman's salary register underlines the symbiotic relationship between the prince's household and the high-ranking members of the *askerî* elite in the area.[46] Moreover, Süleyman's overseer, *lala* Kasım, was a constant consultative and guiding presence in official matters. Given that Saruhan was a large governorship that housed townsmen, farmers, and nomads who engaged in various types of agricultural, commercial, and artisanal activity, it is not surprising that Süleyman would need guidance on how to manage a complex population and economy.

Süleyman's household had a strong martial component as well. In Caffa, he had a skeleton crew of military men, a group of thirty-seven that included armorers, personal guards, and cavalrymen. In Manisa, the military units were organized in companies of ten, which suggests battle-readiness and a clear chain of command. Süleyman was given 144 cavalrymen (listed in three separate units as *ebna-yı sipahiyan*, *ulufeciyan*, and *gureba*), seventy armorers, nineteen bodyguards, and thirteen foot soldiers (*sekban*). His stables had twenty-four saddlers, seven farriers, thirty horse grooms and apprentices, twenty-five camel grooms, twelve donkey grooms, and five cart drivers. Twenty-three men pitched his tents during his excursions, while thirteen carried his standards and played martial music. His hunting birds were seen to by thirty-seven keepers, and his hunting dogs were kept by three men.[47] This was the protective ring immediately surrounding the prince and his residence from the outside.

The large number of tent-pitchers and stable personnel testifies to the extent to which the prince and members of his household moved around, either to the nearby mountain plateaus for the summer or to the hunting grounds around the region. In this sense, a major part of Süleyman's household was an army camp in near-constant motion. Any movement of the prince would be accompanied by companies of military men, walking in orderly ranks, sometimes to the sound of music being played by the martial band. Heightened status went hand in hand with an increased level of ceremonialism, and Süleyman's life was increasingly dominated by formalized relationships even though he continued to seek solace in close personal relationships.

In the coming years, Süleyman's household expanded as he became more settled in Manisa, and his wealth and power grew. Around November–December 1519, for instance, he had a significantly higher number of military men under his command: 561 cavalrymen and 860 armorers. From 1512 to 1519, the group of his chief household officials and pages more than doubled to 148, and the number of gatekeepers rose from fifty-one to 161. The kitchen personnel went from sixty-three to more than two hundred and fifty, with nineteen tasters, sixty-one cooks and a large group of 161 bakers. Compared with thirty-seven at the time of his move to Manisa, he now had ninety-four bird keepers.[48] As an avid hunter, his ability to afford many huntsmen and a large menagerie of birds and dogs must have given Süleyman tremendous pleasure, as well as an occasion to escape from the minutiae of government and the everyday management of the household.

He could escape from official matters only temporarily, however. Süleyman's administrative record in his governorship covered a range of activities. One was of a legal nature. Shortly after reaching his district, he had requested instructions from Constantinople for dealing with the mischief-makers and thieves of the area. Indeed, the overall impact of the 1511 rebellion and the succession struggles must have upset many districts across Anatolia, and economically motivated crimes must have increased.[49] Selim sent his son a set of legal instructions, which only partially survive as part of a court register. These informed Süleyman, and by extension all members of the *askerî* elite in the district, on how to deal with cases of adultery, home invasion, abduction, murder, banditry, and theft, as well as the management of the land and the treatment of the subjects.[50]

Another task for Süleyman, a crucial one for creating and maintaining legitimacy, was the distribution of favors and charity.[51] Recipients of his charity included members of his household, such as his chief eunuch Ali who received a farm as property, a local donor to a mosque whose sons were rewarded with jobs, and a Sufi sheikh by the name of Esedullah Efendi who received a gift of three thousand *akçes*. The sheikh, who stated in a letter that he prayed day and night for the prince's good fortune, affectionately called him "my son" in his grateful reply to Süleyman's gesture.[52]

Furthermore, Süleyman communicated with various officials within and outside the district on a variety of matters. In these letters, he used his own stylized stamp, as seen in a request sent to the palace stables for the granting of horses to Süleyman's men. Despite his status, the prince addressed the chief of the stables, an official of his father's household, as "*lalam*," my overseer, in an act of deference.[53] Even though he was the only son of a ruling sultan, he had

FIG. 3.2 A stamp of Süleyman from his years as district governor. Detail from Topkapı Palace Museum Archives, E. 745/26. Courtesy of the T.C. Cumhurbaşkanlığı Milli Saraylar İdaresi Başkanlığı.

to respect existing hierarchies. He must have felt a tremendous political and cultural pressure about performing well as a governor and establishing a good reputation in the eyes of his father and the high officials.

These administrative functions constituted only one part of Süleyman's life. Another part took place in the innermost core of his household, in the secluded harem where he lived as the only sexually active male allowed into a protected zone. Just as hunting may have given him an outlet away from the burden of his formal duties, it seems that the harem similarly served as a refuge where he could relax outside the competitive world of Ottoman dynastic culture. His mother Hafsa was a constant presence there. While she was not as publicly visible as Süleyman's *lala*, tutor, and other officials, she played a unique role by overseeing her son's health, his state of mind, his relationship with concubines, and his overall wellbeing. She was expected to inform Constantinople if she faced major issues she could not resolve, which gave her significant power in her relationship with her son.

Süleyman's changed status as sole heir to the Ottoman throne was further underscored during these years as he became a father and the progenitor of the next generation of heirs. Concubines had been part of his household already in Caffa, where his son Mahmud may have been born in 1512.[54] In 1515, he had another son. The auspicious news reached Selim in Edirne on October 19, 1515, and he asked for his grandson to be named Murad.[55] In 1516 or 1517, Süleyman had a son with Mahidevran, one of the concubines listed in the salary register, and he named him Mustafa.[56] It is likely that he had other children who died in their infancy and are not mentioned in the sources.

Not everything was as peaceful as it seemed in the life of the household, however. Princely households could turn into literary salons or drinking dens, indeed both. The use of intoxicants was part of everyday life. One of Selim's brothers, Şehinşah, had nearly died on one occasion due to an over-consumption of opium. Another brother, Âlemşah, was reported to Constantinople by his mother for his overindulgence in alcohol in the company of his overseer, tutor, and physician.[57] The distance from Constantinople, the prince's relative financial autonomy, and his youth and inexperience could present an opportunity to those keen on ingratiating themselves with him and climbing up the social ladder. One such instance is reported in a letter from Süleyman's *lala* Kasım to Constantinople.[58] In his letter, Kasım first reminds the sultan that, just before Süleyman was sent to Saruhan, Selim had pulled him aside to personally give him instructions. He had particularly emphasized that, when a high official acted improperly, Kasım should first issue a warning; in case of disobedience and continued impropriety, he should write to Constantinople. Kasım then proceeds to report the actions of one of Süleyman's treasurers, a man named Ferhad.

Ferhad reportedly wanted to look grandiose and magnanimous, according to Kasım. He held his own administrative meetings (*divan*), and he even hired his own scribe. He issued exemptions and pardons in the name of the prince, distributed stipends, and gained advantages for his associates. He went so far as to have the same table service as the prince twice a day, with seven or eight kinds of choice dishes. While Kasım does not specify any course of action, he clearly expected Ferhad to be removed and perhaps punished. The letter does not mention Süleyman. It is likely that the prince had a good relationship with Ferhad and was aware of his actions. Otherwise, it is difficult to imagine Ferhad receiving the same table service without some sort of approval. The overseers of bureaucratic rectitude and royal etiquette thought differently, however. The supervising eye, an extension of the Sultan Father, was ever-present in the prince's life.

## Selim and Süleyman in the 1510s

Besides his service as district governor, Süleyman was required to reside in Edirne during Selim's extended military campaigns. There, he was exposed to a new level of administrative activity, much different in scale and complexity compared to what he would have encountered as district governor. His experiences in Edirne were crucial both in terms of practice (chancery formulas, customs, rules) and in terms of familiarizing himself with high offices and office holders themselves as preparation for his own sultanate.

Süleyman's first stay in Edirne extended from March–April 1514 to July 1515. He traveled from Manisa in the company of his *lala* Kasım, his treasurer Sinan, and his tutor Hayreddin. He kept an eye on the situation on the Balkan front, received reports from governors, and issued orders under the scrutiny of his and his father's high officials. The everyday flow of administrative tasks could extend from important tactical decisions to seemingly mundane matters. In one instance, he received alarming news from Bâli, the district governor of Semendire (today Smederevo in Serbia). Despite the ongoing truce, Hungarian troops had crossed to the eastern bank of the river Danube, near Semendire. Süleyman ordered other district governors in the area to assist Bâli; he then wrote to the viziers who accompanied his father to inform them of the situation.[59] On another occasion, he ensured that the *tımar* of a *sipahi*, who was away on campaign, would not be tampered with.[60] In addition to regular correspondence, Süleyman was also sent two "letters of victory" (*fethname*) from the army camp. The first one was about his father's victory over Ismail at the Battle of Çaldıran in August 1514. The second one relayed news of Selim's capture of the strategic fortress of Kemah from the Safavids in April 1515.[61]

In the spring of 1516, Süleyman was once again ordered to relocate to Edirne, around the time Selim left for a campaign against the Mamluk Sultanate in Syria and Egypt, and he spent more than two years there, until August 1518. Many officials and scribes were left behind to assist the prince. Süleyman's responsibilities were the same as before. He relayed news from the other side of the realm to his father's camp in Syria and then Egypt, including critical information about plans for a new crusade under the initiative of the papacy. He also corresponded with Ottoman officials and non-Ottoman actors in the Balkans and the Mediterranean, issuing orders and conveying information about his father's victories, of which he was informed by a detailed letter of victory sent in February 1517.[62]

Süleyman saw his father in person on only a few occasions during these years, in Edirne and Constantinople. In the relationship, unlike Selim vis-à-vis Bayezid II, Süleyman adopted a profoundly deferential attitude. He kissed Selim's hand and presented him with gifts during their personal encounters. He wrote congratulatory and deeply respectful letters in reply to news of his father's impressive victories over the Safavids and the Mamluks, in which he described himself as a servant of utmost, indubitable loyalty. His loyalty was rewarded through gifts he received and increases made to his annual revenue. As the only son waiting for this turn on the throne, he was in a sense locked into a formal relationship, with someone as tempestuous as Selim to boot. In addition to anecdotes that widely circulated concerning Selim's violent temper, Süleyman watched his father's wrath manifest itself during a stressful stay in Constantinople in the summer of 1515.

The visit started inauspiciously. As the prince and his retinue entered Constantinople through the Silivri Gate, one of his standard-bearers mistakenly hit the masonry and the flagstaff broke into half, which would have been interpreted as a bad omen by those present. As Süleyman awaited his father's permission to return to his district, Selim launched a long investigation into the unruly behavior of the janissaries during his previous campaign and eventually ordered the execution of several prominent officials. His anger and suspicion then turned toward Süleyman's officials. He denied the prince's request to leave and ordered an inspection into his expense registers.

Süleyman's officials appeared before the imperial council to explain any discrepancies, but the prince must have felt the weight of his father's order, which implied potential improprieties or mismanagement under his watch. He was eventually allowed to depart and was indeed sent out with a parade in great fanfare, but he had been forced to stay for nearly a month in Constantinople.[63] Then, in December 1516, he had to abide by his father's dismissal of his *lala* Kasım. Süleyman had developed a close relationship with him, but he was obliged to wait until his father's death before bringing Kasım back from retirement, and honoring him with the title of vizier.[64]

Other signs of potential tensions between father and son have survived in diplomatic reports and Ottoman historical and literary works. For instance, there is an Italian-origin story about a poisoned shirt sent by Selim to Süleyman. The prince's death would have been averted at the last minute by the intervention of a loyal servant or his mother. Similar anecdotes are found in a number of Ottoman texts. According to one, Selim ordered for Süleyman to be executed but the executioner could not bring himself to follow the order. He murdered a decoy and disguised the prince as a

gardener working in the palace. When Selim admitted a few years later that
he regretted his decision, the prince was brought to him and father and son
were reunited.[65]

It is difficult to imagine any Ottoman sultan ordering the execution of his
only son, even though other heirs to the throne, Süleyman's sons, had been
born. It is also easy to disprove most of the above-mentioned anecdotes. For
instance, it is irrefutably recorded that Süleyman was either in Manisa or in
Edirne in an official capacity during the time he supposedly was in hiding as
a palace gardener. Stories such as these are likely to be exaggerations based on
stock images about paternal wrath and filial victimhood prevalent in a patriarchal society. At best, they are rumors based upon other rumors. Since rulers
were the celebrities of their time, stories about them circulated on a spectrum
that ranged from fantasy and wishful thinking to the bizarre. At the same
time, it has to be admitted that these stories carry distorted yet genuine traces
of Selim's impetuous behavior and his violent treatment of foe and friend.
Like everyone else, Süleyman had to tread carefully when it came to his relationship with his father.

His personality aside, Selim's military campaigns had long-lasting
repercussions for regional and global history, and their outcomes determined
a major part of Süleyman's political agenda after he came to the throne. In
1514–1515, Selim moved against Safavid supporters in Anatolia, and then
against Ismail himself, whom he defeated at the Battle of Çaldıran in August
1514, in the first major military encounter between the Ottomans and the
Safavids. Victory was secured by the supremacy of the Ottoman standing
army and its gunpowder weapons over the Safavid cavalry and light infantry.
Selim was thus able to contain the westward spread of the Safavids. In 1515,
by turning the Dulkadır principality on the Ottoman-Safavid frontier into a
protectorate, he further consolidated Ottoman control of the eastern frontier. In 1516–1517, under the pretext of supposed Mamluk collaboration with
the Safavids against the Ottomans, Selim marched through Syria to Cairo.
In two major battles, in 1516 at Marj Dabiq in Syria and in 1517 at Ridaniyya
near Cairo, he defeated and subsequently killed two Mamluk sultans and
brought these areas, together with the Holy Cities of Mecca and Medina,
under Ottoman sovereignty.[66]

Through these conquests, Selim significantly expanded the territories
and communities under Ottoman rule. The demography of the Ottoman
realm changed through the addition of majority-Muslim areas in the Middle
East, while the dynasty gained new sources of revenue thanks to the rich
agricultural, manufacturing, and commercial wealth of the newly acquired

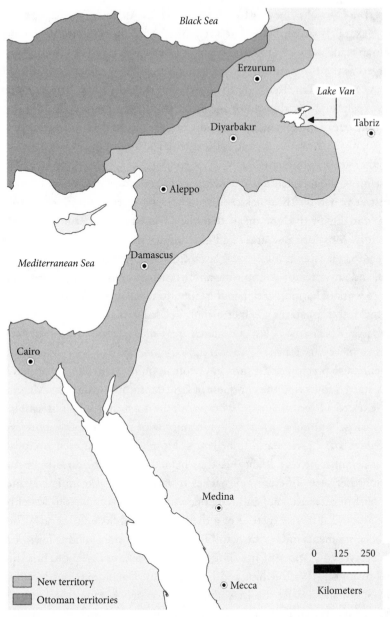

**FIG. 3.3** Selim's conquests. Map by Jordan Blekking, based on Emecen, *Yavuz Sultan Selim*, 432.

areas. The control of new urban centers such as Aleppo, Damascus, Cairo, and Alexandria strengthened the Ottomans' hold over Mediterranean and Eurasian trade networks but also brought in new rivalries. For instance, they emerged as the competitors of the Portuguese, whose recent forays into the Indian Ocean and the Red Sea had been part of their overall attempt at world-wide expansion.[67] At the end of the 1510s, the growing regional and indeed global stature of the Ottomans was more of a prospect than a reality, however. Süleyman was the one who had to deal with the long-term consequences of his father's quick conquests.

Selim's conquests led to the emergence of additional challenges of an ad-ministrative nature. The quick capture of large territories in eastern Anatolia, Syria, and Egypt did not mean that the Ottomans could rule over them smoothly. Most of these areas had been under the rule of various Muslim powers for many centuries. Local laws, customs, and rules were well devel-oped, and any attempt at imposing an Ottoman administration required an intense work of harmonization and negotiation. A larger, more commanding administrative apparatus was increasingly needed to make the Ottoman pres-ence sustainable in the newly conquered areas and to ensure the extraction of resources necessary for the Ottoman military machine.[68]

Selim also precipitated a shift in Ottoman political ideology that had al-ready started following the conquest of Constantinople in 1453 by Mehmed II. He asked Ottoman jurists, who were Sunni Muslim religious scholars, to issue legal opinions (*fetva*) in conformity with the Sharia that portrayed the Safavids as heretics and unbelievers. He positioned himself politically as the defender of true Islam. He thus helped solidify the already existing divisions between different approaches to Islam.[69] He also initiated a new relationship between state and religion, whereby correct religious belief be-came a political matter instead of a theological or philosophical one. There had been moments in Ottoman and Islamic history when central authorities had intervened in cases of non-normative approaches to religion, but these were exceptions. With Selim, and his chief rival Ismail, religious rectitude, in its Sunni and Twelver Shiite variants, increasingly became a matter to be regularly supervised by the powers that be. Very much like the strategical outcomes of Selim's conquests, these ideological implications were left for Süleyman to deal with.

Between August 1518, when he returned to Edirne from Egypt, and September 1520, Selim did not engage in any major military operations. News of his swift victories over the Safavids and the Mamluks had led to a renewal of crusading plots under the leadership of Pope Leo X, who believed Selim would eventually focus his energies on the European front.[70] In fact, Selim watched the frontiers of his realm cautiously, renewing his father's peaceful relationship with Hungary and Venice, and trying to impose a commercial blockade against the Safavids with mixed results. A rebellion in Anatolia in 1518–19 was a stark reminder that the eastern part of the realm was far from pacified. One of Selim's activities during this period was to prepare for an amphibious campaign against the island stronghold of Rhodes controlled by the Order of St. John. In addition, there were persistent yet vague plans about another large-scale campaign against the Safavids.[71] None of these were acted upon, however.

Around mid-July 1520, Selim left Constantinople to spend the fall and winter in Edirne, whose proximity to hunting grounds he particularly appreciated. He had noticed an infected boil on his back before his departure but had refused treatment. His condition worsened on the road, immobilizing him near the town of Çorlu, at the location where his and his father's men had fought nine years earlier. This inauspicious place, as some contemporaries could not help but remark, would be Selim's final stop. After a month and a half spent in the throes of a raging infection, he died there, on the night of September 21–22, 1520.[72]

The death of an Ottoman sultan created a vacuum fraught with tensions. At worst, it instigated a civil war among the princes. Even though Süleyman was the only heir, Selim's death opened up a period filled with uncertainties. First of all, the news had to be kept secret within a close circle of attendants and high officials. Peace, order, and security were very much associated with a sultan's presence on the throne. With his death, the lynchpin of an entire political system disappeared. Rioting, looting, and other acts of violence, usually by the soldiery, were common occurrences in the aftermath of sultanic deaths.[73] In Selim's case, the janissaries had been left behind in Constantinople, and high officials were particularly concerned about the spread of the news to the capital and subsequent riots.

Sultans' deaths weighed heavily on the morale of the high officials as well. Those who owed their careers to their personal and professional relationship with the deceased faced an unpredictable future under the new sultan. For a new sultan like Süleyman, replacing his father on the throne was never a straightforward process. He had to establish his authority and reputation, figure out how to rule with the assistance of the high officials inherited from his father, and handle the many threats and challenges that often followed the passing of a monarch, such as tensions within the elite, rebellions, diplomatic crises, and war.

Following the concealment of the news of Selim's death, the next crucial task was to bring Süleyman to Constantinople. The transfer of power was completed only with the arrival of the prince in the capital and his sitting on the throne. The grand vizier Pirî Mehmed immediately sent a letter to Manisa with a reliable messenger. While Süleyman may have been informed of his father's medical condition, it seems he was caught unprepared by the news of his death. The messenger found him in his summer quarters in Bozdağ, at a mountain pasture 50 miles southeast of Manisa. The letter, written in the name of the high officials and carrying their stamps, relayed the grim news to the young prince and invited him to the capital.

Aware of the risks involved, Süleyman did not return to Manisa. He left in a hurry, rushing toward Constantinople in the company of a small group of servants. On September 30, eight days after Selim's death, and four days after receiving the letter, Süleyman and his men reached Üsküdar, across the Bosphorus from Constantinople. They had covered 300 miles, riding almost constantly.[74] This was the beginning of the next stage of Süleyman's life.

# 4

# *Ascent: The First Years on the Throne, 1520–25*

STARTING WITH SEPTEMBER 30, 1520, Constantinople became Süleyman's main place of residence and remained so for forty-six years, to the end of his reign.

The city had been transformed into the administrative, cultural, and economic center of the Ottoman realm after 1453. Following a long political and economic contraction from the 1150s to the 1450s, it had begun to regain its position as a commercial hub that connected various economic zones from eastern and central Europe and the Italian peninsula to eastern Anatolia and western Iran, and from the Ukrainian steppe to the Red Sea. Its population had risen from around a hundred thousand in 1477, already a significant number that reflected the impact of Ottoman resettlement policies, to around two hundred thousand by the end of the fifteenth century. It would reach four hundred thousand by 1535 and surpass half a million by the end of Süleyman's reign.[1]

Non-Muslims made up more than 40 percent of the city's inhabitants. Around 1520, its rich human landscape included Armenians from Caffa, Karaman, and various parts of Anatolia; Greeks from the various ex-Byzantine possessions in the Balkans and Anatolia; Romaniotes, Karaites, and Hispanic/Sephardic Jews; Venetians, Florentines, Genoese, and other Europeans; and Muslims, including recent converts, from the entire realm. The large and rapidly growing population meant that particular attention had to be paid to the city's provisioning in basic foodstuffs to prevent social unrest.[2] Ensuring the availability and relative affordability of food was a fundamental component of the symbiotic relationship between the city and the sultan.

In 1520, Ottoman efforts at resettlement and rebuilding after 1453 notwithstanding, Constantinople prominently displayed traces of its Byzantine
past. Byzantine walls surrounded it on all sides, and churches, monuments,
and other remnants dotted the urban landscape. The Ottoman impact was
visible through new buildings, such as large and small mosques, fountains,
soup kitchens, mansions belonging to officials, and dervish lodges, as well
as houses and commercial spaces. The city's marketplaces and workshops,
its shipyards and arsenal, and its building sector relied on the activities of
merchants, artisans, and skilled and unskilled workers. Labor was supplied in
the form of slaves, war prisoners, and migrants from the countryside.

Living in Constantinople was a matter of distinction, almost a matter of
personal pride, for both the Ottoman elite and the commoners, as it had been
under the Byzantine Empire.[3] Constantinople was indeed seen as a city of
many wonders and myths, a "rarity of the times," and its attractions were a
constant theme in Ottoman literature.[4] The contemporaries' feelings about
the city are best conveyed in a work completed around 1525 by the Ottoman
poet and scribe Latifî. In Latifî's text, the New Palace, with its imposing
buildings, embodied the provision of justice and punishment; crowded
marketplaces represented the pursuit of wealth and offered everything from

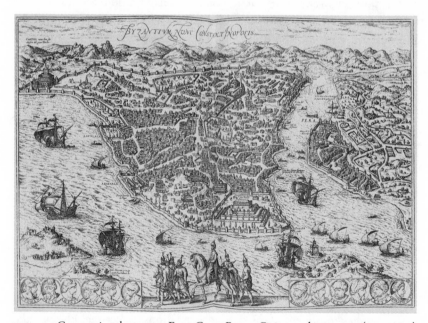

**FIG. 4.1** Constantinople, ca. 1520. From Georg Braun, *Civitates orbis terrarum* (1574–1622).
Courtesy of the Lilly Library, Indiana University, Bloomington, Indiana.

food and clothes to luxury goods and slaves; drinking establishments and areas of recreation outside the city walls provided ample opportunities for the pursuit of pleasure; convents, mosques, and tombs, on the other hand, served as constant reminders of the pursuit of salvation.

Latifi's narrative exudes a sense of awe at the city's beauty and wealth, but also a level of estrangement and anxiety that echoes critiques of urban life across centuries: rampant inequality and poverty, dishonest shopkeepers, alcohol and drug addicts, and an overall sense of moral depravity.[5] The city was filled with busy merchants and artisans, but also swindlers, beggars, and the urban poor who flocked to soup kitchens. Additionally, like many other cities of the period, Constantinople was prone to fires and epidemics, and its location near a major fault line made it vulnerable to earthquakes. Despite the palace's efforts at control, delinquency and violence, from petty crimes to riots, were not infrequent.[6] Anxieties of urban life were compounded by stories that placed the city within an eschatological narrative. Accordingly, as part of the tribulations that preceded the end times, the city would be attacked by Christian armies and destroyed.[7] These apocalyptic anxieties became particularly pronounced in the years following Süleyman's accession, as he engaged in an intense ideological competition with rivals east and west.

On September 30, 1520, however, the foremost thing on Süleyman's mind must have been to cross the Bosphorus from Üsküdar into Constantinople.[8] News of his arrival, which also implied that Selim was dead, had spread to the capital immediately. A vessel was sent to help Süleyman cross the Bosphorus. As he reached the quay closest to the New Palace, his ultimate destination, he was met by palace servants and janissaries. The commander of the janissaries, probably to keep his riot-prone men under close watch and to ingratiate himself with the new sultan, had ordered the corps to leave its barracks to greet Süleyman. The judge of Constantinople, the highest legal official in the city, was also present.

A horse hastily prepared and adorned for the occasion took Süleyman up the hill, surrounded by janissaries, palace servants, and probably urban folk who would have rushed out of their homes and shops to watch the procession. Süleyman had ridden on the same road when he had arrived in Constantinople for the first time from Caffa, in 1512. This time, however, he was marching through *his* capital city, toward *his* palace. Still, despite the pomp that surrounded him, he was quickly reminded of his duties. As the procession reached the palace gates, the janissaries regrouped in orderly ranks and demanded their "accession gift," a customary payment since the accession

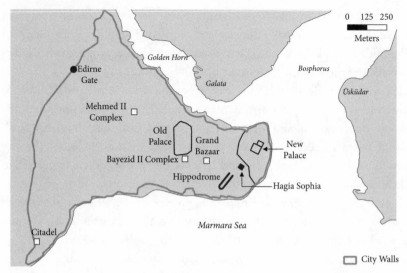

**FIG. 4.2** A few landmarks of Constantinople, ca. 1520. Map by Jordan Blekking, based on Kafescioğlu, *Constantinopolis/Istanbul*, map 2.

of Mehmed II in 1451. Süleyman promised to disburse it soon and entered the palace. The first step of the transition of power was completed.

While Süleyman had been riding toward Constantinople, other developments were unfolding in Selim's encampment. Probably having received a dispatch from the prince about his departure for the capital, the grand vizier Pirî Mehmed finally announced the sultan's death to the household troops and the servants who had traveled with Selim. The second and third viziers, Mustafa and Ferhad, were instructed to bring Selim's corpse to Constantinople. Pirî Mehmed had more important matters to attend to. He rushed to the capital, arriving in Constantinople on the afternoon of September 30, a few hours after Süleyman, and immediately proceeded to the New Palace.

The prince and the grand vizier, who knew each other from Süleyman's time in Edirne, had a meeting that lasted into the evening, during which the details of the transition must have been discussed. Pirî Mehmed was a seasoned administrator, having served Selim as chief treasurer, vizier, and then grand vizier. He was well aware that Süleyman's arrival, the procession, and the entry into the palace constituted an informal recognition of the new sultan. After the meeting ended, he sent word to all members of the *askerî* elite in the city for a ceremony of allegiance to be held early the next day.

On October 1, 1520, right after the morning prayer, around sunrise, a throne was set up in the palace in front of the Gate of Felicity, which led to the third courtyard and the private quarters of the sultan.[9] Pirî Mehmed entered through the gate and came out with Süleyman, who wore dark clothes in mourning for his father. The new sultan was immediately greeted by the prayers of the palace pursuivants. Unlike the previous day's somewhat impromptu reception, the allegiance ceremony was carefully managed. It is true that it was organized by a grand vizier anxious to secure a smooth transition, and thus with some haste. Many high officials, commanders, and members of the household troops were still on the road to Constantinople with Selim's corpse. Still, the first and second courtyards of the palace brimmed with those who had stayed in Constantinople, servants of the palace household, and janissaries.

After the initial acclamation of the pursuivants came the old Islamic ritual of accession, the *bay'a* (*biat* in Ottoman). Originally a pledge of allegiance that was symbolized by a clasping of the hands between caliph and follower, the ritual had evolved in the Ottoman case into a more submissive act in the form of hand-kissing. First the scholars (whose expertise in religious and legal matters gave particular significance to their acquiescence), then the grand vizier, then other officials walked up to the throne, kneeled in front of Süleyman, and kissed his hand.[10] This was the first of many similar occasions during which Süleyman as sultan received expressions of allegiance from his servants, in return for his recognition of their service in the form of gifts, remuneration, and promotion. In other words, mutual obligation formed a crucial part of the sultan-servant relationship.

Following the allegiance ceremony and formal accession to the throne, there was one more pressing task to be accomplished: Selim's funeral. On the same day, October 1, around noon, news reached the palace that Selim's corpse was approaching the gates of the city. As funeral chants broke out from the mosques to announce the impending funeral prayer, Süleyman, still wearing his dark mourning clothes, rode outside the city, through the Edirne Gate. Selim's coffin was taken down from its cart and a procession was formed. The funeral cortege walked through the gate to the mosque of Mehmed II, the city's conqueror. Süleyman marched at the head of the procession (or rode on a horse, according to a Venetian observer),[11] while notables carried his father's coffin on their shoulders amid chants and recitations from the Quran. Following the funeral prayer at the mosque, Selim's corpse was interred on the sixth hill of Constantinople, overlooking the Golden Horn. The procession of officials, soldiers, members of religious confraternities, and city folk,

which had gathered on the occasion of the funeral, then accompanied the
new sultan on his way back to the palace.

It is difficult to gauge Süleyman's true feelings upon the passing of an overbearing, larger-than-life paternal figure, whose persistence and audacity had
opened the road to the Ottoman throne for both of them. Contemporary
descriptions of Süleyman's demeanor during the funeral offer images of profound grief that often sound stylized, indeed exaggerated. This does not mean
that the emotional burden of burying Selim was negligible.[12] Death, particularly the death of a sultan, invited reflections about the futility of worldly
glory and the fragility of life on earth. Süleyman had to reckon with Selim's
complicated legacy both as son and as the new sultan. Also, between the hasty
four-day ride to Constantinople and the ceremonial events he had to attend,
he must have been physically exhausted.

Still, it looks like he was able to create a favorable impression during his
first appearances as sultan. For instance, acting as dutiful son and munificent
sultan, he had alms distributed to the urban poor, and food was served to the
entire city from soup kitchens in his father's memory. Ottoman observers' frequent references to his youth and vigor may be seen as metaphors about the
renewal of the sultanate and the beginning of a new reign; they may also stem
partly from their appreciation that Süleyman had performed flawlessly during
a difficult and taxing period. The fact that the transition from father to son
had been executed smoothly added to the overall sense of relief. As a contemporary observer remarked after his description of Selim's funeral, peace and
security had not been harmed, and disorder and disturbance had remained
dormant. Complete comfort filled the hearts of all, and all became merry and
joyful.[13] It was now time for Süleyman to attend to the various duties of the
sultanate.

## Süleyman's First Weeks on the Throne

Becoming sultan meant that Süleyman began to live in the New Palace, beginning on the afternoon of September 30, 1520. The Old Palace, the first
royal residence built in Constantinople by the Ottomans, was mostly occupied by the sultan's harem. The New Palace (saray-ı cedid-i âmire, the New
Imperial Palace as the Ottomans called it, today known as the Topkapı
Palace) was constructed between 1465 and 1478 on the orders of Mehmed
II. While the Old Palace had a residential emphasis, the New Palace was the
embodiment of a new imperial vision whereby the sultans interacted with
their servants and their subjects through an elaborate court ceremonial. Its

structures and layout also reflected the emergence of a more specialized, more crowded sultanic household that fulfilled various domestic as well as military duties.

The New Palace was built on three courtyards accessed through three monumental gates, with each courtyard serving different functions. The first courtyard, a transition space between palace and city, was accessible to the elite and the non-elite. It housed service buildings such as royal workshops as well as dormitories, small kitchens, and prayer spaces for the use of those who worked in the palace. The second courtyard, accessed only on foot for everyone except for the sultan out of deference to the monarch, had an administrative function. It housed the Council Hall, the meeting place of the imperial council, the Public Treasury, the Royal Kitchens and Stables, and the Tower of Justice. The third courtyard, the innermost part of the complex, had significantly restricted entry from the outside world. The Chamber of Petitions, the Inner Treasury, and the palace school for training pages were located there, together with the Privy Chamber, where the sultan lived. There were also living quarters for a small group of concubines who might spend some time there in the sultan's company.[14]

A daunting task awaited Süleyman as the new sultan.[15] His households in Caffa and Manisa had been microcosms of the sultanic household. He initially had a few, then multiple hundred, people gathered around him, and he

**FIG. 4.3** The New Palace seen from the Golden Horn, ca. 1590. Detail from Heinrich Hendrowski, *Bilder aus dem türkischen Volksleben*, Österreichische Nationalbibliothek, Cod. 8626, 159v. Courtesy of ÖNB.

was supported by a small inner core that consisted of his mother, his tutor, and his overseers. Decisions he made as governor, often in consultation with Constantinople, resonated across a limited geography. During his father's absences on campaign, Süleyman had familiarized himself with some of the high officials, as well as issues pertaining to the realm's management. However, he had done so in the capacity of a caretaker and a prince-in-training whose actions were supervised and, if necessary, corrected. On October 1, 1520, he was for the first time at the helm, surrounded by a multitude yet also alone, at the center of everyone's attention.

From an administrative perspective, being sultan required primarily the management of the large and stratified *askerî* elite, which in turn helped manage, protect, and expand the realm. A survey of those who received stipends from the central treasury, prepared right after Süleyman came to the throne, provides a detailed panorama about the size and specialization of the elite, especially those who worked for/in the palace household and those who fulfilled military functions.

In the record, the janissaries are counted as 8,361 souls, and the number of the palace household troops, from cavalrymen to armorers and artillerymen, is 7,606. These constituted Süleyman's standing army. In and around the palace, nearly 8,600 individuals worked for the sultan and kept him company. Of those, 2,837 cared for the sultan's horses and pack animals. Others relayed his messages and kept order within the palace grounds, tended to the palace gardens, managed the kitchens that fed the palace and the urban poor, waited at the gates, worked as artisans in the workshops, watched the sultan's birds of prey, carried his standards, played martial music, and pitched his tents. The sultan could rely on the services of his own physicians, personal servants, astrologers, musicians, and food tasters. A striking number of young men are listed in the same document as pages: 3,190. They had been taken in as *devşirme* recruits and were raised in the palace before they entered the palace service or one of the permanent military units.[16]

The *askerî* elite extended far beyond the palace. The *tımar*-grantees joined the army during campaigns, served as fortress guards, and helped keep the peace at their assigned areas; they numbered close to forty thousand.[17] Madrasa teachers, legal officials, and judges constituted a group that ranged between fifteen hundred and two thousand.[18] Viziers, treasurers, military judges, and a nascent bureaucracy, who fulfilled the functions of an advisory-administrative body crucial for the supervision of the military-political elite and the realm, constituted a much smaller group of several dozen individuals. The realm itself, after Selim's rapid conquests, spread over 2.5 million square miles, with an approximate population of twenty million.[19] This population consisted overwhelmingly of people who made their living from agriculture. Christian subjects of the empire were the largest group, with a slight edge over the Muslims. Members of all these groups, whose loyalty and labor were necessary for the realm's wealth and survival, expected a form of equitable, indeed favorable, treatment from the sultan.

From a political perspective, being sultan required establishing authority over the entire *askerî* elite, which could take a long time. It also required creating images and conveying messages that appealed to a variety of interlocutors, from the subjects of the sultan to his competitors east and west. Süleyman's task in this matter was made particularly arduous by his father's career. As an oft-quoted couplet by Kemalpaşazade Ahmed states, Selim's reign was comparable to the afternoon sun: it was short-lived, yet it cast a long shadow.[20] The civil war Selim instigated with his brothers, his replacement of his father Bayezid, and his rapid and widespread conquests were awe-inspiring events that had attracted widespread commentary during his reign. Indeed, a subgenre, the *Selimname* (The Book of Selim), had emerged as a result. At least nine works, focusing on Selim's princehood, his rise to the throne, and his rule, were completed by the time of his death in 1520, and others were composed in the early years of Süleyman.[21]

Even histories that did not focus mostly or solely on Selim, including those that dealt with the reign of Süleyman, continued to perpetrate Selim's myth. He was typically presented as a relentless warrior, a hard-working and selfless monarch, and an accomplished poet.[22] His struggle with the Safavids was praised; if he had not died early, many historians predicted, he would have conquered the entire inhabited world.[23] Writing in the second half of Süleyman's reign, Lütfi, who served Süleyman as grand vizier between 1539 and 1541, summarized the overall perception of the father and the son around 1520. Selim, according to him, "faced the troubles of this world, cleared its thorns and thistles, and transformed it into an orchard [while] Sultan Süleyman received and possessed the fruits of that orchard without any trouble or hardship."[24]

European observers echoed the initial impressions of the Ottomans about Selim and Süleyman. Given Selim's martial reputation, many in Europe had feared that he would turn his attention to the European front after defeating the Safavids and the Mamluks. When Süleyman came to the throne, there was a sense of relief.[25] Physician and clergyman Paolo Giovio, observer extraordinaire and historian of Renaissance politics, remembered the atmosphere of jubilation in a work on the Ottomans he published in 1531. It was as if an angry lion, Selim, had left its place to a meek lamb, Süleyman.[26] As Giovio notes, this view would soon prove to be deceptive, but in October 1520 there was not yet much evidence to the contrary.

Süleyman's first actions on the throne were meant to convey that he would be generous and just. First of all, he disbursed the accession gift in cash: three thousand *akçe*s per head for the janissaries, and one thousand *akçe*s per head for the palace household troops. The latter also received increases to their daily stipends. Süleyman used the occasion to show his munificence to the members of his old household in Manisa as well, all of whom were granted increases to their stipends and *tımar* assignments.[27] By all accounts, he was generous almost to a fault, spending large sums. The amount he distributed was close to a full year's stipends for the entire palace household.[28] At the same time, as a new ruler without a martial reputation, it is to be expected that he would work to establish a positive relationship with the members of his standing army.[29]

The delivery of the Friday sermon in his name in mosques, and the minting of coins bearing the new sultan's name and monogram, two age-old symbols of sovereignty in Islamic dynastic cultures, were among other tasks to be accomplished upon accession. These were fulfilled at different times in different parts of the realm, depending on when news of the accession was received. Indeed, another crucial task was to send letters to inform Ottoman officials, such as the governor of Egypt, Khayr Beg; allies and associates, such as the Khan of Crimea and the hereditary ruler (*sharif*) of Mecca; and others such as the Republic of Venice, with whom the Ottomans maintained close economic and diplomatic ties.[30] With the exception of the letter to Venice, dated October 10, these announcements were sent a few days after accession, illustrating the urgency with which they were composed and dispatched.

The group of letters announcing Süleyman's accession reflect the full range of the literary skills used by the Ottoman chancery: elaborate titles for the addresser and the addressees, frequent Quranic references, and the use of multiple languages (Ottoman Turkish for Crimea and Egypt, Arabic for Mecca, Greek for Venice). As the first pieces of official correspondence sent out by Süleyman, these had several interrelated functions. On a practical level, they informed allies and associates of the transition of power and asked them to announce the news in the domains under their control or supervision. Reinforcing the sense that Selim's funeral constituted a critical moment of closure, Süleyman, speaking in the first person, requested funeral prayers to be held for his father. The letter to Khayr Beg, an Ottoman governor, is quite detailed in its expectations of good government, just treatment, and the preservation of order in the recently acquired province of Egypt. The letter to Venice confirms the friendship and peace between the two sides and states that the Venetian envoys, merchants, citizens/subjects, and ships may come and go without any impediments, as was the case during the reign of Selim.

The letters as a group also offer clues about the image Süleyman wanted to project at the very beginning of his reign. The letter to Venice identifies him, at the beginning, as the emperor of Arabia, Persia, Syria and Egypt, and Asia and Europe, a fairly standard form of Ottoman titulature. The letters to Mecca, Crimea, and Egypt, addressed to fellow Muslims and allies and officials, are more elaborate in this regard. There, Süleyman is presented as the Shadow of God on Earth (*zıllullah*). His God-given mandate to rule and his justice are emphasized, and he is described as the holder of both caliphate and sultanate. These are notions that Süleyman had inherited from his forebears, particularly his father. He laid claim to these titles as soon as he came to the throne, even though he had yet to prove himself as sultan.

On a more personal level, Süleyman wanted, and needed, to distinguish himself from his father and to establish his own reputation. One of his first actions after accession was to order the return of individuals and families deported from Egypt and brought to Constantinople by his father after the conquest of 1517. In a similar vein, he ordered restitutions to be paid to those merchants whose properties had been sequestered and who had incurred losses because of Selim's commercial blockade against the Safavids. Turning his attention to the members of the *askerî* elite and their infractions, Süleyman dismissed Cafer, who had been appointed commander of the fleet under Selim. Ever careful that his actions were being watched by many, the young sultan did not ask for a summary execution. Instead, an investigation into Cafer's crimes against the life and property of commoners was conducted, and he was executed only after he was found guilty.

Süleyman did not spare members of the palace household either. Five members of the palace armorer corps were executed for raiding the houses of some viziers, and their commander lost his position. Süleyman's first campaign at reputation building seems to have achieved its intended objective, as it is reported in great detail by almost all chroniclers of his reign.[31] The main theme that emerges from their narratives is Süleyman's justice (*adl*). This is presented as his respect for the rights of both the elite and the subjects, and his struggle against oppression (*zulm*), thanks to which order and harmony are said to have been restored across the entire Ottoman society.[32] The execution of a high-ranking official like Cafer seems to have left a particularly strong impression, filling members of the *askerî* elite with dread, according to a contemporary observer.[33]

While Ottoman works of history present Süleyman as the main agent, these actions were realized with the assistance of the governing apparatus and the palace household he had inherited. Pirî Mehmed, with his considerable experience in fiscal and administrative matters, remained grand vizier. The second and third viziers, Mustafa and Ferhad, also kept their positions. The governor-general of Rumeli Ahmed, with a martial reputation second only to Selim's, retained his post as well. Mustafa and Ferhad were slaves of the sultan, having been taken into Ottoman service as Christian children. Mustafa was married to one of Selim's daughters, and Ferhad would soon marry another, tying them further to the dynasty. In contrast, Pirî Mehmed was a born Muslim, the scion of a venerable central Anatolian family, and a man with a madrasa education. Ahmed also descended from a Muslim family with deep ties to Selim since the days of his governorship in Trabzon; he had been in Selim's company throughout the turbulent years of his career from prince to sultan.[34]

The presence of these officials was another challenge for Süleyman. He clearly needed them, but he was also eager to promote those with whom he had a close personal relationship. One of them was his former *lala* Kasım, who had been dismissed in 1516 on Selim's orders.[35] Kasım was brought in from retirement in Salonica with the rank of vizier, joining Pirî Mehmed, Mustafa, and Ferhad at the top of the Ottoman administration. Moreover, 117 individuals were transferred from Manisa to Constantinople after Süleyman's accession. They included his tutor Hayreddin, his physician Ramazan, and other familiar faces whose presence would give Süleyman a sense of comfort as well as security, from chief household officers (*ağa*) to scribes, pursuivants, musicians, food tasters, and messengers.[36] The transfer of Süleyman's close associates was completed a few weeks later with the arrival of his mother Hafsa, his sons Mahmud, Murad, and Mustafa, and his concubines.[37] However, a new element of formality was already introduced into their relationship. The members of the harem resided in the Old Palace, instead of at the New Palace, with Süleyman.

The most intimate depiction of Süleyman during this critical time of transition, without any embellishments, comes from the Venetian resident envoy in Constantinople, Tomà Contarini. Contarini was invited to the New Palace to kiss Süleyman's hand on the occasion of his accession, and he had an audience on October 6.[38] He seems to have been less impressed by the new sultan's physical characteristics than some Ottoman chroniclers. He informed his

FIG. 4.4 A portrait of Süleyman as a young man by Hieronymus Hopfer, ca. 1530. Courtesy of the Trustees of the British Museum.

interlocutors in Venice that Süleyman "is twenty-five years old. He is tall but slim, with a delicate complexion. He has a neck that is slightly too long, a small face, an aquiline nose, a faint mustache, and a sparse beard. Still, he is quite graceful. His skin color is closer to white, but a pale white." As for Süleyman's character, the envoy was more positive: "It is said about him that he is wise, that he likes to study, and that everyone has high hopes for his reign. . . . He is a very prudent man."

## Süleyman's First Military Challenges

Soon after coming to the throne, the "very prudent man" was faced with two major challenges that illustrated the potential dangers that awaited new rulers.

The first, an internal one, was a rebellion in Syria by an Ottoman governor-general. The second, an external one, stemmed from a diplomatic crisis with the Kingdom of Hungary around the renewal of a pre-existing peace agreement. These challenges exposed the personal nature of political authority in this period, whereby the death of a monarch, in this case Selim, might be used as an excuse to delegitimize the treaties, alliances, and other political relationships he had established. The Ottoman-Hungarian tensions also illustrated the limits of diplomacy and the over-reliance on warfare by political and military elites of the time.

In early November 1520, following news of Selim's death, the governor-general of Damascus, Janbardi al-Ghazali, declared his independence. He had been a high-ranking military official under the Mamluks, before the Ottoman conquest. Following Selim's victory over the Mamluk sultan Qansuh al-Ghawri and the latter's death at the Battle of Marj Dabiq in 1516, al-Ghazali had changed sides. He was appointed governor-general of Damascus in 1518. The Ottoman conquest of Syria and Egypt involved both dislodging the Mamluk military elite and co-opting those of its members who were willing to submit to Ottoman authority. They received revenue grant assignments and positions commensurate with their ranks under the previous regime. In return, they administered a wealthy but as yet unfamiliar region with its own well-entrenched political, economic, and scholarly establishments that predated the Ottoman conquest.[39]

Al-Ghazali's rebellion displayed the risks inherent in this policy of co-optation. Indeed, he believed he could count on the support of other ex-Mamluks like him. Süleyman's accession to the throne as a prince inexperienced in military matters may have been a further inducement, at least as a psychological factor, for an experienced and confident military commander like al-Ghazali. The possibility of Ismail's involvement made the rebellion particularly critical for the Ottomans, given the proximity of Syria to the Safavid domains, and the likelihood of communication between al-Ghazali and the Safavids.

The rebellion also demonstrated the vital importance of the high officials Süleyman had inherited from his father. It gave those officials the opportunity to prove themselves to the new sultan, especially since it required large-scale military operations. The grand vizier Pirî Mehmed quickly sent Ferhad from Constantinople at the head of a contingent that included four thousand janissaries, half of the entire corps. Al-Ghazali had gathered thousands of foot soldiers and cavalrymen with whom he laid siege to Aleppo. Hearing of Ferhad's approach, and unable to take Aleppo, he decided to withdraw to

Damascus, his power base. He was defeated there in a field battle, and his severed head was sent to Constantinople.

The military victory was only the first step for the Ottoman officials. Next, Pîrî Mehmed and Ferhad conducted a thorough investigation in Syria to find out which *tımar* holders had lent their support to al-Ghazali. Instead of appointing another ex-Mamluk, the new governor-general of Damascus was selected from among the ranks of the sultan's servants: he was a product of the Ottoman *devşirme* practice named Ayas. The ex-Mamluk Khayr Beg, governor-general of Egypt, was allowed to remain in his position. He had denied his support to al-Ghazali, thus seriously undermining the rebellion's chances of success. This was the same Khayr Beg who had been instructed by Süleyman, in his letter of accession, to preserve order in his governorship, and he had indeed followed orders.

The rebellion in Syria later came to be seen as a minor incident of Süleyman's reign, since its instigator was defeated quickly. Contemporary accounts, on the other hand, devote considerable space to it and convey a distinct sense of surprise and anger. These reactions indicate how great the risk of losing Syria, and perhaps Egypt and other territories in the east, must have seemed at first.[40]

While those risks were averted, to the relief of the inexperienced sultan and his officials, tensions between the Ottomans and the Hungarians came to the fore, eventually culminating in the first military campaign that Süleyman participated in and nominally commanded. The crisis stemmed, on the surface, from the Hungarians' reluctance to renew a peace agreement dating from March 1519. Instead, they chose to delay and then detain an Ottoman envoy sent to Buda with the news of Süleyman's accession. Despite the cessation of major military operations between the two sides by the late 1450s, the Ottoman-Hungarian frontier was the scene of a war of attrition with a high cost in human and financial resources. The frustration of the Hungarian and Croatian nobility, especially those who were involved in frontier warfare, may have led to an eagerness to face the enemy once and for all. Additionally, expectations of a crusade in support of Hungary, news of the al-Ghazali rebellion, and rumors about Süleyman's peaceful disposition all seem to have played a role in the Hungarian decision not to renew the previous agreement with the Ottomans.[41]

The Ottoman decision to go to war was the result of equally complex considerations. Many contemporary observers and modern scholars emphasize the role of long-term dynamics and policies, such as the century-long Ottoman-Hungarian competition. They explain the campaign as the first step of a deliberate Ottoman plan to conquer Hungary in stages, or the first military expression of Süleyman's claims to universal sovereignty.[42] While the impact of a larger vision cannot be discounted, other factors were equally important. One was related to Selim's legacy: he had not been active on the European front, and this had led to expectations on the part of the *askerî* elite that the next military target should be in the west. Also, an attack against the major Christian rival of the Ottomans could help Süleyman build a much-needed martial reputation.

Still, many among Süleyman's close associates were conflicted. An account of the Hungarian campaign, written in Arabic by the sultan's physician Ramazan, shows that there were discussions about whether an attack against the Safavids would be preferable.[43] Ismail was still alive, and the al-Ghazali rebellion had reminded everyone of the tenuous control the Ottomans had over the newly acquired territories in the east. However, the proponents of a campaign against the Hungarians, including Ottoman frontier lords in the Balkans and Ahmed, the governor-general of Rumeli, prevailed. Ramazan also suggests that many viewed a campaign in the west as less arduous than one in the east, given the shorter distances, the relative ease in provisioning due to a more bountiful natural environment, and the strength of the Ottoman supply lines.

Ottoman sources on Süleyman's first military campaign further show how warfare was an integral component of elite mentality. Since the early days of the Ottoman enterprise, waging war had been a major political, economic, and cultural tool in the hands of the Ottoman dynasty. Fighting was a major component of a ruler's image and reputation, as well as the professional identity of the high officials and the soldiery.[44] It also brought in wealth in the form of slaves, material goods, and land that enriched both the sultan and the *askerî* elite. All contemporary Ottoman historians unanimously emphasized the duty of a Muslim sultan to wage holy war against infidels and approached warfare with unbridled enthusiasm in their works.[45] For instance, two of the most accomplished historians of Süleyman's reign, the jurist and religious scholar Kemalpaşazade Ahmed, and the bureaucrat Celalzade Mustafa, often regaled their readers with descriptions of the capture of cities, the enslavement of women and children, and the slaying of enemy troops.

The buoyant approach of the Ottoman elite to warfare was supported by its considerable success in it. Ottoman warfare relied on the relative efficiency of a bureaucratic and financial apparatus that collected taxes and conducted communications with Ottoman officials spread over a large territory. That apparatus maintained a standing army in Constantinople, *sipahi*s across the realm, a fleet, a network of fortresses, and countless military specialists and auxiliaries. Technical know-how, in the form of battle tactics as well as the use of gunpowder weapons from muskets to cannons; technological capacity, in the form of armaments production in the capital and elsewhere; and logistical skills, in the form of supply networks for war materiel and food during a campaign—these gave the Ottomans a major advantage over their Hungarian, Habsburg, and Safavid rivals. They were particularly adept at siege warfare, which required massive firepower as well as the ability to feed large numbers of soldiers and animals.[46] These capabilities notwithstanding, factors such as timing and duration, the weather, the distances traveled, the terrain over which the army traveled, and the presence or absence of epidemics very much helped determine the outcome of any military endeavor.

Despite the congratulatory tone of Ottoman chroniclers, there was always a strong element of uncertainty and contingency in any campaign, as Süleyman soon discovered. He left Constantinople on May 19, 1521, in the company of the janissaries and the household troops, and marched west, toward Hungary. On the road, his forces swelled with the arrival of governors and their men from different parts of the realm, and the supply networks functioned well. The relatively orderly progression was soon upset, however, because of tensions among the high officials about the objective of the campaign. Later in June, these tensions spilled out at a dispute during a meeting attended by the sultan.

Ahmed, the governor-general of Rumeli, was an advocate of the idea of advancing deep into Hungary, toward the capital city of Buda, with the intention of facing the king himself. The grand vizier Pirî Mehmed, on the other hand, advocated for a siege of Belgrade (Nándorfehérvár in Hungarian), arguing that leaving the city unattended would expose the Ottomans to a potential attack from the rear. Süleyman was unable to dictate a single objective to his officials and forces. While he chose to advance with Ahmed deeper into Hungary, he had to consent to Pirî Mehmed's demand to split the Ottoman forces and lay siege to Belgrade. Süleyman and Ahmed took the fortress of Szábacs (today Šabac in Serbia) in early July while the grand vizier took the fortress of Zemun and then laid siege to Belgrade.[47]

The following few weeks were spent in suspense. Pirî Mehmed was not able to take the city quickly and follow Süleyman, but he was unwilling to abandon the siege, to the point of refusing the sultan's orders to join him. He communicated with Süleyman's tutor Hayreddin and the second vizier Mustafa to influence the sultan's thinking. Süleyman seems to have been reluctant to advance into Hungary without the grand vizier. He finally yielded to Pirî Mehmed and marched back east to Belgrade. The city fell on August 8, shortly after Süleyman's arrival with the bulk of the army and the more powerful siege weaponry. The citadel resisted longer, but eventually fell on August 29. The next three weeks were spent securing the city and the fortress, repairing the walls, and clearing out the vicinity by sending out raiders. Leaving behind a garrison, laden with loot and enslaved captives, Ottoman forces departed in the third week of September and reached Constantinople in the third week of October.

What had started as a general campaign against the kingdom of Hungary, with the aim of marching on to its capital Buda and forcing its king to a field battle, thus ended with the conquest of Belgrade, which itself was a result of the grand vizier's insistence and his risky departure from the main Ottoman force. Contemporary Ottoman sources, however, are skillful enough to hide these tensions and the arbitrary nature of decision-making during the campaign. Their depictions of the campaign's outcome convey the considerable strength of Ottoman literary culture. In victory proclamations (*fethname*, "letters of victory"), such as the one sent to Ottoman judges to be recited publicly, and in contemporary and near-contemporary works of history, whose numbers proliferated under Süleyman, there emerges a coherent narrative about the conduct and outcome of the campaign.[48]

Indeed, these testimonies leave the impression that Belgrade was the main target of the campaign from the beginning and that Süleyman made all the crucial decisions by himself. They often emphasize that, while Süleyman's illustrious great-grandfather Mehmed II had failed to take Belgrade in 1456, the great-grandson had finished the task, even bringing back to Constantinople the cannons left behind by Mehmed's retreating army. The recovery of the fortress of Szábacs, built by the Ottomans in 1470 as Böğürdelen and later captured by the Hungarians, pales in comparison with the capture of Belgrade in these narratives. Chroniclers underline the strength of Belgrade's fortifications and the difficulty of capturing such a city, built on a promontory surrounded on three sides by the Danube. Propaganda is a word heavy with negative connotations; it often refers to willful deception. Here, beyond deception, what we see is an ability to create narratives tailored to the requirements of a specific situation.

Süleyman's personal reactions to the campaign's events are mostly unrecorded. How did he feel about his first encounter with violent warfare, during the sieges of two major fortresses? What did he make of the tremendous efforts required to manage the campaign logistically, such as the provision of food and fodder, the daily setting up and dismantling of the army camp, the construction of roads and bridges, the transportation of war materiel? More importantly, as a ruler inexperienced in military leadership, what role did he really play during the important junctures of the campaign? While these questions have to remain unanswered, it is well established that he played a significant ceremonial role. He was aware that the campaign would have a major impact on his reputation. For instance, after Szábacs fell, he stated that, since this was his first conquest, the fortress needed to be rebuilt appropriately. He knew that his name was now forever associated with the place.

Despite frictions with the grand vizier and his inexperience in military matters, Süleyman found many occasions to project his authority and munificence during his first campaign. Before the departure from Constantinople, he visited the tombs of his ancestors: the conqueror of Constantinople Mehmed II, his grandfather Bayezid II, and his father Selim. According to some sources, he also laid the first stone for the foundation of the mosque constructed in memory of his father. The following day, after the morning prayer, he left the New Palace on his horse; in the company of the janissaries and the household troops, he marched to the Edirne Gate. Throughout the campaign, he visited cities with great pomp, received gifts from city-dwellers, listened to complaints, and had his hand kissed by officials. He watched a bridge being built over the Sava River from under a parapet and encouraged the builders. He surveyed the fortifications of Belgrade and the Ottoman positions. After the fall of Belgrade, he entered the city to attend the Friday prayer in the city's cathedral, which had been converted into a mosque. He hunted in the vicinity, scouting his new territory. He rewarded various officials, military men, and members of his household for their services during the campaign.

The state of mind of the sultan and the high officials in the aftermath of Belgrade's capture is portrayed in a diplomatic report (*relazione*) prepared by Marco Minio, the Venetian ambassador sent to Constantinople to negotiate a new peace agreement. On the one hand, there was a sense of elation and pride, accompanied by a sober assessment of the conquest's significance. The Ottomans had breached the southern defenses of Hungary and gained a major strategic advantage for future operations.[49] On the other hand, the high officials were very concerned that the Ottoman capture of Belgrade might lead to a unified front among the European Christians. They quizzed Minio about the activities of the papacy, the newly elected Holy Roman Emperor Charles V (king of Spain, r. 1516–56; Holy Roman Emperor, 1519–56), and the king of France Francis I (r. 1515–47). As for Süleyman, in contrast to earlier assessments of him as meek and under the influence of high officials,

Minio thought that the young sultan was war-like and that he did not allow himself to be governed by others.[50]

Despite these anxieties, the time around Selim's death and Süleyman's accession was a fortuitous one for the Ottomans. A united European front against them was hampered both by the logistical difficulties of organizing a crusade and by developments across Europe. The competition between Charles and Francis over the election of the Holy Roman Emperor in 1519 had turned into open hostility in June 1521, when imperial troops invaded the north of France. Charles was also preoccupied by a revolt of Castilian townsmen concerned about the loss of their liberties to increasing Habsburg control. Another major concern was the growth of Protestantism, which fostered a strong theological and political opposition against the papacy and its allies and protectors.[51] The Ottoman position was strengthened further when the Venetians, after a brief period of hesitation following Süleyman's accession, signed a new treaty in December 1521.

Süleyman's next campaign was waged against this backdrop. It targeted the Order of St. John and their main base, the island of Rhodes.

## The Capture of Rhodes and a New Image for Süleyman

The Order of St. John, established after the armies of the First Crusade captured Jerusalem in 1099, had relocated to the island of Rhodes in 1306. Between 1306 and 1522, the Order established a presence in the eastern Mediterranean, competing and interacting with the Venetians, the Mamluks, the Byzantines, Anatolian Turko-Muslim principalities, the Ottomans, the kingdom of Cyprus, and a variety of Catholic, Orthodox, and Muslim potentates, soldiers of fortune, corsairs, and merchants. The Order continued to recruit from Europe through its zealous religious rhetoric. It became well adapted to the dynamics of the eastern Mediterranean, surviving through a mixture of predatory military activities and pragmatic arrangements with the surrounding powers.[52]

The increase in the naval capabilities of the Ottomans and their expansion into the eastern Mediterranean under Mehmed II eventually put them and the Order on a collision course. In 1480, the Order successfully resisted a three-month siege by an expeditionary force sent by Mehmed II; in 1482, it sheltered the runaway Ottoman prince Cem after defeat by his brother Bayezid II. Following their conquest of Syria and Egypt, the Ottomans had even more reasons to be concerned about Rhodes' position in the middle of the lanes of communication and travel between Constantinople and Alexandria.

The ideological impetus was equally strong. The Order's enslavement of Muslims facilitated the Ottomans' formulation of a religious justification for the campaign. Contemporary Ottoman chroniclers particularly emphasize the capture of Muslim pilgrims on the way to Mecca. Since the Ottoman sultans were the protectors of the two holy cities of Mecca and Medina after 1517, they were responsible for the safety of the pilgrims, so it was claimed.[53] In any case, Rhodes was never too far from the thoughts and fantasies of the Ottomans. For instance, a prognostication from around 1512, about Selim's future campaigns against his brother Ahmed and the Safavid Ismail, predicted that Selim would capture Rhodes after a campaign of four and a half months.[54] Before he died, Selim had indeed ordered preparations for a campaign against Rhodes. Süleyman, in a way, set out to complete a task left unfinished by both his great-grandfather Mehmed II and his father.

The second military campaign Süleyman led turned out to be particularly difficult logistically.[55] First of all, since Rhodes is an island, a successful siege required joint naval and land operations. The fleet was sent in advance while Süleyman marched south from Constantinople with the bulk of the army. Disembarking men and supplies from the ships to the island; transferring thousands of soldiers and animals and large quantities of equipment from the Anatolian peninsula to Rhodes; and setting up camp on a rocky island under defensive fire was only the beginning. The walls of the island's main fortress were extremely difficult to breach. Their high towers allowed the defenders to target Ottoman forces with deadly precision, while the strong fortifications and the rocky terrain made the task of demolishing the walls and digging mines particularly challenging.

Due to these difficulties, the campaign lasted from early June 1522 to the end of December, which posed another problem. Being on campaign after late summer and early fall was a major vulnerability for the Ottomans, given the challenges of provisioning, housing, and keeping large numbers of men and animals warm and healthy. However, abandoning the siege and returning to Constantinople was, it seems, costlier for the new sultan than losing considerable resources and manpower. Thus, after many weeks of battles that exerted a terrifying toll, and despite the beginning of the autumn rains, the sultan and his officials convened on November 1 and decided to continue the siege. In the days after the meeting, the hardships of the siege continued to cause tensions among the Ottoman officials. They openly quarreled over the tactics to adopt and blamed one another, while Süleyman exhorted them to do their best.

The expected break came thanks to the deterioration of the situation inside the main fortress, which was due to dwindling supplies and military resources, illnesses, and declining morale. Philippe de Villiers de l'Isle-Adam, grand master of the Order, asked for terms of surrender, and Süleyman granted him *aman* (literally "safety"). According to the Sharia as well as historical practice, grantees of *aman* could leave with their lives and possessions, while those who wanted to stay would be recognized as "protected non-Muslims," free in their worship yet subject to certain restrictions in public life.[56] This had been the arrangement in Belgrade as well, the defenders asking for a negotiated surrender after a long siege. De l'Isle-Adam and the Order left; after spending the following years without a permanent base, they received the islands of Malta and Gozo from Charles V and relocated there in 1530.

The granting of *aman* is presented in Ottoman sources as yet another sign of Süleyman's magnanimity. Similarly, the freeing of the island's Muslim captives is enthusiastically described. The end of the hostilities gave Süleyman the opportunity to engage in more pleasant pursuits. He received de l'Isle-Adam and the Order's notables and exchanged gifts with them; he toured the island and visited the Garden of Cem, named after his great-uncle; on January 2, 1523, he attended the Friday prayer in the cathedral of St. John, converted into a mosque. He then crossed over to the Anatolian peninsula and marched on to Constantinople. As usual, he made time for hunting; his other entertainments included watching a fight between camels, a practice encountered among the Turkish-speaking nomads of western Anatolia.

Just as Süleyman was leaving Rhodes, other, more unsavory matters were also handled. According to Ottoman dynastic practice, there could be no surviving legitimate claimants to the throne other than a ruling sultan and his sons. Rhodes was home to three such figures: the son of the runaway prince Cem and his two sons, Cem's grandchildren. Cem had taken refuge in the island in 1482; as he was sent over to Europe, his son had been left behind. All three princes were located by the Ottomans and executed, and female members of their families were sent to Constantinople. Süleyman himself was back in his capital city on February 9, after an absence of eight months.

The capture of Rhodes, like the Hungarian campaign, was utilized by the sultan, the high officials, and the literati in their ongoing construction of Süleyman's reputation. Around his accession, the emphasis had been on justice and generosity. His new image included elements of military prowess and magnanimity. He acted against his enemies for legitimate reasons, not solely out of a desire to wage war. He did not refrain from showing his appreciation to his men and his kindness to the defeated.[57] For instance, a letter sent to Venice on December 29, 1522, while Süleyman was still on the island, mentions the Order's depredations against both Muslims and Christians, the tremendous efforts involved in the campaign, and the mercy shown by Süleyman to the defenders.[58] A letter to the judge of the city of Bursa, an Ottoman official charged with adjudicating on the basis of Sharia and dynastic law (*kanun*), initially gives more weight to the theme of holy war, and then proceeds by emphasizing Süleyman's military achievement, his magnanimity, and his protection of the realm of Islam from its enemies. The judge is duly instructed to share the news and organize celebrations.[59]

News of Süleyman's achievements also circulated throughout Europe. European audiences had already been exposed to a plethora of works about the Ottomans since the Ottomans expanded into the eastern Mediterranean and southeastern Europe from the mid-fourteenth century on. As the Ottomans and the European Christians became more profoundly entangled with one another through diplomacy and war, the "Turk" (the ethno-linguistic name the Europeans used for the Ottomans) was variously portrayed as the follower of a misguided faith, the relentless enemy of Christianity, a scourge from God, the harbinger of the end times, a cunning politician, and a skilled soldier. He (for he was almost always depicted as a man) was reviled, respected, abhorred, and emulated in equal measure. The fall of Rhodes, one of the last Christian strongholds in the eastern Mediterranean, was met with particular alarm because it had come after several decades of relative Ottoman inactivity on the European front.[60]

In the years after Rhodes, works like Jacques Fontaine's *De Bello Rhodio libri tres* ("On the Battle of Rhodes, Three Books," 1524) and Jacques de Bourbon's *La Grande Et merveilleuse et trescruelle Oppugnation de la noble cite de Rhodes* ("The Great and Awe-Inspiring and Very Brutal Siege of the Noble City of Rhodes," ca. 1525) told the European reading public both about the unrelenting enmity the Ottoman sultan harbored against Christian religion, and his military and financial might and his chivalrous behavior toward the grand master of the Order of St. John. Thus, rather than a faceless enemy, or the latest representative of a generic Muslim/Turkish foe, Süleyman began to emerge as a distinct figure in European texts around this time. This was the beginning of the European fascination with him. In the coming decades, he and the Ottoman Empire became the subject of a variety of genres and media, from travel narratives, religious polemics, dramatic works, and histories to diplomatic correspondence, news sheets, sermons, songbooks, and woodcuts.[61]

Süleyman's profile rose in the Islamic world as well. Ismail, his father's old enemy, sent a letter after the Rhodes campaign to present his condolences on Selim's passing and his felicitations on Süleyman's victories over the "infidels." The shah of Shirvan, a Sunni and a potential ally for the Ottomans against the Safavids in the Caucasus, sent a letter on the occasion of Selim's passing and Süleyman's accession around the same time. Both letters were answered by the Ottomans in the original Persian, by using the high literary style of Islamic chanceries.[62] Three years after coming to the throne as a relatively un-known, almost universally underestimated prince, Süleyman spoke in these letters with a mature voice, addressing senior monarchs as his peers.

## Süleyman and His Family in the Early 1520s

Süleyman's first years on the throne were not only a time of political and mili-tary challenges, but also a period of important transformations in his personal life. There too, he showed that he was ready to defy established practices as he sought to assert himself and seek close, intimate relationships.

Having intercourse with concubines, siring children, and ensuring the dynasty's continuity was a duty that was imposed on princes and sultans by tradition. Affection, choice, and consent, components of an intimate rela-tionship from a modern perspective, were not often discussed. Süleyman had followed established tradition during his years as district governor. His sons Mahmud, Murad, and Mustafa were born to different concubine mothers. We know the name of Mustafa's mother, Mahidevran, and of another concu-bine, Gülfem, who may have been the mother of either Murad or Mahmud. Süleyman had at least one daughter, and perhaps more, whose names are not mentioned in the sources. All of them were brought to Constantinople after his accession and housed in the Old Palace.

Then, in the years following his accession, Süleyman formed what may be called a special connection with a woman named Hürrem, who had been brought to the Ottoman lands after being enslaved in the Ukrainian steppe.[63] While some reports claim that she had been taken into his harem in Manisa, it is more likely that she was acquired later, perhaps as one of the slaves presented to the sultan as gifts during his accession. Known as Roxelana, "the Ruthenian girl," to European observers, she was named Hürrem, "the joyful one," in the harem.

Upon arrival into the harem, Hürrem had to have undergone a physical check-up, to ensure that she was in good health, and that she was still a virgin. She would have been converted to Islam, been taught spoken Turkish, and learned basic reading and writing skills. She may have received lessons in sewing and embroidery, singing, and playing an instrument. In general, she would have been instructed in how to present herself to the elusive sultan if he were to demand her company. That instruction would have included everything from self-care and cleanliness to the clothes to be worn and the demeanor to be adopted. These skills were meant to impress the sultan during the first encounter and maintain his interest and desire, ideally until pregnancy.

Hürrem eventually became Süleyman's lifelong companion, in defiance of dynastic tradition. It is quite likely that their relationship blossomed at a moment of profound grief and anxiety for Süleyman. In the fall of 1521, as he was returning from Belgrade, he was informed of the death of his son Murad. Shortly after his arrival in Constantinople, in late October 1521, his son Mahmud also died. While he had missed Murad's funeral prayer and burial, he was present for Mahmud's. Murad and Mahmud were buried in the vicinity of their grandfather Selim's mausoleum, and alms were distributed to the city's poor.[64] Ambassador Marco Minio, in a letter to Venice, notes that a daughter also died around the same time. More importantly, he provides a reason for Murad's death: smallpox.[65] It is possible that either the harem or the entire city was hit by an outbreak.

Süleyman now had only one surviving son, Mustafa, and he would be expected to produce more heirs to the throne. This is the time when Hürrem became pregnant with their first child. Their son Mehmed was born in September 1522, when Süleyman was at the siege of Rhodes.[66] Typically, the relationship between concubine and sultan ended after the birth of a male child, and the concubine mother became the lifelong protector of her son. However, Süleyman and Hürrem maintained their connection. After Mehmed, they had three more children in quick succession: Mihrümah (their only daughter, b. 1523), Selim (b. 1524), and Abdullah (b. 1525).

Hürrem must have been judged suitable by others in the harem to be presented to Süleyman. The initial meetings between the two would have been arranged by the harem officials, whose job it was to entertain the sultan and place him in the company of sexual partners. Hürrem had to be particularly intelligent and savvy, in order to engage in and then maintain a mutually pleasant relationship with Süleyman and to navigate the hierarchical, competitive world of the harem. She must have had allies and advisors, such as the concubine Gülfem, who became her close companion. She had to know how to handle the eunuchs who served as overseers and gatekeepers, the washerwomen, the physicians, and the other concubines to be able to receive services, remain informed, and have access to necessary goods.

The reasons behind Süleyman's decision to defy tradition and form a long-term, exclusive relationship with Hürrem have been debated across centuries, often speculatively, in the absence of direct testimonies. Süleyman's search for intimacy and companionship, already seen in his transfer of many close associates from Manisa, may have been a reason. After a childhood and youth spent under the influence of an overbearing father, with the threat of violent death looming over his head for many years, it is understandable that he would seek a stable relationship with a sexual partner that involved companionship. It is likely that, after the sudden death of his two sons and his daughter in the fall of 1521, he was particularly receptive to affection, which he must have found in Hürrem.

Marco Minio, who was in Constantinople from September 1521 to January 1522, noted in his official report that Süleyman frequently visited the Old Palace around that time.[67] Minio interpreted that as a sign of lasciviousness. In fact, the visits must have been related to the burgeoning relationship between him and Hürrem. By the fall of 1524, it was common knowledge in Constantinople that the sultan spent his nights with the same woman and did not seek other sexual partners.[68] It also appears that he paid close attention to the rearing and health of his children. For instance, a marginal note in a revenue register records significant sums of money paid by Süleyman and his mother Hafsa to a healer named Abdi Dede for Prince Mehmed's recovery from an unspecified illness.[69]

Despite the growing intimacy between Süleyman and Hürrem, Mahidevran, as the mother of Mustafa, the eldest surviving son, continued to occupy a privileged place within the harem. Concubines who spent time with the sultan in the New Palace were moved to the Old Palace upon pregnancy and lived there with their children. Hürrem had to share common spaces with Mahidevran, in full knowledge that their sons would become rival contenders to the throne following Süleyman's death.[70] Moreover, she had to live under the shadow of Süleyman's mother Hafsa, the most senior female member of the dynasty. Hafsa's objection to Hürrem as a suitable partner could have ended the budding romance between her son and the concubine. Hürrem must have been able to ingratiate herself with Hafsa, or Süleyman must have been persuasive enough with his mother, who represented established tradition within the life of the harem. Of course, she also depended on Süleyman for financial support as she set out to establish her own reputation.

Indeed, like many other close associates of Süleyman throughout his life, Hafsa was eager to promote herself, change established practice, and leave

behind a self-curated legacy. Even though she lived in a male-dominated society, she was aware that she held a form of political capital that was informal
yet quite real. Thus, after Süleyman's accession, and quite probably with
her son's acquiescence, she began to sign her letters as "the sultan's mother"
(*valide-i sultan*). This was not an official title, yet it was easily recognizable
by all. More importantly, Hafsa was most likely the first sultanic mother who
consistently, indeed persistently, utilized that appellation.

Hafsa was a source of support for many individuals in these years, and she
offered succor particularly to women who were associated with the dynasty in
various ways. For instance, when their mother died in the early 1520s, daughters of Prince Âlemşah (d. 1510), Süleyman's uncle, lost their main source of
sustenance. They contacted Hafsa, who wrote to Süleyman and asked for
them to receive regular food supplies. Similarly, after Khayr Beg, the ex-
Mamluk who had joined Ottoman service, died during the siege of Rhodes, a
female member of his harem sent word to Hafsa. She had been sent to Cairo
from Constantinople to join Khayr Beg's harem, and she asked not to be
left alone in a foreign land. After explaining the situation to her son, Hafsa,
business-like, reminded Süleyman that the concubine's wish to return had to
be considered carefully. If she were to be brought back to Constantinople, the
palace household would need to provide her with money and food. In her
letter, Hafsa addressed Süleyman in a respectful yet affectionate tone, calling
him "the light of my eye, the joy of my heart."[71]

Hafsa seems to have been the dominant female voice in the life of Süleyman
during the early years of his reign. She used scribes to write most of her letters,
and those letters sound highly formulaic at first sight, filled with the chancery
formulas used to address the sultan. In between the lines, however, an intimate tone makes itself heard. In a letter that asks Süleyman to bring Hafsa
from Manisa to Constantinople immediately after his accession, she tells her
son that even the shortest moment spent without his company is a significant
loss.[72] In another, in which she wishes Süleyman victory over the "devilish
infidels," she speaks as an anxious mother who prays for the safe return of her
son from his campaign.[73]

The intimacy between mother and son becomes palpable in a rare letter
by Hafsa's own hand, in which she bemoans a missed opportunity to see
Süleyman. She then tells him an amusing story about one of her household
servants. He apparently had been promised a robe made of precious Indian
cloth; not having received it, he began running around, shouting "where is
my robe?" She asks Süleyman to save them from the servant's folly and order a
robe. The letter ends by Hafsa telling Süleyman she sent him black-eyed peas.

"Eat them in health," she says, and adds, "even a whole treasure would not be enough of a gift for you."[74]

There were times, however, when the limits of Hafsa's influence were tested. The most blatant example is the execution of Ferhad, the husband of Hafsa's daughter and Süleyman's sister Beyhan. Ferhad was an official Süleyman had inherited from his father, in this case as third vizier. His military skills were useful to Süleyman in the early years of his reign. After Süleyman returned from Rhodes, however, Ferhad was accused of crimes dating back several years, such as misappropriation of property and mismanagement of the sultan's troops. Some believed that Süleyman decided to have his brother-in-law executed. He changed his mind, possibly due to Hafsa and Beyhan's intercession, and instead demoted Ferhad to the district governorship of Semendire, several hundred miles away from Constantinople.[75] Then, near Semendire, in August 1523, forces under Ferhad's command were routed by the Hungarians, as a result of which he was dismissed from all positions.[76]

Hafsa and Beyhan interceded with Süleyman once again, and the sultan agreed to grant an audience to Ferhad on November 1, 1524, in Edirne. During their meeting, Ferhad was unable to convince Süleyman of his innocence. Frustrated, he started to shout that he was a victim of conspiracy at the highest level, and Süleyman ordered pursuivants to remove him. When Ferhad continued to loudly protest outside the audience room and pulled out his dagger, he was jailed and then executed by decapitation. Süleyman reportedly told Hafsa that he had only wanted Ferhad to be imprisoned, but that he did not have a choice when his brother-in-law became violent. Beyhan, Süleyman's sister, was inconsolable after her husband's execution. After chiding her brother to his face, she left the palace and went into seclusion. Süleyman and Beyhan would never see each other again.[77]

Her failure in this incident notwithstanding, Hafsa was extremely successful in ensuring her legacy in the form of a charitable complex built in her name in Manisa. The complex's name, Sultaniye, announced her high status to all observers as the sultan's mother. In comparison, the mosque built in the name of Selim's mother Gülbahar in Trabzon was called Hatuniye, "the Lady's Mosque." The construction of Hafsa's mosque and attached buildings, which had probably started during Süleyman's governorship in Manisa, was completed in 1522–23.

An endowment deed was then prepared in late June–early July 1523. Typical for such projects, it listed the sources of revenue for the complex's expenses as well as the charitable functions envisaged by Hafsa. The witness signatures on the deed are proof of her prestige. The viziers Ahmed, Ayas, and

Kasım are there, together with the chief treasurers İskender, Abdüsselam, and Mahmud. They are followed by the chancellor and then all the chief officers of Süleyman's household: head of the Privy Chamber İbrahim, head of the Inner Treasury Süleyman, head of the larder Davud, and head gatekeeper Bali. The endowment deed was inspected and approved according to the Sharia by the two highest-ranking magistrates, the military judges of Rumeli and Anadolu.[78]

For the women of the Ottoman dynasty, displays of charity and religiosity were particularly important. These were their main outlet for public visibility and the performance of piety, and Hafsa was no exception in this regard. The uniqueness of her endeavor comes from the fact that her main charitable project was much larger in scope than similar works patronized by dynastic women before her. An impressive amount of revenue was assigned to Hafsa's complex, mainly from areas close to Manisa, in the form of agricultural, commercial, and animal taxes and rents from shops. Some of these revenue sources would have been accumulated slowly by her, through purchases with her own money and in the form of grants from Selim and Süleyman. Others were donated by Süleyman for this particular purpose.

Hafsa's complex was centered around a mosque, and a large number of Quran readers were assigned to it. In addition to a mosque, the complex included a soup kitchen, a madrasa with one classroom and ten rooms for students, an elementary school for poor and orphaned children, and a dervish lodge for a sheikh and ten disciples. The endowment deed stipulated that the sheikh of the lodge had to be a devout Sunni, a further indication of Hafsa's orthodox stance at a time when non-Sunni forms of piety were popular among Muslims. As a final touch, an inscription above the main door of the mosque reminded to the recipients of her charity that their benefactor was "*umm al-sultan*," an Arabic phrase that meant "the sultan's mother."

Süleyman did not forget to honor the memory of his father either, despite their complicated relationship. Selim had ordered the building of a mosque carrying his name shortly before his death. Süleyman saw to its completion, the construction starting in May 1521. He also commissioned the construction of a mausoleum for Selim, a soup kitchen, an elementary school, and a bathhouse, which constituted his father's mosque complex. This was his first major act of architectural patronage and institutional charity. Representing one more step in the Ottomanization of Byzantine Constantinople, the mosque complex bearing Selim's name became part of the city's new silhouette as seen from the Galata side: the New Palace on the left and a concatenation of mosques on a slight northwest-southeast axis, dotting the summits and slopes of Constantinople's hills.[79]

## A New Grand Vizier for Süleyman

Just as he built for himself a new relationship within the intimate space of the harem, Süleyman eagerly sought to identify new associates in political life. There too, he made unprecedented decisions despite the considerable potential for criticism and dissent. The new images crafted for him in 1522–23 reflect a growing confidence and a new sense of authority over the realm and the elite. As the conqueror of Belgrade and Rhodes, he soon embarked on a series of actions he must have been considering for a long time: the reshaping of the highest echelon of the Ottoman administration, starting with the grand vizierate.

The grand vizier, a post that had existed since the early days of the Ottoman dynasty, was the highest official in the realm. He served as a deputy who oversaw political, economic, and military affairs. Especially under Süleyman, the grand vizier would become a sort of supreme coordinator who harmonized the workings of the administrative and financial branches of the Ottoman government. The first grand viziers mostly came from a Muslim background, and their presence near the Ottoman sultan reflected the alliance between the Ottomans and old Anatolian families. However, Mehmed II, the transformer and codifier of palace protocol and administrative hierarchy, recruited most of his grand viziers from the Byzantine and Balkan nobilities, who served him after converting to Islam. By Süleyman's reign, viziers were mainly men of *devşirme* origin, educated and socialized within the Ottoman ethos following conversion in childhood.[80]

Süleyman's first grand vizier Pirî Mehmed was an exception, coming from a Muslim background. His military performance during the Hungarian and Rhodes campaigns was not stellar, but he was quite talented in bureaucratic and financial affairs. He played a prominent role in diplomacy as well, as attested to by a Venetian ambassador to Constantinople.[81] Süleyman's dismissal of some of his most capable administrators and commanders, starting with Pirî Mehmed, remains one of his most controversial decisions. Ottoman chroniclers, depending on their proximity to specific figures and factions within the palace, provide conflicting evidence about the reasons behind the sultan's actions. Some claim that Pirî Mehmed was a victim of rivals such as Ahmed, who plotted and schemed to bring about his downfall. Others claim that he was guilty of receiving bribes, as concluded by an investigation ordered by Süleyman. Eventually, Pirî Mehmed quietly went into retirement, assisted by a significant revenue assignment by the sultan.

The strongest candidate to the grand vizierate after Pirî Mehmed's dismissal was another vizier from a Muslim family, Ahmed. Like Pirî Mehmed, he had a long history of service under Selim, and he had continued to serve the dynasty well during Süleyman's first years by distinguishing himself as a capable commander. The conquests that formed the basis of Süleyman's new image were in part due to his prowess. The sultan recognized his worth by promoting him after the Hungarian campaign from governor-general of Rumeli to vizier. Ahmed indeed thought he was about to receive the position he believed he truly deserved. Then, suddenly and unexpectedly, İbrahim, head of the sultan's Privy Chamber, was appointed grand vizier in June 1523.

Frustrated, Ahmed openly voiced his discontent in imperial council meetings and other occasions. Then, in August 1523, he was dispatched to Egypt as governor-general. Some contemporaries argue that Ahmed had asked the sultan for the governorship as soon as he was denied the grand vizierate. By this, they imply that moving to Egypt was part of Ahmed's personal and political agenda. It is also possible that Süleyman may have wanted to send him away from Constantinople, due to his disruptive behavior following İbrahim's appointment. Moreover, given the turbulent state of Egypt and the outbreak of a rebellion there earlier in the summer of 1523, appointing a skilled commander to this wealthy yet restless province may have looked like a wise decision.[82]

What Süleyman wanted to do was to completely reshape the upper echelon of the elite. He did not even spare his brother-in-law Ferhad, who was dismissed from his position as vizier around this time. Other high-ranking positions were filled with Süleyman's handpicked appointees in the first half of 1523. While İbrahim's rise was the most meteoric, he was not the only inner household official to be elevated by several ranks. For instance, the head of the inner treasury, a man also named Süleyman, was made commander of the fleet.[83] Thus, by the end of summer 1523, the high officials the new sultan had inherited from his father were gone, with the exception of the docile Mustafa, who kept his vizierate.

The new grand vizier İbrahim had entered Süleyman's household as a slave. His family origins were a source of much speculation during and after his lifetime. The most likely story has him hailing from Parga, a Venetian possession on Albania's Dalmatian coast; his father would have been a fisherman, probably an Orthodox Christian, and a Slavic-speaker. İbrahim may have been "collected" by Ottoman officials as part of the *devşirme* practice. As such, he may have entered Selim's or Süleyman's households as a servant at a relatively young age. This would support some Ottoman sources' references to İbrahim's presence in Süleyman's company since childhood. Another possibility is that İbrahim was captured in a raid and subsequently sold as a slave in an Ottoman market. This version is more plausible, since there are also stories, circulated during İbrahim's lifetime, about how he had been gifted to Süleyman by one of his sisters around 1516, when both were in Edirne. Reportedly, her husband, an Ottoman official named İskender, had purchased İbrahim.

Given the hierarchical chasm between members of the dynasty and low-level servants, it is difficult to imagine that a prince and a servant would develop a friendship that would then culminate in the latter's grand vizierate. It is more likely that they met while both were around twenty years of age. İbrahim joined Süleyman's household as a gift from a beloved sister, and thus a slave with a special status, rather than as a child. He was close to Süleyman in age; reportedly, he was a skilled violin player, a charming conversationalist, and a person of pleasant company overall. With Süleyman's rise to the throne, İbrahim moved from Manisa to Constantinople, where he served the sultan as chief officer of the Inner Falconers and head of the Privy Chamber. These functions allowed him to spend considerable time with Süleyman, both during the frequent hunts he organized and as someone with access to the sultan's private living spaces.

The relationship between the two must have reached a certain level of closeness already before they moved from Manisa to Constantinople. This is indicated by the refurbishment and expansion of a pre-existing mansion on the Hippodrome, the city's main public place, to be given to İbrahim as his "palace." Construction began in 1521, early in Süleyman's reign. It was unprecedented for an active servant of the inner household to live in a separate mansion whose construction expenses were paid for by the sultan himself.[84] Thus, from the very beginning of Süleyman's sultanate, İbrahim's privileged status was announced to all.

Still, İbrahim's appointment to the grand vizierate must have surprised many, even though it may have been planned for a long time. Someone like him, a member of the sultan's inner household, could become grand vizier after a series of promotions and appointments. He would first progress through the ranks of the palace household units, which İbrahim had achieved by becoming head official. He would then need an appointment as district governor. After years in the provinces and in the sultan's company during war, having acquired the necessary skills, he could return to the capital as vizier, depending on merit as well as patronage, and then become grand vizier.[85] However, with his appointment in 1523, İbrahim had leapt several ranks and a few decades.

This radical move may be explained, as many contemporaries tended to do, by the deep personal relationship between the two men. Another reason was Süleyman's strong desire to be rid of his father's men and to rule in his own way. The trust and confidence built through years of intense friendship must have been a precious asset for both sultan and grand vizier during a time of transitions. Moreover, as it became clearer in the coming years, the bond between the two stemmed both from a profound sense of camaraderie and a shared political and cultural agenda. Indeed, İbrahim was positioned subsequently as an intermediary between the sultan and his servants and officials, allowing Süleyman to withdraw to a less accessible, loftier position from where he could preside over a new vision of political and spiritual leadership.

Not everyone was ready to accept the sudden promotion of the sultan's confidant. Many members of the *askerî* elite must have been upset even further when İbrahim was also given the rank of governor-general of Rumeli around the same time as his appointment as grand vizier. The Rumeli governor-general was the governor with the largest revenue assignments. He played a prominent role in the supervision of the empire's European front and the conduct of military operations in times of war. Perhaps the strongest reaction to İbrahim's appointment came from Ahmed. After he arrived in Egypt at the end of August 1523, he began to establish his own power base by mobilizing the remaining networks of Mamluk military men. He may have been spurred on by rumors from Constantinople that Süleyman and İbrahim planned to have him executed; perhaps he was carried away by his arrogance and ambitiousness, as many Ottoman chroniclers argued he did.

Ahmed's bid for independence reached its apogee when he declared his sultanate on February 12, 1524, one day after the much-awaited and much-speculated-upon Great Conjunction of Venus and Jupiter, seen as the harbinger of a time of great tribulations. He also asked a descendant of the Abbasid family of caliphs who lived in Cairo to recognize and validate his sultanate. These highly symbolic acts show the wide circulation as well as transferability of ideas of sovereignty in the Islamic world at the time. Someone like Ahmed, from a Muslim family yet without any dynastic past, could make a bid for the title of sultan on the basis of astrological speculation and Abbasid/caliphal sanction. This must have particularly irritated, indeed concerned, Süleyman and İbrahim, who were about to embark on their own redefinition of sovereignty.[86]

Ahmed was defeated relatively quickly and executed, thanks to the collaboration of some of his men with the authorities in Constantinople. As the first challenger of Süleyman and İbrahim, his name was stamped with the label of traitor (*hain*) by contemporary chroniclers. Even his family past was erased, and he was reinvented as a *devşirme* of Georgian or Albanian origin, an impetuous and ambitious man who had dared rebel against his master.[87]

Ahmed's actions proved the value of personal loyalty and further cemented the alliance between Süleyman and İbrahim. Within the *askerî* elite, however, not everybody would have interpreted Ahmed's defeat as a positive development. In fact, some critics of İbrahim's appointment to the grand vizierate as an inexperienced individual saw Ahmed as someone who had been pushed into the ultimate act of betrayal by Süleyman and İbrahim's actions. Thus, building a reputation for İbrahim was sorely needed in order to prove his qualities and ingratiate him with (indeed, impose him on) the *askerî* elite and the inhabitants of Constantinople.

The first step in the construction of İbrahim's glory was a major wedding celebration held in late May–early June 1524, after news of Ahmed's defeat had reached Constantinople. It had been common practice to have Ottoman officials marry women of the Ottoman dynasty. All of Selim's daughters were married, however, and Süleyman did not have any grown daughters. The solution was to have İbrahim marry one of Süleyman's nieces: a girl named Muhsine, the daughter of his sister, the one who in most likelihood had purchased İbrahim and given him as a gift to Süleyman.[88]

Much like İbrahim's unprecedented promotion, the large-scale celebration of his wedding was a novelty. Weddings between Ottoman officials and women of the dynasty were celebrated, but they had not previously been the occasion for the organization of a major multi-day event, involving the participation of thousands of individuals and extending into the fabric of the capital city. İbrahim's wedding celebrations began with banquets, over several days, given to the janissaries, the different units of the household troops, palace servants, high-ranking officials (including religious scholars who worked in Ottoman service), and members of religious confraternities. The Hippodrome was the designated space for the exhibition of tents, expensive clothes, garments, bejeweled weapons, and other war booty, taken from the Safavids and the Mamluks and brought from pillaged Tabriz and Cairo. These objects displayed the empire's might and established a link between the victories of Selim and Süleyman.

As part of the celebrations, a public debate by religious scholars was organized. The participants were asked to discuss a verse from the Quran, on the
notion of the caliphate. Their discussion helped enhance the political message of the event, and clearly established that Süleyman, as much as İbrahim,
was at the center of the festivities. Other, lighter entertainments were never
too far away. Constantinopolitans invited to the Hippodrome watched
mock fights, wrestling matches, and archery contests. Strongmen broke apart
chains, soldiers climbed on long poles smeared with grease to win a prize,
and a man dressed as a stork walked on long sticks. There was a public feast
toward the end of the celebrations where throngs of spectators were invited
to loot large amounts of food left in the middle of the Hippodrome. At night,
fireworks illuminated the sky. The entire city was generously fed and lavishly
entertained for two weeks.[89]

Shortly after the wedding celebration, in recognition of the severity of
the situation in Egypt despite Ahmed's defeat, İbrahim was sent on an inspection tour to the province.[90] This was intended to settle the administrative problems in Egypt as well as start building a reputation for İbrahim as a
skilled administrator. It was another unprecedented act, since grand viziers
usually accompanied the sultan and conducted the business of government
by correspondence instead of travelling to different parts of the realm. Some
of the most talented individuals in Süleyman's service, such as the scribe
Celalzade Mustafa, the treasury official İskender, and the sea captain Pirî Reis
were ordered to assist İbrahim during his journey.

İbrahim and his company traveled to Rhodes by ship, leaving
Constantinople at the end of September 1524. Unable to continue via sea
due to stormy weather, they crossed over to the Anatolian peninsula. After
a difficult trek, the new grand vizier, considerably delayed, reached Aleppo
in January 1525. He then moved to Damascus, and arrived in Cairo at the
beginning of April 1525, after having traveled for six months. In Aleppo and
Damascus, he gave audiences to the inhabitants and received their complaints,
criticized mistakes by Ottoman officials, and worked to redress past injustices.
He adopted a similar stance in Cairo.

While İbrahim dealt harshly with Arab tribes that had supported
earlier revolts in the area, he acted generously toward the inhabitants of
the city by repairing old mosques, ransoming those who languished in
debtors' prisons, and disbursing money to orphans. He also supervised
the drafting of a new law and tax code, with the intention of establishing
better control over both the remaining Mamluks and their revenue
sources, as well as the finances of the province of Egypt as a whole. The

code included provisions that favored merchants and commercial activity as a counterpoint to the agricultural sources of revenue and possibly against increased Portuguese influence around the Arabian peninsula and in the Indian Ocean.[91]

İbrahim's return was precipitated by riots that broke out in Constantinople. Following his confidant's departure for Egypt, Süleyman had moved to Edirne, where he spent a considerable amount of time hunting. Even sympathetic observers claim that the affairs of state had slowed down considerably, and that the imperial council met infrequently. One can only speculate about the rumors that raged around the capital about the sultan's absence from Constantinople and the controversial grand vizier's long stay in Cairo. Perhaps to fend off potential reactions, Süleyman left Edirne in late March 1525. However, when he took up residence in his mansion in Beykoz, on the northeastern shore of the Bosphorus, instead of returning to the New Palace, tensions boiled over. Janissaries and armed youth looted the houses of Ayas, a new vizier appointed around the same time as İbrahim, and the treasurer Abdüsselam, who was instrumental in helping Süleyman manage his finances after his accession.

In the coming days, the troubles spread across the capital. Houses belonging to Jewish inhabitants and shops in the Grand Bazaar were looted. The next night, rioters attacked and damaged the façade of İbrahim's mansion. Süleyman reacted harshly, and the targets of his anger clearly show that this was not random mob violence. The commander of the janissaries, the senior imperial council scribe Haydar, and the chief household officer of the vizier Mustafa were among those who were executed.[92] Summoned by the sultan to Constantinople, İbrahim left Cairo in June and reached the capital in September, once again dispensing justice and punishment on the road back and behaving with quasi-sultanic authority. He was reunited with Süleyman in mid-September. The scene was set for new ventures.

# 5

## Growth: A New Imperial Vision, 1525–33

İBRAHİM'S SWIFT APPOINTMENT to the grand vizierate, his marriage with Süleyman's niece and the ensuing celebrations, and his tour of inspection in Egypt were the first steps of a new imperial vision on the part of the sultan and his confidant. That vision is outlined in a long document, which serves as the preamble to the law code of Egypt. The law code was prepared toward the end of İbrahim's stay in Egypt, and it was intended to help the Ottomans better manage this wealthy province. The preamble itself was composed under İbrahim's supervision by the talented, madrasa-educated scribe Celalzade Mustafa, a close collaborator.

The preamble was seen as a document of such critical importance that Süleyman was sent a draft and his approval was obtained before the text was finalized. Sultans did not usually involve themselves directly with the matters pertaining to provincial administration, but the preamble is a different kind of statement. It expresses notions of sovereignty that are much more sophisticated than Süleyman's earlier claims to rule as a just sultan and a successful warrior. Moreover, for the first and the last time in Ottoman history, it describes a symbiosis between a sultan and his grand vizier who worked as partners to realize a global mission: universal rule under the mantle of the Ottoman sultan.[1]

### New Visions of Sovereignty

The preamble truly was a declaration of intent. It granted Süleyman both a form of overarching legal and political authority and a mystic, transcendental aura. It promoted Süleyman and İbrahim's partnership as a relentless fight against oppression and injustice across the face of the earth. While relatively new to the throne, the divinely sanctioned sultan, called the Shadow of God on Earth, assumed the task to usher in a new age of peace and prosperity through the perfect application of the Law and with the support of a virtuous servant.

After the customary praise for God and Muhammad, the preamble proceeds by presenting Sunni Muslim piety and the Law (both in the form of Sharia as well as the dynastic/customary *kanun*) as the dual foundations of Ottoman rule. It gives a short cameo to Selim as the conqueror of Egypt, and then introduces Süleyman as his rightful heir. Not satisfied with a simple emphasis on dynastic transition, however, the preamble then compares Süleyman to the major figures of ancient and Islamic history to draw attention to his saintly and prophetic qualities.

Next, the preamble introduces İbrahim as a loyal friend, just as Prophet Abraham (İbrahim in Turkish) had been an intimate friend to God. He is described as the ideal grand vizier and the perfect servant of the sultan, thanks to his unconditional devotion to Süleyman, his moral virtues, and his intellectual capacity. The text also justifies Süleyman's recent dismissal of high officials and his controversial promotion of İbrahim. Just as Süleyman needed to provide perfect justice to his subjects, he also needed to replace his father's officials with a perfect servant. İbrahim is given credit for the conception of the tour of inspection to Egypt, where he is said to have distinguished himself by correcting the mistakes of the Mamluks as well as those of previous Ottoman governors.

One of the central concepts in the preamble is the caliphate. Ottoman uses of the title of caliph, especially after the conquest of Egypt, have been misinterpreted as reflecting the transfer of the title from the Abbasid caliph al-Mutawakkil III (d. 1543) to Selim. In fact, it seems that the Ottomans mainly saw the last Abbasid caliph as a figurehead who could potentially help them establish control over Mamluk society. Selim took him to Constantinople after the conquest, but Süleyman sent him back to Cairo. There he resided to the end of his life, a respected yet somewhat ineffectual figure, a relic of the past.[2]

The caliphate Süleyman claimed was not narrowly defined as the historical Sunni Muslim caliphate. That institution had emerged after the death of Muhammad in 632 as an elected communal leadership. It evolved into a dynastic institution with the Umayyads (661–750), experienced its heyday as well as its political decline with the Abbasids (750–1258), and, after the Mongols sacked Baghdad in 1258, spent its lackluster final centuries in Cairo under Mamluk protection. The notion of the caliphate found in the pre-amble, on the other hand, was the product of debates among Muslim scholars and literati of western Asia in the fifteenth and early sixteenth centuries. Those debates redefined the caliphate from an ethical and political perspective. They placed the caliph atop the cosmic hierarchy from which he acted as God's vicegerent, through his purity of mind and soul as well as attributes such as justice and munificence.[3]

The preamble adopted this new definition and applied it to Süleyman. Writings from Selim's reign reflect a similar understanding of the caliphate, particularly after his victories over the Safavids and the Mamluks. What is surprising in Süleyman's case is his rather early adoption of the title. Already in his letters of accession to allies, he was presented as a caliph. Next, the notion of the caliphate as a form of universal spiritual and political leadership was publicly discussed by a group of scholars at İbrahim's wedding in the summer of 1524.[4] The preamble brought these strands together in a strong, single statement.

There were other titles that were adopted by and ascribed to Süleyman at this juncture. Like the caliphate, the Ottomans appropriated these titles from their Muslim neighbors, particularly the Mamluks and the Akkoyunlu. Diplomatic correspondence, the circulation of texts in the original Arabic or Persian as well as in Ottoman Turkish translation, and the constant movement of scribes, scholars, and Sufis brought the Ottomans in touch with the learning of the Islamic world past and present. A significant term the Ottomans borrowed was Master of the Auspicious Conjunction (*sahib-kıran*). Used as early as the eleventh century in Persian poetry, it denoted, in its simplest form, astrological predestination to rulership for an individual born under a specific conjunction of the celestial bodies. When fifteenth-century writers utilized it to explain the dazzling rise of Timur to power in the second half of the fourteenth century, they recast *sahib-kıran* as a divinely ordained absolute sovereign ruling at a time of eschatological tribulations.[5]

In Süleyman's case, claiming to be a *sahib-kıran* referred to a form of astrological—hence nonhuman, transcendental, unquestionable—form of legitimacy. It also represented a political and cultural claim to the legacy of past rulers who were deemed worthy of the title, such as Timur, Genghis Khan, and Alexander the Great. As in the case of the caliphate, Selim had been called Master of the Auspicious Conjunction during his reign. Süleyman once again appropriated and further expanded a critical concept, particularly by deploying it later against the Hungarians and the Habsburgs.[6]

Another critical term in circulation was _müceddid_ (renewer), which denoted an individual sent by God at the beginning of each century to renew Islam and protect it from corruption. The notion of a _müceddid_ was based on oral traditions attributed to Muhammad. Similar to the redefinition of _sahib-kıran_ in the fifteenth century, the _müceddid_ had come to be associated with the _mehdî_ (the Divinely-Guided One), a messianic figure whose arrival was seen as imminent after 900 AH/1494–95 CE, close to Süleyman's birthdate.[7] The _mehdî_ would unify the entire humanity under a single religion, eradicate oppression, and rule with justice.

Ottoman writers strategically used all of these titles around the time Süleyman departed on a campaign against the Hungarians in the spring of 1526, as seen in two contemporary accounts that were written shortly after the campaign's end. Celalzade Mustafa, the same scribe who penned the preamble of the Egyptian law code, presented Süleyman as _müceddid, sahib-kıran, and mehdî_ of the end times (_âhirüz'z-zaman_).[8] Kemalpaşazade Ahmed also utilized eschatological references, from calling Süleyman _sahib-kıran_ to positioning Ottoman sultans as defenders and promoters of Muhammad's message until the Day of Judgment. Echoing deep-seated Ottoman beliefs about the apocalyptic dimension of their competition with the Hungarians, he announced that Süleyman was marching against the Blond Peoples (_Benî Asfer_), the enemies of Islam who were foretold to attack the Muslims during the end times.[9]

The notion of a leader with messianic attributes, fighting for a righteous cause, was not unique to the Ottomans or the Muslims. Both Muslim and Christian traditions include a strong eschatological dimension. They inform their followers of the inescapable end of humanity's worldly existence, offer a narrative about the tribulations that will precede the end times, and paint a dual picture of punishment and salvation. Thus, expectations of apocalyptic tribulations and messianic leadership, which widely circulated across Europe, the Mediterranean, and western and central Asia around this time, were easily recognizable by all adherents of Abrahamic religions, regardless of whether they were Ottoman subjects.

What particularly distinguishes the era under discussion here is, on the one hand, the growing certainty, from the late medieval period onward, of the imminence of the end. Developments such as the Mongol invasions, the Black Death, the decline of papal authority in Europe, the disappearance of the Abbasid caliphate in the Islamic realm, Ottoman incursions into Europe, and the European "discovery" of the Americas with its large non-Christian communities were all seen as signs pointing out the coming of the end.

Apocalyptic and messianic expectations played a prominent role in shaping the agendas of the empire-builders of the sixteenth century. This was not a simple matter of political pragmatism either. It is likely that the rulers of the time, be they Charles V, Francis I, Ismail, or Süleyman, believed, at least for a time early in their careers, in their divinely sanctioned political and military mission.[10]

In addition to the preamble of the law code of Egypt, Süleyman and İbrahim's mindset in this particular period is described in a report by the Venetian resident ambassador in Constantinople, Piero Bragadin. Writing in early February 1526, Bragadin first mentions large-scale preparations for a military campaign against Hungary, with its capital city of Buda as the main target. This news would not come as a surprise to his interlocutors in Venice since an Ottoman campaign in the west was widely expected. However, the narration then takes an intriguing turn. These large-scale preparations, writes the ambassador, are actually meant for a further plan: an attack on Rome. After the campaign against Hungary, Süleyman will spend another winter preparing for this. He will then land in Puglia, on the southeastern tip of the Italian peninsula, and then march on to the seat of the papacy.

Bragadin then narrates an audience he had with İbrahim. The grand vizier told the ambassador about an old book he had read with Süleyman in their youth. That book prophesied that an individual named İbrahim would rise to the grand vizierate and the governorate-general of Rumeli without holding any high offices beforehand. Following that İbrahim's rise to power, the Ottoman ruler of the time would be able to achieve unprecedented things and would become the Roman emperor. He would organize a major campaign against the Christians; he would lose the first two encounters but would prevail over them in the third and final one, and he would capture the leader of the Christians, together with all of his notables and officers. The Ottoman ruler would free them all, and then a new faith would be ushered in with peace and love.

As İbrahim must have insisted and the ambassador felt the need to report, all of this was bound to happen soon.[11] İbrahim knew that these details would be relayed to Venice and, from there, circulate across Europe. It is possible that he appropriated the period's widespread beliefs about a decisive encounter between Muslims and Christians to intimidate the Ottomans' rivals. It is also possible that he and Süleyman genuinely believed in their divine mission, since the grand vizier's conversation with the ambassador described their partnership as a prophetically predicted companionship dating back to their youth.

These prophetic and eschatological themes gave a particular sheen to Süleyman's military campaigns, starting with 1526. Next to his duty of holy war as a Muslim ruler, he now fought to bring in and preside over a new age of universal peace that would encompass Muslims and Christians alike. Warfare, always an instrument for the enrichment of the *askerî* elite, also served as a tool to implement the ideal of universal rule.

## Süleyman's First Field Battle and the Collapse of Hungary

The Ottoman campaign against Hungary in the spring and summer of 1526 was the first military venture of the Süleyman-İbrahim partnership. Like Süleyman's earlier campaigns, this one had a complicated background. There were many factors, domestic as well as international, short-term as well as long-term, that motivated the Ottomans to march against Hungary.[12]

One factor was strategic. After the Ottoman capture of Szábacs and Belgrade in 1521, skirmishes, which at times turned into larger confrontations, intensified on the Ottoman-Hungarian frontier. The Hungarian side sought to muster military and financial resources necessary for a counterattack, including seeking support from allies within Europe. King Louis II worked, with limited success, at reining in the Hungarian aristocracy to fight with the Ottomans under his leadership. Ottoman frontier forces, on the other hand, worked at gradually weakening Hungarian border defenses to prepare the ground for an eventual Ottoman offensive.[13] A report sent to Constantinople the year before the 1526 campaign, by a prominent frontier commander, described the situation as favorable and assured the sultan of victory over the Hungarians.[14]

Overall, the Ottomans preferred a diminished Hungary as a buffer zone between themselves and the Habsburgs, whose recent advances they had watched from a safe distance. To face the king of Hungary in battle and to have him submit to the Ottomans as their vassal were probably ideas that prevailed among the sultan and his high officials before the campaign. If any additional territories were gained as a result of the operations, that would be a welcome benefit. The rich agricultural potential of the Pannonian plain must have looked appealing to the cadres of an empire whose military and financial success and vitality relied on the capture, taxation, and management of new territory.

The prospect of a revived Hungary concerned the Ottomans a great deal, especially since they thought it might spearhead a joint attack by European

Christians. The future grand vizier Lütfi, who was a district governor in the Balkans around this time, reported the widely circulated rumors of a crusade in a history he wrote a few decades later. According to him, members of the Order of St. John had embarrassed the European kings by blaming their lack of support for the loss of Rhodes. Ashamed, the European kings nominated the king of Hungary as their commander. The papacy, Spain, and France apparently provided money and soldiers. Every single Christian, claimed Lütfi, donated half of their possessions for the coming "holy war" (he interestingly uses the word *gaza* to refer to Christian holy war), whose preparations were already underway.[15]

For Kemalpaşazade Ahmed, on the other hand, the coming war with the Hungarians was the tail end of a long historical competition.[16] As he surveyed Ottoman expansion on the European front in his historical work, he informed his readers that the eventual submission of Hungary had been at the forefront of the Ottoman sultans' agenda for nearly a century and a half. Misfortunes such as the Interregnum of 1402–13 or the escape of Prince Cem to Europe had immobilized the Ottomans; strong leaders on the Hungarian side (he meant John Hunyadi and Matthias Corvinus) had pushed back the Ottomans successfully; finally, the necessity to subdue the Safavids and the Mamluks had delayed an Ottoman reaction against Hungary. As an avid reader of history, Süleyman's views of Hungary must have been partly shaped by these anecdotes. Finally, the time for action had come.

There was another critical factor: a plea Süleyman received from the French king Francis I, who had been taken captive by the Habsburgs at the Battle of Pavia in February 1525. An envoy, sent by Francis' mother Louise of Savoy, reached Constantinople in December 1525.[17] Süleyman officially responded in January 1526, in a letter directly addressed to Francis.[18] The first half of the letter follows Ottoman chancery practice, by invoking the support of God, Muhammad, and the first four caliphs, and describing Süleyman as the ruler of many realms captured by his ancestors as well as himself. Süleyman is presented to his new audience as the Shadow of God on Earth, as a king of kings who distributes crowns to other rulers, and in whose abode other rulers seek refuge. Then, a surprisingly earnest voice tells Francis that losing battles and being captured is not an unusual occurrence for rulers. Süleyman advises Francis not to worry. Like his ancestors, states the voice in the letter, Süleyman is always ready to campaign, conquer lands, and take fortresses, his horse saddled and his sword girded at all times. The letter closes by telling the king that further information, which would be too sensitive to put on paper, can be obtained orally from his envoy.

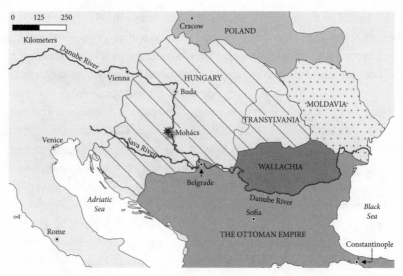

FIG. 5.1 Central-southeastern Europe, ca. 1526. Map by Jordan Blekking.

The new campaign against Hungary thus reflected the growing involvement of Süleyman and the Ottomans in European imperial rivalries. The Ottomans were aware of Charles V's election as Holy Roman Emperor and the rivalry between him and Francis.[19] The Venetians, suspicious of both Francis and Charles' designs over the control of Italy, and particularly concerned about Charles after Pavia, supplied them with ample information. Therefore, the 1526 campaign may also be seen as the first step of the Ottoman-Habsburg rivalry, albeit indirectly. The attack against Hungary, assumed to be an ally of Charles, could be presented as a response to Francis' plea, as Kemalpaşazade Ahmed argued in his history. More importantly, Ottoman observers note Charles' universalist claims with some irritation. Already in 1526, they were poised to declare Charles a usurper and to promote the Ottoman sultan as the true universal emperor.[20]

Süleyman and İbrahim left Constantinople on April 23, 1526, a date that was determined by astrologers as the most auspicious beginning for the campaign.[21] İbrahim, for whom this was an opportunity to prove his leadership skills to the *askerî* elite, commanded the experienced Rumeli troops as governor-general in addition to his title as grand vizier. He marched ahead of Süleyman, and the Ottomans proceeded through Edirne, Sofia, and Belgrade to the northwest, into Hungary. The army advanced in orderly fashion, and the Sava and Danube rivers, two important natural barriers, were crossed without great difficulty. On the way, the Ottoman forces also captured a number of fortresses, most notably Petrovaradin (Pétervárad in Hungarian), to prevent Hungarian attacks from the rear.

Toward the end of August 1526, they reached the swampy plain near Mohács, where Louis and his army awaited them. This was going to be Süleyman's first field battle, and his only one, although he did not yet know that in 1526. His father Selim, whose legacy continued to weigh on Süleyman, had won three in as many years. Besides his father's seemingly unsurpass-able example, he must have had other concerns. Ottoman soldiers had been marching for four months, sometimes under heavy rain, crossing rivers, and carrying large amounts of provisions and materiel. Moreover, rumors about the strength of the Hungarian army, which had circulated for the past few weeks, had made for a tense atmosphere in the Ottoman camp.

On the night of August 28, the eve of the battle, public criers, storytellers, bards, and Quran reciters were sent around the army camp to motivate and encourage the soldiers in anticipation of the next day. On the morning of August 29, there was a battle council meeting, attended by the sultan, İbrahim, high officials, and Ottoman commanders serving on the Hungarian frontier, whose knowledge of Hungarian tactics was of critical importance. It is not clear whether the Ottomans were intent on attacking the Hungarians first, and whether they meant to do so on the 29th or the next day. Ottoman forces, around eighty thousand, were considerably larger than the Hungarian army, estimates for which range from twenty-five to forty thousand. A large section of the Ottoman army was still in the process of taking positions, and this may have motivated the Hungarians to move first. The early attack should have given an advantage to the Hungarian side, whose forces entered the Ottoman lines in the late afternoon.

The initial attack of the Hungarian light cavalry was able to push back the Rumeli contingents, but the follow-up by the heavy cavalry, the strongest part of the Hungarian army, and the infantry, was repulsed by Ottoman musket and cannon fire. Through a mixture of defensive warfare, diversionary retreats, and counterattacks, but mostly thanks to the strength of their gun-powder weapons (nearly four thousand muskets and three hundred cannons), the Ottomans prevailed before sunset, destroying most of the Hungarian army and forcing the rest into a confused retreat. Süleyman watched the battle from an elevation, clad in armor, surrounded by members of his house-hold troops. There were times when the attacking Hungarian cavalry got close to his position, and there are anecdotes about arrows or bullets hitting Süleyman's armor without piercing it. Regardless of the veracity of these, he must have had a good view of everything from his vantage point. As for Louis, he was among the retreating forces and drowned when he was thrown off his horse while fording a river.[22]

This was a moment filled with pride as well as uncertainty for Süleyman. After quickly celebrating the victory and rewarding his commanders, he marched toward the Hungarian capital, Buda. The Ottomans did not yet know that Louis had perished, and they may have expected to face him again and/or have him sign a truce. On September 11, Süleyman entered a defenseless city. Most of the inhabitants had left before the arrival of the Ottomans. Among them was Maria, wife of Louis, and sister of the Habsburg brothers Charles and Ferdinand. The capture of Rhodes had given Süleyman the occasion to act as a merciful, graceful ruler vis-à-vis the Grand Master of the Order of St. John. At Buda, he and İbrahim organized another performance: the symbolic takeover of a rival monarch's possessions.

Indeed, contemporary Ottoman observers note with particular delight that Süleyman and İbrahim stayed in the king's palace, used his hunting grounds, held court, and organized entertainments. Whatever remained from the king's treasury and armory, including manuscripts from the famous royal library, were loaded on to vessels on the Danube and sent to Belgrade. The loot included two cannons left behind by Mehmed II after his failed siege of Belgrade in 1456, which had been transported to Buda by the Hungarians. Two large golden candelabras were taken from a church for use in the mosque of Hagia Sophia. Three bronze statues, commissioned by Matthias Corvinus several decades earlier, were carried away to be displayed on Constantinople's Hippodrome. Two thousand Jewish households, inhabitants of Buda, were likewise relocated to Ottoman territory.

One of the two major Muslim annual holidays, the Eid al-Adha, coincided with the stay in Buda. The celebration in a non-Muslim city of the Feast of Sacrifice, which commemorated Abraham's willingness to sacrifice his own son as an act of obedience and devotion to God, must have added to the Ottoman feeling of superiority.[23] However, the usual acts of conquest, such as the conversion of churches to mosques and the appointment of a garrison for the city, were not carried out. The victory at Mohács had caught the Ottomans by surprise and it seems that they had not planned to rule over Buda and the Hungarian kingdom in the near future. This confusion extended to the behavior of the soldiers. They were used to be allowed to loot newly conquered cities, and instructions to keep order in Buda could not stop their marauding. Against Süleyman's wishes, some neighborhoods and churches were looted and burned down. The atmosphere was so volatile that janissary guards were posted to the king's palace, where Süleyman and İbrahim stayed, to save it from destruction.

After ten days in Buda, Süleyman crossed to the other side of the Danube, the city of Pest, where he met with anti-Habsburg Hungarian nobles. Presumably, there were discussions about the future of Hungary following the disappearance of Louis without any heirs. Then began the return journey to Constantinople. The sultan and the grand vizier adopted a double-pronged march, eliminating the remnants of the Hungarian armed resistance and allowing the soldiers, who had complained about not being permitted to loot Buda and Pest, to pillage to their heart's content. Contemporary Ottoman observers all agree about the large numbers of slaves that were obtained during this stage of the campaign, and they rejoice over the destruction wrought upon Hungary, which they saw as a divine punishment for the vanquished and a prize for the victors.

The 1526 campaign added much to the prestige of the partnership between Süleyman and İbrahim at home and abroad. In case there were any remaining critiques of the grand vizier, their voices were silenced by the resounding praises found in Ottoman works of history. News of the Ottoman victory, soon joined by the even more alarming news of Louis' death, shocked European audiences. After Belgrade and Rhodes, Süleyman was already viewed with awe and dread. His victory at Mohács, his entry into Buda, and the ravages of his raiders and soldiers further accentuated his reputation. Themes such as the tremendous wealth of the Ottoman ruler, the undying loyalty he received from his men, his plans to subdue the entire Christian world, and his ruthlessness reverberated widely, from conversations among courtiers to popular songs.

Reasons behind the Hungarian debacle were amply debated across Europe, but with considerable disagreement among the discussants. Some blamed the youth and inexperience of Louis and the rashness of the decision to engage the Ottomans in open battle. Others pointed out the abandonment of the Hungarians by their fellow Christians, who had failed to do their share to stop the Ottoman onslaught. The lack of peace among European princes, and particularly the rivalry between Francis and Charles, was often blamed. The Protestants were likewise accused of having sown discord.[24] This is in striking contrast to the picture of a unified European Christianity presented by Lütfi with great concern before the 1526 campaign.

Once we get beyond Ottoman self-congratulation and European self-flagellation, the complicated outcome of 1526 becomes clearer. The Ottomans had a larger-than-expected victory on their hands, one that exposed the tensions between imperial vision and reality. In the summer/fall of 1526, they were not ready to impose Ottoman rule on an area as large as the kingdom of Hungary. In addition, Louis' death and the ensuing turmoil among the surviving members of the Hungarian aristocracy prevented the quick identification of a potential ally. Logistically, it was not feasible to keep the bulk of the Ottoman forces in Hungary over fall and winter until a solution was found. These questions must have preoccupied Süleyman and İbrahim as they spent time in Louis' palace and hunting grounds. To make matters worse, as they were on their way back to Constantinople, they received news of rebellions in Anatolia. The situation was severe enough to require İbrahim to command an expedition against the rebels in the coming months. In this environment, it was difficult for the sultan and the grand vizier to devote most of their attention to Hungarian affairs.

In the meantime, two figures stepped forward to fill the vacuum left behind by Louis and the Ottomans. The first was John Szapolyai, lord (*voivode*) of Transylvania. Szapolyai was one of the wealthiest members of the Hungarian nobility, and his prominence grew further upon the death of many high-ranking noblemen at Mohács. Moreover, late to join Louis' ill-fated battle, the forces under his command had remained intact. He had a long record of fighting against the Ottomans with some success, even though his belatedness to battle in 1526 led some to speculate about a possible understanding he had reached with the enemy.

Szapolyai was supported in particular by the lower nobility, whose members did not harbor much sympathy for the Habsburgs. He was elected king of Hungary at a meeting of the Hungarian Diet, the kingdom's legislative body, in November 1526. Members of the League of Cognac, the anti-Habsburg alliance established in May 1526, soon recognized him as king. The impressive list of the League's members in late 1526 included France, Venice, England, the papacy, and the dukes of Bavaria. However, diplomatic recognition did not translate into tangible support against the Habsburgs. Szapolyai's own overtures toward them did not produce the expected results either.

Indeed, one of the most undesirable outcomes of Louis' death, for the Ottomans, Szapolyai, and many others across Europe, was the opportunity it presented to the Habsburgs. The notorious Habsburg skill at securing favorable marriages had led to the union of Charles's brother Ferdinand with Louis' sister Anna in May 1521. This was followed by Louis' marriage to Charles and Ferdinand's sister Maria in January 1522. Around the same time, in 1521-22, Charles had given his brother Ferdinand control over various family possessions in central Europe, making Ferdinand archduke of Austria.

Ferdinand and Louis had thus become neighbors and brothers-in-law. With Louis' death, Ferdinand utilized his marital ties to come forward as heir to the Hungarian crown, with the full knowledge, however, that he needed to be elected to it.

Ferdinand was named king of Hungary in December 1526, by a small group of pro-Habsburg Hungarian nobles who had convened their own Diet. He then secured the crown of Bohemia in October 1526 and that of Croatia in January 1527, assembling all the components of the crown of Hungary. Next, he marched against Szapolyai in the summer of 1527, buoyed by his brother Charles' financial support. He occupied the capital, Buda, and his forces defeated Szapolyai. Ferdinand had himself crowned king of Hungary in November 1527 in Székesfehérvár, at the historic coronation church used by Hungarian monarchs, while Szapolyai was eventually forced to take refuge in Poland. As he planned his next steps, he also sent an envoy to Constantinople in late 1527.[25] The question of Hungary was about to pull the Ottomans even more deeply into the intricacies of European politics and diplomacy.

## Süleyman and İbrahim between War and Diplomacy

Diplomacy, from displays of feigned friendship to the negotiation of agreements, had been a cornerstone of Ottoman expansion since the early days of the polity. The view of the Ottomans as an "Oriental" empire whose rulers were out of touch with developments outside their own realm has been debunked long ago. Similarly, the facile classification of Islam versus Christianity, with its references to unbridled aggression and heroic defense, fails to describe the complicated relationship between the Ottomans and the Europeans and its long history of pragmatic arrangements.[26] The complexities of inter-European political and economic relations had led to a significant expansion of diplomacy after 1400, within which major powers as well as smaller entities like the Italian city-states found new ways to assert their agendas.[27] The Ottomans were increasingly involved in this "Renaissance diplomacy" from the second half of the fifteenth century onward.

One distinguishing feature of Ottoman-European relations under Süleyman and İbrahim was the intensification of diplomatic ties. Concomitantly, the scope of diplomacy expanded from mostly political, military, and commercial affairs into ideological debates. Süleyman and İbrahim were particularly enthusiastic in engaging with European audiences, and their enthusiasm was reciprocated. Humanist scholars, merchants, pilgrims, information-gatherers, and middlemen of all sorts dwelled within the Ottoman realm with greater frequency. Venetians played a crucial role as intermediaries and brokers of information, while envoys from the Habsburgs, the Hungarians, the French, Poland, Muscovy, Ragusa, and others arrived in Constantinople, which became one of the centers of regional and global diplomacy.[28]

Always keen to impress their audiences, and mindful of hierarchy and order, Süleyman and İbrahim introduced new diplomatic protocols. The Venetians, the closest observers of Ottoman politics, were the first ones to note the changes. Marco Minio, who was on a diplomatic mission to Constantinople in 1521–22, and who returned as Venetian ambassador in 1526–27, saw that the ceremonial elements of diplomatic reception had become more elaborate compared to his earlier visit, and the palace facilities better appointed.[29] The viziers accompanied the diplomat into the sultan's audience, where he kissed Süleyman's hand and respectfully withdrew, without being allowed to address Süleyman. Süleyman did not utter a word either.[30]

As the Ottomans were increasingly drawn into the struggle over Hungary, İbrahim emerged as the face of Ottoman diplomacy on the European front. In the winter and spring of 1528, he met with Szapolyai's envoy Hieronymus Łaski and Ferdinand's envoys Janos Hoberdanecs and Sigismund Weixelberger. He questioned Łaski about Szapolyai's delay in getting in touch with the Ottomans, although everyone involved knew that the Ottomans were an ally of last resort for him. İbrahim then comforted Łaski by announcing that the Ottomans would recognize Szapolyai as king and promised support against Ferdinand. Hoberdanecs and Weixelberger, who reached Constantinople around the time Łaski's negotiations were concluded, had a more frustrating experience. They tenaciously presented Ferdinand as the rightful king of Hungary, but their detailed arguments about Ferdinand's legitimacy were met with outright refusal. Indeed, they were treated quite haughtily. In one instance, when they relayed Ferdinand's demand to have the Hungarian fortresses recently acquired by the Ottomans returned, the grand vizier answered them sarcastically. "Why not ask for Constantinople?," he retorted.

İbrahim used the negotiations to convey to the Habsburgs, in a quite persistent manner, the argument that the Ottomans were the major imperial power on the European front. Several rulers, such as the kings of Poland and France, but also the papacy, Venice, and Szapolyai himself, had entered into agreements with Süleyman and sought his help. Why would Ferdinand refuse to do so? Thus, already in 1528, the Ottomans claimed to act as the guarantors of peace within Europe against Habsburg encroachments. Religious and cultural differences did not prevent them from seeing themselves as an integral part of a system of alliances and rivalries across Europe and the Mediterranean.[31] However, warfare was never too far away from their thoughts. Moreover, the specter of Ferdinand's brother Charles continued to hover in the background. İbrahim openly told the envoys that they expected Charles to attack the Ottomans once he had defeated his current foes, meaning the League of Cognac and the Protestants.

Süleyman and İbrahim utilized the negotiations as a stage upon which they performed their new public identities and gave voice to their agendas. İbrahim emerged as the witty, well-informed, cunning yet friendly statesman, while Süleyman acted as the distant and punishing monarch, unreachable except while having his hand or the hem of his robe kissed in submission. On the rare occasions when he gave an audience, he fixed a steady gaze upon the Habsburg envoys and communicated his wishes by whispering into İbrahim's ear. When the envoys, through translators, relayed an idea he did not find agreeable, his anger and frustration became visible to all in attendance.

As the sultan and the grand vizier reached an impasse, they started preparations for another campaign.The defeat of the recent rebellions in Anatolia, the turmoil in the Safavid realm following Ismail's death in 1524, and a renewed agreement with Poland allowed them to focus on the European front without any concerns about an attack from the east or the north. Before leaving for a campaign against Ferdinand, there was one more task to be accomplished: the further promotion of İbrahim by assigning him new powers and a new title.

These were articulated in a diploma (*berat*), which was publicly recited to the high officials and the household troops in March 1529. Four years ago, the preamble to the Egyptian law code had accorded İbrahim an unprecedented place in the Ottoman hierarchy. However, its sections about the partnership between the sultan and the grand vizier constituted an abstract statement that was contained within a legal text, and it was not necessarily meant for widespread circulation. In contrast, the diploma was made public immediately. Also, it focused solely on İbrahim's privileges.

İbrahim was given a new title next to that of grand vizier: *serasker* (head of the soldiery, i.e., commander-in-chief). All servants and subjects of Süleyman were ordered to obey him as if he were the sultan. He could appoint governors-general and provincial governors, and give out *tımar* assignments. He could punish any officials who mistreated Ottoman subjects, as well as anyone who strayed from the law, both religious and dynastic. Like his appointment to the grand vizierate, his title of commander-in-chief and his new prerogatives were unprecedented in Ottoman history. With this diploma, İbrahim truly emerged as Süleyman's all-powerful representative, indeed his surrogate.

What were the reasons behind this development? Ottoman sources close to the sultan cite the expanding affairs of the empire. It is true that the growing ideological rivalry with the Habsburgs, coupled with attempts at increasing political and fiscal control throughout the 1520s, required a new level of administrative institutionalization. However, these do not suffice to explain the extraordinary promotion of İbrahim. Also, was it Süleyman who gave his grand vizier these new powers, or did İbrahim ask for them? Were the Ottomans inspired by the relationship between Charles and Ferdinand, and Ferdinand's formal titles, including lieutenant of the emperor, which the Ottomans translated as *ser-leşker*, also meaning commander-in-chief? There was a major difference between Ferdinand and the grand vizier, however: İbrahim remained a slave of Süleyman from a legal perspective, and he owed his political authority and economic wealth to the sultan, not to any inheritance or natural right.

Contemporary observers of the 1529 campaign place the companionship and perfect harmony between sultan and grand vizier at the center of their narratives. In contrast, they portray Ferdinand as a usurper of the Hungarian crown and of the title of Master of the Auspicious Conjunction, which he supposedly began to use after declaring himself king. While Ferdinand did not use this specific title, the Ottoman interpretation shows the seriousness of the ideological rivalry between the sides, since Master of the Auspicious Conjunction was a political title with universalist connotations. Another reason behind the campaign is presented as support for John Szapolyai, who is described as an Ottoman ally and a rightful king of Hungary. Of course, the perennial Ottoman concern about a concerted attack against the Ottoman realm from the direction of Hungary, which had become even more likely after Ferdinand's capture of Buda, was an additional motivation.[32]

The 1529 military campaign was launched on May 10. Once again, it started as a struggle against the elements, as severe rains delayed the march of the army. After multiple incidents involving muddy roads, destroyed bridges, and the flooding of the army camp near Philippopolis, Süleyman reached the plain of Mohács, the location of his great victory of 1526, in mid-August. At that highly symbolic location, he met with John Szapolyai and his forces. The true Master of the Auspicious Conjunction graciously received his newest ally in his tent as he got up from his throne and took three steps toward his guest. Szapolyai was allowed to sit on a low chair, and he and Süleyman conversed. While details of the conversation are impossible to ascertain, Ottoman sources convey the sense that the two monarchs discussed recent developments, Szapolyai's claims to the Hungarian throne, and his political future. İbrahim was with them, sitting like the sultan and the king, while the other viziers were standing.

As can be expected, the meeting had a ceremonial dimension that extended far beyond the intimate conversation between the sultan and the king. The entire army stood at attention as Szapolyai initially made his way to Süleyman's tent: janissaries, troops under the command of the governors-general of Anadolu and Rumeli, raiders, and the household troops, constituting a force of around one hundred and fifty thousand. Szapolyai was invited to kiss Süleyman's hand and received ceremonial robes and various gifts from him. Then the joint forces marched on to Buda, which had been occupied by Ferdinand's men. The defenders surrendered after a few days but were slaughtered during their departure from the city.

In Buda, Szapolyai was placed on the throne a second time, in a ceremony attended by Hungarian nobles as well as janissaries. Süleyman did not participate, probably finding it unworthy of his grandeur; instead, he preferred to spend his time hunting in the city's vicinity. Alvise Gritti, a confidant of İbrahim and a long-term resident of Constantinople with ties to the Venetian aristocracy, was left in Szapolyai's company to act as a go-between. Gritti's task was to represent Ottoman political and economic interests in Hungary, serve Szapolyai as an advisor, thanks to his political and diplomatic connections, and establish a system of supply for the Ottoman troops.[33] That Gritti was imposed on Szapolyai shows the weight of İbrahim's associates in Ottoman affairs, and also reveals the suspicions of the sultan and the high officials about Szapolyai's intentions and capabilities.

It was already the middle of September when Szapolyai was put on the Hungarian throne, and the campaign season was nearing its end. Still, the Ottomans decided to march against Vienna. The city did not represent a strategic priority, but it was important in terms of the ideological conflict between the Ottomans and the Habsburgs. It was Ferdinand's capital, and Ottoman sources claim they expected to meet him on the battlefield, even though it was soon discovered that he was not in the city. Proceeding through difficult terrain, the bulk of the Ottoman forces arrived in front of Vienna on September 27. The conduct of the operations was left to the new commander-in-chief, İbrahim, and the doomed siege began.

There are significant discrepancies between European and Ottoman sources about it: the former hail it as a major achievement by a small garrison defending a city whose fortifications were in disrepair, while the Ottomans portray a strong city zealously defended by a determined garrison.[34] It indeed appears that the city was defended by a combined infantry and cavalry contingent of twenty-five thousand, not counting the local militia, and that it was well stocked with supplies. Ottoman sources draw particular attention to the fact that Süleyman's large-caliber cannons, which would have obliterated the city walls, had been left behind during the difficult trip from Buda to Vienna. Perhaps more importantly, the onset of cold weather turned into a major advantage for the city's defenders.

Following an unsuccessful general assault in mid-October, the decision to lift the siege was made. Ottoman sources refer to the compassion of the sultan for his soldiers as a motivation behind the lifting of the siege. The distribution of cash bonuses to the janissaries indicates that Süleyman was genuinely concerned about a negative reaction on the part of his most skilled soldiers. While Vienna was thus saved, to the relief of many across Europe, the true casualties of the siege were the civilian population living in areas near the city and along the route of the Ottoman army, who bore the brunt of attacks by Ottoman raiders.

Just as the campaign had started as a struggle against nature, it ended in the same way. This time, over an arduous two-month march from Vienna back to Constantinople, Süleyman and his forces had to endure the cold and the wet. Resources diminished every day. Muddy roads and swamps sucked in men, carts, and beasts of burden. Still, one more task had to be fulfilled. The main component of Hungarian royal regalia, the crown of St. Stephen, had not been available during Szapolyai's enthronement in August under Ottoman protection. An Ottoman official had been designated especially to locate the crown and its guardian, a Hungarian nobleman named Péter Perényi, and he had brought Perényi and the crown to the Ottoman camp in early September. On the way back from Vienna, in late October, the crown was sent to Szapolyai with Alvise Gritti, who was accompanied by two high-ranking Hungarian officials: Perényi himself, as the guardian of the crown, and the archbishop of Ezstergom and primate of Hungary, Pál Várday.

Perényi was a figure who balanced his allegiances among the Habsburgs, the Ottomans, and Szapolyai, while Várday was known for his pro-Ferdinand stance. Regardless, they were brought together by the Ottomans' attention to the details of Hungarian royal traditions. After he received the crown, the final piece in Szapolyai's restitution to power was thus completed.[35] Wearing a crown was not part of Ottoman dynastic practice, but a crown, as a symbol of European/Christian monarchy, seems to have fascinated them. For instance, contemporary Ottoman observers rarely fail to mention the "*korona*" as an object through which Charles supposedly claimed universal rule, conflating the physical object with Charles' title of Holy Roman Emperor. It can be surmised that they were similarly entranced by the Hungarian crown.

Another critical task was to take stock of what had happened and to inform friend and foe before returning to Constantinople. A letter sent to Venice from Belgrade, dated November 13, 1529, outlined in Süleyman's voice the recent struggles over the Hungarian crown, from Louis II's defeat to the recent re-coronation of Szapolyai and the stages of the 1529 campaign. The letter may be seen as part of Ottoman attempts to explain and propagate their own position over Hungary to a larger audience across Europe, since they knew that the letter's contents would eventually circulate from Venice to the other capitals.

In the letter, Süleyman emerges as the only figure with the right to dispose of the crown of Hungary, by dint of his victory over Louis, the last legitimate king. Szapolyai had sent an envoy to Constantinople, the letter states, and Süleyman "confirmed" him as the king of Hungary. Ferdinand, whom the letter calls king of Bohemia, archduke of the "German realm" (*Alemagna*), and brother of the "king of Spain," rose against Szapolyai, took his capital and his crown, and occupied the realm of Hungary. The first-person narrator then describes the important stages of the Ottoman campaign. He places particular emphasis on the army's march, Buda's recovery from Ferdinand's forces, Szapolyai's enthronement, the castles and towns captured by the Ottomans, the punishment inflicted upon Ferdinand's subjects, and the latter's failure to face Süleyman. The unsuccessful siege of Vienna is briefly mentioned, after which Süleyman proceeds back to Buda, where he has his hand kissed by Szapolyai and the crown of St. Stephen is given to the latter.

The letter was sent to Venice with Yunus, Süleyman's chief translator and a prominent figure in diplomatic exchanges at the time.[36] After dispatching this critical missive, Süleyman resumed his march. He must have been relieved when he finally reached Constantinople in mid-December, both for having accomplished his initial objective of placing Szapolyai on the throne, and for finally leaving behind the taxing climate and growing logistical problems of the campaign's final months.

The buoyant tone of the letter to Venice and the praises of Ottoman historians aside, the 1529 campaign produced a mixture of results that were not all intended by the Ottomans. They were able to hold on to important Hungarian fortresses they had recently acquired, like Belgrade, Szabács, and Pétervárad. However, Ottoman sources fail to mention that Szapolyai had to rule over a truncated Hungary. While he had been enthroned and crowned, the main objective of the campaign, Ferdinand's ultimate defeat, was not reached. Parts of the realm of Hungary remained under Ferdinand's control, and many towns and fortresses that had surrendered to the Ottomans during their march to Vienna reverted to him after Süleyman's departure from the region.

## A Clash between Emperors

The Ottomans and the Habsburgs had been on a collision course in central Europe and the Mediterranean since Charles V's election as Holy Roman Emperor and Süleyman's enthronement as Ottoman sultan. The question of Hungary finally brought them face to face and activated a rivalry that extended from the battlefield to the written page, and into the minds and hearts of their subjects, allies, and enemies.

Süleyman, İbrahim, and their supporters had built a new imperial agenda on a wide basis of influences that extended from Roman/Byzantine and Islamic notions of ecumenical leadership to the legacies of Genghis Khan and Timur. Similarly, Charles and his close associates had appropriated and expanded European late medieval ideas of universal empire. The Ottoman-Habsburg rivalry became the battleground for these rival imperialisms. Moreover, the apocalyptic and messianic visions of the period, adopted and deployed by both sides, gave their struggles a transcendental dimension and a sense of overwhelming urgency. Although the urgency abated around the middle of sixteenth century, the period from the mid-1520s to the late 1540s witnessed one of the most intense imperial rivalries in Eurasian history.[37]

Thanks to the Ottoman threat, the Habsburg dynasty was able to present itself as the defender of Christian civilization while maintaining its dreams of re-conquering Constantinople, subduing Protestantism, and ushering in a new age of universal Christianity.[38] One tangible outcome of that position at the end of the 1520s was the rapprochement between Charles and Pope Clement VII. The two had been rivals until recently, and the pope had been imprisoned after the sack of Rome by Habsburg troops in May 1527. At the end of June 1529, Charles and Clement signed the Treaty of Barcelona, whose aim was both to establish peace in Italy and to fight against the Ottomans. Francis I, whose hope for papal support thus vanished, signed the Treaty of Cambrai with Charles in August 1529, relinquishing his claims to Milan, Naples, Flanders, and Artois.

The Ottoman envoy Yunus, who reached Venice with Süleyman's letter in mid-December 1529, was not able to dissuade the Venetians from entering into an agreement with the pro-Habsburg camp, even though he received Venetian assurances that the republic would not take up arms against the Ottomans. Charles' prestige reached an ever-greater height when he was crowned Holy Roman Emperor by Clement VII in Bologna in February 1530, an occasion for elaborate ceremonies. Holy Roman Emperors did not have to be crowned by the pope after 1508, and Charles was indeed the last one to receive a papal coronation. The chief function of the event in February 1530 was not ecclesiastical or constitutional, but purely political.[39]

This was a time when Charles' prestige was at its apogee. Even some of the most strident critics of the Habsburgs felt compelled to revise their earlier positions. For instance, Martin Luther had initially portrayed the Ottomans as the scourge of God sent to induce Christians into improving themselves. He had refrained from supporting anti-Ottoman military efforts, which he saw as instruments for increasing the power of the papacy and the Holy Roman Empire at the expense of the Protestants. He did not necessarily abandon his profound suspicions vis-à-vis the papacy and the empire in the late 1520s, as he continued to criticize them for their exploitation of German wealth and their lack of action against the Ottomans. Nevertheless, in his *Vom Kriege wider die Türken* ("On the War against the Turks"), published in 1529, he came around to the idea of actively opposing the Ottoman advance. This should not be a crusade, but it could take the form of defensive warfare.[40]

Similarly, in the German-speaking areas of the Holy Roman Empire, which had a strong Protestant population, the siege of Vienna gave rise to a few thousand pamphlets and broadsheets that decried the atrocities of the "Turk." These

FIG. 5.2 A medal with Charles V (front), Süleyman (right), and an angel. The inscription, addressing Charles, states: "It behooves you, fortunate Caesar, to advance further (*plus ultra*). The present head [an allusion to Süleyman] will fall by the imperial sword." Possibly Netherlandish, ca. 1530s. Courtesy of the Metropolitan Museum of Art.

included a strong visual element, from images of Ottoman soldiers carrying away captives or massacring children to depictions of the siege.[41] The shifting mentalities within Europe may also be observed in Desiderius Erasmus' *De bello Turcico* ("On the War against the Turks"), written after the siege of Vienna and finished in 1530. Unaware of Luther's change of mind, Erasmus, one of the most prominent humanist authors of the time, offered a strong criticism of Luther's earlier position about the Ottomans. While, like Luther, Erasmus refrained from advocating a crusade, he nevertheless argued for peace among Christians and a just war against the Ottomans.[42] At this critical juncture, in 1530, the Habsburgs were the obvious leaders for any such endeavor.

The first Ottoman response to Charles' growing stature was a three-week celebration held in Constantinople in June-July 1530.[43] The event was organized on the occasion of the circumcision of Süleyman's sons Mustafa, Mehmed, and Selim, and it promoted Süleyman as the father of three healthy princes aged fourteen, nine, and six. The festivities extended from exhibitions of objects taken from the enemy to mock battles, and from shows by jugglers and strongmen to reenactments of recent battles. Süleyman occupied a pivotal role, watching everything from a loggia built in the Hippodrome, and being watched in return by a large audience. İbrahim was never far from the center of the action, supervising the proceedings and presenting lavish gifts to the sultan and the princes.

Süleyman's generosity was prominent throughout. Clad in beautiful garments, he threw gold and silver coins to the performers. Banquets were organized for the sultan's servants and officials, while the palace and the soup kitchens churned out large quantities of food for the entire city. Palace bands played during the day, and fireworks illuminated the sky at night. Although İbrahim's wedding in 1524 had been an elaborate affair, it had mostly involved the members of the *askerî* elite in the capital, while the celebrations in 1530 pulled in the entire city of Constantinople. Envoys from Venice and Hungary, invited for the occasion, also watched the festivities. The Venetians reported back about them, and news of the celebrations circulated in Europe as yet another sign of the sultan's good fortune.

During this time, the Ottomans and the Habsburgs continued to communicate through diplomatic channels. However, negotiations conducted by Ferdinand's envoys Nikola Jurišić and Joseph von Lamberg in Constantinople during the final months of 1530 failed to produce an agreement, due to both sides' insistence on their respective positions. Ferdinand claimed to be the legitimate king of Hungary, while the Ottomans argued that, since they had taken Hungary through the force of their sword, it was their prerogative to give it away to a king who was, in this instance, John Szapolyai. Discussions between the envoys and İbrahim were not limited to the fate of Hungary. Indeed, these may be seen as long conversations on the state of Europe, the Ottoman view of European politics and diplomacy, and the ever-growing rivalry between Charles and Süleyman.

It is clear that the retreat from Vienna continued to rankle the Ottomans, since İbrahim insisted to the envoys that it had not been the Ottomans' intention to take Vienna. That is why large-caliber cannons had been left behind. The main objective had been to fight Ferdinand, but he had fled. The grand vizier's mistrust of Ferdinand extended into his peace proposals, which, he claimed, were apparently meant to distract the Ottoman side as Charles made preparations for an attack. İbrahim then mocked Charles' recent voyage to Italy and his coronation. A true Caesar, he said, would establish an empire with his sword, like Süleyman; that is the reason why the Ottomans did not recognize Charles as emperor. İbrahim further criticized Charles' imprisonment of Francis after the Battle of Pavia, and his imprisonment of Clement VII after the sack of Rome. He also intimated that the recent peace agreements among the Habsburgs, the French, the papacy, and the Venetians lacked a strong foundation.[44]

The discussions were filled with sarcasm and veiled threats on both sides, even though Ferdinand's envoys had to be more subtle. In a political culture in which a military victory or a peaceful agreement had repercussions on the reputation of a monarch, both the envoys and İbrahim were careful to protect the honor and integrity of their respective rulers. The personalization of continent-wide geopolitical struggles rendered a precarious situation even more so, and subsequent developments exacerbated it further. In late 1530–early 1531, Ferdinand's forces laid siege to Buda, but the city was relieved thanks to the arrival of Ottoman forces stationed in the region. Ferdinand's election as King of the Romans in January 1531, which made him heir apparent to the title of Holy Roman Emperor after Charles, must have further irritated the Ottoman side. They may also have heard of negotiations between Ferdinand and the Safavids, which, if successful, would create the specter of a joint attack from east and west.

The Ottoman answer was a large-scale military campaign to start in the spring of 1532. It is called the *Alaman* ("German") campaign in Ottoman sources. The "German realm" referred in the Ottomans' mind to Ferdinand and Charles' possessions in German-speaking territories; it also signified the land that formed the territorial basis for Charles' claims to be Caesar. Thus, just as the political objective of the 1529 campaign was to weaken and undermine Ferdinand, the 1532 campaign was directed against Charles and his growing prestige.[45]

Süleyman and İbrahim left Constantinople in late April 1532 with lavish ceremonies that had become customary for the sultan's departure. The army followed the usual route of Edirne, Philippopolis, and Sofia, and reached Nish on June 10, where Ferdinand's envoys Leonhard von Nogarola and Joseph von Lamberg awaited. They had been sent to negotiate a truce. The Ottomans, who clearly wanted to impress the envoys, made them watch the military units' procession. According to an Ottoman source, these included three hundred artillery carts and twelve thousand musket-carrying janissaries. The sultan's household troops, the soldiers under the governors-general of Rumeli and Anadolu, the raiders, and the cavalry sent by the Khan of Crimea amounted to around one hundred and eighty thousand.

The envoys' reception by İbrahim, and later by the sultan, expanded the ceremonial dimensions of the negotiations as they took place in the middle of the army camp, in tents and pavilions set up for the occasion. A jewel-studded tent, filled with a paraphernalia of swords, maces, bows, and arrows, stood to one side, underlining the majesty and strength of the sultan. Martial bands played and janissary units fired their muskets into the air in unison. The ceremonies continued as Antonio Rincón, Francis' representative, joined the Ottomans in early July, near Belgrade. Habsburg and French envoys were received on the same day, to the unease of the Habsburgs, who saw this as a breach of diplomatic protocol. The Ottomans were not bothered, however, since they were thus able to display their affinity with the French, even though Francis had recently signed a treaty with Charles.

The objectives of the French envoy are difficult to reconstruct. The French wanted to have outside observers believe that their intention was to intercede between the sultan and Ferdinand for the sake of all European Christians. Others across Europe believed that the French wanted to divert the Ottomans from Hungary and Austria toward Italy, which would then give Francis an excuse to return to the Italian peninsula under the pretext of fighting against the Ottomans.[46] The negotiations between the Habsburg envoys and the Ottomans, on the other hand, are better documented.

While the Habsburg envoys were there to stop the Ottoman advance and secure a truce, their conversations with İbrahim extended into the respective political and diplomatic stances of the two sides. In addition to the now standard discussions about the legitimate rights of Ferdinand and Szapolyai over the Hungarian throne, the Ottoman side was harshly critical of Charles. İbrahim continued to accuse Charles of having treated Francis and Clement VII unjustly, and for oppressing the Christians of Europe by collecting money from them under the excuse of fighting against the Ottomans. He often emphasized that the main objective of the Ottomans this time was to ignore

Ferdinand, whom the grand vizier described as a figure of no importance, and face Charles himself on the battlefield. This argument was repeated in a letter to Ferdinand sent on July 12.[47]

The Ottoman army continued its march in the meantime, but it was bogged down by heavy rains, muddy roads, and swollen rivers for much of June and July. In August, food stocks began to diminish to a critical level, but the Ottomans pressed on. The main force marched through Habsburg territories in today's western Hungary and southeastern Austria, reaching the vicinity of Graz around mid-September, while raiders fanned out farther throughout central Europe. For nearly two months, the entire area was devastated in what ended up being a punitive expedition against Ferdinand and Charles. Ceremonial elements were never absent, however: many towns and fortresses, whose names are recorded obsessively by the Ottoman sources, submitted their keys to the sultan and escaped his wrath, apparently. The Ottomans' aim was not to capture territory, as Ottoman sources insist, but to display their military might.

Charles, in the meantime, had approached Vienna with a large force that nearly equaled the size of the Ottoman army: around a hundred cannons, an infantry of one hundred and twenty thousand, and twenty thousand cavalrymen, according to one estimate. The much feared, much expected, and much prophesied encounter between the two emperors did not happen, however. As Charles entered Vienna on September 23, the Ottomans had begun to turn back. Süleyman arrived in Belgrade in mid-October; there, in tune with the ceremonial character of the campaign, he distributed gifts to the governors-general and other high-ranking officials and sent messengers to convey the news of a successful venture throughout the Ottoman realm. Upon his arrival in Constantinople in late November, a five-day celebration was ordered.

The 1532 campaign is mostly forgotten today. From the perspective of an outcome-oriented approach to warfare, which privileges territorial gain, it is difficult to explain such a military venture as anything but a failure, an even bigger one than the siege of Vienna in 1529. For contemporary observers, however, the campaign was seen in quite different terms. Many in 1532 felt they were witnessing an event that would culminate in the inescapable encounter between two contenders to universal rule. The prospect of that encounter both fueled fears about the end of the world and fostered expectations about the arrival of a new messianic age. İbrahim had, after all, been confident enough to tell his Venetian interlocutors in 1526 about the coming battles between Süleyman and a supreme Christian ruler. In 1528, he reported that a saintly woman had foretold an Ottoman victory if Süleyman marched through Hungary.[48]

Similar prophecies circulated among the Habsburgs themselves. Charles' influential chancellor Mercurino Gattinara, who played a crucial role in creating a cultural and administrative agenda for the emperor, was as skilled as İbrahim in couching his visions in eschatological terms. Already in 1527, he had informed the Venetian ambassador to Spain about Charles' eventual victory over the Ottomans. Accordingly, after taking Hungary, the Ottomans would march to the middle of *Alemagna*, and they would be defeated there and pushed back by a member of the German nation. Gattinara identified that future leader as the emperor Charles.[49] Erasmus himself, who anxiously observed the developments, expected a decisive clash between Charles and Süleyman. Writing to a friend in 1531, he likened them to two suns: the world could not support them both.[50]

In addition to its apocalyptic overtones, the 1532 campaign may be interpreted as a long and elaborate ceremonial procession from Constantinople to Austria, a show of force in front of European audiences.[51] Notably, Ottoman

**FIG. 5.3** A depiction of Süleyman wearing the tiara displayed during the 1532 campaign by Agostino Veneziano, ca. 1535. Courtesy of the Metropolitan Museum of Art.

claims to universal rule, and their denunciation of Charles' titles, were given voice through an impressive piece of headgear. The object was made by Venetian goldsmiths, but the design quite likely originated with İbrahim and his close associate Alvise Gritti. The headgear mimicked the emperor's crown and the pope's tiara but surpassed them both by the addition of a fourth tier to a traditionally three-tiered object. Süleyman probably never wore this Ottoman version of the *korona*. However, the object was displayed ceremonially throughout the campaign, and depictions of Süleyman wearing the four-tiered tiara soon circulated throughout Europe.

The high stakes of the ideological competition between the Ottomans and the Habsburgs, and the extent of Venetian involvement, are also seen in a manuscript composed in Venice around 1532. The work starts by giving the Ottomans and the French a common genealogy as the offspring of the Greek god Apollo and Cassandra, daughter of Priam, king of Troy. It then proceeds with a concise account of Ottoman history, including the recent battles fought by Süleyman. It hails the Ottoman ruler as the true emperor of the age thanks to his achievements on the battlefield, his many virtues, as well as divine support. In between the lines, the text emphasizes Süleyman's clemency toward the defeated, possibly to counteract European criticisms of Ottoman cruelty. In its final paragraph, the voice of the anonymous author sends a final salute to Süleyman: "Live and conquer more happily than Augustus, better than Trajan, more fortunate than Alexander the Great!"[52]

The Ottomans may not have secured any territorial gains in 1532, but their military advances nonetheless continued to have an impact on European politics. The Diet of Regensburg was convened in the first months of 1532, against a background of growing news about an impending Ottoman campaign. The Diet brought Charles together with his imperial constituency, which included prominent Catholic and Lutheran leaders as well as delegations from fifty-five towns. The matters to be discussed included religious and political conflicts between Catholics and Lutherans, the prospect of a joint struggle against the Ottomans, and the problem of France.

At Regensburg, Charles not only distanced himself from his brother Ferdinand's policy of reconquering Hungary, an unpopular prospect among the constituents, but also promised to negotiate a religious truce with the Lutherans. The idea of a defensive warfare against the "Turk," expounded by Luther a few years earlier, offered a common ground to both parties, and resulted in Charles obtaining aid from both Catholics and Lutherans.[53] The culmination of this rapprochement was the Religious Peace of Nuremberg signed in July 1532, when Süleyman and İbrahim were in central Europe.

Charles suspended the Edict of Worms of 1521, which had banned Luther's writings and declared him a heretic. The suspension would last until a general council to be convened by the pope; in the meantime, the Lutherans would supply and finance forty thousand infantrymen and eight thousand horsemen.

The diplomatic gains they made in Europe did not stop Ferdinand and Charles from continuing to negotiate with the Ottomans. Hieronymus of Zara was sent to Constantinople in January 1533 on behalf of Ferdinand. Cornelius de Schepper joined him there in May, carrying a letter from Charles even though he claimed he too was sent by Ferdinand. Communicating with Charles had been a political and cultural objective for İbrahim and Süleyman, who saw the emperor as the sole European ruler on a similar footing with the Ottoman sultan. The first official contact between Charles and Süleyman was thus established. This was a major development that concerned other parties. In the middle of the negotiations, Alvise Gritti arrived from Hungary, always mindful of his own position vis-à-vis all sides involved. Soon after, Szapolyai sent his own envoy Hieronymus Łaski to Constantinople. The Venetians also kept an anxious eye on the negotiations, to ensure that any subsequent settlement would not be to their detriment.

The first frictions emerged as Charles' letter was read. The titles used by Charles' chancery, such as King of Jerusalem, Duke of Athens, and Lord of Tripoli, not to mention his imperial title, bothered the Ottomans. While İbrahim informally admitted that Charles was a mighty ruler, he reminded the envoys that Jerusalem, Athens, and Tripoli were all under Ottoman rule. Did Charles want to take them by force? The envoys apologized, emphasizing that these were simply chancery formula, nothing more. On another occasion, İbrahim displayed his knowledge of recent developments while poking fun at Charles' inability to prevail over the Protestants. Informed on the negotiations at Nuremberg the previous summer, including a council that had yet to be convened, the grand vizier offered his help in bringing Luther and the pope together around the same table.[54]

The Ottoman position was articulated further in letters sent from the sultan and the grand vizier to Ferdinand and Charles. After a succession of Süleyman's titles and an enumeration of the lands under his rule, Charles was called merely "king of Spain and of all dependencies of Spain." Both letters also emphasized Süleyman's conquest-based rights over Hungary and the legitimacy of his decision to grant its crown to Szapolyai.[55] The intransigent tone of these letters overshadows the nuances of the overall negotiations. For instance, Ottoman sources do not mention the dispatch of an Ottoman envoy to Ferdinand in the early months of 1533. Accompanied by Hieronymus of Zara's son, the Ottoman envoy was met with great pomp by Ferdinand in Vienna.

Even though neither Habsburg envoy represented Charles formally, concerns of importance to him, such as the activities of Muslim corsairs in the western Mediterranean, were discussed. Charles' suggestion of signing a peace agreement that would involve all Christian princes was another reflection of Ottoman-Habsburg tensions across a wider landscape. The Ottomans refused, arguing that they were already at peace with France, Venice, and Poland. Finally, the differences between Charles and Ferdinand became further pronounced during the negotiations, since Charles viewed Hungary as a minor concern and was closer to a truce, while Ferdinand was more eager to fight for what he saw as his legitimate right.

The Habsburg envoys and İbrahim had the opportunity to discuss other matters as well. At one point, İbrahim, showing that the Ottomans were aware of their representation in Europe, felt the need to explain himself. He asserted that war inescapably led to the suffering of civilians. He then argued that he always strove to prevent unnecessary bloodshed. In fact, during campaigns, he had freed thousands of captured Christian women and children, allowing them to escape in the dark of the night and hide in forests. He told the envoys that, contrary to what the Christians thought of the Ottomans, they were not "inhumane barbarians or cruel people (*barbaros inhumanos aut crudeles*)."[56] On another occasion, as a gesture of reverence toward Charles, he solemnly received the emperor's letter, which he then took his lips, and then to his forehead. He offered the diplomats a tour of the Bosphorus on a small galley he could provide. Another day, he told Hieronymus he could arrange for him to attend Easter services at a Catholic church in Galata.

Indeed, the outcome of the negotiations was not on a par with the intransigent tone of the correspondence between the two sides. After months of deliberations, the first formally recognized peace agreement between Ferdinand and the Ottomans finally emerged. In it, Ferdinand received fatherly compassion from Süleyman and brotherly amity from İbrahim, an Ottoman official of slave origins. Still, he kept the parts of Hungary that were already controlled by him in return for an annual payment to the Ottomans, just as Szapolyai preserved his lands in an awkward settlement that would continue to produce much violence in the coming years. In the summer of 1533, however, a three-year truce was the foremost achievement for all involved.

The aftermath of the 1532 campaign, including the negotiations themselves, was a time of unease for the Ottoman side, as the Habsburg envoys noticed on several occasions. One reason was the capture of Koroni, a strategic Ottoman fortress on the southwestern tip of the Peloponnesus, by a naval expedition while the Ottoman army was in central Europe. The expedition was led by Andrea Doria, a Genoese admiral who had recently entered Charles' service. This foray into the eastern Mediterranean was a major strategical achievement and a psychological blow that starkly reminded the Ottomans of their relative weakness on the naval front.

Charles' presence in Italy during the last months of 1532 and the first months of 1533, and his meeting with Clement VII in Bologna in December 1532, must have been reported to the Ottomans by the Venetians, ever fearful of the loss of their freedom to Charles. For the Ottomans, the emperor's extended presence in Italy meant the possibility of an expedition by both land and sea, Koroni constituting perhaps the first step of such a campaign. The Habsburgs' offer to return Koroni in exchange for granting Hungary to Ferdinand was perceived as both insincere and inappropriate by the Ottoman side.

Süleyman, by several accounts, was angry and frustrated. Hieronymus of Zara heard from some of his informants in Constantinople that the sultan intended to have the Church of the Holy Sepulcher in Jerusalem destroyed and all priests, indeed all Christians, expelled from Ottoman lands. These rumors must have stemmed from a mixture of propaganda and apocalyptic anxiety since similar events were foretold as part of the tribulations that would precede the end times. Other unsettling rumors were reported by Cornelius de Schepper in a diary of his journey to Constantinople.[57]

For instance, a servant of the second vizier Ayas, who gave his Christian name as Hieronymus of Bratislava, told the envoys that Süleyman could not vanquish Charles or the Safavid shah on the battlefield. That much had been ascertained through the science of letters, a form of prognostication based on numerical values assigned to Arabic letters. Therefore, Süleyman felt obliged to send one of his viziers against the Safavids, instead of commanding the army himself.[58] Another story Cornelius heard was about a block of marble on whose face was carved a lion holding a bull by the horns. The lion faced west before the Ottomans captured Constantinople, but the block turned by itself to face the east ("Asia", says Schepper) during the Ottoman conquest. The block changed direction by itself at the time of the Battle of Mohács. In 1533, it turned once again, this time to announce an Ottoman defeat.

These were not the only stories Schepper had heard about ominous signs. For instance, Alvise Gritti told him about the apparition of two warriors over Constantinople, one speaking Latin, the other Turkish. They both declared that Fortune, which had been on the side of the Ottomans, would favor

Christians from then on. These rumors were rounded out by yet another story about how the Ottoman Empire would be destroyed by a bastard, son of a great lord. Alvise Gritti, illegitimate son of a doge of Venice, clearly fit the description in Schepper's mind, and perhaps in Gritti's. The onset of an epidemic, which killed around fifteen hundred people a day by the end of June, must have rendered the atmosphere in Constantinople even more sinister.[59]

Schepper may not have been an impartial observer, but the anecdotes he relayed align with similar concerns encountered in Ottoman works, such as Mevlana İsa's *Câmiü'l-meknunat* ("A Compendium of Hidden Things"), one of whose versions were composed around 1533.[60] According to the author, the world was beset with violence and destruction, and the end was near. Süleyman and his officials were destined to play prominent roles in the last decades of human life on Earth. This is the environment in which the final venture of the Süleyman-İbrahim partnership, a campaign against the Safavids, was conceived and organized.

## Managing and Recording the Realm

Apocalyptic anxieties, inconclusive military campaigns, and diplomatic negotiations were not the only things Süleyman and İbrahim had to manage. A long passage in a historical work by Celalzade Mustafa, their close collaborator, exposes the variety of the issues they faced during the first years of their partnership.[61]

One was the outbreak of violence in parts of south-central Anatolia in 1526–27. The primary cause was the palace's efforts at surveying properties and resources in the district of Bozok, recently established on the lands of the Dulkadır principality. Expecting higher taxes and more intrusion by the Ottoman center, the remnants of the tribal aristocracy rose up. One of their first acts was to kill the Ottoman officials who were conducting the land survey. That spark ignited similar outbursts of protest in different parts of the region. Typically, the rebels resorted to the anti-Ottoman, non-Sunni, salvationist message of the Safavids. The absence of many *tımar*-holders from the area, who were away on campaign in Hungary, contributed to the loss of control. Only İbrahim's arrival at the head of a large military contingent and negotiations with the tribal elements in the region finally brought an end to the rebellions.[62]

After the rebels were defeated, İbrahim and Süleyman encountered a different kind of disturbance in Constantinople. A Muslim scholar named Kabız began to argue that Jesus was superior to Muhammad as prophet. Kabız expounded his ideas publicly, and he seems to have found many followers. His arguments contravened Islam's claim that Muhammad is the last prophet and that his message abrogated previous revelation. Kabız was reported to the authorities by other religious scholars. In November 1527, he was brought to the imperial council for a trial. The two military judges were unable to refute his arguments, however, and he was released. Süleyman, who watched the proceedings from behind a window that gave him a view of the council chamber, was alarmed. He ordered Kabız to be brought back, and asked the most prominent scholar of the time, the chief jurist Kemalpaşazade Ahmed, to handle the interrogation. After a tense trial and debate, Kabız was executed for contravening the Sharia.[63]

Shortly after the trial and execution, Constantinople was rocked by a heinous crime. One night in late January 1528, intruders killed the inhabitants of a house near the mosque of Sultan Selim and stole all their property. Suspicions fell on young Christian men who worked in menial jobs across the city. Palace pursuivants, gatekeepers, and guards were sent to scour the streets, marketplaces, and drinking establishments. Around eight hundred non-Muslims, working as non-skilled labor, many of them recent migrants to the capital, were rounded up and publicly executed.

Disturbances continued, however. The palace discovered next that the judge of Aleppo had embezzled large sums on the pretext of inspecting properties. He had shared his illicit gains with the men around him, and his friends in the administration had made sure that complaints about him did not reach Constantinople. Locals decided to mete out their own justice. In April 1528, in a dramatic move that must have shocked many in the city, they attacked the main mosque during the Friday prayer and killed the corrupt judge and his men, including a market inspector (*muhtesib*). Around the same time, complaints reached Constantinople about a district governor in the Balkans who had been enslaving the children of Christian subjects illegally.

A system of rule based on the domination of a military-political elite over a largely rural population regularly produced similar problems. Several factors, ranging from population increase to the appeal of the Safavid message of salvation beyond Sunnism, challenged the rule of the Ottoman sultan and his officials. The *askerî* elite itself, from the smallest *tımar*-holders to the viziers and religious scholars at the center, had to be managed and cajoled in return for their service. The sultan and his associates chose to see these problems as exceptions and as products of human ambition and error. At least, this is how Celalzade Mustafa preferred to present them. He also described the sultan's justice as rightful and swift. The rebels were defeated, Kabız was executed, the corrupt notables of Aleppo were exiled to Rhodes, and the provincial governor was hanged.

While instances of disorder were seen as aberrations to be handled on a case-by-case basis, Süleyman and those around him were aware that other matters needed constant attention. One was the collection of revenue. Süleyman and İbrahim's ambitious imperial policy abroad largely relied on war, and war required money. The Ottoman central administration was able to manage the financing of war fairly well during the first decades of Süleyman's rule.[64] Still, new policies imposed unforeseen costs. For instance, naval activities by Habsburg allies in the Mediterranean in 1531 and 1532 pushed the Ottomans to instigate an extensive ship-building program.[65] In general, even though low-ranking members of the *askerî* elite obtained benefits through pillage and enslavement, most of the campaigns in this period produced a negative balance for the central treasury. Moreover, the crowded palace household required large sums of cash for everything from stipends to expenses for the kitchens, the stables, and the workshops. Expensive tastes in luxury goods, introduced by İbrahim and soon adopted by Süleyman and others, and the patronage of a large number of poets and historians, imposed additional costs.

Süleyman, İbrahim, and their associates, and particularly the chief treasurers, were concerned about multiple dynamics. Preventing the spread of private property at the expense of sultanic ownership and supervising the establishment of tax-free endowments to make sure they did not become tax havens were two such worries. Besides, merchants of various nations had to be given incentives and offered protection to foster regional and international trade, a major source of tax revenue in cash. Overall, collecting and redistributing tax revenues in an efficient manner was the most critical task. In particular, the political center had to allocate sufficient revenue to the *askerî* elite to keep its allegiance, while at the same time trying to prevent the over-taxing of the agricultural, artisanal, and commercial classes. Peasant flight from land was a serious problem the central authorities tried to handle through incentives as well as fines.

The financial administration of the empire revolved around this balancing game. The idea of sultanic justice as equitable treatment for all supported this equilibrium from a political standpoint. Of course, the same notion of justice also protected existing social and economic relationships by presenting them as permanent components of a particular concept of society. Within that static notion, members of different social and professional groups eternally fulfilled their specific duties and functions under the watchful gaze of the sultan and his men.[66]

Süleyman and İbrahim successfully increased the revenues of the empire during this period. Following İbrahim's inspection visit to Egypt, the revenues of the province, which sent an annual sum to Constantinople instead of being divided into *tımars*, increased twofold. Between 1524–25 and 1527–28, while expenditures of the central treasury increased by nearly 50 percent, its revenues nearly doubled.[67] In an indication of the economic control exercised by the center, the revenue generated by freehold properties and endowments in the entire realm in 1528 was only around 12 percent of the revenue generated by sources controlled by the sultan and the *askerî* elite. More strikingly, around half of the collected revenue accrued to the sultan, to be utilized for various expenses mentioned above.[68]

Süleyman and İbrahim's financial success was partly a result of bureaucratic activity. In the second half of the 1520s, in addition to existing land surveys that were regularly conducted, general surveys of Anatolia and Rumeli were ordered. These provided information about population, *tımars*, the number and type of settlements, and military and public buildings (fortresses, mosques, dervish lodges, baths, madrasas). Overall, they offered a snapshot of the empire's economy for the central authorities. The preparation of a detailed budget in 1527–28 served a similar purpose. Of course, the drafting of land surveys could elicit strong reactions that included rebellions, such as the ones in Anatolia 1526–27. Süleyman and İbrahim proceeded regardless.

Another major concern was to manage all existing and future *tımar* assignments, large and small. In an imperial decree from 1531, Süleyman, speaking in the first person in the text, gave his instructions to the governor-general of Rumeli and all the officials of the governorate. The intention was to regularize the hodge-podge nature of prior assignments, some of which had been given to individuals who did not belong to the *askerî* elite. Ever mindful of his image as a just sultan, Süleyman ordered that none of the current holders of *tımars* should be dismissed, regardless of their social background. This was clearly directed at preventing dissent by those military men who had served the dynasty for many years and now faced dismissal.

With the same decree, the sultan instructed his officials that, from then on, the larger *tımar* assignments should be executed with his approval and with an imperial diploma, in contrast to earlier practice. This instruction significantly limited the power of the governor-general over the distribution of revenue and emphasized his subordinate status to Constantinople.[69] The sultan's gaze, and his writ, were to reach all corners of the empire. Moreover, central control over *tımar* assignments allowed Süleyman to send out more and more members of the palace household, slaves raised within an ethos of service to the sultan, to the provinces.

The further elevation of the office of the grand vizier as a general supervisor for all imperial affairs was another important measure. The sultan withdrew from the nitty-gritty of government, befitting his new claims of temporal and spiritual authority. İbrahim stepped in as the most influential grand vizier the Ottoman enterprise had seen until that time. The importance of the grand vizierate, one of the oldest positions in Ottoman government, had grown exponentially as the Ottoman enterprise expanded. In the earlier centuries, sultans overshadowed their viziers and grand viziers, who are portrayed in Ottoman chronicles as important yet secondary actors. Pirî Mehmed, Süleyman's first grand vizier, was a transitional figure. If he had not been sidelined by the sultan, he could have been the first truly powerful grand vizier. Instead, the opportunity was presented to İbrahim, and he relished it. He assumed increasing responsibilities in imperial policy at home and beyond, and vigorously took initiative. He helped transform the office from one of advisor and subordinate to one with considerable executive powers. He was the harbinger of a series of Ottoman grand viziers whose reputations eclipsed those of the sultans they served.

The expansion of bureaucratic activity led to several other changes. For instance, between 1525 and 1529, new offices were built in the second court of the New Palace for the imperial council and the treasury.[70] A latticed window up high in the imperial council hall reminded all in attendance that the sultan could be silently and invisibly watching from there, as he had during the trial of Kabız. Meeting days and times of the imperial council were regularized. According to a Venetian report, those days were Saturday, Sunday, Monday, and Tuesday.[71] The number of viziers, which had fluctuated in earlier reigns, was fixed at four.

The imperial council had existed in one form or another since the early years of the dynasty and had been developing into a more formal unit of administration since the mid-fifteenth century. Under Süleyman, it became a cabinet-like body, with the same set of officials (the grand vizier and viziers, treasurers, military judges, the chancellor, the chief jurist, etc.) in regular attendance. The number of scribes serving the council and the treasury doubled, from around forty to around eighty. The employment of migrant scholars and scribes mostly ended as the growing specificity of Ottoman administrative practices required on-the-job training. Many of the new scribes who joined the bureaucratic career were freeborn Ottoman Muslims who, after a madrasa education, were drafted through merit or patronage.[72]

The other response Süleyman and İbrahim produced to deal with the challenges of the period was cultural and literary in nature. They were not alone in that endeavor. The early years of Süleyman's reign witnessed the emergence of many works written by various individuals who were motivated by the sultan, the grand vizier, and the new imperial project, and who utilized their talents to support them and their agendas. While the Ottomans were always interested in history both as practical knowledge and as an art form, Selim's violent march to power and the intense imperial competition of Süleyman's first decades lent a particular poignancy to history. The field of history-writing in Ottoman Turkish, which had been fairly narrow until the last decades of the fifteenth century, considerably expanded under Süleyman. Poets, scribes, religious scholars, judges, viziers, and others dabbled in history, and inscribed their own agendas and expectations into the story of Süleyman's reign. This was not a mere matter of patronage whereby texts were produced in return for money and promotion, although that dimension cannot be entirely discounted.

Historical works produced during Süleyman's long reign include event-based accounts, such as the descriptions of a single campaign, but also dynastic chronicles, regnal histories, and universal histories. Some of these works, enriched with illustrations, are among the most impressive representatives of Ottoman visual arts.[73] Many other forms of writing with a historical character abounded. Poets were encouraged to present chronograms to mark important events, such as a military victory, the birth of a prince, a wedding, or the construction of a building. Scribes kept detailed campaign diaries that recorded the advance of the army and the critical developments of a campaign. Letters of victory sent to foreign rulers and to Ottoman judges to be recited to the public provided snapshots of military achievements.

Works of history composed during the first decade and a half of Süleyman's reign are significantly different than those produced in his later years on the throne.[74] These early representatives reflect the agendas and interests of Süleyman and those around him during a time of transitions. One important consideration was to define the legacy of Selim and establish the continuity between father and son, but also promote Süleyman through his own achievements and his justice. A typical example is the Arabic account of the Belgrade campaign by Süleyman's physician Ramazan, who devotes the first one third of his account of Süleyman's first campaign to a reassessment of Selim's reign. There, Selim is hailed as an accomplished warrior, yet his failure to fight against the Christians of Europe is also underlined. Süleyman is presented as the one who opens the gate of holy war that had been closed under his father. Another example is Sad b. Abdülmüteal's *Selimname*. Almost nothing is known about the author, who seems to have been close to Selim and Süleyman. In his work, Selim's succession struggles and his eventful reign seamlessly leave their place to Süleyman's rule, and Süleyman, in an implicit critique of Selim, is first and foremost described as a just sultan.

Another objective encountered in historical writings from this time is the creation of a record of Süleyman's activities. Campaign-based narratives emerged after the capture of Belgrade and continued to be produced to the end of Süleyman's reign. In these early years, they constituted the bulk of history-writing. Süleyman's physician Ramazan wrote accounts of his first two military campaigns in Arabic, a classical language of the Ottomans' cultural universe. The majority of works from this period, however, is in Ottoman Turkish. These were written by younger people whose enthusiasm for Süleyman's agenda is palpable. One of them was Mustafa, later known as Bostan Çelebi, who composed an account of the period between 1520 and 1523 around 1523–24.[75] At the time, he was an advanced madrasa student nearing graduation as a candidate to a judgeship or a professorship. As a student of Süleyman's tutor Hayreddin, he had access to one of Süleyman's closest associates, and he must have been particularly motivated by that affinity. Similarly, the young scribe Celalzade Mustafa, who was about to become a close collaborator of Süleyman and İbrahim, and his brother Celalzade Salih, another student of Hayreddin, composed accounts of military campaigns.

Many of these historical works are significant in terms of their approach to the partnership between Süleyman and İbrahim. For instance, Sad b. Abdülmüteal's *Selimname*, which ends with an account of İbrahim's grand vizierate and his inspection tour to Egypt, praises the relationship between sultan and grand vizier as an auspicious beginning for the new reign.[76] Celalzade Salih, in the introduction of his account of the 1526 campaign, likewise eulogizes sultan and grand vizier together, presenting their collaboration as a unique moment in Ottoman history.[77] Another junior scholar, Baharî, echoes their sentiments in his own work on the 1526 campaign, in which he presents Süleyman as a Second Solomon and İbrahim as Asaph, recognized in the Islamic tradition as Solomon's vizier.[78]

Süleyman and İbrahim's attention to the recording and commemoration of history is evident in a variety of works they commissioned. There is a strong indication that Kemalpaşazade Ahmed was asked by Süleyman to continue his account of earlier Ottoman sultans by writing on the reigns of his father and himself.[79] The sultan also ordered a translation, from Arabic into Ottoman Turkish, of al-Tabari's (d. 923) forty-volume Islamic history from

Creation to the early tenth century.[80] One of the most significant examples of the intellectual rapport that tied sultan and grand vizier to the literary and scholarly elite is an encyclopedic work presented to İbrahim in 1529. The work includes sections on politics and morals, rhetoric, the wonders of the world, and history. Very tellingly, it places Selim and Süleyman at the end of Islamic and caliphal history, making them the current representatives of the Prophet and his successors.[81] İbrahim also asked Pirî Reis, an Ottoman captain, to write his *Kitab-ı Bahriye* ("The Book on Navigation"), an atlas and navigation guide of the Mediterranean.

The patronage of poetry was another prominent aspect of the new cultural agenda. İbrahim, in particular, is described in contemporary works as a connoisseur of good poetry and an extremely generous patron.[82] The treasurer İskender, another close associate, also emerged as a major patron in this period. The money collected through his efforts thus underwrote both military campaigns and a new level of conspicuous consumption and literary activity. For instance, many poets submitted odes that commemorated İbrahim's wedding in 1524 and the princes' circumcision in 1530. Composing poetry in Ottoman Turkish, for the consideration of an ever-growing reading public, was another prominent cultural dynamic in the early years of Süleyman.[83]

İbrahim's approach to poetry seems to have been rather utilitarian. Süleyman shared his grand vizier's enthusiasm in supporting poetry as an instrument for conveying a cultural and political message. He also had a deep personal connection to it. He had started writing poetry while serving as district governor in Manisa. In the 1520s, he was still in the process of finding his own poetic voice. His early poetry revolves, a tad superficially and in a tone that is not yet distinct, around the usual themes of earthly and mystic love.[84] He was going to establish his own style in the coming years, by reading, learning from the poets around him, and tirelessly applying himself, to the point of becoming one of the most prolific poets of the Ottoman tradition.

## Süleyman between Family and Friends

The period from 1525 to 1533 was crucial both in terms of Süleyman's public image and his intimate relationships. Ottoman sources of the time are replete with depictions of Süleyman as a centerpiece of ceremony, from his Friday processions to the mosque to his departures for a military campaign. Ironically, as he became more visible publicly, he became less accessible personally. Palace household officials and viziers served as conduits to Süleyman and barriers around him. This seclusion in the midst of splendor must have increased the value of those with whom he was professionally and personally intimate. Among those, his concubine Hürrem and his grand vizier İbrahim stand out in particular.

Pietro Bragadin, a Venetian diplomat, left behind a description of Süleyman and Hürrem circa 1525. The sultan had a pale, pasty face and an aquiline nose. He was lean, with a long neck. He was melancholic by nature, but very passionate, generous, magnanimous, quick to act, but humble on occasion. As for Hürrem, whom Bragadin did not see in person, she was reputed to be young. She was not a beauty, but she was graceful and of small stature. Süleyman harbored a great love toward her; indeed, he had spent one hundred thousand ducats for her clothes and jewels.[85] (In comparison, the entire sum distributed in the form of cash disbursements and stipend increases after his accession was around five or six hundred thousand ducats.)

Between 1525 and 1533, Süleyman and Hürrem's relationship was further strengthened. After Mehmed, Mihrümah, and Selim, they had a son in 1525, Abdullah, who died a year or so after birth. Two more sons followed: Bayezid in 1527, and Cihangir in 1531.[86] They abstained from having more children after 1531, even though Hürrem was still of childbearing age. Barring any unknown medical complications on either side, this may be a conscious decision about not to increase the number of potential heirs after a safe number was reached.

The end of reproduction-centered sexual activity signified the arrival of a different period in Süleyman and Hürrem's life. As seen in the circumcision celebrations of 1530, Süleyman's image as the father of healthy princes became an important component of his identity. Süleyman and Hürrem's parental attention was directed to the formation of their children as appropriate candidates for the sultanate. This included supervising the first steps of their education, which ranged from reading and writing skills to horseback riding. Also, Cihangir was born with a birth defect, a spinal malformation that required constant monitoring and treatment.[87] Thus, in the midst of the harem, Süleyman and Hürrem established what looked like a nuclear family.[88]

While Hürrem is not identified by name in Süleyman's poetry, it has been assumed that the anonymous beloved in his verses often referred to her, as in the following lines:

*My very own queen, my everything, my beloved, my bright moon;*
*My intimate companion, my one and all, sovereign of all beauties, my*
*sultan.*

*My life, the gift I own, my be-all, my elixir of Paradise, my Eden,*
*My spring, my joy, my glittering day, my exquisite one who smiles on*
*    and on.*

*. . .*

*My Istanbul, my Karaman, and all the Anatolian lands that are mine;*
*My Bedakhshan and my Kipchak territories, my Baghdad and my Khorasan.*

*My darling with that lovely hair, brows curved like a bow; eyes that*
*    ravish: I am ill*
*If I die, yours is the guilt. Help, I beg you, my love from a different*
*    religion.*[89]

Hürrem's feelings for Süleyman may be gleaned from two letters she sent him in the spring and summer of 1526.[90] Both were written as replies to Süleyman's letters, which did not survive. Süleyman was away from Constantinople on the campaign that would end with victory at Mohács. The anxiety of separation from the beloved and the sorrowful state of the lonely lover permeate both of Hürrem's letters. She was quite likely pregnant with their son Bayezid at the time, which must have rendered their correspondence particularly valuable for each other.

Poetry plays a prominent role in her letters from this time. It is likely that Süleyman read his poetry to Hürrem and included verses in letters to her. This is her reply, in the second letter:

*Go, gentle breeze, tell my Sultan: "She weeps and pines away*
*Without your [rosy] face, like a nightingale, she moans in dismay."*

*"Don't think your power can heal her heartache in your absence:*
*No one has found a cure for her woes," that's what you should say,*

*"The hand of grief pierces her heart with its painful arrow;*
*In your absence, she is sick and wails like that flute, the ney."*[91]

It is unclear whether Hürrem had, by the mid-1520s, acquired the necessary skills to compose poetry or even write these letters, which are filled with the stock expressions of literary Ottoman Turkish. It is possible that she dictated them to someone who was knowledgeable about how to properly address the sultan, but who used Hürrem's own expressions, such as "the star of my happiness" and "my graceful, delicate sultan." Even if she used the service of scribes, her tenderness and caring still come through.

On one occasion, Süleyman apparently complained about the shortness of one of her earlier letters and teased her for not fully reading his messages.

Hürrem replies that the suffering of separation prevented her from writing further. She then reminds her beloved of the love of their children for him and emphasizes that the entire family is yearning for his safe return. Her fear for his safety is one of the major themes in the second letter. She implores God to protect him from all sorrows and illnesses; she invokes God, Muhammad, and the saints to ask for Süleyman's victory over the "ill-natured, dirty infidels" (*küffar-ı bed-kirdar-ı hak-sar*). The letter was sent with a talismanic shirt, brought by a holy man all the way from Mecca. Hürrem asks Süleyman to make sure to wear it at all times.

Others close to Süleyman and Hürrem make appearances in the letters. One of them is Gülfem, one of Hürrem's close companions and a senior concubine. There is a message from her appended at the end of Hürrem's letter or sent together with it. Clearly written by someone used to entertaining Süleyman, the message begins with a funny story. Süleyman had sent Gülfem some money and a box of sweets that included a mild intoxicant (*kolonya*). Gülfem ate the entire box by mistake and became lethargic. Those around her, including some guests, tried to revive her but she slept through most of the day. She teases Süleyman for making a laughingstock out of her and says they will talk more when he returns. She then tells him, briefly, about a delicate matter. Süleyman had instructed her to check and see whether an unnamed sultanic concubine (*kadın*) had enough allowance left. Gülfem talked to someone, probably a eunuch in the harem, and found out how much she had left. It is possible that the unnamed concubine was Mahidevran, Mustafa's mother. Even though Mahidevran had fallen out of favor with Hürrem's rise, Süleyman would ensure that she and their son Mustafa lived comfortably.

While the relationship between Süleyman and Hürrem deepened through mutual affection and many children, Mahidevran must have maintained a level of prestige as the mother of Süleyman's eldest son. Bragadin reported that, after Süleyman had turned away from her, Mahidevran spent all her time caring for her son. Mustafa was known to be smart and daring. He was much liked by janissaries, apparently, and was expected to become a mighty warrior.[92] The relationship between the two mothers and their children seems to have been formal. In her first letter, Hürrem asks Süleyman to forward a message from her to Mustafa, rather than contacting him directly. Looking back to this period from the 1540s and 1550s, it is tempting to search for elements of a rivalry between Hürrem and Mahidevran, but they are not yet visible. Hürrem properly addresses Mustafa as "sultan" in her letter, for instance.

Mustafa's subsequent appointment as district governor of Saruhan in 1533 is another indication that the prince was treated fairly. Saruhan, Süleyman's old seat, was seen as a favorable location for a prince. If Hürrem had had the intention or power to do so, it would have been wiser for her to lobby for a location farther from Constantinople. Throughout 1520s and 1530s, it seems that civility and custom prevailed between the mothers of the princes. Moreover, Mahidevran's departure from Constantinople with her son may have been a relief for Hürrem, as it put a considerable physical distance between them and Süleyman.

In addition to his unprecedented relationship with Hürrem, another unconventional partnership Süleyman maintained in this period was his association with his grand vizier İbrahim. Rumors in the capital about their friendship found their way into Bragadin's report. According to the Venetian diplomat, Süleyman could not spend a moment without İbrahim's company. Against custom and precedent, İbrahim spent many a night in the New Palace, in the sultan's Privy Chamber. There, they slept in two beds joined at the head.[93] Ottoman sources of the time concur about the time the two spent together. The sultan and the grand vizier went on long hunting trips for instance, some of them lasting for a month.[94]

Bragadin, who negotiated with the grand vizier as a Venetian diplomat, describes İbrahim as a thin man with a small face, pale skin, and short stature, who was graceful and eloquent. He had broad interests. He liked to listen to epic stories (*romanzi*) about Alexander the Great, Hannibal, wars, and various things of the past. He enjoyed composing music with an Iranian who lived in his household. He was interested in the situation of other rulers of the world, the lands they ruled, and many other things. He purchased every exquisite object he could.[95]

The extent of İbrahim's cultural and material interests was only matched by the extent of his power, it seems. Bragadin called him the sultan's "heart and breath" (*il cuor e il fiato*). He could do whatever he wished, and Süleyman did not act without consulting him. He had been much detested when he was appointed grand vizier, but Süleyman's love for him pushed all, including Hafsa, Hürrem, and the other viziers, to maintain a good relationship with him. While Ottoman sources do not always provide the sort of personal details found in diplomatic reports, they wholeheartedly agree with the Venetians about İbrahim's virtues, skills, rhetorical talent, and hard work, which were said to make him an unprecedented grand vizier.[96]

The first signs of İbrahim's declining fortunes seem to have emerged in the early 1530s. He had been at the forefront of Ottoman imperial policy since 1524 and had done much to attract attention and criticism. The expenses involved in the refurbishment of his residence on the Hippodrome, the funds

spent for the purchase of precious objects, the jacket covered with gold leaf he
wore in public, his gem-encrusted rings, and the statues brought from Buda
erected in front of his residence must have all contributed to an undercurrent
of displeasure.[97] Bragadin also reports that İbrahim had brought his mother
and two of his brothers to Constantinople from his native Parga. The brothers
had been placed in palace service, and his mother, who had converted to
Islam, lived in a house near her son's. A year later, Marco Minio relays that
İbrahim's father had come to Constantinople and that his son wanted him
to convert to Islam, like other family members.[98] There were instances when
Christian-origin Ottoman officials reconnected with family members, but,
reuniting the old family in the capital sounds like something only İbrahim
would and could do.

Competition with others like Hürrem for Süleyman's time and attention must have exposed İbrahim to additional criticisms from within the
harem, as seen in one of Hürrem's letters from 1526. Toward the end of the
letter, we learn that Süleyman had asked her why she was displeased with
İbrahim. She briefly tells him this is best discussed in person upon his return. To emphasize that the matter is not too important, she purposefully
adds her greetings to the grand vizier. Indeed, neither the arrival of İbrahim's
relatives, nor his conspicuous consumption, or the outbreak of tensions and
rivalries within Süleyman's inner circle would have been enough to discredit
him in Süleyman's eyes initially. However, it is likely that these small and large
criticisms and accusations accumulated over the years and became particularly salient in the light of the mixed results of the 1529 and 1532 campaigns
championed by İbrahim.

The Venetian diplomat Daniello de Ludovisi, who visited Constantinople
in late 1533/early 1534, is one of the first observers to discuss the changing
perceptions of the grand vizier. İbrahim was away from Constantinople in
Aleppo during the diplomat's visit, which must have facilitated the exchange
of rumors about him. It appears that, in the grand vizier's absence, there had
been a reckoning with his career in the palace circles. In order to become and
remain grand vizier, the diplomat was told, he had schemed for the dismissal
and demise of the sultan's most talented servants: Ferhad, who was executed;
Ahmed, who was sent to Cairo and killed there; and Pirî Mehmed, who was
exiled and supposedly poisoned later on İbrahim's orders.

The diplomat also relates a recent incident, without knowing that one of
its protagonists was to become one of the most important officials of the empire in the coming decades. Accordingly, İbrahim was so jealous of Süleyman
that he continued to monitor him even from Aleppo. He thus found out

that Süleyman often conversed with a palace official named Rüstem, head of the stables. He immediately ordered Rüstem to be appointed to a district in Anatolia. Rüstem, saddened, asked Süleyman's permission to stay. However, the sultan chose not to defy the grand vizier. He simply told Rüstem he would talk to İbrahim upon his return.[99]

İbrahim was clearly aware of his declining fortunes, and he adopted different personas in order to manage different audiences. One such instance was witnessed by the Habsburg diplomat Cornelius de Schepper, who was in Constantinople in early 1533. When Celalzade Mustafa, chief scribe of the imperial council, and Yunus, chief translator, joined the negotiations, the grand vizier adopted a harsh, accusatory tone toward the diplomats. When they were not in the room, he was more understanding and civil.[100] İbrahim was increasingly seen in the capital as being too accommodating toward the Christians, and it looks like he wanted to act in a way to disprove these perceptions in the presence of Süleyman's close collaborators Mustafa and Yunus.

Perhaps most importantly, despite years of costly campaigns in central Europe, ambitious plans such as defeating the Habsburgs, marching on to Rome, and establishing universal rule had not been realized. That frustration may have led İbrahim to throw his weight behind another military campaign, this time against the Safavids. He may have seen an easy victory over them as a way to restore his reputation. He could not have known that this was the beginning of the end of the partnership between him and Süleyman.

# 6

## Maturation: The Middle Years, 1533–53

AS THE OTTOMAN-HUNGARIAN and Ottoman-Habsburg rivalries took center stage in political and ideological debates from 1520 to 1533, Süleyman did not organize any major campaigns in the east. Still, the Safavid enemy continued to preoccupy the Ottomans in a variety of ways.[1] The estrangement felt by the Ottomans vis-à-vis the Safavids was both deeper and more ambiguous than their enmity toward the European Christians. First of all, the Safavids, according to the Ottomans, were heretics who had departed from the true interpretation of Islam. Ongoing proselytization of the Safavid cause among Anatolian Muslims continued to concern the Ottomans from a religious standpoint. They also believed that Safavid propaganda was behind major threats to Ottoman order, such as the Anatolian rebellions in 1527.

The Ottoman bureaucrat and historian Celalzade Mustafa voiced the opinions of many when he called the Safavid realm the "sedition-filled, Sharia-abrogating Orient."[2] The cultural affinity between the two sides, which did not necessarily exist between the Ottomans and the Habsburgs, further complicated the rivalry. Thus, even though they clashed over whether the Sunni or Twelver Shiite variants were the correct versions of Islam, learned Ottomans and Safavids used Persian as a high literary language and shared a corpus of Arabo-Persian belles lettres, extending from poetry to history-writing.[3]

Even for those among the *askerî* elite who might not care about the cultural and theological aspects of the rivalry, the logistical difficulties of campaigning in eastern Anatolia and western Iran were a cause for concern. Tabriz, the Safavid capital, was farther away from Constantinople than Vienna. The inhabitants of the region, from urban dwellers to pastoralists, sympathized with the Safavids and their message. The difficult terrain, which included rugged highlands and semi-arid flatlands, was not suited to the march of a large army, particularly one laden with food, the heavy equipment necessary for gunpowder weapons from muskets to cannons, and large numbers of pack animals. Moreover, the relative scarcity of resources in the region and the long distances rendered Ottoman supply chains less effective.[4]

The frontier between the Ottomans and the Safavids covered a large area that included the southern Caucasus, Azerbaijan, eastern Anatolia, parts of western Iran, and present-day Iraq. Georgian nobles tenuously held on to their lands in the north, while chiefs of Turkish nomadic tribes and Kurdish noblemen exerted political and military power over most of the frontier, under the watchful eyes of Ottoman officials posted nearby. There, nomads lived in a tense balance with agriculturalists and townsmen, and Georgian, Armenian, and Assyrian Christianity coexisted with various forms of Sunnism and Shiism. Despite the enmity between the Ottomans and the Safavids, or perhaps because of it, the geographical frontier witnessed a significant level of mobility. Merchants traveled alongside old trade routes. Safavid proselytizers crossed over into Ottoman territory. Ottoman spies traveled in the opposite direction. The rivalry also gave soldiers, scholars, artists, and others the opportunity to change loyalties and seek their fortunes on the other side.[5]

As Süleyman and İbrahim were busy creating and implementing their new imperial agenda, Ismail died in 1524, and his ten-year-old son Tahmasb (r. 1524–76) succeeded him. Ismail had acted both as political leader and spiritual guide for members of Turkish tribal confederations, which constituted the bulk of the military-political elite in the early decades of the Safavid dynasty. Following his death, the tribal confederations entered into a violent competition for power and autonomy. The situation was made worse by the near-constant military threat posed by the Sunni Uzbeks from central Asia, under the leadership of the Shaybanid dynasty. This was a time of turmoil and transition for the young Tahmasb. Scribes and scholars provided a certain level of stability, but they constituted a much smaller group compared to the military elements. They worked at consolidating a dynasty-centered political and religious identity based on Persian bureaucratic traditions and Twelver Shiism, but their progress was gradual.[6] The near-immobilization of Tahmasb under the strain of internal and external threats helped the Ottomans focus their attention on the European front.

Ismail's delay in congratulating Süleyman right after his accession had irritated the Ottomans, but the subsequent exchange of letters between the two sides in 1523, following the capture of Rhodes, was courteous. Süleyman soon after adopted a different stance toward the Safavids, which is clearly seen in a letter addressed to Tahmasb, sent in 1525. The letter is called "a letter of threat" (*tehdidname*) in Ottoman sources.[7] It was written shortly after the introduction to the Egyptian law code, by the same scribe who worked closely with Süleyman and İbrahim. The letter sent to Ismail a few years earlier was composed in a stylized Persian, but the one sent to his son is in Turkish, with a rich vocabulary yet direct style, addressing Tahmasb in the informal second person singular.

The letter presents Süleyman as the Master of the Auspicious Conjunction and caliph. Süleyman then directly speaks to the Safavid shah. He calls him "*Tahmasb bahadır*" (Tahmasb the warrior), diminishing his counterpart to the status of a soldier of fortune. The ten-year-old Safavid ruler is chastised for not having sent envoys to Süleyman to express his subservience. The letter calls the Safavids misguided and states that Tahmasb has worn the headgear of "heresy" (*ilhad*), a reference to the headgear worn by Safavid followers. Süleyman informs Tahmasb that his imminent march to the east has been delayed due to his impressive victories over the Hungarians and the Franks (that is, the Order of St. John). However, he is bound to move soon against Tahmasb. Even if Tahmasb were to turn into an ant and hide in the ground, or become a bird and fly into the skies, Süleyman intends to find him and cleanse the face of the earth of his evil existence.

For those in the know, these threats must have sounded hollow since Süleyman was getting ready to move against Hungary when the letter was sent. This letter is important primarily for attesting to the persistence of anti-Safavid attitudes among the Ottomans, even though İbrahim and Süleyman were becoming increasingly entangled in European affairs. The tone of the letter was later echoed in a poem by Süleyman, probably written shortly before his first campaign against the Safavids. Earnest-sounding and appealing to the sense of duty and heroism of a male audience, it must have been intended to be widely circulated and recited. In it, writing under his penname Muhibbî, Süleyman expresses the wish to follow the example of Abu Bakr and Umar, recognized by the Sunnis as rightful caliphs, who were notorious for their military campaigns against the enemies and rivals of the early Muslim community. Süleyman also calls upon his supporters to raise the imperial banner and endure the difficulties of the long road ahead.[8] The jingoistic tone of the poem becomes particularly apparent in its derogatory use of "Red Heads" (*kızılbaş*) for the Safavids, a strong ethno-religious insult in Ottoman usage.[9]

Süleyman's poem may have been a response to one written by his childhood friend Yahya, a madrasa teacher at the time. Yahya's poem is both a reflection of the anti-Safavid and anti-Shiite sensibilities among the Sunni

Ottomans, and the ongoing relationship between two childhood friends. Yahya describes the Safavids as treacherous heretics, and as the greatest enemies of the Ottoman realm. Counting on their friendship, Yahya uses a direct tone while addressing the sultan. He tells Süleyman that the entire Sunni community awaits his orders, implying that he should not waste any more time. He also advises him, quite bluntly, to follow the example of his father Selim. Finally, he invites the sultan to behave with honor and dignity to inspire his soldiers to fight well.[10]

## Süleyman and İbrahim's First Campaign in the East

The long road ahead, mentioned in Süleyman's poem, emerged as a result of a variety of factors that ranged from Sunni triumphalism and imperial hubris to simpler ones like skirmishes on the frontier.[11] Almost all Ottoman sources offer both strategic as well as theological and political reasons for Süleyman's first campaign against the Safavids. According to them, the Ottoman sultan intended to end the Safavid problem once and for all by decisively defeating Tahmasb and restoring Sunni Islam in the lands of heresy. Similar overarching arguments were also produced against the Habsburgs and the Hungarians. However, fighting against what was seen a corruption of Islam from within gave a particular vehemence to the Ottoman position.

In the wake of the mixed results produced by their campaigns against the Habsburgs, Süleyman and İbrahim may have seen a victory over the Safavids as a rejuvenation of their imperial agenda. There were several factors that may have reassured them about a positive outcome to their campaign. It was common knowledge that, despite Tahmasb's growing authority in recent years, the Safavid military-political elite was deeply divided, and the power of the shah was limited. While the Ottomans enjoyed the advantage of a large army and sophisticated gunpowder weaponry, the Safavids lagged behind in military recruitment as well as technology.[12] None of these may be singled out as the main reason behind Süleyman's first expedition against the Safavids, and it is quite likely that they were all mentioned and discussed in different contexts, depending on the identity of the interlocutors.

There was one immediate factor that precipitated the enmity between the sides into open warfare. It all began with a military man named Ulama, initially an Ottoman *sipahi*, who had gone over to the Safavids in the early 1510s. He and his tribal confederation, the Tekelü, competed with other confederations in the years following Ismail's death. Toward the end of 1531, at a time when the Tekelü were losing ground against their rivals as well as

Tahmasb, Ulama crossed the frontier in the other direction and returned to the Ottoman fold. In the absence of a reliable provider of information like Venice in the west, the Ottomans often depended on figures like Ulama, who quickly gained access to the grand vizier. It seems that he convinced İbrahim that many on the Safavid side would join the Ottomans in the event of an invasion.

As if to prove his point, Ulama engaged in military operations in the southern part of the frontier in the summer of 1532, clashing with a prominent Kurdish noble named Sheref Han and inadvertently drawing Tahmasb to the region. Safavid sources of the time place the blame for the subsequent violence on Ulama's ambitions, as well as İbrahim's covetousness and gullibility. Interestingly enough, an Ottoman observer like Celalzade Mustafa, who participated in the campaign in the company of İbrahim, echoes the Safavid portrayal of Ulama as an ambitious, unreliable schemer. Entering a somehow foreign, faraway region under the dubious guidance of a double turncoat: thus began the campaign that brought about the end of the partnership between the sultan and the grand vizier.[13]

Süleyman's first eastern campaign was carefully planned.[14] In October 1533, shortly after a peace agreement was reached with Ferdinand's envoys, İbrahim was sent to Aleppo. He spent the winter and early spring there for military preparations and intelligence gathering. As he found the situation in the region and inside the Safavid realm favorable for a larger operation, the grand vizier wrote to Süleyman in April 1534 to inform him that he could leave Constantinople in May with the bulk of the Ottoman forces.[15] For Süleyman, this was not the most accommodating time. Two of his closest acquaintances and supporters had died recently, news as yet unbeknownst to İbrahim: in March 1534, his beloved mother Hafsa, and in April, the chief jurist Kemalpaşazade Ahmed, who had been instrumental in building an anti-Safavid position through his historical and religious writings and his legal opinions.

Süleyman left Constantinople after some delay, in mid-June, and proceeded to a part of his empire he had never visited before. In a couplet appended to a love poem, written at the time of his departure, he informs his reader/beloved that he raised the army of Islam against the "Red Heads" and that, by God's help, he is marching against the land of Iran.[16] As usual, his march became the occasion for him to indulge in his favorite pastime, the hunt. On the long trip, he made a point of spending time in Konya, where he visited the tombs of the Anatolian Seljuk sultans. At the tomb complex of the famous thirteenth-century Sufi Celaleddin Rumi, Mevlevi dervishes treated the sultan to their traditional ceremony with music and whirling. Also in Konya, Süleyman saw the Melami sheikh Pir Ali Alaeddin Aksarayi, who was notorious for dabbling in occult sciences. The sheikh presented the sultan with a copy of a work by the thirteenth-century mystic and prognosticator Ibn Arabi, whose corpus was one of the foundations of Ottoman occult practices. He pointed out a passage in which the meeting between him and the sultan (identified only by their initials), its location, and its date were foretold.[17]

As Süleyman progressed through the Anatolian peninsula, after receiving prophetic confirmation about his campaign, İbrahim marched on toward Tabriz, the Safavid capital, and reached it around mid-July. Bearing his title of *serasker* (commander-in-chief), with all the powers granted to him by the sultan in 1529, İbrahim behaved like a conqueror. He appointed many officials, some of whom had recently left the Safavids and joined the Ottomans, to newly instituted governorates around western Iran. His imposition of the Ottoman military-administrative system on newly captured, barely controlled areas shows the hubris that prevailed in the early stages of the campaign. Süleyman was informed of these developments, and it is likely that he was made to believe there would be a quick and comprehensive victory. The hubris extended into İbrahim's entry into Tabriz without waiting for Süleyman. One of his first acts was to attend the Friday prayer with great fanfare.

The midday prayer on Friday is the major Muslim communal gathering, and attendance is obligatory for adult Sunni males. Next to its religious significance, it is also politically important since, typically, the ruler's name was mentioned in the sermons. There were discussions among Twelver Shiites about its validity after the disappearance of the Twelfth Imam, who was expected to return as a restorer of true faith before the Day of Judgment. Thus, while the Safavid dynasty wanted to use the Friday prayer as a political occasion, the Shiite clergy were reluctant to legitimize its practice.[18] The Ottomans, aware of these discussions, often criticized the Safavids by claiming that they shunned the Friday prayer in contravention of the Sharia, going so far as to imply that the Safavids and their followers had abandoned all forms of prayer.

As a result, the Friday prayer had become one of the central components of the Ottomans' performance of Sunnism. Holding the Friday prayer in Tabriz had another meaning for them as well. A sizeable Sunni community continued to live in the city and in its vicinity, despite Ismail's militant anti-Sunnism. The location chosen for the Ottoman-sponsored Friday prayer reinforced the message of Sunni restoration. It was the city's central mosque that was built by Uzun Hasan (d. 1478), the Sunni Akkoyunlu ruler whose domain had been taken over by the Safavids after his death.

The triumphalist atmosphere subsided when news of Tahmasb's march toward Tabriz was received. An attack led by the shah in person was a fearful prospect. İbrahim immediately contacted the sultan, who hurried to join him, reaching Tabriz at the end of September 1534. The arrival of the sultan meant more soldiers and firepower, while the sultanic presence also boosted the morale in and around Tabriz. That was one aspect of political power, charismatic authority, which İbrahim could not replicate, despite his titles and the wide network of patronage he had established.

It was now Tahmasb's turn to worry. Defections, indecisiveness, and concerns about Ottoman military prowess already had reduced the number of confederates who had gathered around him. Instead of attacking the sultan, Tahmasb retreated to a safe distance and waited for the next Ottoman move. As he admits in his memoirs written a few decades later, he was aware that facing the sultan in open battle was a losing proposition. Tahmasb's solution was a scorched-earth campaign that reduced resources available to the Ottomans inside Iran. He also adopted a sort of guerilla warfare that was more suitable for the Safavid forces, whose bulk consisted of light cavalry units. Knowledge of the terrain, the support of the local population, and the comparative slowness of the Ottoman army allowed the Safavids to attack supply lines, harass advancing columns, and eventually recover lost territory after the Ottoman army retreated from the areas it had captured during the campaign season.

Süleyman and İbrahim must have known all this, but it seems that their imperial agenda once again carried the day and forced them into a difficult venture, like the "German" campaign. Instead of being instructed to winter around Tabriz and fortify the city, Ottoman forces were ordered to pursue Tahmasb inside Iran. Süleyman and his men marched more than 200 miles southwest to reach Soltaniyeh in mid-October. They received the submission of a few high-ranking Safavid officials, but the shah, who had been thought to be in Soltaniyeh, was nowhere to be seen. The cold weather, which brought heavy snowfall, and food scarcity, led to considerable losses in Ottoman ranks, and it was decided to find a suitable location to spend the winter.

The large but dwindling Ottoman force proceeded to Hamedan, around 150 miles south, reaching the city at the end of October. Some supplies were procured there, and the difficult march resumed, this time toward Baghdad, almost 400 miles to the southwest. The freezing weather continued to weigh on the Ottomans, and the bare nature of the region did not offer much for firewood. Winds were strong enough to blow down tents. Rivers overflowed, making crossings life-threateningly difficult. The old capital of the Abbasid

caliphs was finally reached at the end of November. The city's Safavid governor had fled with some of his men, and the Ottomans entered Baghdad
without resistance.

After sending most of his military units to suitable winter quarters,
Süleyman began turning Baghdad into another stage for ceremonialism.
The tomb of the scholar Abu Hanifa (d. 767), the founder of the Sunni
legal school followed by the Ottomans, had been ruined under Safavid rule.
In a show of respect, his tomb complex was rebuilt as a fortified structure.
Süleyman also visited the tombs of scholars and Sufis who had flocked to
Baghdad across centuries to live in the capital of the medieval Islamic world,
and he spent large amounts of money to embellish and maintain these holy
structures.[19] The names of the first three caliphs of Islam (Abu Bakr, Umar
and Othman), recognized by Sunnis but reviled and at times ritually cursed
by the Safavids, were placed on the walls of the city's mosques. The Ottomans
had also captured Najaf and Karbala, towns that housed some of the holiest
Shiite tomb complexes and shrines, including those belonging to the foundational figure Ali, his son Husayn, and many of their descendants. As these two
towns were situated near Baghdad, Süleyman did not miss the opportunity to
visit them.

Sunni triumphalism aside, the military campaign continued to produce
mixed results while Süleyman was in Baghdad. Tahmasb counter-attacked and
recovered Tabriz at the end of 1534. He then progressed west and laid siege
to the fortress of Van. Süleyman left Baghdad in April 1535 while Tahmasb
once again retreated, and he entered Tabriz a second time in July. He repeated his usual ceremonial gestures there, by staying in Tahmasb's palaces,
and attending the Friday prayer in the city's main mosque. Locating Tahmasb
was another matter, however. Ottoman forces followed the trajectory of the
previous year's expedition toward Soltaniyeh, in better weather this time, but
they returned empty-handed to Tabriz after a month. Süleyman and İbrahim
left Tabriz at the end of August. In early January 1536 the sultan and the grand
vizier were back in Constantinople, where they were greeted with a five-day
celebration after their long absence. As for Tahmasb, he recovered Tabriz
shortly after the Ottomans' departure. He even occupied Van as the Ottoman
forces left the region.

Süleyman's first campaign against the Safavids is called *sefer-i Irakeyn*,
the "Two Iraqs" campaign, in the Ottoman historical tradition. The idea is
to underscore that both the Arab Iraq and the Persian Iraq, that is, western
Iran, had been targeted. The capture of Baghdad is promoted as the crowning
achievement of the campaign, and it is presented as both a carefully planned

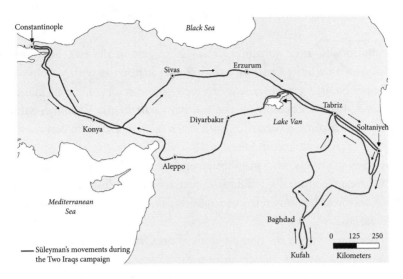

**FIG. 6.1** Süleyman's movements during the Two Iraqs campaign. Map by Jordan Blekking, based on Matrakçı Nasuh, *Beyan-ı menazil*, ed. Yurdaydın, insert after page 307.

operation and a legitimate act. Many historians mention that Baghdad and the surrounding area had been offered to Süleyman by an ex-Safavid tribal leader who had captured the city in 1528, but he had been killed by Tahmasb's forces the following year. Thus, they imply, the Ottomans had a right to be there. One historian argues that Süleyman's victory exposed the falsehood of Safavid claims about the support they received from the Twelve Imams of Shiism. Their belief that the head of the Safavid dynasty had the powers of "sainthood" (*velayet*) and "prophecy" (*keramet*) was proven to be incorrect as well. In fact, it was Süleyman himself, the Master of the Auspicious Conjunction, who had displayed those qualities and used them to prevail over his enemy.[20]

Gaining control over territories with considerable historical and cultural significance for all Muslims, particularly for Shiites, was a milestone in the history of Ottoman imperialism and Sunnism in the sixteenth century. Like Selim's conquest of Aleppo, Damascus, and Cairo, and his control over Mecca and Medina, the capture of Baghdad and the Shiite shrine towns of Karbala and Najaf symbolized a major transfer of cultural and political capital. The Ottomans could now claim to rule over most of the territory of the first Muslim caliphates, together with their possessions in Anatolia and Europe. Sunnism became even more prominent in Ottoman imperial ideology in the decades after Süleyman's first campaign against the Safavids, overshadowing and eventually replacing the messianic and apocalyptic themes of his earlier years.[21]

Additionally, after remaining relatively passive in the east for nearly a decade and a half, the Ottomans thus renewed their ties with various allies in the region. The establishment of a new governorate-general in Erzurum increased their supervision on the northern part of the Ottoman-Safavid frontier in the coming years. The potential to extend Ottoman control from Baghdad into Basra and the Persian Gulf was instantly recognized by contemporary observers as a major gain against the Portuguese and a boon for Ottoman commerce.[22] Tahmasb had remained elusive, however, and Ottoman forces had suffered severe hardships and losses next to tremendous financial costs.

Indeed, tensions at the highest levels of the Ottoman administration had manifested themselves already during the campaign, following the costly march inside Iran and the forced fall back to Baghdad. Quite tellingly, the chief treasurer İskender was dismissed from his post shortly before Süleyman reached Baghdad. İskender, who acted as superintendent of the army during the campaign, had been instrumental in managing and increasing the empire's revenues over the previous decade. The fall from favor of such a prominent figure is an indicator of the sultan's wrath. Within a few months, while Süleyman was still in Baghdad, İskender was executed.

İbrahim's reputation suffered as well. Writing shortly after the end of the campaign, a few Ottoman historians criticized him for having marched on to Tabriz instead of attacking Baghdad as his first objective. Even though they primarily blamed ambitious figures around the grand vizier, most of them ex-Safavids, for his mistake, the message was clear. It is thus tempting to draw a link between the campaign's events and the sudden demise of İbrahim. He was killed on the night of March 14/15, 1536, on the sultan's orders, while staying at Süleyman's palace.

## The End of the Partnership: İbrahim's Demise

İbrahim's execution remains one of the biggest mysteries of Süleyman's reign. Why did the sultan order the murder of his closest collaborator? Did İbrahim suspect anything when he went to the New Palace to spend the night? How did it reflect on Süleyman's reputation to draw his grand vizier into a mortal trap? Was İbrahim strangled during his sleep, or did he fight with his executioners? Was his corpse thrown into the sea, or was he buried somewhere in Constantinople? Was the execution justified on the basis of the

Sharia or the dynastic *kanun*? If he was buried, where is his tomb? A thick sediment of rumors and fantasies have accumulated over the centuries around these questions.

İbrahim's reputation had been declining in the years before Süleyman's first eastern campaign. Anti-İbrahim gossip was widespread in Constantinople. Since the early days of his grand vizierate, there had been stories about how he had undermined other officials to come to and remain in that position. Habsburg diplomats heard even more damning rumors in the first half of 1534, which claimed that İbrahim intended to deliver Süleyman to his Christian enemies; apparently, this is why he always advocated for campaigns on the European front, during which he might find a suitable occasion to do so. While the Habsburg diplomats found this difficult to believe, they felt that İbrahim had made too many enemies and could not remain grand vizier much longer.[23] Guillaume Postel, who was in Constantinople with a French diplomatic mission at the time of the grand vizier's execution, records similar speculations: İbrahim was secretly allied with Charles V; he was allied with Tahmasb; he was allied with Prince Mustafa, whom he wanted to make sultan in Süleyman's place; he was a secret Christian.[24] Like the Habsburgs, Postel found these rumors beyond belief and set out to refute them one by one in a work he published in 1560.[25]

Complementing the observations of the European visitors, many similar rumors are repeated in a popular work of Ottoman history completed around 1541–42. Written by an anonymous author who did not belong to the Ottoman elite, the work displays the negative image of İbrahim among the city's middle and lower classes. İbrahim is blamed for the execution and dismissal of several officials, and their replacement by people like the second vizier Ayas, called a "bribe-taker" (*rüşvethor*). This popular history brims with enmity toward the grand vizier. He is described as "a mischievous man, of short stature, with the voice of a girl" (*Bir kısa boylu kız avazlu fettandı*). He took over the sultanate and manipulated Süleyman as he wanted.[26] He had a secret agreement with the defenders of Vienna in 1529, and he tricked Süleyman to lift the siege. As they abruptly withdrew, thousands of Ottoman raiders were left behind in enemy territory, and many were killed or captured.[27]

These allegations about İbrahim probably reflected growing displeasure in the capital with the grand vizier's ostentatiousness, as well as frustration with the uncertain outcomes of the military campaigns on the European front he had promoted. Indeed, reactions against İbrahim came from too many fronts for him to manage. Perhaps the most memorable outburst of anti-İbrahim sentiment from the time is a Persian couplet attributed to the poet Figanî:

> *In earth's temple have Ibrahims twain appeared;*
> *Idols were by one o'erthrown, by one upreared.*[28]

Here the first İbrahim is the Prophet Abraham, who destroyed idols, and the second İbrahim is the grand vizier, who erected statues in the Hippodrome to celebrate the 1526 victory over the Hungarians. The poet lost his life for this couplet, being arrested and hanged on İbrahim's orders in 1532.[29]

İbrahim had other detractors who were much more powerful than a poet. One of them was quite possibly Hürrem. Almost no evidence about the tensions within Süleyman's close circle has survived, but there are a few clues that point to their existence over time. For instance, already in the spring of 1526, as seen in a remark in one of her letters, Hürrem was irritated by İbrahim, but she sounded confident that the problem could be resolved upon Süleyman's return. Other signs of troubles are found in a letter İbrahim wrote to his wife Muhsine during the Two Iraqs campaign. Muhsine, who was Süleyman's niece, apparently had a falling out with Hürrem. She even refused to attend a banquet that was given on the occasion of the princes' circumcision in 1530. In his letter, İbrahim advises Muhsine to at least pay a visit to offer her condolences upon Hafsa's death, since failing to do so would be very disrespectful.[30]

Beyond matters of etiquette, Hafsa's death may have contributed to the further deterioration of the relationship between Muhsine and Hürrem, with the potential of dragging in their partners. Hürrem became the most prominent female member of the dynasty after Hafsa. While the coldness between Hürrem and Muhsine would have been tempered by Hafsa's conciliatory presence, her death meant that Hürrem did not have to treat Muhsine as an equal of sorts. The way İbrahim and Muhsine presented themselves to the others may have been another source of tension. For instance, like Hürrem and Süleyman, the couple had named their eldest son Mehmed. İbrahim referred to him with the royal title of "shah" in his letters, presumably because his mother was a member of the dynasty. It is likely that he did so publicly as well, which would have led to further observations and criticisms about his pretentiousness.[31]

Contemporary Ottoman observers who left behind accounts of İbrahim's demise provide two sets of explanations for his execution. According to Bostan Çelebi, İbrahim's mind was filled with pride. He lost his foresight as well his manners, to the point of calling himself "commander-in-chief and sultan" (*serlesker sultan*) in his letters.[32] Celalzade Mustafa, who had worked closely with the grand vizier since 1524, agreed with Bostan that İbrahim underwent a change of character. In his earlier days, he was respectful of Sharia and *kanun*. During the Two Iraqs campaign, however, he began listening to the advice of a group of ignorant people. As a result, he strayed from the Sharia by permitting unnecessary bloodshed. Moreover, were it not for İbrahim's laxity and his wasting of time, the true aim of the campaign, the defeat of Tahmasb, could have been achieved.[33] In fact, the only ones in the Ottoman literary elite to say good things about İbrahim after his death were the poets who had lost a generous patron.[34]

Unable to remain oblivious to these rumors and criticisms any longer, Süleyman must have had a sudden change of heart and order the execution of his closest associate. That change must have been so sudden and so well-concealed that İbrahim did not have any immediate cause for concern when he came to spend the night at the palace on March 14, 1536, in the midst of intense negotiations with French diplomats about a Franco-Ottoman alliance. This was death by a thousand rumors, by a growing avalanche of criticisms: İbrahim's ostentatiousness attracted the ire of the entire city as well as the elite, his unabashed panache added further fuel to the fires of envy, and Hürrem and others inside the palace found him irritating, to say the least.[35]

The execution was also a warning to all: despite all his power, in the end İbrahim was but a mere slave of Süleyman, easily dispatched by a single order of the sultan. His considerable wealth was sequestered and returned to the treasury. His young son Mehmed died a few years later, in October 1539.[36] Nothing is known about his wife Muhsine's later years, but she must have suffered the fate of other female members of the Ottoman family who lost their male protector: a difficult life on the margins of the dynasty, as a recipient of occasional charity.

Süleyman, not for the first time in his life, sought consolation in prophecy at this difficult juncture. Haydar the geomancer, another close associate, and another detractor of İbrahim, came to his help by locating a passage in a work of occult sciences. The passage stated, "Do not be heedless of İbrahim for he is a cursed Satan." In the following pages of the same manuscript, under the name of İbrahim, the following commentary was provided: "Dominion has vanished, his name is a cover, his essence is infidel. That is, he was cloaked by this noble name, but his form and fact were known and attested to by the *ulema* of God."[37] In this way, the deceitful character of the grand vizier was ascertained through the power of prophecy.

While Süleyman may have been consoled by Haydar's speculations, at least temporarily, losing his closest associate had a lasting impact. For the rest of his life, he refrained from making other close friends, becoming increasingly lonely at the top of the edifice of the state. In terms of the new imperial agenda Süleyman and İbrahim had devised in 1524–25, this was a turning point as well. The ambitious claims of Ottoman imperialism, based on an idea of universal rule over east and west, had practically run their course. After years of expectations and speculations about a resounding victory over their enemies, the Ottomans were left with stalemates on both fronts, even though they were not yet fully cognizant of this stark reality around 1536.

## Imperial Pursuits after İbrahim

İbrahim had played a prominent role in shaping Ottoman imperial policy in the 1520s and 1530s, both domestically and internationally. After his execution, while Ayas was appointed as grand vizier, Süleyman was obliged to play a larger role in negotiations and problematic situations that used to be managed by İbrahim. He thus entered one of the busiest, most taxing periods of his entire career, during which imperial rivalries became more complex than ever before. The Ottomans were dragged into a series of engagements with high financial cost yet low returns, both economically and politically.

The chief preoccupations of Ottoman imperial policy in the mid-1530s are seen in negotiations conducted in April–June 1534 by Cornelius de Schepper.[38] Schepper had returned to Constantinople with letters from Charles V and Ferdinand to represent both the emperor and his brother. He had audiences with the sultan, as well as conversations with the second vizier (soon grand vizier) Ayas, members of Ayas' household, and Alvise Gritti. Throughout, Schepper repeated Ferdinand's demands for the restitution of Hungary, defended Charles against allegations that he had mistreated Francis I, and denounced the Venetians for providing partial information to the Ottomans, while the Ottoman side insisted on their right to give the crown of Hungary to whomever they wished. Süleyman was quite adamant about his advocacy of the French. Echoing Francis' position, he claimed that peace between the Ottomans and Charles could only be realized after Charles restored the territories he had captured from the French.

By the end of Schepper's mission, it became clear that, as in 1533, Ferdinand was willing to negotiate separately with the Ottomans to continue the ceasefire in central Europe. Moreover, the Mediterranean, already an area of contention, was becoming a new military frontier between Charles and the Ottomans, and the Ottoman-French alliance was becoming stronger. Venice, on the other hand, was increasingly seen by the Ottomans as insufficiently supportive against the Habsburgs. Dreams of universal monarchy and large-scale conquest persisted. Schepper was told by an alarmed Gritti that European Christians should exploit the war between the Ottomans and the Safavids. Otherwise, following the end of their victory over the Safavids, the Ottomans would march on Rome.

Schepper's report about his time in Constantinople also reveals the changed atmosphere in the capital in İbrahim's absence, even though the grand vizier was only away on campaign. The second vizier Ayas, Schepper's main contact, presented himself as a simple intermediary between the envoy and the sultan, while İbrahim had usually established a lively dialogue with diplomats. Süleyman had played a mostly ceremonial role in Schepper's earlier visit, as İbrahim had done most of the talking in his presence, sometimes whispering into Süleyman's ear. In the spring of 1534, Süleyman's voice was heard more prominently. İbrahim's lenient approach in diplomacy and his tendency to make grand promises had frustrated Süleyman, apparently.

In the grand vizier's absence, Süleyman asked questions, interrupted the chief translator Yunus to make a point, and inquired about several details. Süleyman warned Schepper that Gritti, İbrahim's associate, could only discuss Hungarian affairs, and only with Ferdinand. He voiced his dissatisfaction with the vagueness of Charles' demands for peace and his reluctance to fully commit to negotiations. He was clearly angry with the behavior of the Habsburg occupiers of Koroni who, against all decency, had carried away the town's inhabitants and artillery belonging to the Ottomans as they withdrew. Schepper was particularly concerned when he heard that a fleet of eighty ships had left Constantinople in mid-May to fight against the Habsburgs, under the command of Hızır Hayreddin (d. 1546), known throughout the Mediterranean as Barbarossa ("Red Beard" in Italian).

A greater naval presence in the Mediterranean had been on Süleyman and İbrahim's agenda for some time, and Habsburg forays into the eastern Mediterranean in 1532 had quickened their reaction. One Ottoman response was to build new ships at the arsenal in Constantinople. The other was to extend an offer of alliance to Barbarossa.[39] Barbarossa, a Muslim corsair born in the eastern Mediterranean, had established himself as a prominent military and political figure in the western Mediterranean in the early decades of the sixteenth century. He had communicated with Selim around 1519 but a comprehensive alliance, including joint operations, had not been achieved. From

his base in Algiers, on the northwest African coast, Barbarossa interacted and
competed with Arab Muslim and European Christian magnates, merchants,
and pirates on the Ibero-African frontier.[40]

There, too, Charles' growing stature and the slow yet assured expansion
of Habsburg power forced unlikely figures to become allies. Barbarossa had
been contacted by the French in 1533 and he signed an agreement with them
in 1534. Just before, in the fall of 1533, he traveled to Constantinople at the
invitation of Süleyman. This was yet another case of a smaller, regional power
being subsumed by expanding empires and dynastic states. Barbarossa, who
had styled himself "sultan of Algiers," and who was known by that title to a
variety of audiences around the Mediterranean, had to end his long and tumultuous career as an Ottoman official.[41]

When Barbarossa arrived in Constantinople at the beginning of
December 1533, with a fleet of twenty ships, he went to great lengths to make
an impressive entry. He showered the sultan with precious gifts, which fea-
tured valuable goods brought from north Africa as well as the loot taken by
Barbarossa and his men on the way to the capital. These included twenty-
five enslaved boys, two Black eunuchs, cups and ewers made of precious
metals, several wild cats, a large quantity of precious clothes, and two clocks.
Süleyman duly reciprocated, and Barbarossa was lodged in a palatial residence
on the Hippodrome. The sultan personally put a fur-ringed coat around his
shoulders during an audience and called the corsair "my holy warrior elder"
(*mücahid lalam*); to further show his affection, the usually distant Süleyman
patted the corsair on his back three times.

Still mindful of İbrahim's role as grand vizier and commander-in-chief,
Süleyman then sent Barbarossa to Aleppo, where the grand vizier was
spending the winter before the campaign against Tahmasb. Barbarossa was
met with great pomp there as well. After the reception, the seasoned corsair
and the skilled negotiator must have discussed European politics, a topic on
which both were particularly knowledgeable. İbrahim, using his authority
to appoint officials, named Barbarossa head of a newly instituted unit: the
governorate-general of the "Mediterranean ports and islands" (*cezair-i Bahr-i
Sefid*). He also became "captain of the sea" (*kapudan-ı derya*), that is, commander of the fleet.[42] This was a mutually beneficial agreement. Barbarossa,
the experienced sailor, relinquished some of his autonomy to the sultan. In
return, he received help in the form of men, ships and other materials, money,
and political/diplomatic support. The fact that he was already in contact with
the French was another advantage at a time when France and the Ottomans
were getting closer.

In the initial years of his service to the sultan, Barbarossa's activities produced mixed results. In the summer of 1534, after raiding the southern Italian coast, he captured Tunis from its Arab Muslim rulers, the Hafsid dynasty, in August. This led to a counterattack by Charles, who took Tunis in July 1535 and restored the Hafsids, his Muslim allies, to power. Barbarossa escaped. He reportedly received another warm welcome from Süleyman when they met in the spring of 1536, despite his defeat and escape. Apparently, the sultan teasingly called him "my runaway elder" (*kaçagun lalam*) first, but he then switched to his earlier appellation, "my holy warrior elder." He assured Barbarossa that he could keep his position as commander of the fleet. Elated, the corsair pulled out from his bosom a rosary with beads of pearl, a diamond ring mounted with a compass, and a golden watch studded with jewels, gifts that were both practical and fashionable, and presented them to the sultan.[43]

On the other side of the Mediterranean, Barbarossa's defeat had given Charles a major opportunity for burnishing his reputation further.[44] After necessarily adopting a defensive position vis-à-vis the Ottomans between 1529 and 1535, he had now personally organized an expedition against the Muslim enemy and commanded a difficult amphibious operation with considerable skill. After taking Tunis, and full of pride and glee, Charles traveled to Naples, from where he marched on to Rome to meet with the recently elected Pope Paul III. He organized processions and celebrations along the way. Charles' victory was further circulated, in text and image, by writers and painters who had accompanied him during the expedition. The most striking cultural outcome of the campaign is a series of tapestries ordered by Charles in 1546. The tapestries became one of the most precious heirlooms of the Habsburg dynasty and they were displayed often on ceremonial occasions in subsequent centuries.[45]

Another important development around this time was the renewed vigor of the Ottoman-French alliance. After Charles' election over Francis as Holy Roman Emperor in 1519, the competition between the two had revolved around the leadership and defense of Christianity. In an age of seemingly unstoppable Ottoman expansion and profound Catholic-Protestant divisions, Francis' image in Europe was harmed by his portrayal by Habsburg propagandists as pro-Ottoman. This is one of the reasons why, despite making the first overtures to the Ottomans in 1525–26, Francis had been reluctant to fully commit to joint action. The Ottomans, careful observers of European politics, were aware of Francis' oft-changing position vis-à-vis the Habsburgs, which could quickly shift from enmity to treaty, and they were frustrated. Still, they found it useful to portray themselves as the friends and protectors of Francis in their negotiations with the Habsburg envoys.[46] Of course, given the means of communication of the period and the logistical challenges of mounting joint campaigns, even a perfect agreement between the French and the Ottomans might not have produced the desired outcome.

When the French found it convenient to get closer to the Ottomans once again in the early 1530s, the Ottomans were ready to oblige. The first step of this new era was the mission of the French envoy Jean de la Fôret, which started in 1534. He was first sent to North Africa to communicate with Barbarossa; he then proceeded to Constantinople, from where he traveled with Süleyman to the east during the Two Iraqs campaign. De la Fôret's negotiations seem to have extended into the legal and economic privileges to be granted to French and French-protected merchants. Even though a formal agreement was not signed, French commerce in the eastern Mediterranean and the Ottoman territories grew considerably in the coming decades. The increased rapprochement and ensuing mobility also led to the production of multiple works by French travelers on the lands, culture, and society of the Ottomans from the late 1530s onward.[47] One of the earliest arrivals was Guillaume Postel, a scholar of languages, cosmographer, and advocate of universal religious comity, who traveled with de la Fôret.[48]

While the economic and cultural relations took time to unfold, de la Fôret's negotiations, completed under the shadow of İbrahim's execution, produced two immediate outcomes. The first was the institution of a French resident envoy in Constantinople, which made the French a permanent presence in Ottoman political and diplomatic life. The second was a joint military campaign targeting the Italian peninsula. This was in accordance with instructions given by Francis to de la Fôret. The king of France was aware of the entangled nature of alliances and counter-alliances across Europe in the 1520s and 1530s. According to his instructions, even though the German princes, many of them Protestant, did not necessarily obey Charles, they lent their support to the emperor when their own lands were under threat. The Ottomans should therefore be dissuaded from campaigns in central Europe. An attack against Italy or Spain was better, since the German princes would not fight for those lands.[49] Of course, this might also allow Francis to enter Italy once again, either as an Ottoman ally or under the guise of the defense of Christianity.

The initial plan was for the French to attack the Habsburgs in northern Italy, as they had already done so the year before, while the Ottomans invaded the south, and their joint fleets chased the Habsburgs and their allies in the Mediterranean. Another reason behind the campaign was to draw the

FIG. 1 Süleyman painted in European style, ca. 1530s. Venetian origin, attributed to Titian. Courtesy of the Kunsthistorisches Museum Wien.

**FIG. 2** Prophet Solomon on his throne, placed above saintly figures, kings, military men, and creatures of the unseen world. Uzun Firdevsî, *Süleymanname*, Chester Beatty Library, T 406.1 © The Trustees of the Chester Beatty Library, Dublin.

FIG. 3 Süleyman's accession to the throne. *Sulaymannama*, 17b. Courtesy of the T.C. Cumhurbaşkanlığı Milli Saraylar İdaresi Başkanlığı.

FIG. 4 Süleyman is entertained by musicians and dancers. Detail from *Sulaymannama*, 71a. Courtesy of the T.C. Cumhurbaşkanlığı Milli Saraylar İdaresi Başkanlığı.

**FIG. 5** Süleyman (in the center) at the hunt. *Sulaymannama*, 115a. Courtesy of the T.C. Cumhurbaşkanlığı Milli Saraylar İdaresi Başkanlığı.

**FIG. 6** Süleyman (in the center, on a black horse) at the Battle of Mohács, 1526. *Sulaymannama*, 219b. Courtesy of the T.C. Cumhurbaşkanlığı Milli Saraylar İdaresi Başkanlığı.

FIG. 7 Süleyman is brought the crown of St. Stephen, the main component of Hungarian royal regalia, in 1529. Detail from *Sulaymannama*, 309a. Courtesy of the T.C. Cumhurbaşkanlığı Milli Saraylar İdaresi Başkanlığı.

**FIG. 8** Süleyman listens to a scholarly debate during the circumcision celebrations in 1530. Detail from *Hünername*, 123a. Courtesy of the T.C. Cumhurbaşkanlığı Milli Saraylar İdaresi Başkanlığı.

**FIG. 9** Süleyman receives the famed sea captain Hayreddin Barbarossa in 1533. Detail from *Sulaymannama*, 360a. Courtesy of the T.C. Cumhurbaşkanlığı Milli Saraylar İdaresi Başkanlığı.

FIG. 10 After his execution on the night of March 14/15, 1536, İbrahim's corpse is taken out of Süleyman's palace and loaded onto a vessel. *Hünername*, 165b. Courtesy of the T.C. Cumhurbaşkanlığı Milli Saraylar İdaresi Başkanlığı.

**FIG. 11** While out hunting, Süleyman listens to the grievances of an old woman. *Hünername*, 152b. Courtesy of the T.C. Cumhurbaşkanlığı Milli Saraylar İdaresi Başkanlığı.

**FIG. 12** Süleyman hunts in the company of his sons. *Sulaymannama*, 462b. Courtesy of the T.C. Cumhurbaşkanlığı Milli Saraylar İdaresi Başkanlığı.

**FIG. 13** Following their execution on October 6, 1553, the corpses of Prince Mustafa (bottom center) and two of his close associates (bottom left) are exhibited. *Hünername,* 71a. Courtesy of the T.C. Cumhurbaşkanlığı Milli Saraylar İdaresi Başkanlığı.

**FIG. 14** Süleyman asks for God's wrath against his rebel son Bayezid. *Hünername*, 212a. Courtesy of the T.C. Cumhurbaşkanlığı Milli Saraylar İdaresi Başkanlığı.

FIG. 15 During his final campaign, unable to ride on his horse anymore, Süleyman is helped by the grand vizier Sokullu Mehmed to dismount; he will be transferred to his carriage, shown bottom left. *Hünername*, 276a. Courtesy of the T.C. Cumhurbaşkanlığı Milli Saraylar İdaresi Başkanlığı.

FIG. 16 Süleyman's funeral in Constantinople. Seyyid Lokman, *Tetimme-i Ahval-i Sultan Süleyman*, Chester Beatty Library, T 413, 115v © The Trustees of the Chester Beatty Library, Dublin.

Venetians forcefully to the Ottoman-French side and dissuade them from supporting the Habsburgs. The resulting campaign of 1537 is alternately known as the *Pulya* (after the southeastern Italian region of Puglia) or the Corfu campaign in Ottoman sources. The Ottoman fleet indeed raided the Italian shore, and particularly Puglia, and landed soldiers in Otranto; later in the campaign, the Venetian fortifications on the island of Corfu were besieged.

This was Süleyman's first campaign in the post-İbrahim period. Given its high stakes, such as an eventual invasion of the Italian peninsula, and the power vacuum at the top, Süleyman personally assumed responsibility for leading the Ottoman forces toward Italy in May 1537. He is thus presented in near-contemporary sources as the supreme decision-maker and ultimate commander. Moreover, this was the first campaign in which two of his sons, Mehmed and Selim, accompanied him. Their presence in a military campaign, very much like their public appearances in 1530 during the celebration of their circumcision, gave a message of dynastic continuity. At the same time, the growth of the princes made Süleyman a mature figure, increasingly closer to the threshold of old age. He was in his mid-forties in May 1537, when he left Constantinople with his sons in the direction of Italy.[50]

In early July 1537, Süleyman and his sons reached Avlonya (today Vlorë) in Albania, across from Puglia on the other side of the Adriatic. There, to Süleyman's frustration, it was discovered that the promised French attack on northern Italy had not taken place, rendering moot Ottoman plans to enter southern Italy. The only sign of the alliance was the arrival of a small fleet under the command of the Baron of Saint-Blancard, a sort of French exploratory force assessing the economic and environmental conditions in the eastern Mediterranean.[51] As the prospect of a joint Ottoman-French campaign collapsed, the Ottomans spent their time reestablishing alliances with tribal leaders in Albania, whose willingness to help the Habsburgs and their allies had been a matter of concern. Next, the Ottomans turned to the Venetians at Corfu, an island close to the southern Albanian coast, to punish them for their recent failures to fully support the Ottomans. However, the early arrival of cold weather and strong winds at sea prevented a longer siege.

If the Ottoman sources are to be taken literally Süleyman showed mercy to his warriors and ordered the land and naval forces to withdraw from the area. Tens of thousands of troops, hundreds of thousands of animals, the entire fleet, the palace household and its personnel, and auxiliary troops all over the Balkans had been mobilized for the prospect of a joint attack with the French and the dream of ultimate victory over the Habsburgs and their allies.

The invasion of Italy by the Ottomans, an event that was much anticipated and feared by believers in apocalyptic speculations among both Muslims and Christians, had been downgraded into the pacification of a group of Albanian tribal chiefs.

To further frustrate the Ottomans, Venice, the papacy, and the Order of St. John, alarmed both by the 1537 campaign and by clashes in Croatia between Ferdinand and Ottoman forces, formed the Holy League with the Habsburgs in early 1538 as both a defensive and offensive alliance. According to the treaty that underwrote the league, Charles was to be emperor of Constantinople following victory over the Ottomans.[52] The French then signed the Truce of Nice with the Habsburgs in June 1538, rendering the 1537 campaign entirely futile.

Süleyman's next military venture, in 1538, was similarly a result of and a response to the complicated imperial rivalries across Europe and the Mediterranean. Following the failed invasion of Italy, many in Europe expected another attack in Italy or central Europe.[53] Süleyman's invasion of the principality of Moldavia must have surprised those observers. Contemporary Ottoman sources provide vague reasons for it. These include the unreliability of the Moldavian rulers, who had paid an annual tribute to the Ottomans since the mid-fifteenth century, and the recent activities of the current *voivode* Petru Rareş, who had reportedly refused to submit to the Ottomans and engaged in activities harmful to Muslims.[54] As usual, these vague passages hide a more complicated reality.

Petru Rareş was yet another regional ruler who was drawn into the dangerous waters of the Ottoman-Habsburg rivalry. Lately, he had been sliding toward Ferdinand. The king of Poland Sigismund I, Petru's northern neighbor, was concerned about Habsburg expansionism in central and eastern Europe. Signatory to a comprehensive treaty with the Ottomans in 1533, Sigismund advocated the removal of Petru, an unruly and covetous neighbor, and offered help in case of war. To make matters worse for himself, Petru had been implicated in the assassination of Alvise Gritti in Transylvania in 1534. Even though Gritti mainly followed his own agenda of self-enrichment and political ascent, he was a crucial interlocutor between the Ottomans and several European powers, and his death was a major diplomatic incident.

From a wider perspective, Wallachia and Moldavia, vassals of the Ottomans with their own rulers called *voivodes*, occupied an area that was critical both for the security of the Ottoman realm and the control of the Black Sea and north-south trade.[55] These different factors came together to form the background for a military campaign. The naval front could not be ignored this time either, since it had become an active zone of confrontation between the Ottomans, the Habsburgs, and their allies. The recent establishment of the Holy League gave strategic as well as ideological salience to the presence in the Mediterranean of Barbarossa, who left Constantinople in early July 1538.[56]

For Süleyman, this was not a campaign organized with a sense of urgency, as evidenced by the late departure from Constantinople, toward the end of July. The overemphasis on his ceremonial role in the post-İbrahim period was once again manifested: the unfurling of seven banners and four horsetail standards in the palace courtyard, symbolizing Süleyman's rule over the seven climes and the four corners of the world; a slow procession through decorated streets by the sultan and his sons Mehmed and Selim; the dramatic farewell, at the city gates, by religious scholars and dervishes, who prayed for the sultan's good fortune and victory over the infidel. This was to be Süleyman's least challenging campaign, of which he must have had an inkling beforehand.

Indeed, Petru faced a large coalition that rendered any defensive action by him moot. As Polish forces entered his realm from the north, the Ottomans, joined by Wallachian and Crimean troops, plundered Moldavia. Petru's treasury, including precious objects ranging from icons and bibles to cups and weapons, fell into the hands of the Ottomans as the city of Suceava surrendered. Petru escaped, and his nephew Stefan was made *voivode* by the Ottomans, just as they had anointed John Szapolyai king of Hungary nearly a decade previously. Perhaps more critically, the *voivode* was treated as a sort of Ottoman official, instead of a tribute-paying ruler. Stefan's accession was approved during a meeting of the Ottoman imperial council. He was asked to swear on a copy of the Bible and on the cross to serve the Ottomans. He was presented with a copy of the document underlining the new relationship, and he was given a red skullcap with golden braids to be worn as a sign of his appointment by the Ottomans. Always mindful of strategic issues, the Ottomans also annexed a part of Moldavia in the southeast, thus increasing their control over the Black Sea shore and the north-south trade between Constantinople and Lviv.

Following Charles' victory at Tunis, and the insignificant outcome of the 1537 campaign, the fortunes of Ottoman imperialism had turned one more time. Contemporary Ottoman observers thought as much. As Süleyman returned from Moldavia, after having acted again as distributor of crowns, he received news of a major naval victory against the fleet of the Holy League. The two foremost naval tacticians in the Mediterranean, Barbarossa and Andrea Doria, came to blows near the port of Prevesa on September 28, with Barbarossa prevailing against Doria and his larger battle fleet. This was the beginning of the end for the Holy League, which became inactive despite the pleas of Pope Paul III. In the summer of 1539, the Venetians finally sent an envoy to Constantinople to negotiate peace.[57]

The boost in imperial self-confidence was seen in another circumcision ceremony, organized for princes Bayezid and Cihangir in Constantinople, between November 26 and December 8, 1539. Similar to their brothers' circumcision in 1530, the palace and the entire city were mobilized. Envoys from Ferdinand, the French, and the Venetians were present during the celebrations, visible to all in their loggias in the Hippodrome. Viziers, governors-general, district governors, members of the palace household, janissaries, scholars, and city dwellers joined the atmosphere of jubilation through parades, banquets, mock battles, performances of music, and shows with jugglers and trained animals, all brought together through the sultan's largesse.[58]

The celebrations also marked the wedding between Süleyman's daughter Mihrümah and an accomplished career official named Rüstem. While two more of Süleyman's sons stepped into the limelight through this rite of passage, the family further expanded with the arrival of a new son-in-law who also happened to be a capable administrator.[59] The positive mood continued unhindered in 1540, buoyed by a peace treaty with Venice in October of that year. The treaty was very much an outcome of Barbarossa's recent activities, which had disrupted Venetian commerce in the eastern half of the Mediterranean. Venice agreed to pay a hefty sum of three hundred thousand

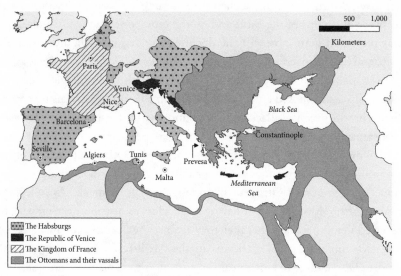

FIG. 6.2   Major powers around the Mediterranean, ca. 1550. Map by Jordan Blekking.

ducats and relinquish its claims over a number of islands and fortresses recently captured by the Ottomans. A strong presence in the Mediterranean, sought by Süleyman and İbrahim since the early 1530s, was finally established.[60] However, the imperial rivalries were unrelenting, and the triumphal atmosphere of 1540 provided only a brief respite.

## Süleyman's Return to Hungary

John Szapolyai's reign in Hungary had depended on his careful maneuvering between Süleyman and Ferdinand. Alvise Gritti's assassination in 1534 freed him from an overseer who both represented the Ottomans and pursued his personal interests. In this environment, he sought a rapprochement with Ferdinand.

Szapolyai was unmarried and childless for most of his life. In the second half of the 1530s, it seems that his main priority was to make sure he remained king until his death. After lengthy negotiations, begun in 1535, Ferdinand and Szapolyai entered into a secret agreement in February 1538. With the Treaty of Grosswardein/Nagyvárad (today Oradea in Romania), Ferdinand recognized Szapolyai as king over the Hungarian territories already under his control, while Szapolyai recognized Ferdinand's rule over the western one-third of Hungary he held. More importantly, he accepted Ferdinand's right to inherit the entire kingdom after his death. In case he were to have an heir (which looked unlikely at the time of the signing since he was unmarried), the heir would inherit some of Szapolyai's ancestral lands with the rank of duke.

The treaty disregarded the electoral privileges of the nobility by turning Hungarian kingship into a purely dynastic institution under the Habsburgs. Anti-Habsburg Hungarian nobles, concerned about losing their privileges, forced Szapolyai into a marriage in 1539. The bride was Isabella, the daughter of the king of Poland Sigismund I, who had his own reasons to be wary of the Habsburgs. In July 1540, the couple had a child: John Sigismund, named after two kings, his father and his grandfather. When Szapolyai unexpectedly died two weeks after his son's birth, the fate of Hungary once again became a matter of contention, pitting Ferdinand and the Ottomans against each other, with Queen Isabella and the baby John Sigismund in the middle.[61]

Ferdinand, arguing that Szapolyai's death gave him the right to rule over Hungary, entered into negotiations with Queen Isabella and sent an envoy to Constantinople, while a contingent of his men took Pest and laid siege to the Hungarian capital Buda in the fall of 1540.[62] His persistence worried the Ottomans, in terms of both their ideological rivalry and the prospect of a growing Habsburg presence in central-eastern Europe. News about Safavid missions to the Habsburgs, to establish an anti-Ottoman alliance, gave them further cause for concern.[63]

Ferdinand's envoy to Constantinople, Hieronymus Łaski, describes Ottoman reactions in the diary he submitted to Ferdinand after his mission.[64] Łaski had been one of Szapolyai's closest supporters and representatives between 1526 and 1534, but had joined Ferdinand's side after a falling out. As someone who knew well all the issues at hand and who had been to Constantinople before, he was a shrewd choice. Indeed, he appears to have skillfully defended Ferdinand's position. In addition to the earlier claim to the Hungarian throne through marriage, Łaski brought up the secret agreement between Ferdinand and Szapolyai. He even intimated that John Sigismund may not have been Szapolyai's son.

During these negotiations, Süleyman was accompanied by his son-in-law Rüstem, recently promoted to the rank of vizier. The Ottomans answered Habsburg claims with their own argument that it was their right, thanks to their victory in 1526, to determine the next king of Hungary. The angry reactions of Süleyman and Rüstem toward the Habsburg envoy are palpable in these pages, written in Latin by a diplomat under considerable stress. Some of their anger must have been a performance, meant to put pressure on Łaski. It is also quite likely that Süleyman took his commitments seriously, and saw them as matters of personal honor.

Thus, both Rüstem, probably eager to make his mark at this early stage of his vizierate, and the sultan, uncharacteristically raised their voices during the negotiations, frustrated by Łaski's defense of Ferdinand's actions. Süleyman asked about Charles V as well. When he heard that the emperor was at Regensburg to attend a diet of the imperial constituents, he became agitated. This meant, as the sultan knew well, another attempt to create Christian unity under Charles' command and to secure financial and military support from the German princes. "It is now winter," Süleyman uttered, "but summer will surely come." This was a barely veiled threat of violence, since summer was the season during which the sultan typically led his army into battle.

Süleyman initially wanted to preserve the Kingdom of Hungary as a buffer zone. In the fall of 1540, he had welcomed Hungarian envoys sent by Queen Isabella and promised his father's throne to John Sigismund, who was elected king by the Hungarian Diet in September 1540.[65] The failure of the negotiations with Łaski and another Habsburg siege of Buda in spring–summer 1541 forced the Ottomans to react differently.[66] Süleyman first sent a contingent to rescue the besieged city. Given the gravity of the situation and some initial reversals suffered by the Ottoman forces, he himself left for Hungary in late June, accompanied by his sons Mehmed and Selim. In the meantime, the grand vizier Süleyman was sent to the east, with a few thousand janissaries, for fear of a Safavid attack in coordination with the Habsburgs.

Even though the sultan's camp was flooded near Constantinople, he rallied quickly and continued his march. As he progressed, the Ottoman forces sent ahead of him defeated the Habsburg besiegers of Buda. Süleyman reached the city's vicinity at the end of August. There, he was presented with weapons, banners, small and large drums, and other equipment captured from Ferdinand's forces. This macabre ritual of Ottoman supremacy included three thousand war prisoners, whom Süleyman ordered to be executed. For the second time in fifteen years, the Hungarian capital now lay before him, almost completely defenseless.

As in 1526, the Ottomans were in the position of determining the political future of Hungary. This time, however, they opted for a different solution. The Ottoman conquest of Hungary had been a major theme in apocalyptic tales for nearly two centuries, but it seems that more pragmatic reasons were at the forefront in 1541. Even though the Ottomans had been inclined to recognize John Sigismund as king, he was a toddler. The varying loyalties of the Hungarian nobles and clergymen gathered around him were an additional source of concern. The inability of the Hungarian kingdom to serve as a military counterweight against the Habsburgs was another reason. Also, the Ottoman enterprise relied heavily on the capture of territory and resources to the benefit of the sultan and the *askerî* elite, and the annexation of large parts of Hungary obviously represented an opportunity in that regard.[67]

Little did the Ottomans know that their possessions in Hungary would constitute an important financial burden in the coming decades, due to the near-constant state of war on the frontier. Moreover, as in the case of many other Ottoman military advances, the partitioning of Szapolyai's kingdom led to yet another wave of panic, self-recrimination, and crusader zeal across Europe. Finally, Ferdinand, whom Ottoman observers thought of as foolish for spending large resources for an impossible dream, remained as determined as ever to rule over the entire territory of pre-1526 Hungary.[68]

Before entering Buda, and always concerned with legality and ritual, Süleyman ordered that Queen Isabella and John Sigismund be brought to his encampment. One Ottoman observer remarks that Süleyman made the little John Sigismund sit on his knees as a sign of affection. He was made *voivode* of Transylvania (*Erdel* in Ottoman), a position his father had held before becoming king. Friar George Martinuzzi, a close collaborator of Szapolyai and the architect of the secret agreement between him and Ferdinand, was to act as guardian of the prince. The remainder of Szapolyai's kingdom was taken over by the Ottomans.

The pre-1526 Hungarian kingdom was thus divided among the Habsburgs in the west and northwest, the Ottomans in the middle, and John Sigismund in the east and northeast. An imperial diploma outlined his new position and promised him the Hungarian throne when he reached the age of majority. However, the establishment of a new Ottoman governorate-general around Buda made that promise ring hollow. The governorate-general was a sign of the Ottoman intention to establish deeper, longer control over the area, one that could not be secured through a vassal kingdom. Moreover, as in the case of Stefan, *voivode* of Moldavia, the diploma and the ceremony clearly indicated that the Ottomans viewed John Sigismund as a subordinate of the sultan, bound by oath and obligation to follow Süleyman's orders.

The intention to establish lasting Ottoman control in the area was further manifested by the march of the Ottoman forces into Buda, the erection of banners on the city walls, and the conversion of the city's cathedral into a mosque as a sign of formal conquest. On September 2, Süleyman entered Buda and attended the Friday prayer in the cathedral. An experienced career officer who had previously served as governor-general of Baghdad and Anadolu was appointed as Buda's first governor-general, and Süleyman began his return journey toward Constantinople in mid-September.

Süleyman must have been further comforted by the prominent role played by his son-in-law Rüstem during the campaign. For the first time after İbrahim's execution in 1536, Süleyman had found the kind of high official he needed: quick on his feet, with a flair for dramatic acts, deferential to the sultan, yet comfortable with taking initiative. On the way back, in a letter suffused with pride, he informed the Venetians of the developments. After a short introduction that underlined the Ottomans' right over the destiny of Hungary, the letter offers a detailed account of the military operations, the defeat of Ferdinand's forces, and the occupation of Buda. The Ottoman annexation is presented almost nonchalantly, as part of a natural progression of events.[69] Once again, Süleyman had exercised his right to appoint kings: in this case, by practically dethroning a king-elect in the person of John Sigismund.

Neither diplomacy nor war were sufficient to alleviate the ongoing tensions in Hungary, however, even though Ferdinand tried both. While he continued to negotiate with the Ottomans and John Sigismund's guardian Martinuzzi, he sent a large force to besiege Pest. The composition of the force (troops committed by the German princes, Hungarian allies of the Habsburgs, and mercenaries) provides clues about how and from where Ferdinand drafted military support. The siege began at the end of September, but it soon dissolved into a disorderly withdrawal due to the absence of co-ordination among these disparate units.[70] Süleyman decided to return to central Europe in 1543 as the Ottoman fleet set sail towards the western Mediterranean: French diplomats, particularly active in Constantinople since 1536, had convinced the Ottomans to undertake a joint campaign, despite the failure of 1537.[71]

Süleyman left Edirne toward the end of April 1543, while Barbarossa sailed from Constantinople a month later. After raiding Sicily and southern Italy, he joined the French in early July. The target was Nice, which belonged to Charles III Duke of Savoy (d. 1553), an ally of Charles V. The attacking force consisted of nearly one hundred Ottoman galleys and fifty French ones. The siege started in early August and resulted in the surrender of the city on August 22, but the citadel remained in the hands of the defenders, possibly due to the French failure to provide sufficient gunpowder to Barbarossa. News of the arrival of a relief army forced the Franco-Ottoman forces to withdraw. Barbarossa and his men, numbering around thirty thousand, including a few thousand janissaries, spent the winter in Toulon, emptied for the use of the Ottomans.

While the Ottoman fleet used its presence in the region to harass Habsburg allies, the costly joint campaign did not turn into a major military operation against Spain or Italy. Its impact on morale was tremendous, however, since the wintering of thousands of Ottoman soldiers in western Europe was terrifying for many across Europe. Francis, it seems, was once again concerned about the extent of his alliance with the Ottomans and his image vis-à-vis his fellow Christian princes.[72] It appears that he could not wait to be rid of Barbarossa and his men.

The land campaign produced better results for Süleyman. His campaigns in 1529 and 1532 had been focused on the display of Ottoman military might and the ideological competition with the Habsburgs. In 1543, he had a specific objective: to consolidate the newly established governorate-general of Buda. Thus, from early July to early September, the Ottomans extended their zone of control around Buda by capturing important fortresses such as Siklós, Pécs, Esztergom, and Székesfehérvár. These were historically Hungarian cities that had fallen under Ferdinand's control after 1526. The latter two had very strong fortifications, and the Ottomans suffered considerable casualties during short yet very violent sieges. Contemporary Ottoman sources talk about the defenders' skilled use of small- and large-caliber gunpowder weapons, instances of close combat across breached walls, skirmishes inside cities, and moats filled with Ottoman and enemy corpses.

These are not simple tales of heroism. Already in 1541, all of the Ottoman observers had noted the Habsburg forces' construction of a fortified encampment (called *istabur* in Ottoman) near Buda for defensive purposes. In 1543, the difficulty faced by the Ottomans, particularly during the capture of Esztergom and Székesfehérvár, was the harbinger of future sieges, where new forms of fortifications and infantry tactics would pose serious challenges to Ottoman domination on the battlefield. Another significant aspect of the 1543 campaign was the presence of Muslim settlers, who quickly took up residence in the conquered cities. This was a further indication that, despite their promises to John Sigismund and Queen Isabella, the Ottomans had long-term plans for their new governorate-general in Buda.

The Ottomans felt extremely proud upon capturing these old Hungarian cities. They were already aware of many myths about their storied past. Székesfehérvár, for instance, had been established by an ancient king five millennia after the fall of Adam, and had seen the days of Alexander the Great. Indeed, only Alexander, the first Master of the Auspicious Conjunction, had previously been able to take that city by force. That honor now belonged to Süleyman. Székesfehérvár's cathedral had been the burial ground for Hungarian kings, and the Ottoman victors were quite impressed by the ornate tombs of past monarchs. Still, as one Ottoman observer dryly remarks, the signs of a faith destined to perdition were erased as the Ottomans turned the cathedral into a mosque.

Süleyman was mindful of other symbolic aspects of campaigning as well. His sons Mehmed and Selim had been assigned to district governorships, but his younger son Bayezid accompanied him in 1543. His son-in-law Rüstem, like in the previous campaign, carried the rank of second vizier and played an important role throughout. Süleyman celebrated the capture of Ezstergom with martial music in front of his tent and attended the Friday prayer in the city's newly converted cathedral. During the ultimate general attack against the walls of Székesfehérvár, he looked on from an elevation, praying with the members of his palace household, visible to his troops. Despite his advancing age and the first signs of an illness that would continue to bother him during the rest of his life, he presented himself as the ultimate authority who decided the fate of nations and kingdoms.

There were no Ottoman campaigns in central Europe for several years. In Europe, there were expectations of an Ottoman push toward Vienna after the conquests of 1543, and the rumors were supported by news of military preparations in Constantinople. However, the preparations were halted later in 1544 for reasons that remain unclear. Seeking peace, treating rivals magnanimously, and being open to negotiation were, very much like heroism in war, important components of the performance of sovereignty in this period. While the military-political elites were unable to fully abandon their martial outlook, they knew well that the absence of war meant the preservation of human life and money, to put it bluntly, and the Ottoman side was ready to negotiate.

Ferdinand had even more reasons to engage in a new round of diplomacy. The replacement of a militarily weaker figure like Szapolyai by the Ottomans was disastrous for him. The new governorate-general in Buda allowed the Ottomans to react to Ferdinand's military and political initiatives quickly and with more power than was ever available to Szapolyai. The lack of financial resources and Charles' reluctance to fully commit to his brother's help further undermined Ferdinand's position, especially given his lack of a strong demographic base for military recruitment and his reliance on mercenary forces and the support of unpredictable allies.[73]

As for Charles, the first half of the 1540s started with a stunning defeat, followed by a stunning victory. A second amphibious operation he organized and commanded, directed at Barbarossa's old base of Algiers, was hit by rain and storms in October 1541, and Charles returned to Spain, beaten by the weather and after a tremendous loss of life and equipment, at the beginning of December. In the coming years, however, a successful invasion of France gave a much-needed boost to his reputation and his self-confidence. The Treaty of Crépy in September 1544 not only ended the war, but also stipulated a dynastic marriage between the French Valois dynasty and the Habsburgs and discussed a joint effort by both rulers against Protestantism. The French also committed to help the Habsburgs seek peace with the Ottomans.[74]

In this environment, Ferdinand, the ruler who most needed a peace agreement in central Europe, made the first steps in that direction by negotiating a ceasefire with the governor-general of Buda, a position that was already becoming the main point of contact between the Ottomans and the Habsburgs of Austria. Ferdinand's haste is also seen in his deputization of a Portuguese envoy on the way to Constantinople to negotiate on his behalf. He then dispatched his own envoy, who reached Edirne in February 1545 but died soon after. A replacement arrived in early summer, followed by French and Habsburg diplomats, who traveled together. The Ottomans had insisted, during previous negotiations with Ferdinand's envoys, that Charles should negotiate with them separately. They finally got their wish with the arrival of Charles' representative Gerard Veltwycjk.

Süleyman's son-in-law Rüstem, elevated to the rank of grand vizier in late 1544, played a crucial role in the negotiations, further cementing his place within the Ottoman administration. An eighteen-month truce was agreed upon in October 1545, and a treaty was signed in June 1547, the first formal agreement between the Ottomans and Charles. The Ottoman version of the treaty recognized Ferdinand's occupation of parts of Hungary in the west and the northwest, in conjunction with the Ottoman claim that they had the final say over the lands of Hungary. It included clauses about limiting the violence on the frontier, securing and protecting the flow of merchants and goods, and returning runaway subjects seeking refuge on the other side. It also had a pan-European dimension: it established a five-year peace between Charles, Ferdinand, the Ottomans, the French, and Venice.

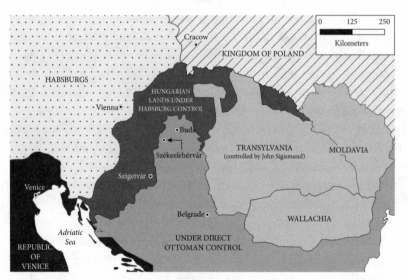

FIG. 6.3 Central-southeastern Europe, ca. 1549. Transylvania, Wallachia, and Moldavia are vassals of the Ottomans. Map by Jordan Blekking, based on an original map by Béla Nagy.

The Ottoman side, as always, was mindful of the symbolic aspects of the diplomatic exchanges. Süleyman was presented as sultan of sultans and the Shadow of God on Earth in the text, while the treaty called Ferdinand "king of Austria," and Charles "king of Spain." Ferdinand agreed to pay thirty thousand ducats a year for the parts of Hungary under his control. The Ottomans preferred not to twist the knife one more time, and they used a neutral word for the annual payment, "*kesim*," which literally means a cut, and which has a meaning akin to rent or share.[75] Ferdinand presented that to his own constituents as a "gift of honor," even though all involved knew that it was an annual tribute.

The Ottomans may have called Charles "king of Spain" dismissively, but the years before and after 1547 represented a high point for the emperor, and for the Catholic cause more generally. Pope Paul III had convened the Council of Trent in March 1545, in an attempt to restore the vigor of Catholic dogma after a few decades of Protestant criticism.[76] Using the respite afforded by the negotiations with the Ottomans, Charles was able to resoundingly defeat the Lutheran forces, who had gathered under the banner of the Schmalkaldic League, at the Battle of Mühlberg in April 1547. Also, four of his rivals and competitors died in quick succession: Martin Luther in February 1546, Barbarossa in July 1546, Henry VIII in January 1547, and Francis I in March 1547.

As for Süleyman and those around him, their concerns and thoughts in the second half of the 1540s were recorded by Charles' envoy to Constantinople, Gerard Veltwyjck, in a perceptive report written in late 1545, addressed either to Ferdinand or to Charles himself.[77] Veltwyjck may have been eager to present the situation in Constantinople as favorable to Charles. At the same time, his report is clearly based on conversations with the chief translator Yunus and the Ottoman viziers, as well as a number of informers, merchants, and others who would have supplied him with current rumors.

Veltwyjck reports that the Ottomans were very much displeased by the 1544 peace treaty between the French and the Habsburgs, and thus had become more amenable to a settlement with the Habsburgs. Moreover, the Habsburg envoy thought that Süleyman was tired of the ongoing war in Hungary and was ready for an honorable solution. An important component of that honorable solution was the preservation of Transylvania, once under Hungary, as John Sigismund's domain and thus Ottoman tributary. Dreams of conquering Vienna were not mentioned anymore. Veltwyjck also noted that tensions between Süleyman's sons, harbingers of a future succession struggle, were serious enough to dissuade the Ottomans from another

campaign in Europe. Just past the age of fifty, Süleyman was already considering the matter of succession. So was Charles, six years younger, as seen in a
long text he prepared for the edification of his son Philip around this time.[78]

The long diplomatic negotiations and the lack of hostilities gave Süleyman
the chance to rest at a point in his life when signs of declining health were
showing themselves. This respite also meant ample time for hunting, his favorite pastime. Moreover, for the first time since 1533–36, he could refocus
his attention on the eastern frontiers of his realm. Veltwyck reported that
news of an alliance between Georgian lords and Shah Tahmasb had given the
Ottomans cause for concern. The defection of a Safavid prince in mid-1547
presented them with an unexpected opportunity.

## Süleyman, a Runaway Safavid Prince, and
## Another Eastern Campaign

Between 1536 and 1547, while the Ottomans were dragged into long and costly
campaigns in Europe and the Mediterranean, Tahmasb kept busy. He further
consolidated his control over the tribal confederations, the bulk of the Safavid
military-political elite. The Safavid bureaucracy and chancery, an instrument
of control as well as cultural self-assertion for Tahmasb, continued to expand
its personnel and its sphere of action. Twelver Shiism, with its hierarchy of
scholars and its emphasis on a centuries-old written tradition, increasingly
replaced earlier religious and political sensibilities of a millenarian mold. The
loss of the Shiite shrine cities to the Ottomans in 1534–35 was compensated
for by an emphasis on the Safavid realm as the religious and cultural center
of Twelver Shiism. The Safavids could not organize a large-scale invasion of
Ottoman territories, but they held their own against Ottoman frontier forces.
They were also able to fend off Uzbek attacks from central Asia, and expanded
further north, across Azerbaijan toward the Caucasus.[79]

Around 1546, four of Ismail's sons were alive. The oldest, Tahmasb, ruled as
the shah. His full brother Bahram, and his half-brothers Alqas and Sam, held
administrative positions under Tahmasb. This was radically different from the
Ottoman practice, in which the prince who came to the throne exterminated
his brothers. The co-existence of the shah with his brothers, deferential yet
vying for more power, was a critical factor for political destabilization in the
Safavid realm. Sam, for instance, had rebelled in Khorasan in 1534–35, but
was pardoned subsequently by Tahmasb.[80] Sam had also been coveted by the
Ottomans as a client around the same time. The next brother to rebel was

Alqas. He had been appointed governor of Shirvan in 1538, where he set out
to build his own power base. There, he rebelled, renegotiated with Tahmasb
and asked for pardon, and then rebelled again and declared himself an independent ruler.

Alqas' agitation, in a region that was then at the northernmost border of
the Safavid realm, led to military action by Tahmasb. Defeated in March–
April 1547, Alqas escaped to the Crimea with a small retinue, and then sailed to
Constantinople, which he reached in May.[81] Beforehand, he had sent a letter
to beseech the help of Süleyman, who was then in Edirne, against his brother
Tahmasb. Süleyman must have been surprised by this unexpected letter. In
it, Alqas, who called himself the lowliest slave, addressed Süleyman with the
utmost respect, through references to Alexander the Great and Solomon and
to Süleyman's embodiment of justice and holy war. More strategically, Alqas
also mentioned a potential invasion of the Safavid domain and offered the
prospect of placing an Ottoman-friendly, indeed Ottoman-supported ruler
on the Safavid throne.[82]

Süleyman quickly left for Constantinople to grant an audience to Alqas.
While still in Edirne, he had ordered the commander of the janissaries and
the commander of the fleet to greet him. A galley was sent to the northern
entrance of the Bosphorus, and the runaway Safavid prince was brought to
Constantinople. At the port, Alqas and his men were mounted on horses as a
sign of respect and a procession took them to a mansion in a central location.

Süleyman arrived in Constantinople a few days later. After a meeting
with the grand vizier Rüstem, during which they must have discussed future
steps, Süleyman ordered lavish gifts to be sent to Alqas: ornamented weapons,
richly accoutered horses, Ottoman-style dresses and headgear, fine fabrics,
and cash. Rüstem presented the Safavid prince with a copy of the Quran, a
gold sword, two prayer rugs, and horses and weapons.[83] Some of the clothes
and dresses for the women of the prince's household were apparently sent by
Hürrem personally.[84] Alqas was also given 1.3 million *akçes*, a sum close to
the annual revenue assigned to an Ottoman grand vizier. His men, including
his vizier Sayyid Aziz and his commanders and companions, received cash
disbursements commensurate with their rank.[85]

A few days later, Alqas was invited to the palace, where he met Süleyman
in person and declared his submission. Ten days later, there was a major feast
in Rüstem's mansion, where Alqas and high-ranking officials ate together
and watched military games. Finally, nearly a month after Süleyman's return,
Alqas attended an imperial council meeting. He and his men first ate with the

viziers and other high officials in a formal yet collegial atmosphere. He was
then given a chance to present his case in front of Süleyman.

Probably speaking in a different dialect, with a vocabulary and accent
that was distinct yet intelligible to the Ottomans, Alqas told the story he
had previously presented to Süleyman in his letter. He had been wronged
by his brother Tahmasb and he was willing to be part of a military action
against him. If he were to lead a military expedition against his brother
with Ottoman help, he could secure the defections of many Safavid
officials. Ottoman sources convey the sense that Alqas was a charismatic,
convincing speaker. Süleyman responded positively. As a a sign of Alqas'
growing stature after the imperial council meeting, he was transferred
from his mansion to İbrahim's old palace on the Hippodrome, one of the
most visible spots in the city.[86] To ingratiate Alqas with the inhabitants of
Constantinople, three thousand akçes were distributed every week to the
city's poor in his name.[87]

Some Ottoman testimonies from the period convey a sense of unease with
regard to Alqas' arrival and the planned military campaign. In the case of central Europe and the Mediterranean, the Ottomans were able to obtain information through spying as well as diplomatic and commercial networks. This
was not necessarily the case for Iran, even though some information flowed
from the Ottoman governors in eastern Anatolia and Iraq as well as various
Sunni allies. Many Safavid governors and commanders may have resented
Tahmasb's centralization efforts, but they were tied to the dynasty through
a shared history of struggle against the Sunni Ottomans and Uzbeks and
adherence to Ismail's religio-political message. Alqas, no doubt aware of the
Ottomans' inadequate grasp of Safavid realities and their lack of prominent
allies, presented himself as the sort of intermediary the Ottomans had been
looking for.

This did not prevent lingering doubts about Alqas' personality. Was he
reliable? According to some, while in Constantinople, he relinquished his
family's religio-cultural identity as Shiites and became a Sunni. In the minds
of others, this was a pragmatic act, not a sincere change of heart. Moreover,
the lavish gifts given to Alqas seem to have led to strong criticisms among the
inhabitants of Constantinople, who found it inappropriate to spend so much
on a non-Sunni deviant.[88] Of course, the positive reception granted to Alqas
did not mean that Süleyman and his associates had abandoned their anti-
Safavid position. That position was articulated in detail in a number of legal
opinions (fetvas) issued around this time by the chief jurist Ebussuud. These
qualified warfare against the Safavids as holy war, described their followers

as "unbelievers" (*kâfir*), refuted the Safavid dynasty's claim of descent from Muhammad, and refused to recognize Safavids as Shiites or members of another legitimate Muslim denomination.[89]

Convinced that Alqas could help the Ottomans achieve a significant victory against the Safavids, Süleyman ordered preparations for a new expedition to the east, which began in March 1548.[90] It was planned as a major military engagement. For instance, the experienced Rumeli troops, which protected the European front, were redeployed to the east, thanks to the recent peace treaty with the Habsburgs. Alqas left Constantinople ahead of Süleyman, in the company of someone who was tasked with supervising his actions. This was Ulama, who had previously played a prominent role before and during the Two Iraqs campaign of 1533–36.

Süleyman followed behind, with the bulk of the army, accompanied by his son Cihangir. They joined Alqas and Ulama near Tabriz in July 1548, and the city fell to their joint forces without resistance at the end of July. As in the Two Iraqs campaign, however, the Ottomans immediately ran into logistical problems. These underscored the fact that Tabriz could not be utilized as a base from which a large army might invade the rest of Iran. Also in Tabriz, the first major disagreements between Alqas and the Ottomans emerged. Alqas, according to the Ottoman side, sought revenge on his brother's subjects unnecessarily and behaved harshly against the city's inhabitants. Moreover, he was unable to control the men under his command, who ended up looting the city.

From Tabriz, Süleyman fell back on Van, already under siege by a separate Ottoman contingent. The sultan's arrival with the heavy artillery decided the fortress' fate, which surrendered on August 24. As with Buda seven years earlier, Van was turned into the center of a new Ottoman governorate-general to ensure a more direct Ottoman presence in the area. Süleyman and the army then retreated further west to Diyarbakır, the largest city in the region and the seat of an Ottoman governorate-general. There, most of the Ottoman units were released to go back to their winter encampments.

Alqas, who was eager to press on, was given a small contingent, some funds, and the right to raise soldiers from the Kurdish tribes in the area. In early October, he crossed with his forces into Iran and attacked various towns and cities in the following months. In the meantime, after spending the month of Ramadan in Diyarbakır and celebrating the Eid holiday, Süleyman had relocated to Aleppo. Benefiting from the warmer weather, he was able to hunt. His son Bayezid, district governor in Konya, came to Aleppo to keep his father and his brother Cihangir company.[91]

As Süleyman rested, Alqas' campaign was unraveling. After an incursion deep into Iran, during which he plundered urban areas and captured members of his brother Bahram's family, Alqas had been unable to rally anyone to his cause. He retreated into Ottoman territory in January 1549, and the troops under his command began to disperse. The hubris he displayed the previous year was replaced by survival instinct. For a while, Alqas bided his time, sending Süleyman precious objects looted in Iran, while re-establishing contact with his brother Tahmasb to ask for mercy. Aware that Alqas had become a liability, the Ottoman side began to withdraw its support.

In the fall of 1549, chased by both Ottoman and Safavid forces, Alqas took refuge with a Kurdish local lord. In October, he surrendered to the Safavids and had an audience with Tahmasb. According to a Safavid source, Tahmasb asked his rebel brother, "What evil have I committed against you that you turned away from me and took refuge with the sultan?" Alqas remained silent.[92] He was imprisoned and eventually killed in April 1550. Tahmasb emerged even more powerful from the Alqas affair, since he had displayed his ability to fend off challenges from within the Safavid polity and dynasty, despite initial Ottoman support for his rebel brother.

Alqas' failure to prevail over his brother, and the absence of any defections from the Safavids to the Ottoman side, meant the utter failure of the campaign's initial objectives. Instead, Ottoman forces spent the summer and fall of 1549 attacking Georgian lords in the Caucasus. Süleyman returned to Constantinople in December 1549 after nearly twenty months, the last few of which were spent in an atmosphere of frustration and recrimination. According to a Venetian diplomat's report, Ottoman soldiers were so exhausted by the weather and the lack of resources that, defying Süleyman's plans to spend another winter in Aleppo, they rushed back to Constantinople in the fall of 1549. The same report mentions that many high-ranking officials were beheaded on Süleyman's orders following his return, and that their corpses were exhibited in the Hippodrome.[93]

Indeed, many in the upper echelons of the elite felt manipulated by Alqas, who was subsequently portrayed in Ottoman sources as a trickster. As a sign of ultimate betrayal, he was said to have reverted to Twelver Shiism in the early months of 1549 while visiting Shiite pilgrimage sites in Iraq. There is also an element of self-criticism in Ottoman sources, which is rarely seen in contemporary accounts of the reign of Süleyman. It is as if high-ranking officials regretted that they had been led by their ambition and greed into an unproductive, wasteful enterprise.[94] In a letter sent to Rüstem a few years after the campaign, a prominent sheikh living in the Balkans voiced his displeasure at the support lent to Alqas, whom he saw primarily as the descendant of a family of heretics.[95] Finally, in terms of imperial policy, in 1549, the Ottomans definitively realized the impossibility of dislodging the Safavid dynasty and eradicating the Safavid movement.

This bleak state of affairs was made worse by Süleyman's illness in the summer of 1549, while he was traveling from Aleppo to Diyarbakır. It seems that the doctors were unable to cure the sultan's ailment. As a result, he was prevented from traveling for more than a month, from late June to late July.[96] A French diplomat reported that Süleyman's legs were swollen. He shouted from intense pain, and his officials placed singers and musicians around his tent so that his voice would not carry and demoralize the soldiery.[97] The rest of his time in the region, through the end of October, was spent recuperating. The French attributed his illness to an excess of black bile, spurred on by mental strain and the hardships of the campaign. In fact, he suffered from gout (*nikris* in Ottoman), which particularly afflicted members of the upper classes whose indulgence in the consumption of alcohol and animal proteins made them susceptible to it. Excess uric acid gathered in the bloodstream, causing swelling and pain in joints and extremities.[98]

The first signs of Süleyman's gout were observed in April 1540, when an acute pain in his big toe prevented him from riding on his horse on the way back from Edirne to Constantinople. Still, to keep up appearances, he left his carriage as they neared Constantinople and entered the city on his horse.[99] In the summer of 1549, when he had to spend more than a month recuperating in the middle of a campaign, the pretense was over. Süleyman was now in his mid-fifties, and this major health crisis was the harbinger of more troubles ahead. In the coming years, his health continued to deteriorate while he and his doctors strove to find cures.

In a report from 1553, Venetian ambassador Bernardo Navagero noted that Süleyman was very careful about his diet and ate very little meat. He had stopped drinking wine, which he had reportedly enjoyed during the grand vizierate of İbrahim. Instead, he drank pure spring water. The ambassador also remarked that Süleyman's intense physical activity, from daily excursions on the Bosphorus to hunts around the city and in Edirne, was meant to alleviate the symptoms of his illness.[100] These measures must have brought little relief, however, since Süleyman's physicians felt obliged to contact a colleague who lived in Safavid Iran. He sent them a drug recipe for digestive problems and gout.[101]

The few years that followed Süleyman's return from Aleppo were among the least eventful of his life. He relocated to Edirne for increasingly longer periods, living far from the tumult of Constantinople, hunting, reading, and conversing with his close companions. On the other hand, the imperial enterprise continued to produce friction and violence, as the Habsburg-Ottoman frontier remained volatile despite the treaty of 1547.

John Szapolyai's widow Isabella and his son and heir John Sigismund had been relocated to Transylvania by the Ottomans in 1543, where the son served as *voivode* and George Martinuzzi acted as regent. The competition between the dowager queen and the regent was intense, and it allowed both the Habsburgs and the Ottomans to meddle in Transylvanian affairs. In early 1550, Isabella told the Ottomans that Martinuzzi was in league with the Habsburgs and asked for help. The following year, she reversed her position and signed a treaty with Ferdinand in July 1551. The treaty transferred Transylvania and the Szapolyai claim over Hungary to Ferdinand, in return for a duchy for John Sigismund in upper Silesia. The Ottomans reacted swiftly and annexed parts of Transylvania in the summer of 1552. Like Buda in 1543 and Van in 1548, the newly annexed territory was turned into an Ottoman governorate-general, around the city of Timişoara.[102]

Central Europe was not the only location where the Ottoman forces were active. In the year 1552, Ottoman fleets occupied Tripoli in Libya and clashed with the Portuguese in and around the Persian Gulf. Ottoman forces gained control of the territory between Baghdad and Basra and fought with the Safavids between Erzurum and Lake Van.[103] A peace treaty with Poland in the summer of 1553 helped maintain some stability in east-central Europe and in the Ukrainian steppe.[104] The eastern frontier was another matter. As the Ottoman commanders found it increasingly difficult to fend off the Safavids, another campaign was planned there for the summer of 1553. The campaign was delayed, however, by an event that shook the Ottoman polity to its core.

## Mechanisms of Empire

The middle years of Süleyman's reign saw the continuation and expansion of the administrative practices and imperial policies of the earlier decades. Experienced bureaucrats and jurists continued to offer their services to the imperial project. Celalzade Mustafa, who had worked closely with İbrahim and for the imperial council, was appointed chancellor (*nişancı*) in 1534. In this capacity, he continued to supervise the correspondence of the sultan and to issue edicts and orders with his signature, as he had done before. Under his new purview, he played a larger role in supervising the *tımar* system, in dialogue with the treasurers. He also helped regularize the formulation of dynastic law (*kanun*) as a major instrument of government, in dialogue with the chief jurist.[105]

Mehmed Ebussuud (d. 1574), who became chief jurist in 1545, similarly rendered a critical service by helping harmonize the Sharia with the secular aspects of Ottoman dynastic law. These two officials helped expand the field of action of the Ottoman government and gave that expanded field of action a strong legal foundation. Ebussuud also filled the void left by Kemalpaşazade Ahmed's death in 1534, both as legal scholar and as figure of authority. The office of the chief jurist (*şeyhülislam*) became a better-organized bureau under him. His clerks, many of whom were students of his from his days as a madrasa professor, were taught to quickly and efficiently answer the multitude of legal questions that flowed from all corners of the empire. Ebussuud's authority and his closeness to the dynasty were displayed on public occasions as well. In 1550, he was asked to lay the foundation stone of a mosque being built in Süleyman's name.[106]

The imperial council continued to supervise the affairs of the empire domestically and abroad. Land surveys, crucial instruments in the accounting and redistributing of resources, continued to be conducted in large numbers. The imperial land registry, an office that had existed since the second half of the fifteenth century to keep records of land surveys, expanded concomitantly. New officials were appointed in the provinces to serve as supervisors of *tımar* assignments.[107] A major actor of bureaucratic institutionalization in this period was Rüstem. Rüstem is a much-reviled figure in the Ottoman historical tradition, which has passed down an image of him as an avaricious, bribe-taking official. Needless to say, these adjectives could be applied to any and all officials in the context of a patriarchal dynastic empire. Rüstem appears to have been a more skilled financial manager than many others. He was insistent in his pursuit of wealth for his own household as well as the imperial treasury, which extended to his order to harvest and sell in Constantinople's markets the produce of the large palace gardens.

More significantly, Rüstem extended the practice of tax-farming whereby the right to collect taxes from sources assigned to the dynasty (such as land, mines, markets) was given to the highest bidder.[108] He also made better use of record keeping, including the creation of orderly and regular registers of *mühimme* (important affairs) for the decisions made at the imperial council. These registers clearly demonstrate the main concerns of the central administration: the management of the *askerî* elite across the empire; the securing of order and peace; the pursuit of those seen as deviants, both rebels and non-Sunni elements; and the conduct of war. Finally, in this period, the creation of new governorates-general, such as Erzurum (1535), Yemen (1539), Buda (1541), Basra (1546), Van (1548), and Timişoara (1552), allowed the Ottoman administration to establish better political and financial control in critical areas.

These financial and administrative measures were particularly helpful since costly imperial ventures continued in the late 1530s and the 1540s. In addition to the engagements in Europe, the Mediterranean, and the eastern front, Ottoman imperial policy manifested itself on an even wider scale in this period. As chancellor Celalzade Mustafa stated, every single problem of the Muslim community was of concern to Süleyman.[109] This argument was related to the Ottomans' recent reworking of the notion of the caliphate. While Süleyman's caliphate in the early years of his reign was described as a form of divinely sanctioned universal rule, the 1540s saw it being redefined with an emphasis on Süleyman's leadership of the Sunni Muslim community. He was promoted as the protector of Muslims against enemies and rivals as varied as the Muscovites and the Safavids, who clashed with various Sunni polities in central Asia, and the Portuguese, who put pressure on Muslim polities around the Indian Ocean.[110]

The Ottoman-Portuguese rivalry had started when the Ottomans established control over the Red Sea after 1517 and intensified after the Two Iraqs campaign. While the Portuguese dominated the Indian Ocean thanks to their carracks armed with heavy artillery, the Ottomans were able to keep them out of the Red Sea and the Persian Gulf. Through engagements such as Hadım Süleyman's Indian Ocean campaign in 1538, the Ottomans even went on the offensive.[111] Their search for allies in the Indian Ocean extended to the Sultanate of Aceh, on the northern edge of Sumatra. In the 1530s, Aceh received a small but well-armed contingent of sailors and musketeers as support against the Portuguese.

Ottoman efforts to control the southern shore of the Arabian peninsula resulted in the establishment of the governorate-general of Yemen in 1539, even though the relationship between the Ottoman officials and the locals remained tense. Basra, in southern Iraq, was made a governorate-general in 1546, and a naval base was built there. The Ottomans subsequently tried to extend further into the Persian Gulf, but their failed siege of Portuguese-controlled Hormuz in 1552 forced them to seek a difficult yet economically viable modus vivendi with the Portuguese. Ottoman military presence in the Persian Gulf and the Indian Ocean remained limited by the Portuguese, but it was commercially beneficial. Basra, especially, served as a major entry point for fabrics and spices from India, and newly established caravan routes tied the town to the markets of Aleppo, whose wealth overshadowed that of Damascus in this period.

However, on the whole, Süleyman's middle years were a time when imperial ventures brought in increasingly diminishing returns, both financially and politically.[112] The Safavids' scorched earth tactics and the Habsburgs' use of new defensive strategies turned campaigns into drawn out, exhausting ventures while naval warfare in the Mediterranean swallowed considerable resources. As a land-based empire whose control over revenue sources and information flows was significant yet limited, the Ottoman enterprise suffered from geographical over-extension and strategic over-commitment in this period. The balance between gains from conquest and military spending began to tilt decidedly toward the latter, as ambitious plans east and west, which had promised absolute victories over the Habsburgs and the Safavids in the 1520s and 1530s, devolved into wars of attrition in Hungary and across the Ottoman-Safavid frontier.

While it is difficult for any imperial establishment to openly acknowledge the shortcomings of its policies, Süleyman and his associates, especially toward the end of this period, began to exhibit a sort of prudence and a palpable war-weariness. There were growing warnings against the waste of resources and the unnecessary oppression of the subject populations on the frontiers with the Habsburgs and the Safavids.[113] Of course, prudence was not the only factor behind the increased drive toward institutionalization, one of the hallmarks of this particular period in the life of Süleyman and the empire itself.

Thus, after seeking ultimate victory over enemies east and west through long and costly campaigns, the sultan and his imperial project refocused their sights on creating a lasting legacy. An important component of this legacy was the issue and implementation of *kanun*, dynastic law, which refers to the law prepared under the authority of the sultan or with reference to custom/tradition. Ottoman rulers had issued *kanun* in various forms, especially after the mid-fifteenth century. However, consistent and regular legislative activity as part of the business of empire came to the fore under Süleyman. This is why he was later given the moniker with which he is still known to Turkish audiences: *Kanunî*, the Lawgiver (or, rather, the *kanun*-giver).

*Kanun* usually pertained to land management, taxation, and criminal law. It could be issued in the form of an individual ruling (e.g., an answer to a petition), a general law code (such as a code of criminal law), or a law code pertaining to a region, such as a district, or to a specific socio-economic and professional group, such as nomads of a region or religious scholars. While *kanun* was different from Sharia law, it nevertheless had to be in harmony with it. It also complemented the Sharia in significant ways. As a body of law developed by scholars mostly outside formal state structures since the early centuries of Islam, the Sharia included many gaps about the specifics of secular government that needed to be filled. This was the task handled by the chancellor Celalzade Mustafa and the chief jurist Ebussuud.[114]

*Kanun* thus became one of the chief instruments for the management of the realm. The existence of a supposedly harmonized body of laws and regulations was also used as an argument to justify the rule of Süleyman and the actions of the Ottoman administration as fair and rational. For the members of the *askerî* elite high and low, *kanun* was seen as a guarantee for meritocracy and a defense against summary demotion and dismissal.[115] This idealization of *kanun* led to high expectations, and the sultan's failure to meet those expectations became a source of stringent criticism already during Süleyman's lifetime, and particularly in the decades following his death.

## *Family, Charity, Aging*

A number of individuals who played important roles in Süleyman's life deceased in the 1530s and 1540s. His mother Hafsa died on March 19, 1534. His grand vizier and close companion İbrahim was executed in March 1536. His tutor Hayreddin died, after a long illness, on December 10, 1543.[116] Hafsa and Hayreddin had been a constant presence on his side throughout most of his life. The chief jurist Kemalpaşazade Ahmed also died in 1534. Widely respected as the epitome of Ottoman scholarship, he had lent his tremendous skills as legal scholar and historian to Süleyman's imperial project.[117]

These losses must have exerted a considerable emotional toll. Hafsa's death, for instance, plunged Süleyman into a deep grief. Reportedly, he cried profusely and only stopped since he knew it was best to resign oneself to the will of God. Hafsa was buried in the vicinity of the mosque of Sultan Selim. As usual, food was distributed to the urban poor, officials and members of the palace household donned dark clothes and paid condolence visits to Süleyman, the construction of a separate mausoleum for Hafsa was ordered, and readers were hired to recite the Quran continuously at her grave.[118]

Perhaps the most shocking loss of this period, for both Süleyman and Hürrem, was the death of Prince Mehmed, their first child. It is likely that Mehmed contracted a disease during the public celebrations of his father's latest campaign in Manisa, where he served as district governor. He died after just a six-day illness, on November 5, 1543.[119] Deceased Ottoman princes were usually buried in Bursa. However, Süleyman once again departed from established tradition. Mehmed's final journey was exceptional in every way. His corpse traveled north from Manisa to Üsküdar, across the sea from Constantinople, where a funeral cortege was formed. The prince's coffin was solemnly taken to the quay, from where it crossed the Bosphorus to Constantinople. There, a large crowd awaited: scholars, elders of religious orders, members of the palace household, city folk, and the sultan himself. The enlarged cortege then walked up the hill to the mosque of Bayezid II for the funeral prayer.

The degree of Süleyman's sorrow may be gleaned from the unprecedented gestures he made after the prince's passing. He ordered a complex, which included a mausoleum, a soup kitchen, a mosque, and a madrasa, to be built in Mehmed's name.[120] He also composed two chronograms, one in Turkish and the other in Persian, to commemorate the prince's death:

*Favorite among princes, my Sultan Mehmed (Turkish: Şehzadeler güzidesi Sultan Mehemmedüm);*[121]

*May Sultan Mehmed's resting place be the Eternal Paradise (Persian: Marqad-e Sultan Muhammad bad firdavs-e abad).*

While his personal life was rocked by these family losses, Süleyman had to fill İbrahim's void as well. Following the execution of his grand vizier and commander-in-chief, he had to become more involved in the daily affairs of the empire, as many European diplomats noticed. In terms of finding a new grand vizier, he chose to respect the existing hierarchy and promoted second viziers to the grand vizierate when the position became vacant.

İbrahim was succeeded by Ayas, Lütfi, and Hadım Süleyman, respectively, between 1539 and 1544. Ayas and Lütfi were seasoned administrators who had started their Ottoman careers as Christian children levied from the Balkans. They had risen through the ranks of the palace and the military-administrative hierarchy. However, they lacked İbrahim's personal charm, his flair for diplomacy, and his remarkable talent for self-promotion. Ayas was best known as an accomplished military commander.[122] Lütfi was a committed administrator who engaged in reforming imperial finances and communication networks and was also known for his interest in history and Islamic sciences.[123] Hadım Süleyman, a eunuch, had served as head of the Inner Treasury before he was sent out as commander of the fleet in 1523. He was known for his long service as governor-general of Egypt and his competition with the Portuguese in the Red Sea and the Indian Ocean.

Ayas' tenure was cut short in July 1539 when he succumbed to the plague. Lütfi's fall from grace was equally sudden. When he ordered the brutal physical punishment of a woman found guilty of adultery, his wife Şah Sultan, the sultan's sister, objected strongly. Lütfi may have hit his wife after being reprimanded by her, and she instigated divorce proceedings. Even in a patriarchal society, violence against a female member of the dynasty was unacceptable. Lütfi was divorced, dismissed, and sent into retirement in March 1541. His replacement was Hadım Süleyman, whose eventual dismissal was similarly inglorious. In November 1544, he had a discussion with another vizier, Hüsrev, over the finances of Egypt at a meeting of the imperial council. The discussion turned into a dispute; strong words were used, and daggers may have been drawn. As a result, both were dismissed and sent into retirement while an inspection was ordered into their administrative record.[124]

More than eight years after İbrahim's execution, Süleyman finally found someone who could be seen as a true replacement: Rüstem, the husband of his only daughter, who served as grand vizier from 1544 to 1553, and then from 1555 to 1561. Rüstem, of Slavic origins, born around 1500, was taken into Ottoman service through the *devşirme* practice. As one of the pages living in the close vicinity of Süleyman, he had distinguished himself on a rather mundane occasion. As Süleyman was standing by a window, an object fell from his hand to the outside. Other pages rushed through the door and down the stairs to retrieve it, but Rüstem made it there first because he jumped out of the window, proving his practicality and dedication.[125] He rose through the palace hierarchy to become keeper of Süleyman's sword, and then head of the stables. From there, he was sent out to a district governorship due to İbrahim's jealousy. He must have impressed Süleyman enough that he was considered a suitable husband for his only surviving daughter, Mihrümah, whom he married in 1539.

Depictions of Rüstem are not very flattering in terms of his appearance: he is described as an unremarkable, indeed unattractive man with a short stature and a reddish complexion. However, both Ottoman and European observers agree that he devoted himself to his work as grand vizier. The long hours he kept, his attention to detail, his negotiation skills, and his financial acumen made him the ideal manager of the business of government.[126] Still, his relationship with his father-in-law was more formal than personal. Rüstem was allowed into the sultan's presence only for official reasons or when summoned by Süleyman. Despite Hürrem and Mihrümah's pleas, Süleyman did not let his son-in-law into the third courtyard of the palace, where the private residence of the sultan was located. He apparently told Hürrem and Mihrümah that it was enough to make a fool of himself once, referring to the mistake he believed he had made by allowing İbrahim to stay there.[127]

This was a time when Süleyman's relationship with Hürrem and their children deepened further. In 1534, with the death of Hafsa, Hürrem finally became the most influential female member of the dynasty. She had probably been freed by Süleyman before 1534, becoming a free Muslim legally. Soon after Hafsa's death, Süleyman and Hürrem were married, and Hürrem moved to the New Palace definitively. Hafsa may have been strict about tradition and protocol. In this sense, her death, although much lamented by her son, allowed Süleyman and Hürrem to defy past practice. Süleyman waited until the end of the Two Iraqs campaign to organize public celebrations for their marriage, during which he and the participants (and possibly Hürrem, sitting behind a latticed window) watched mock battles and jugglers at the Hippodrome.

Compared to the circumcision celebration in 1530, this was a more subdued affair, perhaps in reflection of the recent execution of İbrahim, or in anticipation of a negative reaction in the palace and in Constantinople against the marriage between sultan and concubine. Indeed, while Ottoman sources are mostly silent about the marriage and its celebration, European sources record a sense of awe as well as a surge of disparaging gossip about this unprecedented union. In a deeply patriarchal society, anecdotes about Hürrem's bewitching of Süleyman circulated quickly. Her reputedly nefarious influence

**FIG. 6.4 A & B** Depictions of Süleyman and Hürrem by Matteo Pagan, ca. 1550. Courtesy of the Trustees of the British Museum.

over the sultan became a recurring topic of gossip during the remaining years of their life together and beyond.[128]

The rumors about Hürrem utterly failed to recognize the facts behind her rise to prominence: the genuine love between her and Süleyman, as well as her ingenuity. Hürrem served as an affectionate interlocutor for Süleyman in the midst of a male-dominated, competitive, and violent world, as seen in her correspondence from the 1520s and the early 1530s. Süleyman enjoyed their correspondence tremendously. For instance, in a poem composed during the Two Iraqs campaign, he states that he yearns for letters from Constantinople, which brought the scent of the beloved's hair (perhaps Hürrem sent a lock of her hair together with her letters?) all the way to Baghdad.[129]

Hürrem was not merely the object of Süleyman's affection, however. She established a close-knit family in an environment that precluded such a thing. She also served as a confidante and an ultimately reliable source of information. Her central role in all aspects of Süleyman's life is apparent in her correspondence. In a letter written around 1541–43, for instance, she informs Süleyman, who was on campaign, of a plague in Constantinople. She consulted some sages about it, who told her it would go away as the leaves started to fall. At the end of the letter, she reminds the sultan to send messengers every few weeks with news of the campaign. Otherwise, she says, there arises much agitation and rumor in the city. She concludes, as a devoted mother, by sending her prayers and praises to her sons Mehmed and Selim, who accompanied their father during the campaign. She also relays the love and respect of Bayezid, Cihangir, and Mihrümah for their father and brothers, reuniting the family in her letter.[130]

In another letter written around the same time, Hürrem updates her husband about kitchen expenses, informs him about the treatment of Cihangir's health issues (application of a poultice on his back, resulting inflammation, extraction by lancing), and tells him about the fatal illness of his tutor Hayreddin. She does not forget to send her greetings to Rüstem, her son-in-law, who played a prominent role in the 1541 and 1543 campaigns.[131] Hürrem's correspondence was not limited to her letters to Süleyman. She played a seemingly slight yet symbolically important role in Ottoman anti-Habsburg diplomacy. She wrote to Queen Isabella, mother of John Sigismund, to express her sympathy and offer her protection. She communicated with queen of Poland Bona Sforza, to support her opposition to her son's marriage with a Habsburg princess. When that son, Sigismund August, became king of Poland in 1548, both Hürrem and Mihrümah wrote congratulatory letters, without forgetting to offer their condolences on the death of the previous king, and sent gifts.[132]

Hürrem's growing stature in the period following her marriage to Süleyman also became evident through her architectural patronage and charitable works. Since the conquest of Constantinople in 1453, members of the Ottoman dynasty and the elite had seen the re-population and re-building of the city as a major administrative and cultural project. Building mosque complexes in the names of sultans stemmed from the urge to supplant and surpass Byzantine Constantinople, whose landmarks dominated the cityscape. In general, charity played an important social role in the life of Constantinople and its outer districts. In an urban environment riddled with epidemics, fires, high prices, crime, and various other problems stemming from overpopulation, dynastic, elite, and non-elite charity was fundamental in providing some sort of relief. The large dynastic complexes, consisting of a mosque flanked by soup kitchens, schools, guesthouses, and hospitals, catered to the needs of large numbers of urban dwellers.

Hürrem's uniqueness comes from the fact that she was the first female member of the dynasty to build a complex in Constantinople, which included a mosque (completed in 1539), a madrasa (in 1539–40), a soup kitchen (in 1540), and a hospital (in 1550–51). The complex was called Haseki ("chief consort") Sultan. It was a major sign of self-affirmation for Hürrem, and the epitome of her journey from concubine to wife and mother, and from slave to free woman.[133] Hürrem's patronage extended into other types of buildings and spread throughout the empire, in the form of fountains, dervish lodges, and hostels for travelers and pilgrims. She also had a complex built in her name in Jerusalem. The soup kitchen began serving food by September–October 1551, and the complex, including a small mosque, a guesthouse, and a caravanserai, was completed by 1557. In a city whose population was around thirteen thousand, Hürrem's soup kitchen fed nearly five hundred people twice a day.[134]

Jerusalem, the location of Prophet Solomon's Temple, must have exerted a particular form of attraction on Hürrem and Süleyman, who relished the Solomonic implications of his name and presented himself often as the Second Solomon, or the Solomon of the Age. Before Hürrem's complex was built, Süleyman had the city, which lacked fortifications, surrounded with a wall, built between 1537 and 1541. He had six fountains erected, five of them at central, visible locations, with their inscriptions telling one and all about their benefactor. The old aqueduct, which brought running water to the city, was restored. In 1545–46, the Dome of the Rock mosque was repaired and covered with tiles that reflected a distinct Ottoman taste. At a time of religious

**FIG. 6.5** One of the first depictions of the newly built walls of Jerusalem. From Sebastian Münster, *Cosmographiae universalis* (1555). Courtesy of the Lilly Library, Indiana University, Bloomington, Indiana.

and cultural conflict with the Habsburgs and the Safavids, Jerusalem, which occupies a major role in all Abrahamic religions, thus received Süleyman and Hürrem's imprint.[135]

All of these construction activities belonged to a new cultural agenda that projected sovereignty and munificence through the patronage of architecture. As always, there was a personal dimension as well, which manifested itself in the form of family loyalties. Thus, Süleyman added a public bath in 1538 and a hospital in 1539 to his mother Hafsa's complex in Manisa. Around 1545, he ordered the restoration of the mosque built by his father Selim in memory of his grandmother in Trabzon. A madrasa was added to Selim's mosque complex in 1548/49. Crucially, Rüstem's financial acumen helped collect and redirect considerable resources for these projects.

Süleyman and Hürrem's daughter Mihrümah played an important albeit informal role in dynastic politics in this period, especially after her marriage to Rüstem in 1539. In line with Süleyman's increasing reliance on his family members, his daughter became one of his closest advisors and interlocutors in the last decades of his life. Mihrümah's high status was publicly manifested even before her husband became grand vizier. In 1543, when she was in her early twenties, the construction of her own mosque complex was begun. Completed in 1548, it was located in Üsküdar, in a prominent location on the seashore, near a busy landing. Large numbers of pilgrims, soldiers, merchants, and others traveling to and from the east passed by. That may be why, in addition to a madrasa and a soup kitchen, the complex included a guesthouse and a caravanserai. The mosque design, meant to maximize the light entering the building, may have been a reference to the name Mihrümah, a Persian-based construction that meant "Sun and Moon."[136] In the early years of the 1550s Rüstem joined his mother-in-law and his wife and emerged as a major patron. The grandest of all complexes, however, was to be Süleyman's own, the construction of which also started in the late 1540s.

Despite the considerable level of institutionalization and the construction of a visible architectural and charitable legacy for the dynasty, Süleyman's life during these years remained filled with tensions. The ongoing, unresolved rivalries with the Habsburgs and the Safavids were a source of constant frustration. Mentions in diplomatic reports of his melancholic temper and his outbursts of anger became more frequent from the early 1540s onward. For instance, during an audience with Venetian envoy Alvise Renier, he reluctantly allowed the diplomat to begin presenting his case and then angrily interrupted him several times.[137] The growing prospect of a succession struggle among those of his sons who served as district governors, Mahidevran's son Mustafa, and Hürrem's sons Selim and Bayezid, was another source of anxiety.

For someone who lived in a dynastic culture with a strong masculine ethos, Süleyman's declining health was yet another source of concern, both personally and politically, since a sultan's illness was a constant reminder of impending succession struggles. Perhaps the best expression of his state of mind in the last decades of his life is found in a poem he wrote under the weight of these tensions:

> *Naught among the folk is holden like to fortune fair to see;*
> *But no worldly fortune equal to one breath of health can be.*
>
> *That which men call empire is but world-wide strife and ceaseless war*
> *There is nought of bliss in all the world to equal privacy.*
>
> *Lay aside this mirth and frolic, for the end thereof is death;*
> *If thou seekest love abiding, there is naught like piety.*
>
> *Though thy life-days were in number even as the desert sand,*
> *In the sphere's hour-glass they'd show not as a single hour, ah me!*
>
> *O Muhibbi, if thou cravest rest, withdraw from cares of earth;*
> *There is ne'er a peaceful corner like the hermit's nook, perdie.*[138]

On the one hand, these tensions seem to have induced a sort of restlessness in Süleyman. He had always liked hunting, but he devoted more time to it, both during campaigns and during his stays in Constantinople, even though his deteriorating health limited his movements as he got older. Edirne became a second home to him, where he was joined by Hürrem. The fresh air, the availability of hunting grounds nearby, and the distance from the rumormongering of Constantinople must have made Edirne particularly attractive. On the other hand, he turned inward and increasingly sought answers from the unseen realm.

Prophecies and omens played a central role in the thinking of sixteenth-century denizens, from pauper to king, and messianic and apocalyptic notions of history, politics, and war had important roles in determining imperial policy and diplomacy. In Süleyman's case, it seems that prognostication had a deep personal dimension as well, as seen in his frequent consultation of an Iranian émigré, Haydar the geomancer, from the early 1530s onward. Haydar had honed his skills among the Safavids before migrating to Constantinople. He submitted various reports to Süleyman, in which he addressed personal as well as political issues, ranging from his interpretation of İbrahim's true character to the outcome of planned campaigns, and to Süleyman's identity as a ruler with messianic attributes. He warned, consoled, and cajoled Süleyman thanks to his mastery of occult sciences.

In a report Haydar submitted in the early to mid-1540s, Süleyman's main preoccupations become evident.[139] In this sixty-folio report, the length of a small treatise, Haydar offers a long discourse on Süleyman's identity as the divinely anointed Master of the Auspicious Conjunction, who brings together temporal and spiritual rule under his mantle in the last age of human history. His personal concerns are also answered. Haydar comforts the sultan by announcing that, according to his horoscope, he will live to be ninety years of age. He will continue ruling, without being replaced by his sons. He will live in prosperity, patronizing the building of mosques, caravanserais, and bridges, taking pleasure from food, hunting to his heart's desire, seeing his enemies defeated, completing two compilations of his poetry, and starting a third one. All will be well. Even his foot pain, which must have started around the time Haydar submitted his report, will be cured.

A darker side of Süleyman's life nevertheless emerges from Haydar's report. Süleyman appears in these pages as a middle-aged man who is beset by anger, quick-tempered, upset by unnamed yet no doubt persistent criticisms of his imperial policies. There are long periods, it seems, during which he was completely overwhelmed with anger. Haydar urges him to remain calm, refrain from making decisions while angry, and seek solace in prayer, which is described here almost like a meditative activity, different from the five daily prayers of Islam.[140] If anger may be said to be a form of loss of control, Süleyman in these pages looks like someone who feels he is losing control. In 1553, under the weight of these tensions, angry and suspicious, and spurred on by his son-in-law and grand vizier Rüstem, he proceeded to make one of the most controversial decisions of his life.

# 7

# *Old Age: The Final Years, 1553–66*

IN OCTOBER 1553, Prince Mustafa was executed by strangling in his father's tent in the army camp. The eldest of Süleyman's surviving sons, he was in his late thirties.[1] He had served as district governor for nearly twenty years, first in Saruhan between 1534 and 1541, and then in Amasya. His three half-brothers, sons of Hürrem, were both younger, and less experienced in the affairs of state. Selim, the district governor of Saruhan, was close to thirty years of age. Bayezid, the district governor of Karaman, was twenty-six. Cihangir, whose birth defects and overall physical condition disqualified him from the sultanate, and who lived in Constantinople, was in his early twenties.

At the time of his eldest son's execution, Süleyman was nearly sixty. By sixteenth-century standards, he was an old man. Due to his advancing illnesses, and the presence of several sons eligible for the throne, he had spent the years before Mustafa's death under the threat of an eventual succession struggle among the princes. Many, including Süleyman, must have remembered the demise of his grandfather Bayezid II. Perceived as old and inefficient, Bayezid II had been forced into abdication by Süleyman's father Selim and was quite likely poisoned shortly thereafter. To make matters worse, Mustafa was seen as a particularly strong candidate to the throne. Already in the late 1540s, a Venetian ambassador noted his martial reputation and the janissaries' affection for him and presented him as the prince who was universally favored as the next sultan.[2] Another Venetian ambassador reported the same assessment in the early 1550s, shortly before Mustafa's death.[3]

Mustafa's execution was meant both to preempt the outbreak of violence among the princes and to protect the members of the family Süleyman had established with Hürrem. All, within and outside the Ottoman realm, were aware of the sultan's predicament. For instance, in two letters sent to Henri II in the fall and winter of 1549, a French diplomat reported news of the sultan's illness during the summer of 1549 and discussed the prospect of his death and Mustafa's rise to the throne. According to some rumors, the sultan's illness had so profoundly concerned those around him that Mustafa had been invited to the army camp near Diyarbakır to replace his father in case Süleyman died. The diplomat found that difficult to believe, he says, since it was well known that Süleyman had great affection for his other sons, and that Mustafa's rise to the sultanate would leave them subject to his mercy, meaning that they would be executed.[4]

## *Süleyman's Conflicting Loyalties and the Execution of Prince Mustafa*

Indeed, the impending succession struggle was further complicated by Süleyman and Hürrem's relationship. Against recent Ottoman dynastic practice, they had had four male children, three of whom were alive in 1553. Unlike other concubine mothers of princes, Hürrem had chosen to remain in Constantinople rather than accompanying her sons to their governorships. Still, she maintained a close relationship with them. She visited Selim in Konya and Mehmed in Manisa in 1543, soon after their appointments, in an unprecedented show of maternal affection. In the summer of 1544, a family reunion in Bursa brought Hürrem, Süleyman, their daughter Mihrümah, and her husband Rüstem together with Selim. In 1546, Hürrem was on the road again, to visit Bayezid in Konya and Selim in Manisa.[5] When Selim was sent to Edirne to watch the empire's western frontier, during Süleyman's eastern campaign of 1548–49, Hürrem moved there to keep her son company.

The elevation of her daughter Mihrümah's husband Rüstem to the grand vizierate in 1544 further consolidated Hürrem's power. It also increased the rumors about both Hürrem and Rüstem, and especially allegations of favoritism. Many among the elite and the commoners, already critical of Rüstem's privileging of the state and the palace household over them, and his appointment of allies and supporters to critical positions, blamed the grand vizier for unfairly supporting Hürrem and her sons against Mustafa and for manipulating the sultan. These rumors colored the ways in which the Ottoman public saw the competition among the princes and determined the reactions to the execution of Mustafa in 1553.[6] While it is impossible to ascertain the veracity of these rumors, there are sufficient indicators that many of them were close to the truth.

Süleyman openly displayed his affection for his sons with Hürrem. Cihangir, by all accounts a wise and witty conversationalist, was a near-constant presence in the sultan's daily life. While Mustafa was never asked to accompany his father in a military campaign, Mehmed, Selim, Bayezid, and then Cihangir traveled with Süleyman on several occasions from the late 1530s to the late 1540s. During the campaign against the Safavids in 1548–49, Bayezid, then district governor of Karaman, spent several months in Süleyman's company in Aleppo and its vicinity. During the same campaign, Selim was sent to Edirne as a sort of stand-in for the sultan, just as his father had dispatched Süleyman to Edirne during his absences from Constantinople in the 1510s. The more experienced Mustafa was passed over.

For Mustafa, one of the most obvious signs of the favoritism toward his half-brothers must have been his removal from the governorship in Saruhan, a preferred location for Ottoman princes, and his relocation to Amasya in 1541. It was a move he resented, despite the considerable increase in his annual stipend.[7] While he may not have voiced his displeasure directly, his tutor Sürurî mentioned it in one of his poems.[8] To make matters worse, after a year's vacancy, Saruhan was given to Mehmed, Süleyman and Hürrem's eldest son. After Mehmed's sudden death in November 1543, the district governorship went to their second son Selim in the spring of 1544. In sum, from the early 1530s onward, while the Mahidevran-Mustafa wing of the family increasingly looked banished, the Hürrem side flourished and thrived. It expanded further with the birth of Bayezid's, Selim's, and Mihrümah's children. Mustafa did not have access to this intimate circle, even though he had many sympathizers within the *askerî* elite.

Süleyman was caught in a bind. Notions of justice, custom, and merit, important components of Ottoman political thought, required him to behave equally toward his sons. Members of the elite and the public expected him to do so as well. It is difficult to unearth personal details of his relationship with Mustafa. A unique eyewitness account, which describes a meeting between Mustafa and Süleyman in May 1548, offers a few precious clues in that regard. As Süleyman progressed east with the army, he met with Mustafa near Sivas. It is obvious from the text that the sultan and the prince's relationship had previously been strained. The sultan reportedly used this occasion to show his affection to the prince since he had not been able to do so of late. Mustafa was welcomed with much pomp by high-ranking officials who kissed his hand and received gifts from him. The full army camp stood at attention as the prince then proceeded to his father's tent. There they met, like Jacob and Joseph after a long separation. The prince displayed his "loyalty" (*sadakat*) and "good manners" (*hüsn-i edeb*) toward Süleyman. After conversing with his father, according to the contemporary observer, the prince felt much "relief and joy" (*inşirah*).[9]

Another account of this critical meeting is provided in the history of Süleyman's reign commissioned by the sultan, the *Sulaymannama*, which was completed a few years after Mustafa's execution. There too, Mustafa is presented as having been given an elaborate, ceremonious reception at the army camp in 1548. A group of officials met him where he was stationed. He was brought a richly caparisoned horse from the sultan's stables to ride to his father's camp, where viziers guided him to the imperial tent. As Mustafa prostrated in front of his father, Süleyman made him stand up and embraced him. The prince was released for the day, and he returned the next morning. As Süleyman and Mustafa mounted their horses, the soldiery hailed them with great enthusiasm, moved by their sight. Father and son rode unaccompanied until evening came, and they conversed the whole time.[10] Rather than mentioning any prior issues between father and son, the *Sulaymannama* is at pains to emphasize the exceptional treatment given to Mustafa.

Despite the slight differences between the two accounts, the meeting seems to have been a genuine moment of reconciliation between father and son, but its impact did not last long. Did Süleyman have any non-violent solution in mind for the impending succession struggles? Did he, for instance, consider dividing the realm among his sons, despite the risk of undermining one of the foundations of the Ottoman enterprise? Even if he may have considered this, albeit probably briefly, it is likely that his sons could and would have insisted on fighting until one of them remained. It is more probable that Süleyman accepted it as fate and tried to ensure that succession struggles would not tear apart the fabric of the Ottoman government and society.

As for Mustafa, he could not, and did not, remain inactive. Especially during his tenure as district governor in Amasya, he successfully built a reputation as a patron of poetry and scholarship, a protector of the subjects, a purveyor of justice, and a good companion to the rank and file of the *askerî* elite. It seems that he represented, for his supporters and sympathizers, a reinvigoration of the Ottoman sultanate. They believed he would serve as a warrior sultan who would lead his men to victory and spoils and as a just ruler who would protect the commoners from oppression. Some of these sympathies were related to economic and demographic pressures that were felt in the last decades of Süleyman's reign. Peasants unable to pay their taxes, military men whose *tımar*s were revoked, and city dwellers suffering from the shortage of basic goods and rising prices may have seen Mustafa as an answer to their problems.[11]

**FIG. 7.1** A representation of Süleyman and Mustafa's meeting in 1548. Perhaps to underscore the problems between father and son, the sultan is depicted with bow and arrow in hand, facing away from the prince. Detail from *Sulaymannama*, 477b. Courtesy of the T.C. Cumhurbaşkanlığı Milli Saraylar İdaresi Başkanlığı.

Mustafa went beyond building a reputation, as an undated letter by him, probably from the late 1540s, shows.[12] The letter was sent to an Ottoman governor serving near the Safavid frontier. In it, primarily, Mustafa seeks the support of a high-ranking member of the *askerî* elite in view of the inevitable succession wars, although very carefully and tactfully. He underlines his intention to wait until his father's death, thus stopping short of open rebellion. At the same time, he reminds his addressee of his grandfather Selim's rise to the throne. Like him, Mustafa writes, after becoming sultan, he will reward those who support him, and he will punish those who fail to do so.

In the conspiratorial political world of an early modern empire, where open declarations of intent are rare, the allusion to Selim is as clear a message as could be delivered. The letter is also significant in giving clues about Mustafa's view of himself and his brothers. Apparently, he believed he was the only prince to display the true qualities of a sultan, implying that the other candidates did not. He also told his interlocutor that he viewed his inheritance of the throne as his Sharia-based right, thus making a claim that supersedes Ottoman custom. Mustafa's search for support included diplomatic endeavors as well. Shortly before his execution, he sent an envoy to Venice to ensure political and logistical support during his eventual march to the throne.[13]

The final chapter of Mustafa's life opened with a seemingly innocuous event: the dispatch of the grand vizier Rüstem to Anatolia in late December 1552/early January 1553, at the head of the janissaries and the palace troops. The apparent reason was a new campaign against the Safavids, whose recent resurgence and effective attacks against the Ottoman forces on the frontier had been a cause for concern.[14] However, the march of the Ottoman forces was soon hampered by internal tensions, as persistent rumors circulated among the soldiery about the impending arrival of Mustafa to the throne. Rüstem, beginning to lose control of his men, had to set up camp near Konya. According to an anonymous Venetian report, the situation was so volatile that, against all established practice, a group of janissaries broke ranks and went to Amasya to express their allegiance to Mustafa, whom they saw as their next sultan.[15] Following a positive reception there, the rowdy janissaries returned to the army camp.

Around the same time, other, related rumors were spreading among the soldiers about Süleyman being severely ill, which rendered the situation even more precarious for Rüstem. He had, under his command, some of the most skilled forces of the Ottoman army whose support was essential for a transfer of power, and many among them looked favorably upon Mustafa. If Süleyman were to die, or Mustafa to make a daring step to demand the command of the army, Rüstem and the rest of Hürrem's nuclear family would be condemned to a certain death. This was the point at which the grand vizier probably chose to persuade Süleyman to act definitively against Mustafa.

From the army camp near Konya, Rüstem dispatched messengers to Süleyman with the news that his son was about to make his ultimate move. Since Süleyman had so far resisted acting upon rumors, Rüstem also submitted evidence, apparently. According to a report blaming Rüstem for Mustafa's demise, written most likely by the geomancer Haydar, Rüstem had

a replica of Mustafa's seal made. A letter was then written as if from the prince
to the Safavid ruler Tahmasb, offering an alliance. Not realizing this was a
fabricated letter, Tahmasb sent a letter of acquiescence, which was intercepted
by Rüstem's men. Rüstem forwarded Tahmasb's letter to Süleyman as proof of
the prince's treason, together with news about the rebellious atmosphere in
the army camp.[16] While this sounds like a farfetched conspiracy, Haydar was
a Safavid émigré, and he claims in his report that he had received this information from Safavid diplomats he met in Aleppo after the prince's execution.

Eventually, Rüstem prevailed. As a first step, he and his men were
recalled to Constantinople. Süleyman then assumed the command of the
Ottoman forces for the first time since 1549, and he and Rüstem finally left
Constantinople with great fanfare on August 28. The end of August was close
to the end of the campaign season. The delay may have been due to Süleyman's
ill health and his need to rest. He had to be in good physical condition, not
only to travel and command, but also to impress the soldiery. Moreover,
since campaigns in the east were logistically more challenging, it is possible
that the plan was to travel from Constantinople to Aleppo, spend the winter
there with preparations, and move against the Safavids in the next spring and
summer, weather and logistics permitting. It is also true that discussions between Süleyman and Rüstem on how to deal with Mustafa may have delayed
the departure.

Süleyman left his capital city with great fanfare, as had been his custom;
seven banners, which symbolized his supremacy over seven climes, were again
unfurled. He wanted to prove to all, especially amid rumors that his eldest
son might soon replace the ailing sultan, that he was still the ruler he used to
be. As a sign of the campaign's importance, the bulk of the Ottoman forces
was committed to it, including the Rumeli troops under the command of
governor-general Sokullu Mehmed (d. 1579), the newest rising star in the fir-
mament of Ottoman high officialdom. Cihangir, who had become his father's
closest companion over the recent years, accompanied him, even though his
physical condition was not suitable for the strains of a long campaign. The
sultan, in old age, increasingly disliked loneliness and sought comfort in familiar company.

Süleyman marched east at the head of his forces. Bayezid, who reached
them on September 8, was sent to Edirne to keep an eye on the European
front. Continuing his progress, Süleyman ordered to set camp around Ereğli,
near Konya, on October 5. The same day, Mustafa arrived in the vicinity of the
army camp with his men, to have an audience with his father, as he had done
in 1548. He was met and greeted by officials, and given presents, as befitted an

Ottoman prince. While Mustafa was doubtlessly aware that his rivals plotted against him, this positive reception must have been somewhat reassuring. He perhaps expected that an audience with his father might lead to another reconciliation. In any case, since he had been invited by his father, the refusal to come would have meant rebellion, and he was not at that point yet.

On October 6, around midday, Mustafa rode to the army camp, and then to his father's tent, situated in the middle of it. It was a Friday, near the time of midday prayer, the most auspicious time of the week according to Muslims. The prince dismounted; he left his weapons outside the tent, following custom. The men who accompanied him also stayed outside. After he entered the inner chamber of the tent, he was set upon by executioners and strangled after a struggle. It is unclear whether Süleyman was present, despite many stories that describe him as chastising his son and watching the execution. Mustafa's corpse was immediately exhibited in front of the sultan's tent as a message to his supporters. Some of his men, probably those known to be closest to him, were killed. Other members of his retinue were dispersed across the realm through *timar* grants. His property, including the gifts he had received the day before from the high officials, was sequestered.

After the grim display in front of the sultan's tent, a sparsely attended funeral prayer was held for the prince in the nearby town of Ereğli. From there, his corpse was hastily sent to Bursa, the old Ottoman capital and the burial ground for many members of the Ottoman dynasty. While Süleyman and Hürrem's son Mehmed had been buried in Constantinople, Mustafa was once again denied a privileged treatment. His death meant a downturn in the fortunes of his closest relatives as well. His mother Mahidevran followed her son's corpse to Bursa. Mustafa's young son Mehmed, who had been relocated to the same city in the company of the female members of the prince's household, was soon after executed by strangulation. Mahidevran continued to live in Bursa, in reduced circumstances, to the end of her life in 1581.

As in the case of İbrahim's execution in 1536, it is difficult to find, in contemporary testimonies, a clear explanation for Mustafa's execution. The chancellor Celalzade Mustafa, writing a few years later, tries to shift part of the blame to the prince by pointing out some injustices committed by his men. Aware of the weakness of his argument, however, he ultimately attributes what happened to the inscrutable will of God.[17] In the *Sulaymannama*, Mustafa is accused of being behind unspecified actions that would have led to sedition if he had not been stopped by an angry Süleyman.[18] Very few, in the army camp and beyond, agreed with these arguments. Rather, Mustafa's execution was met with widespread grief, confusion, and shock. To appease the soldiery,

Süleyman immediately dismissed Rüstem from the grand vizierate. The dismissal, and his quick return to Constantinople, probably saved Rüstem's life
from raucous, revenge-seeking soldiers who held him responsible for the
prince's demise.[19]

The anger and dismay felt by many outside the upper echelons of the elite
are best illustrated by a series of poems composed in response to Mustafa's execution.[20] For instance, Taşlıcalı Yahya (d. 1582), a soldier and one of the most
prominent poets of the era, wrote an elegy that became popular, giving voice
to the feelings of many:

> Alas! alas! and a column of the earth is broke atwain;
> For the tyrant Death's marauders Prince Mustafa have slain.
> Eclipsed is his sun-bright visage, away were his helpmeets ta'en;
> Through treason and guile have they wroughten the House of
>     'Osman bane.
> . . .
> Unproved any crime of him, and unknown any infamy.
> Saint! O Martyr! foul is the wrong they have wrought on thee.
> Undone on the face of earth, he returned to his own true land,
> And joyous he went forthright in the presence of God to stand.[21]

Many others followed Yahya's example. Thus, a popular chronogram,
whose letters' numerical values give the date of the execution according to
the Hijri calendar (960), informed all and sundry that the execution was due
to "Rüstem's conspiracy and deceit" (*mekr-i Rüstem*). The poets reacting to
the prince's demise call him "*şehid*" (a martyr). They decry the murder of
Mustafa's innocent, blameless son Mehmed. They deny the accusation that
he was conspiring with Tahmasb. They blame Rüstem, Hürrem (called a
"Ruthenian witch"), and even the chief jurist Ebussuud, who had presumably
issued a *fetva* against the prince.[22] They also criticize Süleyman for lacking affection for his son and for following the guidance of Rüstem, a mere servant.
A similar tone is also encountered in a contemporary Safavid source, which
provides a chronogram on the execution of Mustafa's son Mehmed: "*sitam-e
mukarrar*" (an injustice repeated).[23]

This was one of the most difficult moments of Süleyman's life. Setting
aside the emotional burden of ordering the execution of his own son, he was
on his way to another eastern campaign, surrounded by a soldiery whose sympathy for the dead prince had to be surmounted and transformed. And he had

to achieve all this in the absence of Rüstem, his closest collaborator for the past decade and the true manager of the machinery of the state.

## Peace with the Safavids

Süleyman's last campaign in the east may be seen as a two-stage operation, the first phase of which was to neutralize Mustafa, and the second to march against the Safavids.[24] His first campaign against the Safavids had intended, in line with the high imperialism of the 1530s, to eradicate the Safavid dynasty. On his second campaign, the initial plan was to install an Ottoman-friendly shah on the Safavid throne in the person of Alqas Mirza. The third campaign, in comparison, was a much more subdued affair.

On the surface, an overarching anti-Safavid rhetoric persisted among the Ottomans. This is clearly seen in a campaign narrative in verse written by an Ottoman magistrate, in which Süleyman is presented, in addition to his munificence and his military achievements, as a protector of correct belief (i.e., Sunnism) whose mission is to invite the Safavids to relinquish their errors.[25] In fact, Süleyman and his officials had modest military objectives in his third eastern campaign. Their most ambitious aim may have been to force the Safavids into a peaceful settlement.[26]

Ottoman historians have subsumed the events of 1554–55 under the name of the Nakhichevan campaign, since the main military operations focused on present-day Nakhichevan and southern-central Armenia. The apparent reason was to respond in kind to the Safavid attacks throughout 1552–53, which had wreaked havoc particularly around Lake Van and resulted in the loss of a number of Ottoman fortresses. Rüstem's fabricated evidence about an alliance between Mustafa and Tahmasb may also have played a role. While the campaign was conceived before Rüstem made his allegations, they may have given additional urgency to an already planned operation.

The first major episode of the campaign was the execution of Mustafa on October 6. Although not welcomed by all, Mustafa's death must have reintroduced some stability into the lives of Süleyman, Hürrem, and their children. Sons of the same mother, Selim and Bayezid did not seem likely at the time to declare war against each other. Hürrem, who had worked strenuously to preserve the lives of her children and secure the accession of one of them to the throne, must have been particularly relieved. Cihangir traveled with Süleyman; Bayezid was sent to Edirne for the duration of his father's absence from Constantinople; Selim left his governorship and kept Süleyman company throughout most of the campaign. The family Süleyman and Hürrem had established, against custom and despite criticism, functioned well.

After the conclusion of the Mustafa affair, Süleyman marched to Aleppo and entered the city in early November with great ceremony. Cannons were fired from the citadel, and city folk (scholars, dervishes, notables among them) cheered the sultan. Anthony Jenkinson, an English merchant who saw him enter Aleppo, watched thousands of soldiers parade: light cavalrymen clad in scarlet; janissaries with their muskets, wearing high hats and clothes made of violet silk; palace troops adorned in gold. Süleyman followed on a white horse, in a robe of gold cloth embroidered with precious stones.[27] The performance of sovereignty continued during Süleyman's stay in Aleppo, as he ordered a review of taxes in the area and addressed the inhabitants' grievances. Despite institutionalization, early modern governance still relied on personal intervention and the display of royal justice, and campaigns gave rulers an occasion to travel across the realm and have these personal interactions. For Süleyman, however, these displays of power were soon interrupted by an unexpected tragedy: the death of his son Cihangir on November 27.

At the time of his death, Cihangir was in his early twenties. He suffered from a congenital problem of spinal malformation, which manifested itself as a hump on his back and required constant care. He was mobile enough to assist his father in his daily excursions and even in a long journey such as the 1548–49 campaign. However, another long trip on horseback and in carriages in 1554 may have put too much pressure on his constitution.[28] A variety of Ottoman sources claim that Cihangir's death was the outcome of a deep state of grief, ushered in by Mustafa's execution. While it was impossible to remain impervious to the trauma of the execution, Cihangir's death, which was preceded by a few days of sickness, was more likely a combination of his condition, the impact of the long trip, the stressful situation, and perhaps a contagious disease.

The death of a well-liked prince soon after Mustafa's execution was a significant shock for Süleyman and the army. According to an anonymous Venetian report, some soldiers initially thought that Süleyman had died, instead of Cihangir, and they rioted and looted Aleppo's markets. Süleyman had to come out of his chambers, leaning on a walking stick because gout limited his movements, to appease them. Following the funeral prayer, Cihangir's corpse was sent to Constantinople, to be buried next to his older brother Mehmed, who had died in 1543. After Cihangir's death, Süleyman asked his son Selim to leave his winter quarters and join him in Aleppo. In the coming days and weeks, father and son were often seen hunting together in the vicinity of the city. Despite deaths in the family, the life of the court went on.

There was also a military campaign to be conducted. Süleyman left Aleppo on April 9, 1554, and moved east. The morale of the soldiery must have bothered him. In addition to the impact of the Mustafa affair, some units had been on the move for more than a year. Therefore, on May 15, commanders, high officials, and senior members of various units were invited to an audience with the sultan. In yet another display of sovereign performance, Süleyman, whose ceremonial presence was usually distant and immobile, talked to his men. He reminded them of their duty to fight in the name of God. They were in the east to fulfill that duty; moreover, they were bound to serve their sultan. These reminders were accompanied by gifts, and his men declared their loyalty to Süleyman. Then, from the vicinity of Diyarbakır, where this meeting took place, Süleyman marched north-northeast, through Erzurum to Nakhchivan, arriving there on June 29.

After a short incursion into Safavid territory, Süleyman fell back on Kars on July 5. From there, a letter, full of the usual tropes mobilized by the Ottomans against the Safavids, was sent to Tahmasb: the Ottomans accused their rivals of heretical behavior, chided them for their practice of cursing the Sunni caliphs, denounced their cowardice, and invited them to the battlefield. These threats were followed by the Ottoman forces' move into Nakhchivan, where they spent the second half of July looting and pillaging. Then, upon the arrival of the holy month of Ramadan, Süleyman went back to Erzurum.

The Ottoman letter, full of theological accusations and threats of violence, and the punitive expedition that followed, were typical examples of early modern diplomacy, even though they do not appear so on the surface. The choice of Nakhchivan as a target, instead of a large city such as Tabriz, and the absence of a large-scale invasion of Safavid territory were indications that the Ottomans had in mind a sort of settlement with the Safavids, probably similar to their agreement with the Habsburgs from 1547. However, the hubris of Ottoman imperial rhetoric dictated that the Safavids should be forced to sue for peace, thus demonstrating their inferiority. Tahmasb had received and understood this convoluted message. On August 6, an Ottoman official previously captured by the Safavids brought a letter from senior Safavid officials, addressed to the Ottoman grand vizier Kara Ahmed. The letter ominously warned the Ottomans about a counterattack by the shah, but suggested that, if the Ottomans were willing, a state of peace could be reached between the two sides.

Diplomatic games continued in the coming days. The Ottomans sent two different replies to the Safavid letter. The first, from the grand vizier, restated the claims of their earlier, accusatory and threatening one; the second, from Ottoman viziers, lower in rank than the grand vizier, signaled that, while the Ottomans had not asked for peace, they would not reject Safavid appeals to Süleyman's clemency. The Safavids replied by a letter to the Ottoman governor-general of Erzurum, Ayas, in which, among other things, they provided a strong and confident defense of their dedication to Twelver Shiism against Ottoman allegations. In his retort, Ayas repeated earlier Ottoman claims; he also asserted that they had enough provisions to winter in the region and attack the Safavid shrine city of Ardabil the coming spring.[29]

It was fairly obvious by then, however, that a large-scale military operation was not on the horizon. This war of letters reflected a new reality in the Ottoman-Safavid relationship: the Safavids, for the first time, matched the haughtiness and hubris of the Ottoman letters.[30] This was not only a rhetorical matter. The Ottomans had not been able to dislodge the Safavids from Iran or convince the majority of their supporters to shift their allegiances. Although at a slower pace than the Ottomans, the Safavids had built bureaucratic institutions and defeated their rivals and competitors within and around the territories they controlled. Even though centrifugal forces were always strong in Safavid lands, by the 1550s, the descendants of Shah Ismail had entrenched themselves deeply in the area. Moreover, Twelver Shiism, the Safavid version of correct belief, had gained strong roots through conversion and the development of a clergy working in the service of the dynasty.

The rest of the negotiations reflected this new equilibrium between the Ottomans and the Safavids, as well as the establishment of a more orderly diplomatic relationship. On September 26, a high-ranking Safavid commander brought a letter that declared the cessation of hostilities; he was taken to Süleyman, who told him that the Ottomans were amenable to a peace agreement. This was the end of the Nakhchivan campaign. To accommodate the more comprehensive negotiations that would follow in the coming months, and to appease the region where his son Mustafa had served as district governor, Süleyman decided to spend the winter in Amasya. He reached the city on October 30, where envoys from France, Poland, Venice, and the Habsburgs awaited him.

The expected Safavid delegation entered Ottoman territory in early May and was sent with an escort to Amasya. Tahmasb had dispatched his chief courtier, one of his closest associates, as his envoy. In Amasya, the Safavids were given a mansion where Ottoman palace servants attended to them.

Ottoman viziers conducted negotiations with the Safavid delegation, and Süleyman received them at an imperial council meeting on May 21, following banquets organized by the viziers to honor the Safavid envoy. Lavish gifts that included fine carpets, embroidered tents, swords and shields, and a gilded, ornamented Quran were presented to the sultan, together with a letter from the shah.[31] Tahmasb's letter and Süleyman's written answer (presented to the Safavid envoy on June 1) once again demonstrated the new level of dialogue between the Ottomans and the Safavids.

Religious identity continued to play an important role in the exchanges between the two sides: Tahmasb presented himself as a devout adherent to Twelver Shiism, while the Ottomans chastised the Shiites for their cursing of the Sunni caliphs. However, both sides came together around the notion that they were Muslims. This meant that, at least officially, the Ottomans relinquished their allegations of heresy against the Safavids. The Safavid side committed to refrain from the ritual cursing of the Sunni caliphs, and the Ottomans agreed to allow the Shiite subjects of the shah to visit the pilgrimage sites in Mecca, as well as the Shiite shrines in Iraq that had passed into Ottoman hands in the 1530s. After half a century of accusations, and four major military campaigns, the Ottomans thus granted a sort of political and religious recognition to the Safavids.

This was an uneasy peace, however. For the Safavids, it came at the cost of accepting Ottoman sovereignty over the territories that had been conquered by Selim and Süleyman. On the Ottoman side, despite the political and financial benefits of peace, there were some, such as the chancellor Celalzade Mustafa, who saw the settlement as a concession that had to be accorded yet also somewhat lamented, since it did not solve the problem of religious deviance. On the European side, some observers were concerned that the settlement might bode ill for the Christian powers since it might allow the Ottomans to turn their gaze to the European front once again.[32]

Following the settlement with the Safavids, Süleyman agreed to a six-month ceasefire in east-central Europe after negotiations with Ferdinand's envoy Ogier Ghiselin de Busbecq. He finally left Amasya on June 21, nearly a year after his departure from Constantinople. He was back in the capital at the end of July. Shortly thereafter, his lifelong rival Charles V signed the Religious Peace of Augsburg with Protestant powers, an act of mutual recognition similar to Süleyman's vis-à-vis the Safavids. Charles had already begun to transfer some of his titles to his son Philip the year before. In August 1556, he abdicated as Holy Roman Emperor. His brother Ferdinand, elected King of the Romans already in 1531, took over the title, even though he was formally recognized only in May 1558. Süleyman, on the other hand, could not with-draw just yet. He was still concerned with leaving behind a specific legacy that suited his political and cultural vision. Moreover, he had two sons who could clash over the matter of succession. Despite peace with the Safavids, there was much to be done.

## A Legacy in Stone and on Paper

Throughout his career as sultan, from 1520 to the very end of his reign in 1566, one of Süleyman's chief preoccupations was to build and maintain his reputa-tion and image.[33] Narratives about his exploits were propagated widely, from European woodcuts and newsletters to Ottoman works of history and poetry. This was not a static image; rather, it was a dynamic narrative that adapted itself to the requirements of specific historical contexts as well as Süleyman's personal choices. For instance, from the 1540s onward, the image of a mes-sianic conqueror was gradually replaced by that of a more mature, settled monarch whose rule guaranteed peace and justice. Sunnism as religious con-fession and political identity played an important role in the creation and jus-tification of Süleyman's various images.[34] The building of a mosque complex bearing his name, the Süleymaniye, was conceived of as the ultimate achieve-ment and legacy of a wise, pious, charitable ruler.[35]

The mosque was presented, in contemporary Ottoman sources, as a new temple built by the Second Solomon, meaning Süleyman. Indeed, the complex was meant to be the larger than previous Ottoman examples. The Süleymaniye competed not only with Ottoman antecedents, but with Hagia Sophia itself. The cathedral church of the city under the Byzantines, Hagia Sophia had been built on the orders of emperor Justinian I (r. 527–65) between 532 and 537 to replace an older basilica.[36] It was one of the most imposing buildings of the medieval period, given its size and its internal decorations.

Even before their capture of the city in 1453, Hagia Sophia loomed large in Ottoman dreams of conquest. Byzantine stories about the building's inauspi-cious characteristics, recast within apocalyptic narratives on the destruction of Constantinople during the end times, were transferred from the Byzantines to the Ottomans, which contributed to the Ottoman fascination with the building.[37] The first Friday prayer after the Ottoman conquest happened there, and Mehmed II established his first endowment in Constantinople to support the newly converted mosque and an adjacent school. Located near the Great Palace and the Hippodrome, and at the beginning of the main av-enue leading toward Edirne and the west, Hagia Sophia served as one of the main ceremonial locations of the city. Süleyman often went there for Friday prayer, arriving and leaving in a procession.

Süleyman waited for a considerable time before starting to build his own mosque complex. His advancing age must have been a factor behind his decision. As his chancellor Celalzade Mustafa remarks in a passage where he discusses the building, Süleyman was well aware that this world was transitory, and he knew, as a highly intelligent individual, that good works meant a second life after death. The chancellor does not forget to add that Süleyman also wanted to follow the example of his ancestors who had built similar complexes, without adding that the sultan's complex was meant to surpass them all.[38] It also seems that, as in all else in his life, Süleyman awaited a time that was politically the most suitable.

That occasion presented itself with the 1547 peace treaty with the Habsburgs. The treaty did not much change the status quo in east-central Europe. However, thanks to Ferdinand's agreement to pay a tribute to the Ottomans for the parts of Hungary he held, and Charles' ratification of the treaty, the Ottomans could claim they had finally subdued their Habsburg rivals. Then, the settlement of 1555 with the Safavids underscored Süleyman's image as a Sunni ruler whose enemies had admitted defeat, at least according to the Ottomans. The Safavids' formal recognition of the Ottomans as the protectors of Mecca and Medina, and their promise to end their anti-Sunni rituals such as the public cursing of the caliphs Abu Bakr, Umar, and Uthman, further enhanced the ideological message behind the Süleymaniye project.

The complex was conceived in 1547. Orders to collect building materials went out as early as 1548, and the foundations were laid the same year. The mosque was opened to the public in June 1557, but construction on the complex continued into 1559. The site chosen was the top of Constantinople's third hill, a prominent point on the skyline of the city as seen from across the Golden Horn. The project was designed and built by the chief architect Sinan (ca. 1490–1588), the prolific master who helped forge a new Ottoman architectural style during his fifty-year service under Süleyman and his successors.

Sinan was, like the chief jurist Ebussuud, the chancellor Celalzade Mustafa, and the grand viziers İbrahim and Rüstem, one of the creators of the principal features associated with the reign of Süleyman. The chief jurist and the chancellor helped build legal and bureaucratic establishments and extended the application of the law into new areas. The grand viziers defined new imperial visions at home and abroad, fortified the political center against centrifugal elements, and strengthened the central treasury. They helped foster both the major military achievements of Süleyman's early years as well as his institution-building later on. Sinan, on the other hand, established the most tangible, visible, accessible legacy of all. While the institutional achievements are best appreciated by scholars today, Sinan's designs are spread across the old Ottoman lands, from the Balkans through Anatolia to the Arab provinces. A few hundred examples of his mosques, bridges, caravanserais, water works, hospices, soup kitchens, and other buildings still stand as the most vivid reminders of an Ottoman inheritance, even in countries where modern nationalist movements have been dismissive of the Ottoman past.[39]

Süleyman kept a close eye on the progress of the construction and visited the site from time to time. One of his visits took the form of an elaborate ceremony. On July 8, 1550, he traveled from the palace to the construction site in the company of servants, officials, and religious scholars. The date had been determined astrologically as the most auspicious day for the placement of the mosque's first stone. That important task was fulfilled by the chief jurist Ebussuud. On at least one other occasion, as Sinan mentions in his autobiography, Süleyman visited the site to inquire about when the mosque would be completed. He went so far as to warn Sinan about not spending time with other parts of the project and thus delaying the completion of its central feature. Sinan, fearing Süleyman's wrath, finished the mosque in great haste, appeasing the sultan and eventually receiving from him the honor of being the first one to unlock and open the building's main door.[40]

The attention given to the complex is demonstrated by the keeping of detailed records of expenses on materials and labor. The same records also provide an idea about the scope of the work involved. Around three thousand and five hundred workers were employed in the final stages of construction. Half of them were paid labor, 40 percent were janissary apprentices, and 5 percent were criminals condemned to hard labor. The cost of the complex was considerable. It came to around fifty-four million *akçes*, compared to fifteen million for the complex of Prince Mehmed, and twelve million for the complex in memory of Selim I.[41] Granted, the Süleymaniye complex was much larger than either of the latter and was meant to serve a more ambitious agenda.

Besides embodying the epitome of Ottoman Sunni triumphalism toward the end of Süleyman's reign, the complex reflected the benevolent side of the paternalistic relationship between Süleyman and his subjects. There, one could cater to all the needs of one's body and soul, thanks to the sultan's charity.[42] In addition to a mosque, with an area of 32,000 square feet, the complex included an elementary school (employing one teacher and one assistant), four madrasas for advanced education in religious sciences (for sixty students), one medical school (one professor and eight advanced students), and one school for the study of Muhammad's sayings and the Quran. The Süleymaniye madrasas were placed at the top of the Ottoman higher education hierarchy, further underlining Süleyman's desire to surpass his ancestors. The complex also included a soup kitchen, a hospice, a caravanserai, and a hospital. According to the endowment deed, its different units employed around eight hundred individuals, including the students who attended the new schools and received stipends.[43]

The central feature of the complex, both in terms of physical size as well as ideological function, was the Süleymaniye Mosque.[44] Despite its large size, the mosque was built in such a way as to receive less light through high-placed windows, which gave its interior a more sober atmosphere, and it was illuminated from within by candles and oil lamps. Decorations and ornaments were limited compared to earlier mosques, and the emphasis inside was placed on Quranic inscriptions that invited believers to prayer while reminding them of God's mercy. The names of the first four caliphs—Abu Bakr, Umar, Uthman, and Ali—were placed on columns on the right and left, while the names of God and Muhammad were prominently inscribed on each side of the prayer niche. The soundscape of the mosque was carefully constructed. Chapters of the Quran were read aloud by thirty reciters every morning; a preacher was appointed to give sermons and pray for the souls of Muhammad, his companions, previous Ottoman sultans, and the current ruler; an orator was tasked with reciting Arabic poetry to praise Muhammad.[45]

Indeed, the builders and designers of the space targeted the visual and aural senses of whoever entered the mosque. The message of austere grandeur continued on the outside: the four minarets, the large dome, the half-domes, and the small lateral domes were the only external ornamental elements, rising on top of a grey stone structure. An inscription composed by the chief jurist Ebussuud met those who entered the mosque through the main portal. There, in Arabic, one of his chief collaborators called Süleyman the caliph who ruled by the favor of God and who implemented his orders across the world. Süleyman was the conqueror of east and west; he was the sultan of the Arabs and the Persians; he was the promulgator of dynastic law (*kanun*).[46] The message was clear: he had built this impressive prayer space. All and sundry should be aware of this, until the end of time.

Süleyman's second comprehensive attempt at leaving behind a legacy during the final decades of his life took the form of an illustrated work of history written in Persian verse: the *Sulaymannama* ("The Book of Süleyman").[47] Very much like the monumental Süleymaniye complex, the *Sulaymannama*

**FIG. 7.2** The Süleymaniye Mosque and part of the complex, depicted ca. 1836–37. From Julia Pardoe, *The Beauties of the Bosphorus* (London: George Virtue, 1838). Drawing by W. H. Bartlett. Courtesy of the Lilly Library, Indiana University, Bloomington, Indiana.

represents the high level of cultural and political self-confidence and maturity that was reached toward the end of Süleyman's reign.

The mosque complex and the illustrated history may be seen as two different image-making strategies, two variations on the background of Perso-Arabo-Islamic culture, and two distinct evaluations of Süleyman's legacy. The complex referred to Sunni Islam, strict piety, everyday ritual, religious learning, and the paternalistic authority and charity of the ruler who provided religious direction as well as material comfort to his subjects. Built to withstand any calamity to the end of time, the mosque complex is strong, timeless, immobile. In contrast, the *Sulaymannama*, an account of Süleyman's exploits from the death of his father to September 1555, is a narrative that flows through time, supported by a succession of images in which the viewer may watch Süleyman ride to war, hunt, capture fortresses, and spend time with his sons. In terms of their audiences, the complex appealed to the widest public possible, while the *Sulaymannama*, of which a single copy was produced, was geared toward the palace household and the upper echelons of the elite.

Just as the Süleymaniye was partly an outcome of cultural competition with Byzantine and Ottoman antecedents, the illustrated history of Süleyman's reign was meant to compete and hopefully surpass earlier cultural models. One such model was the poet Firdavsi's Persian *Shahnama* ("The Book of Kings").[48] Completed in 1010 and presented to Sultan Mahmud of Ghazni, this epic work mainly tells the story of ancient Iranian kings. The *Shahnama* quickly became one of the Ur-texts of elite literary sensibility in the Islamic world, especially in areas where learned members of military-political, religious, and commercial elites spoke Persian, or utilized it, next to their native tongues, as the language of belles lettres.

The *Shahnama* served as a linguistic model to be emulated, a source of literary references and, like all great epic stories, a prism through which essential questions such as life, death, time, sickness, human frailty, heroism, and treason were discussed and understood. Its focus on the exploits of ancient Iranian kings particularly appealed to princes and rulers, such as Süleyman, who recognized themselves, their relatives, and the events of their lives in the adventures of the *Shahnama* characters. Süleyman's desire to see himself represented in a work similar to the *Shahnama* shows his respect for the legacy of the Arabo-Persian cultural heritage, as well as his urge to create his own classicized cultural statements from architecture to literature and beyond.

While very few Ottoman commoners spoke Persian, learned individuals, especially those with a madrasa education, were supposed to be proficient in the ideal linguistic trifecta: Arabic, Persian, and Turkish. (Chaghatay, or Eastern Turkish, preserved its relevance to the end of the sixteenth century, constituting a fourth language for the literati to be familiar with.) Multiple authors living in Ottoman territories had produced works in Persian since the early days of the enterprise. Persian poetry was widely read and emulated by educated Ottomans, including Süleyman himself. The knowledge of Persian was not limited to poetry. Works of history in Persian, especially those on the history of Chinggis Khan, the Mongols, and Timur, were popular among the Ottoman literati. Similarly, Ottoman readers were familiar with a large body of works on mysticism in Persian, from the poetry of Jalaluddin Rumi to hagiographies.[49]

What is interesting, and somewhat puzzling, in the case of the *Sulaymannama* is that its composition coincided with a time when Ottoman Turkish was becoming prominent as the main language of historical and literary writing.[50] The use of Persian in the *Sulaymannama* may be seen as a consciously classicist endeavor that favored the intellectual weight of Persian over the political expediency of Ottoman Turkish. The influence of Firdavsi's

*Shahnama* is particularly obvious. The author and artists who produced the *Sulaymannama* borrowed countless topoi from the *Shahnama*. Moreover, the text was composed in the same *mathnavi* form of rhyming couplets, using the same meter as Firdavsi.

The *Sulaymannama* is the fifth volume of a five-volume work on Islamic/ universal history, called *Shahnama-ye Al-e Osman* ("The Book of Kings of the House of Osman"), in another reference to Firdavsi's *Shahnama*. Of its five volumes, only three are extant today. The first, called *Anbiyanama* ("The Book of Prophets"), begins with Adam and Eve, covers some Old Testament prophets and a few ancient Iranian kings, and ends with the story of Muhammad's journey to the heavens. It was finished in early March 1558, and it has forty-eight folios of text and ten paintings. The missing second and third volumes were probably meant to focus on Muhammad and the rise and expansion of Islam, and the history of ancient Turkish rulers including the Saljuks. The incomplete fourth volume, *Osmannama* ("The Book of Osman"), meant to be a history of the Ottoman dynasty before Süleyman, stops in 1402.[51] It includes 205 folios and thirty-four paintings for its coverage of nearly a century of Ottoman history. The *Sulaymannama* is the longest work among the extant three. It contains 617 folios and sixty-nine paintings, four of them double-page spreads; it is written in sixty thousand couplets.

The *Sulaymannama* was finished in late June–early July 1558. The text was the work of Fethullah Ârif (d. ca.1561–62), an Ottoman litterateur with ties to prominent Sufi milieus.[52] He was the first person to carry the title of *şehnameci* (*Shahnama*-writer), and was tasked with writing a comprehensive history of Süleyman's reign in the late 1540s, just as the Süleymaniye complex was being planned.[53] The fact that he was given guidance by the sultan and by the sultan's entourage added an element of collective authorship to the project. The production of the *Sulaymannama*'s paintings involved many artists who worked as members of an atelier, who divided among themselves tasks such as drawing, coloring, applying gold leaf, calligraphy, page ornamentation, and binding.

A distinguishing feature of the *Sulaymannama* is its inclusion of sixty-nine thematically connected images. The art of illustration was very much associated with the Persian cultural universe in the late medieval and early modern periods. Works with illustrations were created outside the sphere of Persian cultural production as well, most notably in Mamluk Egypt. During Süleyman's reign, narratives with illustrations were produced in the Ottoman realm with greater frequency and wider content. However, the *Sulaymannama* represents the rise of the painted scene from ornament or accompaniment to the level of a visual narrative. This is seen both in the level of detail that is included in single compositions, as well as the fairly coherent concatenation of paintings that tell their own story, next to the Persian text.

The *Sulaymannama* projects specific images about Süleyman, his sovereignty, his persona, and his empire. First of all, by positioning the *Sulaymannama* as the last book of a five-volume series on ancient, Islamic, and Turkic histories, the author and his patrons state that Süleyman's reign represented the culmination of sacred and human history. The opening sections of the *Sulaymannama* present Süleyman not only as superior to other Ottoman rulers, but also as a ruler whose secular and divine charisma superseded those of Prophet Solomon. As a whole, the *Sulaymannama* projects a sovereign image that was very much inspired by strands of Sufism as well as apocalyptic and messianic speculations that were widespread during Süleyman's reign. Indeed, it represents a final reckoning with some of the messianic and apocalyptic speculations that had receded during the decades before its composition. In its pages, Süleyman becomes, for one last time, the Master of Auspicious Conjunction and the Renewer (*mujaddid*) of religion.[54]

The bulk of the *Sulaymannama* focuses on the specifics of Süleyman's rule, navigating between the transcendental and the mundane. It offers a detailed narrative of Süleyman's reign, from the time he received news of his father Selim's passing to the appointment of Rüstem to the grand vizierate a second time, in September 1555.[55] It narrates mostly an event-based history, which proceeds from one military venture to another, with Süleyman as the chief actor. The downfall of figures such as İbrahim or Prince Mustafa is discussed yet subsumed within the flow of the overall story. The centrality of Süleyman is reinforced through the paintings, even though he is not placed at the center of all of them. There, in the visual narrative, he hunts, leads the army, receives foreign envoys, meets with his children, and is entertained in the palace. The violence of war is often tempered through the beauty of nature scenes in the background. The Ottomans prevail at every single venture; once again, peace and order reign.

There is yet another component of Süleyman's rule that is given considerable space in the text: the government and the servants of the sultan. The *Sulaymannama* tells its readers, over nearly thirty folios, about topics such as dynastic law and the ranks of military men and palace servants. It talks about scholars, students, and the religious establishment; it provides details about the imperial council (meeting times, attendees, meeting order); and it enumerates the guns and ships that were available to the Ottoman soldiers. This long section is placed between Süleyman's accession to the throne and the first major crisis of his reign, the revolt in Syria. The second illustration of the work, a single-page painting, depicts the recruitment of Christian children as slaves of the sultan, while the text explains the process and praises the service of those ex-Christian servants. The third illustration is a double-page painting of an imperial council session, with all the appropriate officials represented. Thus, the edifice that Süleyman built, the service class he helped expand, and the machinery of government itself are presented as central features of his legacy.

## Matters of Succession Revived

From the mid-1540s to the early 1560s, Süleyman lived under the constant threat of a succession crisis that could turn violent. The execution of Prince Mustafa was meant to preempt that eventuality, but that radical measure failed to stem all prospects of violent conflict, as seen in the revolt of a pretender to the throne, followed by a clash between Süleyman's two surviving sons, Bayezid and Selim. While Ottoman sources typically treat the participants of the revolt as rabble, many from the lowest-ranking members of the *askerî* elite were among them. As small *tımar* holders, they carried a heavy burden during military campaigns, traveling long distances with their small retinues. At other times, they lived close to the peasant communities, benefiting from their labor, but also vulnerable, like the peasants, to economic and climactic fluctuations. Their modest revenues suffered from inflation, a growing concern during a time of monetization and commercial expansion.

During the first months of 1555, in what is today northeastern Bulgaria, a man dismissively called Mustafa the Impostor ("*Düzme Mustafa*") in Ottoman sources rebelled.[56] The area where the rebellion broke out was a zone of transition between long-standing Ottoman governorates to the south and the lands of the tributary principality of Wallachia to the north. The heavily forested area was an ecological frontier as well, where the Ottomans had settled unruly Turkish-speaking nomads from Anatolia. Inhabitants of the area had already joined a rebellion in the early fifteenth century that had promised equality and prosperity. Others were descendants of Safavid supporters who had been deported there.[57]

The leader of the rebellion presented himself as Prince Mustafa, and he claimed he had run away from Süleyman's army camp while a lookalike was executed. Reportedly, he indeed resembled the late Mustafa. His princely pretensions extended into the way he organized his followers: he appointed a chief vizier and military judges, imitating the Ottoman administration.

According to some reports, the pretender and his men appropriated sums that were collected for taxes and redistributed them. While the extent of the redistribution is not known, it must have secured further support for their movement. Ten thousand men or so had initially gathered around the pretender; the numbers apparently swelled to forty thousand. This was an army of *tımar* holders, raiders, and frontiersmen of all sorts: people who knew how to fight, even though they did not have the heavy weapons of the janissaries and the palace household troops. The rebellion continued to grow while Süleyman was in Amasya and his son Bayezid was in Edirne.

Bayezid was the first to intervene. While he informed his father of developments, he made military preparations and sent an experienced district governor to enter into secret negotiations with the pretender's chief vizier. News must have become particularly concerning in June–July 1555, since Süleyman dispatched Sokullu Mehmed with a contingent of household troops and janissaries to quell the rebellion. Sokullu Mehmed had recently been appointed third vizier, but he was well experienced in the affairs of Rumeli thanks to his long service there as governor-general. In the meantime, the district governor sent by Bayezid had been able to convince the chief vizier of the pretender to change sides. The chief vizier then kidnapped and surrendered him to the Ottoman forces. Mustafa the Impostor was sent to Constantinople, where he was tortured and executed.

The rebellion, today seen as another minor incident of Süleyman's reign, greatly concerned the sultan and his officials. Their victory over the pretender is celebrated in a section at the end of the *Sulaymannama*, accompanied by a painting. There, the pretender is depicted in a pose of utter dejection: bareheaded, torso exposed, wearing short trousers that do not cover his calves, hands and feet tied, dragged behind a horse.[58] The movement disbanded after losing its leader, a typical weakness in agrarian rebellions. Once again, the central authority interpreted a social upheaval as a political/administrative problem and worked to restore order. Some of the pretender's supporters were executed, while others were dismissed from *tımar*s, unwittingly creating potential supporters for future rebellions.

The affair of the pretender had a few unexpected outcomes. For one, Bayezid's attitude during the rebellion may have soured the relationship between him and his father. Ferdinand's envoy Busbecq, in his reminiscences of Constantinople, relates several rumors he heard during his stay. Accordingly, some believed Bayezid had started or managed the revolt in order to come to the throne while his father was away. Apparently, Süleyman wanted to punish his son but Hürrem intervened.[59] Passages in Busbecq's *Turkish Letters* about the pretender affair are highly theatrical, and they describe secret meetings involving the sultan, Bayezid, and Hürrem, which Busbecq's informers would not be privy to. Significantly enough, however, the same rumors are recorded by Venetian diplomat Antonio Erizzo, who was in Constantinople as these events unfolded, and who states that Bayezid "aspired to the throne with all his soul" (*aspira all'imperio con tutto l'animo*).[60]

The execution of the grand vizier Kara Ahmed at the end of September 1555 was also attributed by some observers to suspicions that he may have been implicated in the affair of the pretender, even though the extent of his possible involvement, if any, is not explicitly mentioned. The downfall of Kara Ahmed brought Rüstem back to the grand vizierate, almost two years after his hasty dismissal following Mustafa's execution. Rüstem had not spent this interlude idly; to the contrary, he had lived in Constantinople as a man of influence, maintaining his contacts within the elite. As he was known for being pro-Bayezid, his return must have been welcome news to the prince.

The defeat of the pretender provided only a temporary reprieve, however, and tensions related to succession soon resurfaced. After the elimination of Mustafa, the friction between Bayezid and Selim, and between their respective supporters and sympathizers, became increasingly palpable. Like his grandfather Selim before him, and his half-brother Mustafa, Bayezid presented himself as heroic in battle, generous, just, surrounded by poets. He was described as melancholic, prudent, ambitious, and deeply interested in history. Selim, whose reputation for overindulgence in drinking and other courtly pleasures was noted by many, was known as jovial and lovable. He seems to have adopted the role of the docile, mature elder son who did not stray from his father's wishes.[61]

Both princes needed to ingratiate themselves with their father as the ultimate decision-maker, and they often corresponded with him to relay their anxieties and expectations. Bayezid, a better writer than his brother as well as a more ambitious prince, often presented himself as the aggrieved, misunderstood son in his letters. After the pretender affair, Süleyman, either to demonstrate his equal treatment of his sons or under the pressure of Bayezid's supporters in Constantinople, transferred Bayezid to the district governorate of Germiyan, centered around the town of Kütahya. Bayezid's old seat of Konya was farther from Constantinople than his brother Selim's in Manisa. With this reassignment, the two princes were now nearly equidistant from the capital, to which they would rush upon receiving news of their father's death.

Süleyman's health issues continued to preoccupy those close to him, as well as Süleyman himself. Süleyman did his best to disprove rumors about his impending death. In a letter from June 1557, the French ambassador in Constantinople Jean de la Vigne wrote that, as soon as the sultan felt well enough to ride on his horse, he left Edirne and entered his capital city "with great pomp, showing the best face he could, to persuade everyone that he was not close to death, and that his detractors and the janissaries were not about to get what they wished," that is, the sultan's replacement by one of his sons.[62]

The events took a decisive turn following Hürrem's death in April 1558.[63] While known for having a slight preference for Bayezid, she had been able to prevent her sons from engaging in open warfare. A few months after Hürrem's death, in early September, Süleyman changed his sons' gubernatorial seats, sending them farther away from Constantinople and from each other. Selim was moved to Konya, and Bayezid to Amasya. In addition, Selim's son Murad was given a governorship in Akşehir, close to his father, while Bayezid's son Orhan was made district governor of Çorum. These appointments spurred a flurry of new letters. Bayezid, the more prolific writer, complained about the decision, asked his father for new appointments, and generally tried to delay his departure. At this juncture, Süleyman began to use a sterner tone toward his younger son, going so far as to warn him that he was defying his father's orders at his own risk.

Bayezid, unable to get his father to change his mind, left Kütahya at the end of October. He reached Amasya in late December, taking his time in travelling there. His letters from the road expose his impatience, as well as his emotional mindset: they are filled with complaints about his brother Selim's machinations, accusations about his lewd behavior, pretexts for not following Süleyman's orders, and appeals to have his grievances redressed. He goes so far as to blame Süleyman for his lack of affection and his cruelty. It is quite likely that Süleyman was eventually swayed towards Selim by Bayezid's reluctance to move to Amasya, his tone and arguments, and his attempts at soliciting help from Rüstem and Mihrümah. His sister and brother-in-law, albeit sympathetic to Bayezid, were forced to remain neutral, especially after it became clear that the prince was on his way to openly defy the sultan.

Bayezid's recriminations continued after his arrival in Amasya. He asked to be sent back to Kütahya; he solicited new appointments; he wanted to be assigned higher revenues. His letters became increasingly strident and rambling. Bayezid had collected thousands of men around himself while in Kütahya, and had used his long trip to Amasya to fill the ranks with new recruits, who were given daily stipends. His letters and actions clearly indicated

his intention to usher in an armed conflict, even though he presented his behavior as self-defense. The inevitable had thus become even closer in the last
months of 1558.[64]

The struggle between the two brothers also reflected important social and
economic issues. Bayezid, like Mustafa, had the sympathy of those who saw
him as the embodiment of the old ideal of the warrior sultan, and who also
wanted to play a role in the succession. Moreover, badly remunerated *timar*
holders, runaway peasants, nomads, and unemployed young men flocked to
Bayezid in search of money, favors, and justice. Selim, on the other hand,
chose to adopt a deferential attitude toward his father and the establishment.
For instance, he did not contest his new appointment to Konya. That said,
he was genuinely concerned about an imminent attack by Bayezid in the fall
of 1558. Thus, after he left Manisa, he traveled north to Bursa, instead of east
to Konya. It seems that he wanted to be closer to Constantinople and farther
away from his brother, who was dragging his feet on the road from Kütahya to
Amasya. Selim traveled to Konya only after it was ascertained that his brother
was indeed on his way to Amasya, entering the city in the early days of 1559.

Selim's concerns are clearly seen in a letter he sent to Süleyman around
this time. In it, he reports that his brother and his men had purchased horses,
military equipment, and grain, forcing the owners to sell their goods at lower
prices. Countless men rushed to join Bayezid, who was expected to spend the
winter in his quarters but possibly attack Selim in the coming spring. Selim
further complains that Bayezid had many supporters in Constantinople, including in the upper ranks of the elite.[65] Selim was advised by his father to
stay in Konya and adopt a defensive position against his brother. He duly
complied. He was also given a large sum to recruit stipendiary soldiers, in anticipation of his brother's attack. In the meantime, Süleyman tried to appease
Bayezid, writing to him that he was not being mistreated. [66]

Bayezid made the first move. His haste was due to emotional as well as logistical factors. He was impatient, feeling slighted and mistreated by his father.
He believed, like Mustafa before him, that he had the requisite characteristics
of a sultan, while his brother, whom he often mocked in his correspondence
to Selim and Süleyman, was cowardly, indeed effeminate. On the operational
side, he was faced with the difficulty of housing thousands of followers in and
around Amasya for a long time. Also, the men he had gathered were promised
stipends, and continuing to pay them was becoming challenging. In a way,
Bayezid had the problems and prospects of a mercenary army commander: he
had to put his men into action and find them other sources of revenue, if he
did not want them to turn against him or simply to disband.

Thus, he moved out of Amasya in mid-April 1559 with a force of fifteen thousand and marched to Ankara, a critical crossroads between Constantinople and Selim's seat in Konya. He continued to argue, in his correspondence with his father, that his ultimate wish was to be returned to his previous governorship in Kütahya. However, it had become clear that he intended to attack and kill his brother and remain the sole heir to the throne, before Süleyman decided to throw his weight behind Selim. It was too late, however, since news of Bayezid's expedition convinced Süleyman that military action was necessary against his son. He ordered the third vizier Sokullu Mehmed to join Selim with a janissary contingent. The Rumeli troops, under the command of their governor-general Mustafa, joined Sokullu Mehmed, and they left Constantinople in early May. To provide further support, Ottoman officials close to Konya were ordered to help Selim in case of an attack.

Süleyman also mobilized the Ottoman religious establishment against Bayezid. Scholars and legal officials, including both those in active service as well as a few who were retired, were asked to issue legal opinions on the matter. The resulting *fetva*s argued that, if one of the sons of a just sultan were to occupy fortresses, collect money and property from the populace, gather soldiers, and kill people, it was lawful under the Sharia to kill that prince and his followers.[67] Bayezid must have been informed about the dispatch of a military contingent from Constantinople and the *fetva*s. He knew he had been rejected by his father and the entire establishment before his battle with Selim, and that he was fighting for survival.

Before the forces sent from Constantinople reached Konya, Bayezid turned south from Ankara and arrived in the vicinity of Konya at the end of May 1559. Selim, expecting his brother's attack, was already in a defensive position. His forces had been augmented by troops under the command of governors-general and other officials, while Bayezid's smaller army consisted mostly of low-ranking *timar* holders and men he had gathered over the past months. The morale, it seems, was on Bayezid's side. During two days of engagements, on May 30 and 31, his forces fought with conviction and zeal, while the forces on Selim's side exhibited a certain reluctance about pushing further. Still, numbers and better armament, including gunpowder weapons, prevailed. Despite their fierce attacks, Bayezid's forces were unable to root out Selim's men from their defensive positions and lost many of their own during the process.[68]

Tired and defeated, Bayezid returned to Amasya, from where he wrote to his father and the grand vizier Rüstem to be pardoned, while he again tried to recruit men and gather materiel. The forces under the third vizier

Sokullu Mehmed had reached Konya around mid-June, and Selim was ordered to pursue his rebellious brother with their help. From mid-June onward, as seen in orders sent by the imperial council, the entire state machinery was mobilized against Bayezid. Governors and judges on the Black Sea coast, in the Arab provinces, and on the Ottoman-Safavid frontier were alerted to Bayezid's imminent flight through their regions. The Khan of Crimea was similarly informed that Bayezid might try to cross the Black Sea to the north, just as his grandfather Selim had done nearly fifty years earlier.[69]

While these dispatches circulated, Bayezid left Amasya on July 7, the first day of the Eid al-Fitr, the holiday that followed Ramadan, which fell on a Friday that year. Leaving on one of the holiest days of the Muslim calendar, he may have hoped for an auspicious beginning to his travels. He still had nearly ten thousand men. His four sons were in his company, while four daughters and a newborn son were left behind. He quickly marched east, before the central forces sent from Konya, and the local governors ordered to intercept, could reach him. It seems that many local officials preferred not to engage him during his march, despite orders to the contrary. He thus moved from Amasya to Bayburt, and then to Erzurum, where some governors-general finally caught up with him. Possibly hoping to preserve his forces, Bayezid disengaged after quick skirmishes and entered Safavid territory. Before crossing over, he had continued to send letters to Rüstem and Mihrümah, hoping for their intercession. He admitted his rash actions in these letters, but still hoped

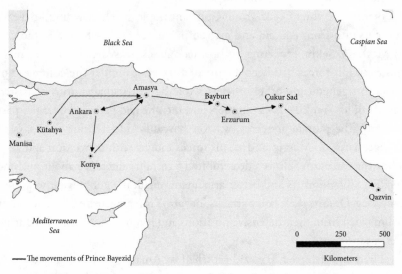

**FIG. 7.3** The movements of Prince Bayezid during the final stage of the succession struggles. Map by Jordan Blekking.

to be pardoned. Receiving no signs to that effect, he did not have any options left other than taking refuge in the Safavid realm.

Bayezid's subsequent actions continued to preoccupy the Ottoman establishment. Since he was accompanied by a large number of fighters, once rested he could return in force to the Ottoman realm. Even worse, he could ally with Shah Tahmasb, perhaps adopting a role similar to the one played by the runaway Safavid prince Alqas Mirza in the late 1540s. To pre-empt any movements against Ottoman territories, additional forces were sent to critical locations on the Safavid border and officials in the area were put in a state of alert. The Ottomans were not the only ones who were reminded of Alqas. In his memoirs, Tahmasb later discussed the Bayezid affair in comparison with the defection of his brother.[70]

While Tahmasb may not have been in a position to organize a large-scale military campaign against the Ottomans or to convince Bayezid to head such a campaign, the prince's presence in his lands gave him a considerable advantage. Thus, on the one hand, he quickly sent his high officials with gifts to Bayezid, and he then received the prince with great pomp in his capital city of Qazvin in late October. Soon after, however, he also sent envoys to Süleyman and Selim to discuss the situation. Intense negotiations ensued, which lasted until the second half of 1562.[71]

Tahmasb's most urgent task was to neutralize any military threats from Bayezid. The prince had, after all, nearly ten thousand men under his command. Despite the agreement of 1555, the Ottomans and the Safavids were rival dynasties whose princes grew up with a strong ethos of enmity toward the other side. As a first step, Bayezid's forces were slowly diluted. Some were stationed farther away from the prince, and others were re-assigned under Safavid units. While Bayezid enjoyed a cautious yet warm welcome initially, he was imprisoned in April 1560, six months or so after his arrival. His imprisonment showed that Tahmasb had clearly decided to play the diplomatic game instead of using Bayezid for military plans against the Ottomans.

In the next two years, Tahmasb maintained a regular correspondence with Süleyman and Selim.[72] Süleyman, possibly embarrassed to ask for his son's execution, and preferring to adopt a more statesmanlike tone, consistently demanded Bayezid's return and offered various incentives, ranging from a large sum of cash to the return of the frontier fortress of Kars to the Safavids. Selim and Tahmasb, on the other hand, were more open about their intentions in the letters they addressed to each other. They discussed the eventuality of Bayezid's execution and the incentives Tahmasb needed to make it happen.

These negotiations happened in the ornate, aestheticized diplomatic language of the time, and all three performed specific roles. Süleyman acted as
the aggrieved father and a more senior figure, while Tahmasb sounded deferential toward him. The relationship was reversed in the correspondence between Tahmasb and Selim, whereby the Safavid shah performed the role of
the more experienced ruler advising the younger Ottoman prince. Aesthetics
and literary prowess, however, did not hide the violence brewing under
the surface. Neither could they prevent the distrust between the two sides.
Indeed, while corresponding with the Safavids, the Ottomans kept a close eye
on developments inside the Safavid domain, sent spies to collect information
and communicated with the neighbors of the Safavids about a potential military action against Tahmasb.

Finally, on July 23, 1562, envoys sent by Süleyman and Selim met with
Bayezid in Qazvin, where he had been imprisoned for more than two years.
The prince was brought to them wearing a simple old dress, a torn skullcap on
his head, his beard shaved: a picture of downfall and desolation. Süleyman's
envoy recognized him, for they had to be sure the right person was going to be
executed. After Bayezid's identity was ascertained, Selim's men strangled him
and his four sons. (His fifth son, left behind as a baby, was soon after strangled
in Bursa, where he had been sent to reside with his mother.) Their corpses, preserved in musk and perfumes, were carried back to the Ottoman side. Although
Süleyman's sons Mehmed and Cihangir had been buried in Constantinople,
Bursa had been the customary burial site for Ottoman princes. The rebel
and his sons had been excised from the dynasty, however. It is true that their
corpses were not left in Safavid Iran, the land of a rival dynasty where Twelver
Shiism prevailed. Still, they were buried outside the city walls of Sivas, deep in
Ottoman territory, but far away from either Bursa or Constantinople.

The Bayezid affair had a number of short-term and long-term consequences.
Tahmasb was not given the 1.2 million gold ducats he had been promised (he
received half a million), nor the fortress of Kars. However, he was able to
ingratiate himself with Süleyman and, more importantly, the heir apparent
Selim, who reached an agreement of peace with Tahmasb that would be, as
it was stated, valid until the Day of Judgment. Perhaps as importantly, the
previous agreement of 1555 between Süleyman and Tahmasb and the ensuing
crisis gave the latter the respite he needed to further entrench the political,
military, and religious authority of the Safavid dynasty.

On the Ottoman side, the conflict mobilized the entire governmental
structure, rendering it impossible for the Ottomans to focus their energies
on any military ventures. This was a period of diplomacy: in addition to the

ongoing correspondence with the Safavids, they signed an armistice, and then an eight-year peace treaty with the Austrian Habsburgs. It was also a period of internal administrative measures. Bayezid's followers inside the Ottoman lands were pursued. Some were punished all the way to being executed, some *tımar* holders were dismissed from their positions, and some were pardoned. The establishment prevailed once again, and the last rebel prince was defeated.[73]

Other repercussions spread over the longer term in such a way that commentators in the next decades, and some modern scholars, saw the Bayezid affair as a major turning point in Ottoman political and social history. Indeed, the militarization of large groups of men, recruited by Bayezid and Selim as stipendiary soldiers, contributed to the spread of gunpowder weapons and military knowhow to individuals outside the *askerî* elite. This led to the increase of non-state armed actors, whose "banditry" and rebellious behavior would preoccupy the Ottoman authorities in the coming decades. Other stipendiary soldiers were promised inclusion into the *askerî* elite, and Selim followed his promise, giving them salaried positions in his retinue as prince and then as sultan after 1566. This represented a significant contravention of established recruitment procedures, which helped maintain a service class mostly staffed by ex-Christian slaves of the sultan.

Rather than constituting deviations from a supposedly ideal form of government, problems such as these stemmed from the challenges presented by an agrarian economy that fed a large military-political elite. Ottoman imperial ideology functioned on the assumption that the sultan and his officials provided justice to all the subjects of the empire to ensure order. As a result, the root causes of severe social and economic issues were to a large extent ignored. At least, this was the position of Süleyman and his officials initially. Any frictions or problems were seen as temporary and extraordinary. They were typically explained with reference to personal attributes such as ambition, lack of loyalty, and a rebellious temperament. During the last decades of Süleyman, however, critical voices about the shortcomings of Ottoman government and the failures of its officials began to emerge.

## Living through Crises

The last decades of Süleyman's reign were a time of reckoning for many among the elite. One of them, who remains anonymous to this day, was probably a low-ranking religious scholar. While he did not advocate for major changes to Ottoman government, his list of critical observations shows that he believed a series of reforms were needed to remedy issues ranging from the over-taxation of the subjects to the misbehavior of judges and market inspectors in Constantinople. *Timar* holders too sick to participate on campaigns should not be penalized; regular inspections should be organized in the provinces, conducted by experienced retired officials rather than palace personnel; and the distribution of charity should be better organized to cater to the widowed, the elderly, the blind, and the orphaned.[74]

Another critical voice heard during the last years of Süleyman was his ex-grand vizier and ex-brother-in-law Lütfi, who penned a treatise on Ottoman politics during his retirement. Similar to the anonymous writer mentioned above, he too cautioned those responsible for the conduct of governmental af-fairs against over-taxation. Aware of the difficulties of appropriately staffing a fast-expanding bureaucratic apparatus, he emphasized the need to find worthy individuals, implying that some of those currently serving were not. Lütfi's criticism did not spare Süleyman either, as he stated that revenues surpassed expenses on his accession while that balance was reversed later on. Under him, *timar* assignments given to non-fighting cadres such as scribes and palace personnel led to a decrease of fighting men. On a personal level, the sultan wrongly empowered individuals like the grand vizier İbrahim and the treasurer İskender by visiting their mansions and socializing with them.[75] Even a posi-tive assessment of Süleyman's reign as a time when just laws were applied felt the need to underline the mutual nature of the relationship between the sultan and his servants, making it incumbent upon the ruler to respect the Sharia as well as the bonds of friendship and civility that tied him to his associates.[76]

While these treatises had limited circulation, negative rumors about Süleyman abounded in the capital as the shock of the Mustafa affair con-tinued to resonate. For instance, it was widely believed that Cihangir had died of sorrow after witnessing the events of his half-brother's execution, and Süleyman and Hürrem may have felt at least partially culpable. The extent of the ongoing criticisms and Süleyman's defensiveness is seen in his falling out with his childhood friend Yahya.

According to one testimony, Yahya, who was in communication with the palace, wrote a few years after the execution to recommend that Mustafa's mother Mahidevran, banished to Bursa after his death, be welcomed back into the palace. With Mustafa's death, she had fallen into poverty and had asked Yahya to intercede. Finding his old friend's request insolent, Süleyman had him dismissed from his teaching position.[77] A Meccan scholar and diplomat, who was in Constantinople in 1558 and visited Yahya, also reports that the childhood friend had chastised Süleyman about Mustafa's execution and had lost his standing vis-à-vis the sultan as a result.[78] Yahya then entered a mystical retreat and rebuilt his life as one of the most prominent Sufis of the capital.

Next to these criticisms, Süleyman and Hürrem had to deal with problems that stemmed from aging. It is well known that Süleyman had been struggling with health problems since the early 1540s, and it seems that Hürrem had her own in the mid-1550s, if not earlier. In a society that segregated women, the physical condition of upper-class women remained a secret kept behind harem walls. Hürrem died in mid-April 1558, from what was probably a combination of declining health and the shock of a recent illness such as malaria. Her funeral prayer, led by the chief jurist Ebussuud, was held in the mosque of Bayezid II, and she was then buried inside the graveyard attached to the Süleymaniye Mosque.[79] A small mausoleum was soon after erected on her tomb, distinguishing her in death after leading an unprecedented, much maligned, and much envied life.

Hürrem's death not only hastened the civil war between her sons Bayezid and Selim, but further added to Süleyman's late-life melancholy. His health declined quickly thereafter. A Venetian diplomatic report from 1562 related

FIG. 7.4 Süleyman as an old man by Melchior Lorck, ca. 1559. Courtesy of the Metropolitan Museum of Art.

that Süleyman spent several months of the year sick, near death, with his legs and other parts of his body swollen. He did not have much appetite either. The same report claimed that there were widespread rumors in the capital critical of Süleyman's cruelty, as someone who had ordered the execution of two sons and several grandchildren. His only consolation, reportedly, was the thought that he had saved the Muslim community from much oppression by preventing succession wars among his sons.[80]

The civil war between Bayezid and Selim was not just a political matter, but a family feud that pulled in Süleyman, Rüstem, and Mihrümah, even though the grand vizier and his wife tried to remain neutral. Indeed, perhaps to prevent Rüstem from becoming entangled in a second affair related to succession, and perhaps in order to ensure his neutrality, the political and military management of the crisis was mostly handled by Sokullu Mehmed, the third vizier. Bayezid's letters reached his father, his sister, and his brother-in-law. Süleyman, in particular, went beyond his role as sultan and answered many of these missives as father. These letters, spread out over a few years, reveal not just the depth of the affection the family members harbored for one another but, at the same time, the height of the anger and frustration Bayezid felt and caused in others.

This was indeed a highly personal crisis for the members of the dynasty and their relatives. Even Hürrem's old confidante Gülfem was dragged into it, by sending a letter to Bayezid in which she recommended the rebel prince to submit to his father's will. One of the most personal remnants of this violent, turbulent period is an exchange of poems between Süleyman and Bayezid. Both were accomplished poets, and the exchange, between the son who asks for forgiveness and the father who asks for genuine repentance, remains one of the most striking examples of classical Ottoman poetry, if one can forgo the violence lurking in the background. Thus wrote Bayezid to his father:

> *Oh, the Sultan of the World from end to end, my Süleyman, my father;*
> *You who are the soul within my being and my soul's loved one, my father;*
> *Dearest one, would you bring on your own Bayezid's destruction, my*
>     *father?*
> *God knows, I have committed no crime, my majestic Sultan, my father.*
>
> *"If a human, God's vassal, is guilty, what can one say?" the proverb goes:*
> *Grant your forgiveness for Bayezid's crime, don't put this vassal in death's*
>     *throes,*
> *God knows, I have committed no sin, my majestic Sultan, my father.*

To which Süleyman replied:

*Oh you! There were times you engaged in tumultuous rebellion, my son;*
*You did not carry around your neck the pendant of my firman, my son.*
*Oh, would I ever put you in death's throes, my own Bayezid Khan, my son?*
*But at least don't say "I am without guilt." Repent, my dearest one, my son.*

*Let us say that you have both your hands steeped in blood,*
*You request our forgiveness and we grant you our pardon, what can one say?*
*I should absolve you of crime, my Bayezid, if you stopped acting this way:*
*But at least don't say "I am without guilt." Repent, my dearest one, my son.*[81]

Displays of piety played a particularly important role in Süleyman's public persona during this tumultuous period. The construction of the Süleymaniye complex was perhaps the most obvious example, but there were other, less conspicuous signs of a deeper, internal yearning for pious behavior. One was the decline in the numbers of goldsmiths and jewelers employed in the palace, from ninety in 1526 to thirty-nine in 1566, which indicated a significant change in consumption patterns and tastes around the palace. Already around 1557, it was reported that Süleyman had stopped wearing cloth of gold. He wore a little silk, but mostly wool. He had stopped using gold and silver cutlery and dishes, preferring china and stoneware instead. He did not want music played in the palace anymore, ordering the pages to break all their instruments.[82] He even decreed the closing of drinking establishments and a prohibition on the playing of musical instruments as further signs of his late-life piety. He wrote to Tahmasb to inform him about his latest acts of devotion, in a rambling letter in which he positioned himself as the purveyor of peace and justice as well as the protector of morality and piety.[83]

Süleyman's interest in poetry continued during the final years of his life, but its public aspect diminished considerably. As he worked on gathering his poems in collections, and exchanged verses with a few fellow poets and officials, his financial support of poets and poetry almost came to a halt. Instead, he patronized Quran scribes from whom he ordered multiple copies, some of which were placed in the Süleymaniye Mosque.[84] He also became closer to the chief jurist and religious scholar Ebussuud, a man of his own age. He memorialized his son Cihangir by ordering Sinan to build a small mosque on a hill overlooking the Bosphorus. Completed in 1559–60, Cihangir's mosque, a square building flanked by a single minaret, looked more like a dervish convent than the majestic mosques built by and for members of the dynasty.

Despite Süleyman's state of mind, the business of government continued as usual. In fact, it became even more independent from him in the last decades of his life. Reliable scribes staffed the central bureaus. This was a period when, under the weight of expanding duties, the financial branch of the government became increasingly prominent compared to the chancery. Money secured in the central treasury and/or controlled by members of the dynasty and the elite through land grants and endowments continued to underwrite their charitable projects.

In the last decades of his life, in addition to the Süleymaniye complex, Süleyman financed the building of a Friday mosque and a hospice in Damascus (completed in 1558–59); roadside complexes (caravanserai, Friday mosque, bazaar, bathhouse), fortified castles, and reservoirs on the pilgrimage road to Mecca; as well as a madrasa in Mecca (completed in 1564–65).[85] Earlier, he had ordered extensive renovations and additions to the Kaaba complex in Mecca, the central location of Muslim pilgrimage rituals. These works were in tune with Süleyman's claim to the caliphate and the protection and service of the Sunni Muslim community. He was active closer to home as well. In September 1563, during a hunt, he was almost carried away by a flash flood, which also destroyed aqueducts outside the walls of Constantinople. He ordered the chief architect Sinan to restore the older structures and build new ones. Expenses for these were higher than the sum spent for the Süleymaniye complex.[86] Mastering nature, and bringing water to the city, were truly Solomonic projects.

Süleyman's family's charity continued through his daughter as well. In the absence of Hürrem, Mihrümah had become the most senior female of the dynasty. Following the death of her husband Rüstem in July 1561, she did not enter into a new marriage, devoting herself instead to charity and supporting her father, even though she was not yet forty. In addition to the complex she had built in Üsküdar, she had a new one constructed on top of Constantinople's sixth hill, between 1562 and 1565. Just as Üsküdar was the city's main gate toward the east, the new complex was located next to the city's main gateway to the west, reminding all who arrived and departed of the dynasty, of Süleyman's family, and of Mihrümah.[87]

Another major concern, as always, was to ensure the dynasty's longevity. While the Bayezid affair raged on, and negotiations continued between the Ottomans and the Safavids, Selim's eldest son Murad was appointed governor of Saruhan. This was a coveted seat that had been occupied in the past by Süleyman, his deceased son Mehmed, the executed Mustafa, and Selim, the heir apparent. Murad, sixteen years of age at the time of his appointment, represented the third generation of the dynasty after his grandfather and father.

In early 1562, Selim was reappointed to Kütahya, closer to Constantinople than Konya, and Bayezid's old seat. Thus, even before Bayezid's execution in Qazvin, the dynasty behaved according to the assumption that Bayezid and his sons were completely out of the picture.

Sokullu Mehmed, who proceeded through the Ottoman hierarchy as fourth vizier (September 1554), third vizier (September 1555), and second vizier (July 1561), married Selim's daughter Esmahan in 1562. This marriage intimately tied to the dynasty yet another high official of Christian background, as had by then been the custom for many decades. In June 1565, upon the death of Semiz Ali, who had held the grand vizierate since Rüstem's death, Sokullu Mehmed finally became grand vizier. Thus, the peculiar Ottoman mixture of meritocracy (the regular advance through the ranks) and family politics (the promotion of officials who married into the dynasty) manifested itself one more time.

With the birth of Murad's first son in 1566, the fourth generation of the dynasty came to the world. Süleyman was asked to name his great-grandson, and he chose Mehmed, the name of his illustrious ancestor Mehmed II as well as his beloved son who had died in 1543.

## Süleyman's Last Campaign

The outbreak of the civil war between Bayezid and Selim a few years after the peace agreement of 1555 with the Safavids, and the continuation of the crisis into the middle of 1562, had prevented the Ottomans from undertaking any major engagements on the European front. They were fortunate as this was a time of transition in Europe as well, during which important actors were more preoccupied with internal issues than international ventures. Charles V, like Süleyman, had been struggling with various illnesses. To secure a smooth transfer of the Habsburg lands, he had left the kingdom of Spain to his son Philip II (king of Spain, r. 1556–98), while Ferdinand had inherited the central European possessions, formally partitioning the Habsburg domain. This partition further underscored the division between two Habsburg visions of imperial policy: one that was more preoccupied with the Ottomans and developments in Europe, particularly central Europe, represented by the Austrian branch; and another one that was geared more toward the Atlantic and the New World, even though it continued to pay attention to the Mediterranean, represented by the Spanish branch.

Ferdinand's position was strengthened by his recognition as Holy Roman Emperor by the Imperial Diet in May 1558, nearly two years after Charles' abdication in his favor. However, his power as emperor was considerably less than that of his brother, and he had fewer resources than his nephew Philip II.[88] The presence of the anti-Habsburg Paul IV (pope, May 1555–August 1559) in the Vatican further weakened the prospect of pro-Habsburg alliances during a critical time for the Ottomans. The Italian war of 1551–59 between the Habsburgs and the French ended with the Treaty of Cateau-Cambrésis in 1559, since both sides had to tackle financial problems and sectarian violence at home.[89] The French also had to manage their own succession crises, which saw the fifteen-year-old Francis II replace Henri II in 1559, who was replaced upon his own premature death by the ten-year old Charles IX in 1560. On the Austrian side, Ferdinand died in July 1564 and was succeeded by his son Maximilian II.

Following Philip's accession to the Spanish throne, the earlier preoccupation with the Mediterranean continued. Thus, in the spring of 1560, a joint Spanish, Florentine, Genoese, and Maltese fleet sailed for an anti-piracy action against Ottoman associates in north Africa and occupied the island of Djerba off the Tunisian coast, the first step of a larger invasion. The Ottoman fleet sailed quickly from Constantinople, catching the allied forces unaware, and dealing them a major blow. Many commanders and admirals were captured, together with numerous flags and banners that were exhibited in Constantinople after the victory. The Ottomans further pursued their actions against the Spanish Habsburgs and their allies by unsuccessfully besieging Malta in May–September 1565, and by capturing the island of Chios from the Genoese in April 1566.

While these developments seem in retrospect like minor parts of Ottoman and Mediterranean political history, the Battle of Djerba and the siege of Malta in particular were major international events of the time. Djerba, like the naval victory at Prevesa in the summer of 1538, demonstrated the ability of the Ottomans to conduct complex naval operations and gave a boost to their confidence. The unsuccessful siege of Malta, on the other hand, and the resistance of the Order of St. John provided succor to many European Christians. As French diplomats reported from Constantinople, Süleyman met news of the failure at Malta with great anger while the Muslim inhabitants of the city were furious, to the point of forcing the diplomats to stay indoors for fear of violence.[90]

Just as the Mediterranean front regained activity in the 1560s, the European front returned to prominence as well. In the early 1550s, Süleyman and Ferdinand had clashed over the status of Transylvania, which Ferdinand wanted to add to the Hungarian lands under his control. The Ottomans, on the other hand, wanted to preserve the area's autonomy under John Sigismund, the only son of the Ottoman-anointed king of Hungary who had died in 1540. Tensions had receded, initially with an agreement on a short-term truce in the summer of 1555, when Ferdinand's envoy Busbecq visited

Süleyman. The truce was renewed in the coming years, helped by the presence of Busbecq in Constantinople until August 1562, when a more comprehensive agreement was reached between the two sides.

The agreement in 1562 included an eight-year truce, the annual payment of thirty thousand ducats by Ferdinand in return for the Hungarian lands he occupied, and Ferdinand's renunciation of his claim over Transylvania.[91] From a diplomatic perspective, this was an important moment in Ottoman-Austrian relations, since the agreement stipulated the residency of a permanent envoy in Constantinople. The agreement also included clauses about the better management of both sides' military elements on the frontier, as well as the prevention of banditry and other forms of violence. These were chronic problems on the frontier around which the Habsburgs, John Sigismund, and the Ottomans coexisted uneasily.

That chronic violence pulled the Ottomans into another open confrontation with the Habsburgs.[92] This time, however, the cause was more than skirmishes between frontier forces, or cross-border raids by roving bands of brigands. It was a fight between Maximilian II, Holy Roman Emperor (r. 1564–76), and John Sigismund, recognized and protected by the Ottomans as the *voivode* of Transylvania. In the first months of 1565, in response to John Sigismund's capture of a fortress he claimed as part of his ancestral lands, Maximilian's forces took a number of towns on the Transylvanian border, most notably the crossroads city of Tokaj. This squabbling over medium-sized fortresses displays very well the precariousness of the political and military balance in the area, where conflicting aristocratic, royal, and imperial claims over land prevented the drawing of an agreed-upon boundary.

The background of the campaign also shows the extent to which the Ottomans were deeply engaged in international diplomacy and were entangled by their own claims and commitments. Even though the matter at hand was relatively unimportant from an imperial perspective, the Ottomans were bound by their guarantees to John Sigismund to protect him and his lands, and the Ottoman position since 1526 whereby they argued that they were the sole power to make decisions over any part of the defunct Kingdom of Hungary, which included Transylvania.

Maximilian sought to establish an agreement with the Ottomans by sending his envoys to Constantinople. The truce of summer 1562 was renewed in February 1565. However, the Ottomans soon found out about the Habsburg capture of Tokaj, and they demanded its return to John Sigismund, which the Habsburgs refused. The situation continued to slide toward a larger confrontation in the summer of 1565, when Ottoman troops supported John Sigismund in skirmishes against Habsburg forces. In October–November, Süleyman informed John Sigismund that he was ready to go to war if Maximilian did not propose a comprehensive peace. In the absence of any concessions from the Habsburg side, he then wrote John Sigismund to tell him that he would lead a campaign in person in the next season, the spring–summer of 1566.

This was to be Süleyman's last campaign. The irony is that, while Süleyman had defended his claim to universal monarchy in the fields of central Europe during his youth, this campaign's objectives were quite unimpressive in comparison: the propping up of a regional ally and the recovery or capture of a few fortresses. It is still quite significant that Süleyman took his role as John Sigismund's protector seriously, especially in his old age, at a time when he was more preoccupied with charity and leaving behind a legacy. Perhaps he read the situation through the lens of morality: he may have thought he had made an oath regarding John Sigismund, and had to act accordingly. Hürrem was the only person who could have dissuaded the sultan from such an adventure, but she was no longer alive. Her absence may have made Süleyman even more susceptible to the idea of engaging in one last heroic act.

On April 29, just before he departed, Süleyman left a few items of value in the palace treasury chamber, with a note to his son Selim. In the note, after telling Selim that his son can recognize his handwriting (by thus confirming that this is by his own hand), he asked the prince to sell the items and use the revenue to bring water to the city of Jidda, in the Arabian peninsula. This was his last act of charity and also one of his last expressions of late-life reckoning with death. The note told Selim that this was to be done to commemorate Prophet Muhammad, the true owner of all things. It reminded the prince that the world was transitory and ended by saying, "I hope I can successfully complete this campaign and return in good spirits."[93] As the sultan himself must have known, he was not strong enough for a long campaign, and it is likely that the departure of the central forces was delayed while waiting for his health to improve. On May 1, later than the customary date of departure for a spring–summer campaign, Süleyman marched west one last time. In his early seventies, the Solomon of the Age was barely able to walk or stand up.

Despite his poor health, Süleyman had to publicly perform his sovereign power during the campaign. One of the most important ceremonial occasions this time was a meeting between him and John Sigismund. The march from Constantinople to Belgrade lasted for over a month, and Süleyman and the soldiery rested there. At the end of June, John Sigismund visited the army camp in full regalia, surrounded by a band of men on foot and on horse, wearing ornamented clothes. Many Ottoman units stood at attention for his arrival, and he was then taken to an audience with Süleyman. As soon as he entered the tent, John Sigismund took off his crown, which signified his claim to the Hungarian throne as king-elect, and kneeled, but Süleyman asked him to stand up. After kissing the sultan's feet, John Sigismund was granted the rare honor of sitting in Süleyman's company, who called him his son.

When the Ottomans left Constantinople, there were two potential targets: Eger (which had been besieged in 1552 but not taken) and Szigetvár. Eger was closer to John Sigismund's possessions in Transylvania, while Szigetvár was closer to the Ottoman-controlled territory, 150 miles south of Buda and 200 miles west of Timişoara. Both fortresses helped the Habsburgs maintain their military presence on the frontier, housing garrisons and serving as a base for the raiders. It seems that the target of the campaign was determined around the time when Süleyman was in Belgrade.

It was thus decided that the sultan would march against Szigetvár, while the second vizier Pertev was sent to the southern border of Transylvania, to besiege Gyula. (Pertev's siege started on July 2 and ended with the garrison's surrender on September 2.) John Sigismund, with the help of Crimean forces, was supposed to take back Tokaj and Szerencs. This would be a campaign directed at shoring up border defenses against the Habsburgs, and a punitive expedition against Maximilian, who had been emperor for a mere two years. Gyula and Szigetvár could also serve as steppingstones for further expansion in the coming years.

Ceremonies moved together with Süleyman. In the middle of July, when a bridge was built on the Drava for the Ottoman army to pass, he conducted an inspection from the river, sailing in his royal boat; three galleys, adorned with flags and banners, accompanied him, giving the inspection a festive air. The campaign and all of these performances must have taken their toll. When Süleyman reached the city of Pécs near Szigetvár, on August 4, one more procession was organized. However, this time, Süleyman was driven in his cart, rather than riding on his horse. The cart was flanked by viziers on horses, while reciters read aloud from the Quranic chapter called the Opening, which promises believers victory over unbelievers.

These ceremonies could not hide the tensions that dominated the campaign since its early stages. A minor official, who served as a judge when he participated in Süleyman's final expedition, left behind a striking testimony about the sultan and his officials' anxieties.[94] Concerned about Süleyman's health, many around him advised the sultan to stay in Constantinople but he angrily refused. On the road, Süleyman apparently wanted to attack Eger, to fulfill his promise of help to John Sigismund, while the high officials pleaded to march onto Szigetvár, a strategically more important target. Heavy rains added to the gloomy atmosphere. Everything upset Süleyman, from the difficulty of advancing on muddy roads to the delayed arrival of supply ships sailing on the Danube. A chief gatekeeper was dismissed and another was given a public beating for failing to secure a smooth journey for the sultan. By the time he arrived in front of Szigetvár, Süleyman was exhausted.

Ottoman scouts reached Szigetvár on August 1, and the siege began in earnest on August 7. Besieging such a fortress was an arduous task. The fortress and the surrounding small city were situated in the middle of natural marshland and artificially flooded areas. Even if some of these were drained, the remaining muddy ground was a challenge for the positioning of artillery. In 1566, the fortress was defended by the Hungarian-Croatian nobleman and career soldier Miklós Zrínyi, assisted by a well-motivated garrison of 2,300 men. However, once more, Ottoman firepower prevailed, helped by the size of the Ottoman forces. As artillery units wreaked havoc, the Ottoman infantry kept advancing, establishing firing positions, digging mines, and attacking breaches. The outer fortress was taken on September 5, and Ottoman soldiers entered the inner fortress on the 7th, killing Zrínyi and the last defenders. The siege had an unexpected end: gunpowder stores in the inner fortress exploded the same day, killing many Ottoman soldiers who had recently entered it.

As the violent siege entered its last stages, Süleyman died on the night of September 6/7, 1566, before the fortress finally fell. The soldiers were not notified of the sultan's death to prevent turmoil and rioting in the army camp. It was the task of the grand vizier to keep the situation under control, just as Pirî Mehmed had done at Selim's death in 1520. The news was shared with a small group of confidants. Imperial decrees were issued in the name of the sultan, and physicians continued to enter his tent to create the semblance of ongoing treatment, while messengers were sent to his son Selim, the heir apparent.

Muslim ritual demanded a quick burial, and Süleyman's corpse was washed, placed in a white shroud, and buried under his tent. Given the need for exhumation and eventual reburial in Constantinople, the corpse was preserved by being bound with wax-treated cloth strips and the application of perfumes and essences. Some reports mention that his internal organs were removed and interred on the spot. The further away from the time of his death, the more fanciful the story becomes, for instance including references to a golden box within which the internal organs would have been buried. It is impossible to ascertain the way in which the corpse was handled, other than the fact that measures were taken to prevent the smell of decay, which would have given away the secret.[95]

In the meantime, Selim travelled to Constantinople after receiving the news of his father's death. He reached the capital at the end of September and sat on the throne, receiving obedience from high officials left behind in the capital. This was an imprudent move since it led to the circulation of news about Süleyman's death. Selim then left Constantinople for the army camp, but he was instructed by the grand vizier to advance no further than Belgrade. As the Ottoman forces began their return from Szigetvár, around October 20, Sokullu Mehmed placed a lookalike in Süleyman's carriage. Finally, on October 24/25, as the soldiers approached Belgrade, Süleyman's death was made public. As feared by the high officials, the news was met with upset and consternation. Selim's refusal to organize a second accession ceremony in Belgrade, and his reluctance to pay out the customary accession disbursement of cash to the janissaries and the household troops, heightened the tensions.[96] As soon as Süleyman died, the much-vaunted order of his establishment was upset, posing the first challenge to the new sultan.

Süleyman, for the first time in more than half a century, did not have to worry about the business of government. His public funeral prayer was held outside Belgrade and the corpse was sent to Constantinople, where another funeral prayer took place, presumably led by his friend, the chief jurist Ebussuud. He was then buried in his final resting place, next to the Süleymaniye Mosque, near Hürrem, and a mausoleum was soon built on his tomb.

While it had been expected for many years, Süleyman's death was nevertheless a considerable shock, especially for those who had been his close companions. Their feelings were summarized by scholar and poet Bakî (d. 1600), who had become one of Süleyman's closest interlocutors in the last years of his life:

> *Good truth, he was the lustre of rank high and glory great,*
> *A King, [Alexander]-diademed, of [Darius'] armied state.*
>
> *Before the ground aneath his feet the Sphere bent low its head,*
> *Earth's shrine of adoration was the dust before his gate,*
>
> *But longing for his gifts would make the meanest beggar rich;*
> *Exceeding boon, exceeding bounteous a Potentate!*
>
> *The court of glory of his Kingly majesty most high*
> *Was aye the centre where would hope of sage and poet wait.*
>
> *Although he yielded to eternal Destiny's command,*
> *A King was he in might as Doom, immoveable as Fate![97]*

Süleyman's worldly life thus ended. His myth, parts of it already built and circulating during his reign, began to live a life of its own.

# Conclusion: Legacies

*The beloved's stature is a cypress tree to some, the letter elif [\]*
*to others*
*They all may have the same intention, but the account*
*differs.*

MUHİBBÎ[1]

SÜLEYMAN, AS THIS couplet by him shows, was well aware that truth was in the eye of the beholder. However, he was not comforted by this conventional wisdom. To the contrary, he was concerned about what others might think of him, and image-making was a major preoccupation for him and his associates.

In histories, poems, and official correspondence from the early decades of his reign, Süleyman was consistently presented as a skilled commander, a just ruler, and a divinely anointed monarch. For his European contemporaries, who called him the "Grand Turk," he was an awe-inspiring figure. His legendary wealth, and the large household and army he presided over, elicited much commentary. At the same time, European authors and audiences also saw him as a tyrant whose conquests dealt mortal blows to Christianity and who cruelly ordered the murder of his own children and grandchildren. A similar ambiguity was exhibited by Süleyman's rivals farther east, the Safavids of Iran. Under the dual threat of military violence and accusations of heresy from their Sunni neighbors, the Safavids treated Süleyman with a mixture of apprehension and grudging respect.

These images persisted throughout Süleyman's reign but, in his later years, the blemishes became too many to ignore. Süleyman did his best to ensure that his legacy would be viewed in certain ways, as seen in the case of the *Sulaymannama* and his charitable works. Stalemates on all fronts, rebellious behavior on the part of his sons, and the deterioration of his health posed serious challenges, however. As diplomatic reports from the last years of his reign show, the austere figure in the *Sulaymannama* was the subject of much rumor, not all of it favorable. Despite his increasing piety and his generosity in dispensing charity, criticisms of the executions of Prince Mustafa and Prince Bayezid lingered. Like an aging celebrity hounded by obsessed fans and rapacious paparazzi, Süleyman went at great lengths to prove he was alive and well, only to further fuel the fires of gossip. Beyond rumors, there were other voices that highlighted more consequential problems, such as cracks within the Ottoman system of elite recruitment and promotion, or over-taxation and bribery. Why, then, has he remained as one of the most easily identifiable and representative figures of Ottoman history?

The first reason may have to do with his longevity. Had he died during the succession struggles of the 1510s at the hands of the men of one of his uncles or hit by a stray cannonball during the siege of Rhodes in 1522 or stabbed by the Hungarian assassins at the Mohács battlefield who were supposedly sent out to kill him, he would have been a tragic, minor figure in Ottoman history. Staying on the throne for forty-six years, during a time of major regional and global transformations, prevented that.

Also, Süleyman lived at a time when there was an explosion in record-keeping and other uses of the written word across Eurasia, extending from the expansion of the printing press in Europe to a burgeoning manuscript culture in Ottoman territories. The consolidation of bureaucracies, the intensification of diplomatic exchanges, and the rise of new reading publics all contributed to the emergence of a plethora of documents that can be used to study the history of the period from various perspectives. As a result, it has been possible to write more comprehensive and layered accounts of Süleyman's reign, compared, for instance, to the short yet eventful reign of his father Selim I or the equally eventful, three-decade long, yet less documented reign of his great-grandfather Mehmed II.

Interestingly, the treatment of Süleyman in the years and decades following his reign was quite multifaceted, especially compared to popular treatments of him in the modern period. First of all, the memory of his reign had to contend with those of his great-grandfather Mehmed and his father Selim for the status of the most accomplished ruler of the Ottoman dynasty. Only over time did his reputation rise above that of his forebears. Moreover, not all treatments of his reign were unabashedly approbatory.

From the last decades of the sixteenth century on, the durability of the structures established by Süleyman and his predecessors were severely tested by disruptions in the Ottoman economy. Fruitless wars, extensions of

Süleyman's imperial expansion east and west, deepened the economic crisis and the overall pessimism. This was a time of reckoning with the past and the present, and a number of bureaucrats set out to diagnose the ills of the times and identify solutions. Süleyman's institutional legacy was first re-evaluated within this atmosphere of critical reflection. On the one hand, since he had made *kanun* a foundational principle of order and justice, many authors looked back at his reign nostalgically, as a time when *kanun* represented a fresh, dynamic, equitable principle through which the realm was kept together. On the other hand, multiple commentators pointed to developments in the reign of Süleyman, such as changing practices of elite recruitment, the pervasiveness of bribery, and the palace's appropriation of lands and resources that could have been used as *tımar* assignments, as the foundations of their ongoing crisis.[2]

As authors got further from the reign of Süleyman, however, and as the empire's government was riddled with more and more problems on all fronts, positive assessments of Süleyman prevailed over critical ones. For instance, in the late eighteenth century, the Ottoman Armenian-turned-translator and Swedish diplomat Mouradgea d'Ohsson presented Süleyman to his European audiences as *Kanunî*, the promoter of *kanun*, in his *Tableau général de l'Empire othoman*.[3] In the mid-nineteenth century, Süleyman's institutional legacy was once again revisited. The analysts this time were bureaucrat-reformers who were trying to prevent the empire's dissolution under the dual pressures of European imperialisms and local nationalisms. They also wanted to curtail the executive powers of the Ottoman sultan to the benefit of the bureaucratic class. The new Süleyman they promoted was recast with reference to modern notions of the law. He became a producer and applier of law in universal fashion, and he was celebrated as a builder of bureaucratic institutions. Süleyman's legislative activities received an unexpected acknowledgment from the other side of the Atlantic Ocean, when a marble relief portrait of him was placed over the gallery doors of the House Chamber in the US Capitol in 1949–50. Today, his image stands there, together with twenty-two other "historical figures noted for their work in establishing the principles that underlie American law."[4]

Süleyman as individual was also a source of attraction for Ottoman authors. An illustrated two-volume history of the Ottoman dynasty, the *Hünername* ("The Book of Skills") devoted its second volume, completed in 1588, to the reign of Süleyman, while fitting all the sultans before him into a single volume. It represented the first step in Süleyman's elevation to a saintly, infallible figure in Ottoman history, which came to co-exist with his image as the builder of a law-based government.[5] *Hünername* expanded on and developed the static figure found in the *Sulaymannama*. For instance, it told its readers about Süleyman's charity and piety; it addressed with greater openness incidents such as the executions of the grand vizier İbrahim and Prince Mustafa; in general, through a series of anecdotes and paintings that reflect the ways in which Süleyman was remembered in oral culture in the decades after his death, it made Süleyman a more relatable, more humane figure.

Süleyman's long journey continued after the end of the Ottoman Empire, which became official in 1922. Initially, the secular bureaucrats of the Turkish nation-state, although raised in Ottoman institutions, saw Ottoman history more as a burden than as a source of pride. As they gave primacy to pre-Ottoman, indeed pre-Islamic Turkish history in school curricula and public life, Süleyman was rendered much less visible. However, from the mid-1940s onward, the rise of more traditionalist ideologies and new middle classes led to a new appreciation of the Ottoman legacy, and Süleyman's central role in Ottoman history was once again promoted. In the late 1980s, as a civilian government of center-right technocrats tried to ingratiate themselves with Western audiences, they sought Süleyman's help as the main representative of Ottoman grandeur. A lavish exhibition of artifacts from the time of Süleyman traveled to the Louvre, the British Museum, the Art Institute of Chicago, the National Gallery of Art in Washington, DC, and the Metropolitan Museum of Art in New York to burnish the image of the Republic of Turkey after years of political turmoil and economic crisis.[6]

As religion-inspired forms of conservatism became more mainstream in Turkey, Süleyman's image as lawgiver and empire-builder was expanded with references to his staunch defense of Sunni Islam against European Christianity and Safavid Shiism. This image was inserted into textbooks, and generations of Turkish schoolchildren grew up with it. It is the image that prevails today, further buoyed by the cadres of the Islamist Justice and Development Party, in power since 2002. In the minds of segments of the Turkish state and society, Süleyman continues to fight. In 2020, a drill ship was purchased and renamed *Kanuni* by the Turkish authorities. It joined *Fatih* (named after Mehmed II) and *Yavuz* (named after Selim I), as the newest representative of an aggressive Turkish foreign policy that looks for energy independence as well as new zones of influence around the Mediterranean and the Black Sea.

As the more popular and politicized images of Süleyman gained further ground in the modern period, the Ottoman bureaucrats' focus on the social and economic conditions of Süleyman's reign was taken over by academia. While not immune from the impact of the dual forces of Turkish nationalism and political Islam, generations of scholars since the 1930s have described and explained specific aspects of Süleyman's reign. For instance, they established the importance of other actors, who are either given secondary roles or no roles at all in sources from the sixteenth century: Süleyman's grand viziers İbrahim, Lütfî, Rüstem, and Sokullu Mehmed; his chancellors Celalzade Mustafa and Ramazanzade Mehmed; prominent religious scholars Kemalpaşazade Ahmed, Ebussuud Mehmed, Kınalızade Ali, Taşköprizade Ahmed, and Birgivî Mehmed; and architects, authors, and poets such as Mimar Sinan, Fethullah Ârif, Latifî and many, many others. While all of these individuals were members of the upper echelon of Ottoman society, their inclusion in the narrative of Süleyman's reign changed its characterization from the sum total of the actions of a single sultan to a group project of sorts. Equally importantly, recent scholarship has promoted the relevance of Ottoman history for European and global history, thus helping put Süleyman on an equal footing with other contemporary monarchs.[7]

As for Süleyman's poetry, it has become nearly invisible. A few excerpts from his output, such as "But no worldly fortune equal to one breath of health can be," continue to circulate as proverbs among modern Turkish speakers. However, his poetry has been relegated to the closed quarters of pre-Republican Turkish literary history, where the Arabic script and the flowery metaphors of the Arabo-Perso-Turkish-Islamic literary tradition reign supreme under the careful watch of a few scholars. This is particularly tragic, since he cared enormously about leaving behind a self-edited, carefully prepared corpus of his own poetry. This invisibility also prevented a wider audience from gaining access to elements of his personality that are mostly absent from his academic and popular treatments: grandeur mixed with humility, melancholic yearnings for divine and worldly love, a voice that alternates between presiding over an empire and seeking truths more profound. There is an openness in his language and a vulnerability in his tone that are not conveyed by any other components of his legacy.

His charitable works, on the other hand, fared better, at least those that survived the passage of time and the impoverishment of their endowments. The aqueducts near Istanbul still stand. One of his biggest commissions, the Süleymaniye complex, has lost many of its charitable functions, but its mosque is still open, visited by throngs of believers and tourists who come to admire its majestic interior or simply fulfill their religious duties. Some of the complex's madrasa buildings today house the Süleymaniye Library, where one of the richest manuscript libraries of the Islamic world resides. The walls he had built, which surround Jerusalem's Old City, were recognized as a

UNESCO World Heritage Site in 1981. The Süleymaniye Mosque was added to the same list in 1985, together with other historical buildings in Istanbul.

Süleyman remains popular with audiences beyond academics and political Islamists. One such treatment of him is a Turkish-made television series, called *Muhteşem Yüzyıl* (*The Magnificent Century*). Widely syndicated in southeastern Europe, North Africa, the Middle East, and South Asia, and eventually picked up by Netflix, the series brought the latest incarnation of Süleyman's life and political career to modern audiences. By using the addictive narrative techniques of soap operas, pushing complicated historical contexts into the background and replacing them with simpler explanations while overly dramatizing life at the Ottoman court, the television series achieved a tremendous success. It portrayed Süleyman as a tragic figure, a ruler whose reign was filled with court intrigues, and a lover and father whose search for happiness and fulfillment often came to naught. The series somewhat democratized the image of Süleyman, by making him more relatable, and moving him away from the tedious narratives of history textbooks. It took away the austerity and sobriety that have been traditionally attributed to him, to the dismay of many prominent conservative politicians in Turkey.[8]

This is where we now find Süleyman, after centuries of mythmaking and scholarship. He lives on under various garbs, offering shelter with his buildings, keeping academics busy, boring school children, and enticing readers and viewers to dream through him of a world filled with sound and fury.

# Notes

ABBREVIATIONS

SK: Süleymaniye Library, Istanbul

*TDVİA: Türkiye Diyanet Vakfı İslam Ansiklopedisi* (*The Encyclopedia of Islam of the Turkish Religious Affairs Foundation*)

TSMK: Topkapı Palace Museum Library, Istanbul

TSMA: Topkapı Palace Museum Archive, Istanbul

ms.: manuscript

E., followed by a number: *Evrak* (Document)

D., followed by a number: *Defter* (Register)

INTRODUCTION

1. Fethullah Ârif, *Sulaymannama*, TSMK, ms. Hazine 1517. Its paintings are reproduced and discussed in detail in Esin Atıl, *Süleymanname: The Illustrated History of Süleyman the Magnificent* (Washington, DC; New York: National Gallery of Art; Harry N. Abrams, 1986), 78–251.

2. The first scholarly biography of Süleyman in English is Roger Bigelow Merriman's *Suleiman the Magnificent, 1520-1566* (Cambridge, MA: Harvard University Press, 1944). Merriman did not know Turkish; as a result, he relied on European materials and a few Ottoman sources in translation. Antony Bridge, an artist and later an Anglican priest, wrote a life of Süleyman for a popular audience, in an exoticizing tone filled with anti-Ottoman and anti-Muslim cliches: *Suleiman the Magnificent, Scourge of Heaven* (London and New York: Granada, 1983). Harold Lamb was able to stay away from many of Bridge's stereotypes in his highly readable *Suleiman the Magnificent, Sultan of the East* (Garden City, NY: Doubleday, 1951), but his book equally suffers from an absence of Ottoman perspectives and testimonies. André Clot, whose French original was translated as *Suleiman the Magnificent* (New York: New Amsterdam, 1992), is the only one among these four authors to offer a multifaceted narrative. The author knew modern Turkish, lived

in Turkey, and used academic studies on Ottoman history in his work. However, he did not conduct his own research. Moreover, he reproduced the Süleyman-centric approach found in many Ottoman sources, telling a story about the achievements of an all-powerful sultan.

3. Denis Crouzet, *Charles V: empereur d'une fin des temps* (Paris: Odile Jacob, 2016); Geoffrey Parker, *Emperor: A New Life of Charles V* (New Haven, CT: Yale University Press, 2019). Even though it does not have the academic heft of Crouzet or Parker, an attempt at a more inclusive approach is John Julius Norwich, *Four Princes: Henry VIII, Francis I, Charles V, Suleiman the Magnificent and the Obsessions That Forged Modern Europe* (London: John Murray, 2016).

## CHAPTER 1

1. This historical background relies on İ. Metin Kunt, "The Rise of the Ottomans," in *The New Cambridge Medieval History*, ed. Michael Jones, vol. 6, *c. 1300-c. 1415* (Cambridge: Cambridge University Press, 2000), 839–44.

2. On early Ottoman notions of holy war, see Linda T. Darling, "Contested Territory: Ottoman Holy War in Comparative Context," *Studia Islamica* 91 (2000): 133–63.

3. Concise treatments of Osman and the first Ottomans are Rudi Paul Lindner, "Anatolia, 1300-1451," in *The Cambridge History of Turkey*, vol. 1, *Byzantium to Turkey, 1071-1453*, ed. Kate Fleet (Cambridge: Cambridge University Press, 2009), 117–21; Cemal Kafadar, *Between Two Worlds: The Construction of the Ottoman State* (Berkeley: University of California Press, 1995), 122–38; Halil İnalcık, "The Question of the Emergence of the Ottoman State," *International Journal of Turkish Studies* 2 (1980): 71–79. For debates on the rise of the Ottomans, see Kafadar, *Between Two Worlds*, 1–117; Colin Imber, "The Legend of Osman Gazi," in *The Ottoman Emirate (1300-1389)*, ed. Elizabeth Zachariadou (Rethymnon: Crete University Press, 1993), 67–75.

4. See Suna Çağaptay, *The First Capital of the Ottoman Empire: The Religious, Architectural, and Social History of Bursa* (London: I.B. Tauris, 2021).

5. For the transition under Orhan and the first forays beyond the Dardanelles, see Halil İnalcık, "Turkish Settlement and Christian Reaction, 1329-1361," in *A History of the Crusades*, ed. Kenneth M. Setton, vol. 6, *The Impact of the Crusades on Europe*, eds. Harry W. Hazard and Norman P. Zacour (Madison: University of Wisconsin Press, 1989), 222–38.

6. On the Ottoman expansion in the Balkans, see Machiel Kiel, "The Incorporation of the Balkans into the Ottoman Empire, 1353-1453," in *The Cambridge History of Turkey*, vol. 1, 138–57. The reasons behind its success are discussed in Dennis P. Hupchick, *The Balkans: From Constantinople to Communism* (New York: Palgrave Macmillan, 2004), 101–23. A volume that brings together recent scholarship on the subject is Oliver Jens Schmitt (ed.), *The Ottoman*

*Conquest of the Balkans: Interpretations and Research Debates* (Vienna: Verlag der Österreichischen Akademie der Wissenschaften, 2016).

7. This quick summary is based on Halil İnalcık, "Ottoman Conquests and the Crusade, 1361-1421," and "The Struggle for the Balkans, 1421-1451," in *A History of the Crusades*, vol. 6, 239–54, 254–75.

8. On the Ottomans' relationship with the Turko-Muslim principalities in Anatolia, see Lindner, "Anatolia 1300-1451," 107–17; a more detailed treatment is Feridun M. Emecen, *İlk Osmanlılar ve Anadolu Beylikler Dünyası* (Istanbul: Kitabevi, 2001).

9. For the first century and a half of Ottoman expansion and consolidation also see Caroline Finkel, *Osman's Dream: The Story of the Ottoman Empire, 1300-1923* (New York: Basic Books, 2007), 22–80; Kunt, "The Rise of the Ottomans," 844–63.

10. For relevant studies on state formation, see Ian Morris and Walter Scheidel (eds.), *The Dynamics of Ancient Empires: State Power from Assyria to Byzantium* (Oxford: Oxford University Press, 2009); Jo Van Steenbergen (ed.), *Trajectories of State-Formation across Fifteenth-Century Western Asia: Eurasian Parallels, Connections and Divergences* (Leiden: Brill, 2020).

11. Halil İnalcık, in *An Economic and Social History of the Ottoman Empire*, eds. İnalcık and Donald Quataert, vol. 1, *1300-1600* (Cambridge: Cambridge University Press, 1994), 55–75.

12. Colin Imber, *Ebu's-su'ud: The Islamic Legal Tradition* (Stanford, CA: Stanford University Press, 1997), 115–38.

13. For an overview of *timar*, see Colin Imber, *The Ottoman Empire, 1300-1650: The Structure of Power*, third edition (London: Red Globe Press, 2019), 159–69. For more details, see Nicoara Beldiceanu, *Le timar dans l'État ottoman (début XIVe-début XVIe siècle)* (Wiesbaden: Otto Harrassowitz, 1980); Linda T. Darling, "Historicizing the Ottoman *Timar* System: Identities of *Timar*-Holders, Fourteenth to Seventeenth Centuries," *Turkish Historical Review* 8, no. 2 (2017): 145–73.

14. For the establishment of Ottoman control over newly conquered territories, see Halil İnalcık, "Ottoman Methods of Conquest," *Studia Islamica* 2 (1954): 107–22.

15. For a quick yet perceptive description of Ottoman *sancak*s, see Imber, *The Ottoman Empire, 1300-1650*, 151–59; for the provinces, see 146–51.

16. On princes as *sancakbeyi*, see Metin Kunt, "A Prince Goes Forth (Perchance to Return)," in *Identity and Identity Formation in the Ottoman World: A Volume of Essays in Honor of Norman Itzkowitz*, eds. Baki Tezcan and Karl K. Barbir (Madison: University of Wisconsin Press, 2007), 63–71; Feridun M. Emecen, "Osmanlı Şehzadeleri ve Taşra İdaresi," reprinted in *Osmanlı Klasik Çağında Hanedan Devlet ve Toplum* (Istanbul: Kapı Yayınları, 2018), 63–68.

17. Gábor Ágoston, *Guns for the Sultan: Military Power and the Weapons Industry in the Ottoman Empire* (Cambridge: Cambridge University Press, 2005), 16–24.

18. For the Ottoman military in the early period, see Pál Fodor, "Ottoman Warfare, 1300-1453," in *The Cambridge History of Turkey*, vol. 1, 192–226. The connection between military recruitment and Ottoman expansion is discussed in Gábor Ágoston, "Ottoman Expansion and Military Power, 1300-1453," in *The Cambridge History of War*, vol. 2, *War and the Medieval World*, eds. Anne Curry and David A. Graf (Cambridge: Cambridge University Press, 2020), 451–68.

19. For a comparative analysis of Ottoman slavery, see Ehud R. Toledano, "Enslavement in the Ottoman Empire in the Early Modern Period," in *The Cambridge World History of Slavery*, vol. 3, *AD 1420-AD 1804*, eds. David Eltis and Stanley L. Engerman (New York: Cambridge University Press, 2011), 25–46. A comprehensive survey of slavery in Islamic history is Bernard K. Freamon, *Possessed by the Right Hand: The Problem of Slavery in Islamic Law and Muslim Cultures* (Leiden: Brill, 2019).

20. Imber, *The Ottoman Empire, 1300-1650*, 103–14, 119–24.

21. On the composition of the Ottoman elite, see İ. Metin Kunt, *The Sultan's Servants: The Transformation of Ottoman Provincial Government, 1550-1650* (New York: Columbia University Press, 1983), 31–56.

22. For the interplay between Sharia and *kanun* in Ottoman practice, see Imber, *The Ottoman Empire, 1300-1650*, 207–35.

23. For further information and a discussion about tolerance and interreligious relations, see Anver M. Emon, *Religious Pluralism and Islamic Law: Dhimmis and Others in the Empire of Law* (Oxford: Oxford University Press, 2012).

24. See Eleni Gara, "Conceptualizing Interreligious Relations in the Ottoman Empire: The Early Modern Centuries," *Acta Poloniae Historica* 116 (2017): 57–91. For a critique of the unqualified use of the notion of pragmatism for the Ottoman case, see Murat Dağlı, "The Limits of Ottoman Pragmatism," *History and Theory* 52 (May 2013): 194–213.

25. Âşıkpaşazade Ahmed, *Tevarih-i Âl-i Osman*, ed. Âlî (Istanbul: Matbaa-yı Âmire, 1914), 7, 19–20.

26. For various components of Ottoman administrative practices, see Kaya Şahin, "From Frontier Principality to Early Modern Empire: Limitations and Capabilities of Ottoman Governance," in *The Routledge History of the Renaissance*, ed. William Caferro (London: Routledge, 2017), 321–36.

27. See, for instance, Gábor Ágoston, "A Flexible Empire: Authority and Its Limits on the Ottoman Frontiers," *International Journal of Turkish Studies* 9 (2003): 15–31.

28. For a discussion of social and economic factors behind rural rebellions, see Yves-Marie Bercé, *History of Peasant Revolts: The Social Origins of Rebellion in Early Modern France*, trans. Amanda Whitmore (Ithaca, NY: Cornell University Press, 1990). Although all three focus on later events, the following works are useful for the study of Ottoman rural rebellions: Mustafa Akdağ, *Celâlî İsyanları (1550-1603)* (Ankara: Ankara Üniversitesi Basımevi, 1963); William J. Griswold, *The Great Anatolian Rebellion, 1000-1020/1591-1611* (Berlin: Klaus Schwarz, 1983);

Sam White, *The Climate of Rebellion in the Early Modern Ottoman Empire* (New York: Cambridge University Press, 2011).

29. For a relevant study, albeit one that focuses on later periods, see Gülay Yılmaz, "Urban Protests, Rebellions, and Revolts," in *A Companion to Early Modern Istanbul*, eds. Shirine Hamadeh and Çiğdem Kafescioğlu (Leiden: Brill, 2021), 555–80.

30. For a theoretical discussion on legitimization that uses the Ottomans as a case study, see Hakan T. Karateke, "Legitimizing the Ottoman Sultanate: A Framework for Historical Analysis," in *Legitimizing the Order: The Ottoman Rhetoric of State Power*, eds. Karateke and Maurus Reinkowski (Leiden: Brill, 2005), 13–52.

31. Timur was not a descendant of Genghis Khan, but he ruled in the name of a puppet Genghisid monarch he had put in place, and he had married a princess from the line of Genghis. See Beatrice Forbes Manz, *The Rise and Rule of Tamerlane* (Cambridge: Cambridge University Press, 1999), 14–16.

32. See Colin Imber, "The Ottoman Dynastic Myth," *Turcica* 19 (1987): 16–20.

33. While the Rumi identity was fully developed over time, its beginnings were in the fifteenth century, as discussed in Cemal Kafadar, "A Rome of One's Own: Reflections on Cultural Geography and Identity in the Lands of Rum," *Muqarnas* 24 (2007): 7–25.

34. See Irène Beldiceanu-Steinherr, "Analyse de la titulature d'Orḫan sur deux inscriptions de Brousse," *Turcica* 34 (2002): 223–40.

35. See Nikolay Antov, "Crusading in the Fifteenth Century and Its Relation to the Development of Ottoman Dynastic Legitimacy, Self-Image and the Ottoman Consolidation of Authority," in *The Crusade in the Fifteenth Century: Converging and Competing Cultures*, ed. Norman Housley (London: Routledge, 2016), 15–33; Imber, "The Ottoman Dynastic Myth," 7–13.

36. For more on Ottoman titulature, see Rhoads Murphey, *Exploring Ottoman Sovereignty: Tradition, Image and Practice in the Ottoman Imperial Household, 1400-1800* (London: Continuum, 2008), 77–83.

37. Murphey, *Exploring Ottoman Sovereignty*, 146–74.

38. Gülru Necipoğlu, "Visual Cosmopolitanism and Creative Translation: Artistic Conversations with Renaissance Italy in Mehmed II's Constantinople," *Muqarnas* 29 (2012): 6–12.

39. *Kânûnnâme-i Âl-i Osman (Tahlil ve Karşılaştırmalı Metin)*, revised second edition, ed. Abdülkadir Özcan (Istanbul: Kitabevi, 2003), 3–26.

40. For fifteenth-century Ottoman history-writing, see Kafadar, *Between Two Worlds*, 90–117.

41. For a discussion of those negative characterizations and an attempt at reorientation, see Linda T. Darling, "Rethinking Europe and the Islamic World in the Age of Exploration," *Journal of Early Modern History* 2, no. 3 (1998): 221–46; also see Giancarlo Casale, *The Ottoman Age of Exploration* (New York: Oxford University Press, 2010), 3–22.

42. On this new age of global expansion, see John Darwin, *After Tamerlane: The Global History of Empire since 1405* (London: Allen Lane, 2007), 50–99; Charles H. Parker, *Global Interactions in the Early Modern Age, 1400–1800* (Cambridge: Cambridge University Press, 2010). A more detailed treatment is found in Jerry H. Bentley, Sanjay Subrahmanyam, and Merry Wiesner-Hanks (eds.), *The Cambridge World History*, vol. 6, *The Construction of a Global World, 1400-1800 CE*, 2 volumes (Cambridge: Cambridge University Press, 2015).

43. For the situation in Hungary after Matthias Corvinus, see Pál Engel, *The Realm of St. Stephen: A History of Medieval Hungary, 895-1526*, trans. Tamás Pálosfalvi (London: I.B. Tauris, 2001), 345–61. For political developments in Europe from 1494 onward, see Richard Bonney, *The European Dynastic States 1494-1660* (Oxford: Oxford University Press, 1991), 79–99.

44. Michel M. Mazzaoui, *The Origins of the Ṣafawids; Šīʿism, Ṣūfism, and the Ġulāt* (Wiesbaden: F. Steiner, 1972), 41–82, and particularly Jean Aubin, "L'avènement des safavides reconsidéré," *Moyen Orient & Océan Indien* 5 (1988): 1–130.

45. John E. Woods, *The Aqquyunlu: Clan, Confederation, Empire*, revised and expanded edition (Salt Lake City: University of Utah Press, 1999), 125–163.

46. About Ismail and his movement's impact on Ottoman territories and subjects, see Ayşe Baltacıoğlu-Brammer, "Neither Victim Nor Accomplice: The Kızılbaş as Borderland Actors in the Early Modern Ottoman Realm," in *Historicizing Sunni Islam in the Ottoman Empire, c.1450-c.1750*, eds. Tijana Krstić and Derin Terzioğlu (Leiden: Brill, 2021), 423–50.

47. For Ismail's life and career, see Roger M. Savory and Ahmet T. Karamustafa, "ESMĀʿĪL I ṢAFAWĪ," *Encyclopaedia Iranica*, VIII/6, 628–636. A concise treatment of his rise to power is Woods, *The Aqquyunlu*, 163–72.

48. For the intellectual climate of the period, see A. C. S. Peacock, *Islam, Literature and Society in Mongol Anatolia* (Cambridge: Cambridge University Press, 2019); Jonathan Brack, "A Mongol Mahdi in Medieval Anatolia: Rebellion, Reform, and Divine Right in the Post-Mongol Islamic World," *Journal of the American Oriental Society* 139, no. 3 (2019): 611–29.

49. Kaya Şahin, "Constantinople and the End Time: The Ottoman Conquest as a Portent of the Last Hour," *Journal of Early Modern History* 14, no. 4 (2010): 317–54.

50. Antov, "Crusading in the Fifteenth Century," 19–23, 24–27.

51. Pál Fodor, "The View of the Turk in Hungary: The Apocalyptic Tradition and the Legend of the Red Apple in Ottoman-Hungarian Context," in *Les traditions apocalyptiques au tournant de la chute de Constantinople*, eds. Benjamin Lellouch and Stéphane Yerasimos (Paris: Harmattan; Istanbul: Institut français d'études anatoliennes Georges-Dumézil, 2000), especially 104–11.

52. For the parallels between Ottoman/Islamic and European Christian apocalyptic traditions, see Cornell H. Fleischer, "A Mediterranean Apocalypse: Prophecies of Empire in the Fifteenth and Sixteenth Centuries," *Journal of the Social and Economic History of the Orient* 61, nos. 1–2 (2018): 18–90; for the global extent of

apocalyptic and messianic visions, see Sanjay Subrahmanyam, "Turning the Stones Over: Sixteenth-century Millenarianism from the Tagus to the Ganges," *Indian Economic and Social History Review* 40, no. 3 (2003): 131–63.

53. For instance, see Ahmed Bican Yazıcıoğlu [attributed], *Dürr-i Meknun: kritische Edition mit Kommentar*, ed. Laban Kaptein (Asch: self-publication, 2007), 575.

54. Celalzade Mustafa, *Tarih-i Sultan Selim*, ms. British Museum Add. 7848, 50a–53a.

55. For a summary of Cem's struggles, see Finkel, *Osman's Dream*, 81–89. A detailed narrative, mostly from a European perspective, is in Kenneth M. Setton, *The Papacy and the Levant (1204-1571)*, vol. 2, *The Fifteenth Century* (Philadelphia: The American Philosophical Society, 1978), 381–482.

56. See Halil İnalcık, "The Ottomans, the Crusade, and Renaissance Diplomacy, 1481-1522," in *A History of the Crusades*, vol. 6, 331–53. An in-depth study of the situation from a Hungarian perspective is Tamás Pálosfalvi, *From Nicopolis to Mohács: A History of Ottoman-Hungarian Warfare, 1389-1526* (Leiden: Brill, 2008), 278–329.

57. See Shai Har-El, *Struggle for Domination in the Middle East: The Ottoman-Mamluk War, 1485-1491* (Leiden: Brill, 1995); for a quick overview, see Finkel, *Osman's Dream*, 90–94, and Cihan Yüksel Muslu, *The Ottomans and the Mamluks: Imperial Diplomacy and Warfare in the Islamic World* (London: I.B. Tauris, 2014), 141–55.

58. Nikolay Antov, *The Ottoman "Wild West:" The Balkan Frontier in the Fifteenth and Sixteenth Centuries* (Cambridge: Cambridge University Press, 2017), 88–89.

59. For Bayezid II and the Sufis, see Derin Terzioğlu, "Sufis in the Age of State Building and Confessionalization," in *The Ottoman World*, ed. Christine Woodhead (London: Routledge, 2012), 92–94.

60. The register was published as İlhan Şahin and Feridun Emecen (eds.), *Osmanlılarda Divân-Bürokrasi-Ahkâm: II. Bâyezid Dönemine Ait 906/1501 Tarihli Ahkâm Defteri* (Istanbul: Türk Dünyası Araştırmaları Vakfı, 1994).

61. Imber, *The Ottoman Empire, 1300-1650*, 164–65, 230–31.

62. Çiğdem Kafescioğlu, *Constantinopolis/Istanbul: Cultural Encounter, Imperial Vision, and the Construction of the Ottoman Capital* (University Park: Pennsylvania State University Press, 2009), 214–26.

63. Cornell H. Fleischer and Kaya Şahin, "On the Works of a Historical Nature in the Bayezid II Library Inventory" and "List of Entries," in *Treasures of Knowledge: An Inventory of the Ottoman Palace Library (1502/3-1503/4)*, vol. 1, *Essays*, eds. Gülru Necipoğlu, Cemal Kafadar, and Cornell H. Fleischer (Leiden: Brill, 2019), 569–96.

64. The catalogue has been published, together with an accompanying volume of ana-lytical studies, as Necipoğlu et al. (eds.), *Treasures of Knowledge*, vol. 1, *Essays*; vol. 2, *Transliteration*.

65. The palace library does not reflect the entire landscape of Turkish literary output, but rather the upper class' cultural preferences. For a more inclusive panorama, see Ahmet Yaşar Ocak, "Social, Cultural and Intellectual Life, 1071–1453," in *The Cambridge History of Turkey*, vol. 1, 407–11.

66. A concise discussion of this transition is in Ferenc Csirkés, "Turkish/Turkic Books of Poetry, Turkish and Persian Lexicography: The Politics of Language Under Bayezid II," in *Treasures of Knowledge*, vol. 1, 673–77. For a survey of the nascent Ottoman intellectual tradition and its subsequent development, see Gottfried Hagen, "The Order of Knowledge, the Knowledge of Order: Intellectual Life," in *The Cambridge History of Turkey*, vol. 2, *The Ottoman Empire as a World Power, 1453–1603*, eds. Suraiya N. Faroqhi and Kate Fleet (Cambridge: Cambridge University Press, 2009), 407–56.

67. *Defter-i Müsveddat-ı İnamat ve Tasaddukat ve Teşrifat ve İrsaliyat ve Âdet ve Nökeriye ve Gayrıhu*, Istanbul Atatürk Library, ms. Muallim Cevdet O. 71, hereafter *Defter-i İnamat*. An analysis and transliteration (to be used with some caution) of the register is İlhan Gök, "Atatürk Kitaplığı M.C. O.71 Numaralı 909-933/ 1503-1527 Tarihli İn'âmât Defteri (Transkripsiyon-Değerlendirme)" (PhD diss., Marmara University, 2014).

68. On the family of Bayezid, see M. Çağatay Uluçay, "Bayazıd [sic] II. in Âilesi," *Tarih Dergisi* 10, no. 14 (September 1959): 105–24.

69. About the origins and transformation of Ottoman succession practices, see Joseph Fletcher, "Turco-Mongolian Monarchic Tradition in the Ottoman Empire," *Harvard Ukrainian Studies* 3–4 (1979-1980): 236–51; Halil İnalcık, "The Ottoman Succession and Its Relation to the Turkish Concept of Sovereignty," in İnalcık, *The Middle East and the Balkans under the Ottoman Empire: Essays on Economy and Society* (Bloomington: Indiana University Turkish Studies, 1993), 37–69.

70. An overview of Ottoman succession in the earlier centuries is Imber, *The Ottoman Empire, 1300-1650*, 73–88.

71. *Kânûnnâme-i Âl-i Osman*, 18. For more on *nizam-ı âlem*, see Gottfried Hagen, "Legitimacy and World Order," in *Legitimizing the Order*, 55–83.

72. On the royal household as one of the main institutions of Ottoman political and cultural life, see Metin Kunt, "Royal and Other Households," in *The Ottoman World*, 103–15. Princely households are discussed in 110–11. Also see Emecen, "Osmanlı Şehzadeleri ve Taşra İdaresi," 72–74.

73. For individuals and groups that belonged to Selim's household throughout his governorship, see M. Hanefi Bostan, "Yavuz Sultan Selim'in Şehzâdelik Dönemi (1487-1512)," *Türk Kültürü İncelemeleri Dergisi* 40 (Spring 2019): 32–41.

74. While there are contemporary and later arguments that portray Hafsa as a noblewoman of Crimean or Turkic origin, her endowment deed uses a formula for her name that is typical for slaves and converts to Islam. See M. Çağatay Uluçay, *Padişahların Kadınları ve Kızları* (Ankara: Türk Tarih Kurumu, 1980), 29–30.

75. Juliette Dumas, "Des esclaves pour époux. . . Stratégies matrimoniales dans la dynastie ottoman (mi-XIVe- début XVIe siècle)," *Clio. Femmes, Genre, Histoire* 34 (2011): 255–75. Also see Leslie Peirce, *The Imperial Harem: Women and Sovereignty in the Ottoman Empire* (New York: Oxford University Press, 1993), 28–45.

76. There is evidence about Bayezid II's search of a concubine for his son Ahmed (d. 1513) in a letter sent by a middleman or a slave trader to the palace (TSMA, E. 760/17). According to the letter, Bayezid II had ordered a search for a comely, not-too-young concubine. In it, the middleman/slave trader informs the palace that he found three suitable candidates and asks for permission to bring them over.

77. See Kecia Ali, *Marriage and Slavery in Early Islam* (Cambridge, MA: Harvard University Press, 2010), especially 176–84. For the diverse functions of concubinage in Islamic history, see Matthew S. Gordon and Kathryn A. Hain (eds.), *Concubines and Courtesans: Women and Slavery in Islamic History* (New York: Oxford University Press, 2017).

78. For a description and critique of similar views, see Irvin Cemil Schick, *The Erotic Margin: Sexuality and Spatiality in Alterist Discourse* (London: Verso, 1999).

79. A short yet characteristic description by the leading Ottoman historian of the modern period is Halil İnalcık, "Harem Bir Fuhuş Yuvası Değil, Bir Okuldu," preface to a new edition of M. Çağatay Uluçay, *Osmanlı Sultanlarına Aşk Mektupları* (Istanbul: Ufuk Yayınları, 2001), 7–15.

80. The summary here relies on Peirce, *The Imperial Harem*, 15–50.

## CHAPTER 2

1. Seyyid Lokman, *Hünername*, vol. 2, TSMK, ms. Hazine 1524, 19a.

2. Fethullah Ârif, *Sulaymannama*, TSMK, ms. Hazine 1517, 6a. This is the date that has been more widely adopted by Ottoman historians writing after Süleyman's death, among them the respected and oft-quoted Mustafa Âli, *Künhü'l-ahbar*, Istanbul University Library, ms. TY 5959, 215a.

3. See İ. Metin Kunt, "Ottoman Names and Ottoman Ages," *Journal of Turkish Studies* 10 (1986): 229–34.

4. See Jan Schmidt, "The Reception of Firdausi's *Shahnama* among the Ottomans"; and Lâle Uluç, "The *Shahnama* of Firdausi in the Lands of Rum," in *Shahnama Studies II: The Reception of Firdausi's Shahnama*, eds. Charles Melville and Gabrielle van den Berg (Leiden: Brill, 2012), 121–39 and 159–80, respectively.

5. For narratives of old Turkic history that circulated among the Ottomans, see İlker Evrim Binbaş, "Oguz Khan Narratives," *Encyclopædia Iranica* (http://www.iranicaonline.org/articles/oguz-khan-narratives), last updated April 15, 2010.

6. The trilateral root is *ḥ.m.d.* Its basic meaning is to praise, commend, laud. See Hans Wehr, *A Dictionary of Modern Written Arabic*, ed. J. Milton Cowan (Ithaca, NY: Spoken Word Services Inc., 1976), 204.

7. Quran 30: 27. The name of the chapter is *Al Naml* ("The Ants"). I use the translation in Seyyed Hossein Nasr et al. (eds.), *The Study Quran: A New Translation and Commentary* (New York: HarperOne, 2015), 933.

8. Seyyid Lokman, *Hünername*, vol. 2, 19b.

9. Seyyid Lokman, *Hünername,* vol. 2, 19b.

10. Sad b. Abdülmüteal, *Selimname*, TSMK, ms. Revan 1277, 115b–116a.

11. H. Erdem Çıpa, *The Making of Selim: Succession, Legitimacy, and Memory in the Early Modern Ottoman World* (Bloomington: Indiana University Press, 2017), 188–91.

12. For the number and names of Selim's daughters I follow Uluçay, *Padişahların Kadınları ve Kızları*, 31–34.

13. Mustafa Âli, *Künhü'l-ahbar*, 348a–348b.

14. For the figure of Solomon in Islam, see Suzanne P. Stetkevych, "Solomon and Mythic Kingship in the Arab-Islamic Tradition: Qaṣīdah, Qurʾān and Qiṣaṣ al-anbiyāʾ," *Journal of Arabic Literature* 48, no. 1 (June 2017): 1–37.

15. See Firdevsî-i Rumi, *Süleymanname*, Chester Beatty Library, ms. T 406.

16. Fethullah Ârif, *Sulaymannama*, 2b, 3a.

17. For the notion of place as well as the links between place, memory, and identity, see Tim Creswell, *Place: An Introduction*, second edition (Malden, MA: Wiley Blackwell, 2015).

18. An old yet still reliable study on the foundation of the Empire of Trabzon is A. A. Vasiliev, "The Foundation of the Empire of Trebizond (1204-1222)," *Speculum* 11, no. 1 (January 1936): 3–37. A quick overview is Donald M. Nicol, *The Last Centuries of Byzantium, 1261-1453*, second edition (Cambridge: Cambridge University Press, 1993), 401–9.

19. See Yaşar Yücel, "Fatih'in Trabzon'u Fethi Öncesinde Osmanlı-Trabzon-Akkoyunlu İlişkileri," *Belleten* 49, no. 194 (1984): 287–311.

20. On pre-Ottoman Trabzon as a commercial center, see Aslıhan Akışık-Karakullukçu, "The Empire of Trebizond in the World Trade System: Economy and Culture," in *Trade in Byzantium: Papers from the Third International Sevgi Gönül Byzantine Studies Symposium*, eds. Paul Magdalino and Nevra Necipoğlu (Istanbul: Koç University Research Center for Anatolian Civilizations, 2016), 323–36.

21. M. Hanefi Bostan, *XV-XVI. Asırlarda Trabzon Sancağında Sosyal ve İktisadi Hayat* (Ankara: Türk Tarih Kurumu, 2002), table CVI on 417–19; Heath W. Lowry, *The Islamization and Turkification of the City of Trabzon (Trebizond), 1461-1583* (Istanbul: Isis Press, 2009), table V on 53.

22. Ruy Gonzalez de Clavijo, *Narrative of the Embassy of Ruy Gonzalez de Clavijo to the Court of Timour, at Samarcand, A.D. 1403-6*, trans. Clements R. Markham (London: The Hakluyt Society, 1869), 65–69.

23. Clavijo, *Narrative of the Embassy of Ruy Gonzalez de Clavijo*, 198.

24. Tursun Beg, *Tarih-i Ebu'l-feth*, SK, ms. Ayasofya 3032, 90a–91a.

25. İbn Kemal, *Tevârih-i Âl-i Osman. VII. Defter*, ed. Şerafettin Turan (Ankara: Türk Tarih Kurumu, 1991), 195–96.

26. Clavijo, *Narrative of the Embassy of Ruy Gonzalez de Clavijo*, 56–60, 198–99.

27. My understanding of Trabzon and its vicinity as a specific natural environment relies on Émile Janssens, *Trébizonde en Colchide* (Brussels: Presses universitaires de Bruxelles, 1969), 7–15 and throughout; and Anthony Bryer and David

Winfield, *The Byzantine Monuments and Topography of the Pontos* (Washington, DC: Dumbarton Oaks Research Library and Collection, 1985), vol. 1, 1–60.

28. Bostan, *XV–XVI. Asırlarda Trabz*on, 390–92, 487–525; Evliyâ Çelebi b. Derviş Mehemmed Zıllî, *Evliyâ Çelebi Seyahatnâmesi. 2. Kitap*, eds. Zekeriya Kurşun, Seyit Ali Kahraman, Yücel Dağlı (Istanbul: Yapı Kredi, 2011), 53–54.

29. The description of the town is based on Clavijo, *Narrative of the Embassy of Ruy Gonzalez de Clavijo*, 62–63; Bessarion, *Encomium on Trebizond*, in *Two Works on Trebizond: Michael Panaretos, Bessarion*, ed. and trans. Scott Kennedy (Cambridge, MA: Harvard University Press, 2019), 127–29, 189–95; Âşık Mehmed, *Menâzırü'l-Avâlim*, ed. and transl. Mahmut Ak (Ankara: Türk Tarih Kurumu, 2007), vol. 3, 1021–26.

30. See Veysel Usta, "Şehzade Süleyman'ın (Kanuni) Trabzon'da Doğduğu Ev Meselesi," *Karadeniz Araştırmaları Dergisi* 26 (Spring 2019): 397–414.

31. Bostan, *XV–XVI. Asırlarda Trabzon*, 82–96; Lowry, *Islamization and Turkification*, 21–22.

32. For conversion in Trabzon after the Ottoman conquest, see Lowry, *Islamization and Turkification*, 27–57. A useful discussion of the factors behind conversion is Anton Minkov, "Forms, Factors and Motives of Conversion to Islam in the Balkans," chapter 3 in Minkov, *Conversion to Islam in the Balkans*: Kisve Bahası *Petitions and Ottoman Social Life, 1670-1730* (Leiden: Brill, 2004), 64–109.

33. See map in Lowry, *Islamization and Turkification*, 43, for the location of Trabzon neighborhoods.

34. See Bostan, *XV–XVI. Asırlarda Trabzon*, table XC on 289 for the town; table C on 317–18 for the district.

35. Bostan, *XV–XVI. Asırlarda Trabzon*, 256, 263.

36. Bostan, *XV–XVI. Asırlarda Trabzon*, 159, 162. Lowry, *Islamization and Turkification*, 27–59, gives a number of ca. 6,700. The discrepancy is due to Bostan's inclusion of members of the *askerî* class who lived in the town, and I adopt his estimate here.

37. Lowry, *Islamization and Turkification*, 31; Bostan, *XV–XVI. Asırlarda Trabzon*, 97.

38. Lowry, *Islamization and Turkification*, table VI on 57. The Greek Orthodox were counted as 4,373 individuals, the Armenians 838, and the Venetians and the Genoese 210.

39. My summary of the built environment is based on a sixteenth-century account and four modern studies, all of which convey the continued presence of the pre-Ottoman urban fabric: Âşık Mehmed, *Menâzırü'l-Avâlim*, vol. 3, 1021–26; Janssen, *Trébizonde en Colchide*, 217–39; Şâmil Horuluoğlu, *Trabzon ve Çevresinin Tarihi Eserleri* (Ankara: Er Ofset Matbaacılık, 1983); Hüseyin Albayrak, *Trabzon Orta Hisâr ve Çevresi* (Ankara: Kozan Ofset, 1998); Bryer and Winfield, *The Byzantine Monuments and Topography of the Pontos*, vol. 1, 178–251.

40. Bessarion, *Encomium on Trebizond*, 195–201.

41. This claim was reported by Theodore Spandounes in the early sixteenth century. Spandounes was the descendant of a Byzantine family that had migrated to Venice

after 1453. See *On the Origin of the Ottoman Emperors*, trans. and ed. Donald M. Nicol (Cambridge: Cambridge University Press, 1997), 11.

42. This detail is found in the account of an Ottoman traveler who probably heard it during his visit to the town in 1640: *Evliya Çelebi Seyahatnâmesi. 2. Kitap*, 53.

43. This point has been made by Heath W. Lowry, "From Trabzon to Istanbul: The Relationship between Süleyman the Lawgiver and His Foster Brother (*Süt Karındaşı*) Yahya Efendi," *Osmanlı Araştırmaları* 10 (1990): 42–43. For a discussion of Süleyman's childhood years by the same author, also see his "Süleymân's Formative Years in the City of Trabzon: Their Impact on the Future Sultan and the City," in *Süleymân the Second and His Time*, eds. Halil İnalcık and Cemal Kafadar (Istanbul: Isis Press, 1993), 29–44.

44. For Yahya's life and career, and an edition and analysis of his poetic output, see Müslüm Yılmaz, *Beşiktaşlı Yahyâ Efendi: Hayatı Tasavvufi Şahsiyeti ve Dîvânı* (Istanbul: Dergâh Yayınları, 2014); Beşiktaşlı Yaḥyā Efendi, *Dīvān: Analysis – Critical Text – Dictionary – Facsimile*, ed. Enis Tombul (Cambridge, MA: The Department of Near Eastern Languages and Civilizations, Harvard University, 2018). In addition to references found in Yahya's poetry, information about their lifelong relationship largely relies on a hagiographic narrative of Yahya's life: Mehmed Dâî, *Menakıb-ı Şeyh Yahya Beşiktaşi*, SK, ms. Hacı Mahmud Efendi 4604.

45. Feridun M. Emecen, *Yavuz Sultan Selim*, revised edition (Istanbul: Kapı, 2016), 39–40.

46. *Defter-i İnamat*, 6b, 74a. The presents after Kamerşah's death were sent in September 1503, and those after Gülbahar's death in November 1505. They must have died several months before these dates.

47. Özkan Ertuğrul, "Gülbahar Hatun Camii ve Türbesi," *TDVİA* (Ankara: Türkiye Diyanet Vakfı, 1988-2013, 2016), vol. 14, 231–32.

48. This information is available thanks to an entry in the *Defter-i İnamat* for money and clothes given from the palace to the two messengers sent by Selim (169a). The same source also records (in 168b) a sum of 40,000 *akçes* and a quantity of clothes sent to the new bride by her grandfather Bayezid II.

49. For two overviews, the first one focusing more on Islam and the second one on Judaism, see Malek Chebel, *Histoire de la circoncision, des origines à nos jours* (Paris: Éditions Balland, 1992); Leonard B. Glick, *Marked in Your Flesh: Circumcision from Ancient Judea to Modern America* (New York: Oxford University Press, 2005).

50. For the role of circumcision in Ottoman dynastic life and culture, see Kaya Şahin, "Staging an Empire: An Ottoman Circumcision Ceremony as Cultural Performance," *American Historical Review* 123, no. 2 (April 2018): 463–92.

51. The list is in *Defter-i İnamat*, 56b; a transliteration is in Feridun M. Emecen, "Kanuni Sultan Süleyman'ın Şehzadelik Dönemine Ait Bazı Yeni Tespitler ve Notlar," reprinted in Emecen, *Osmanlı Klasik Çağında Hilafet ve Saltanat* (Istanbul: Kapı Yayınları, 2020), 183–84.

52. My interpretation of these gifts slightly differs from Emecen, "Kanuni Sultan Süleyman'ın Şehzadelik Dönemi," 183–84.

53. Here, I rely on Konrad Hirschler, *The Written Word in the Medieval Arabic Lands: A Social and Cultural History of Reading Practices* (Edinburgh: Edinburgh University Press, 2012), 12–17, 82–99, 164–75. For notions of child development, see Avner Giladi, *Children of Islam: Concepts of Childhood in Medieval Muslim Society* (Houndmills, Basingstoke, Hampshire: Palgrave Macmillan, 1992), 45–66. A panoramic study of childhood in Ottoman society is Yahya Araz, *16. Yüzyıldan 19. Yüzyıl Başlarına Osmanlı Toplumunda Çocuk Olmak* (Istanbul: Kitap, 2013).

54. For the development and transformation of the symbiotic relationship between scholars and the Ottoman dynasty from ca. 1300 to the end of the reign of Mehmed II, see Abdurrahman Atçıl, *Scholars and Sultans in the Early Modern Ottoman Empire* (Cambridge: Cambridge University Press, 2017), 17–82.

55. A short biography of Hayreddin is in Mecdî Efendi, *Tercüme-i Şekaik* (Istanbul, Daru't-Tıba'ati'l-Âmire, 1269 [1852-53 CE]), 440.

56. For Abdülhalim's biography, see Mecdî Efendi, *Tercüme-i Şekaik*, 385–86.

57. For education and educators, see Ocak, "Social, Cultural and Intellectual Life, 1071–1453," in *The Cambridge History of Turkey*, vol. 1, 411–14. More information is available in Mustafa Bilge, *İlk Osmanlı Medreseleri* (Istanbul: Edebiyat Fakültesi Basımevi, 1984).

58. An edition of Süleyman's Persian poetry is Kasım Gelen, "Kânûnî Sultan Süleymân'ın Farsça Dîvanı" (MA thesis, Istanbul University, 1989).

59. For a quick survey of what Ottoman princes studied, to be read cautiously due to the idealized picture it provides, see Haldun Eroğlu, *Osmanlı Devletinde Şehzadelik Kurumu* (Ankara: Akçağ, 2004), 81–85. Since the Ottomans borrowed aspects of Byzantine dynastic culture, a comparison with Byzantine princes may be useful. For their education, see Dimiter G. Angelov, "Emperors and Patriarchs as Ideal Children and Adolescents: Literary Conventions and Cultural Expectations," in *Becoming Byzantine: Children and Childhood in Byzantium*, eds. Arietta Papaconstantinou and Alice-Mary Talbot (Washington, DC: Dumbarton Oaks Research Library and Collection, distributed by Harvard University Press, 2009), 85–116, especially 105–10.

60. Abdulkerim Abdulkadiroğlu, "Halîmî Çelebi," *TDVİA*, vol. 15, 343–44.

61. For the prevalence of Persian poetry within Ottoman elite circles, see Sooyong Kim, "An Ottoman Order of Persian Verse," in *Treasures of Knowledge*, vol. 1, 635–56. The impact of Persian on Süleyman's Ottoman Turkish poetry, in terms of both poetic sensibility and pedagogy, is discussed in Murat Umut Inan, "Rethinking the Ottoman Imitation of Persian Poetry," *Iranian Studies* 50, no. 5 (2017): 671–89; Benedek Péri, "The Persian Imitation Gazels (Nazires) of Kanuni Sultan Süleyman 'Muhibbi' (1520–1566) as They Are Preserved in a Hitherto Unnoticed Early Copy of his Divan," *Amasya Üniversitesi Sosyal Bilimler Dergisi* 5 (June 2019): 95–120.

62. For the development of a specifically Ottoman poetic tradition, see Selim S. Kuru, "The Literature of Rum: The Making of a Literary Tradition (1450–1600)," in *The Cambridge History of Turkey*, vol. 2, 548–92.

63. For references by Süleyman to other poets, see Coşkun Ak, *Muhibbî Dîvânı. İzahlı Metin* (Ankara: Kültür ve Turizm Bakanlığı, 1987), 24; Kânûnî Sultan Süleyman, *Muhibbî Dîvânı. Bütün Şiirleri*, eds. Kemal Yavuz and Orhan Yavuz (Istanbul: Türkiye Yazma Eserler Kurumu Başkanlığı, 2016), vol. 1, 26–30.

64. For the performative aspects of poetry, see Didem Z. Havlioğlu, *Mihrî Hatun: Performance, Gender-Bending, and Subversion in Ottoman Intellectual History* (Syracuse, NY: Syracuse University Press, 2017), 57–71, 101–37. My overall discussion of the structure and content of Ottoman poetry is based on Walter G. Andrews, *Poetry's Voice, Society's Song: Ottoman Lyric* Poetry (Seattle: University of Washington Press, 1985).

65. For a study of Selim's poetry and an edition of his work, see Benedek Péri, *The Persian Dīvān of Yavuz Sulṭān Selīm: A Critical Edition* (Budapest: Research Center for the Humanities, 2021).

66. İbn Kemal, *Tevârih-i Âl-i Osman. VII. Defter*, 521–24.

67. Hoca Sadeddin Efendi, *Prognostic Dreams, Otherworldly Saints, and Caliphal Ghosts: A Critical Edition of Sa'deddīn Efendi's (d. 1599) Selimname*, trans. and ed. H. Erdem Çıpa (Leiden: Brill, 2022), 70.

68. For Byzantine examples on the physical aspects of princely education, including hunting, see Angelov, "Emperors and Patriarchs as Ideal Children and Adolescents," 105–11. Thomas T. Allsen's *The Hunt in Eurasian History* (Philadelphia: University of Pennsylvania Press, 2006) is the best discussion of the practical as well as cultural aspects of hunting for dynastic elites.

69. Bostan, *XV–XVI. Asırlarda Trabzon*, 269, 277.

70. For the men around Selim, see Bostan, "Yavuz Sultan Selim'in Şehzâdelik Dönemi," 32–41.

71. Bostan, *XV–XVI. Asırlarda Trabzon*, 526–31.

72. See Bostan, *XV–XVI. Asırlarda Trabzon*, 390–525.

73. Emecen, *Yavuz Sultan Selim*, 38–41; Bostan, "Yavuz Sultan Selim'in Şehzâdelik Dönemi," 41–45, 50–53.

74. Şahin and Emecen, *II. Bâyezid Dönemine Ait 906/1501 Tarihli Ahkâm Defteri*, 32, order # 111.

75. For summaries of Selim's activities against the Safavids and the Georgians, see Emecen, *Yavuz Sultan Selim*, 32–37; Bostan, "Yavuz Sultan Selim'in Şehzâdelik Dönemi," 11–20. For a contemporary account, see İbn Kemâl, *Tevârîḫ-i Âl-i Osmân. VIII. Defter*, ed. Ahmet Uğur (Ankara: Türk Tarih Kurumu, 1997), 259–60, 272–76.

76. For representations of Selim in near-contemporary Ottoman histories, see Çıpa, *The Making of Selim*, 132–75.

77. Bostan, "Yavuz Sultan Selim'in Şehzâdelik Dönemi," 47.

78. *Defter-i İnamat*, 110a, quoted in Bostan, "Yavuz Sultan Selim'in Şehzâdelik Dönemi," 17.

79. Şahin and Emecen, *II. Bâyezid Dönemine Ait 906/1501 Tarihli Ahkâm Defteri*, 78–79, order # 281.

80. İbn Kemâl, *Tevârîḫ-i Âl-i Osmân. VIII. Defter*, 243, 251–59.
81. Bessarion, *Encomium on Trebizond*, 121.
82. For examples of those who were displaced by the Safavids and relocated by Selim, see Bostan, *XV–XVI. Asırlarda Trabzon*, 102; for Ottoman subjects who left to join Ismail, but later returned to their lands, see 239, 660, etc.
83. Bostan, "Yavuz Sultan Selim'in Şehzâdelik Dönemi," 47–48. The letter is TSMA, E. 745/21.
84. Bostan, *XV–XVI. Asırlarda Trabzon*, 491, table CXXIX.
85. The letter is TSMA, E. 850/38.

CHAPTER 3

1. For Ahmed's presumed activities against Süleyman and Selim, see Emecen, *Yavuz Sultan Selim*, 42–45; Çıpa, *The Making of Selim*, 34, 44; Nevin Zeynep Yelçe, "The Making of Sultan Süleyman: A Study of Process/es of Image-Making and Reputation Management" (PhD diss., Sabancı University, 2009), 64–67.
2. For a contemporary view on Bayezid's advancing age and his desire to abdicate, see Sad b. Abdülmüteal, *Selimname*, 7a–8b.
3. For these rumors, told from a pro-Selim perspective, see Sad b. Abdülmüteal, *Selimname*, 13b–15b.
4. The letter is TSMA, E. 752/18. A partial trans literation is in Bostan, "Yavuz Sultan Selim'in Şehzâdelik Dönemi," 48–49.
5. *Defter-i İnamat*, 151b.
6. *Defter-i İnamat*, 167b.
7. *Defter-i İnamat*, 167b.
8. For Selim's elaborate plans to obtain Caffa for Süleyman, see Sad b. Abdülmüteal, *Selimname*, 16a–18b.
9. For these appointments, see *Defter-i İnamat*, 102b, 140a, 146b. Osman's appointment is not listed but his date of service may be deduced from the record of a sum of money sent to him to build a residence.
10. Ahmed's son Süleyman was appointed in March 1510; Alaeddin was in Bolu by late October 1510. See *Defter-i İnamat*, 182a, 205b. Other appointments are mentioned in İbn Kemâl, *Tevârîḫ-i Âl-i Osmân. VIII. Defter*, 276. There are a few discrepancies between the documentary evidence and İbn Kemâl's text.
11. Sad b. Abdülmüteal, *Selimname*, 18b–19b. For further proof of Selim's intentions as well as the date of his departure for Caffa, see Andrea Foscolo, "Relazione," in *Relazioni di ambasciatori veneti al Senato*, vol. 14, *Costantinopoli: Relazioni inedite (1512-1789)*, ed. Maria Pia Pedani Fabris (Padua: Aldo Ausilio-Bottega d'Erasmo, 1996), 16–18.
12. Sad b. Abdülmüteal, *Selimname*, 22a.
13. TSMA, E. 759/94.
14. The gifts given to Süleyman's men are listed in *Defter-i İnamat*, 218b.

15. *Defter-i İnamat*, 236a.

16. Yücel Öztürk, *Osmanlı Hakimiyetinde Kefe (1475–1600)* (Ankara: Kültür Bakanlığı Yayınları, 2000), 23–30.

17. For the prince's death and a failed plan to have him marry a daughter of the Khan of Crimea, see İbn Kemâl, *Tevârîḫ-i Âl-i Osmân. VIII. Defter*, 239–41.

18. See Öztürk, *Osmanlı Hakimiyetinde Kefe*, 200–84 for a detailed demographical analysis, and 285–86 for a snapshot.

19. See Öztürk, *Osmanlı Hakimiyetinde Kefe*, 339–411 for revenues from 1520 and 1542.

20. İnalcık, *An Economic and Social History of the Ottoman Empire*, vol. 1, 185–87, 283–85.

21. For the lives of slaves within the Ottoman economy, see Yvonne J. Seng, "Fugitives and Factotums: Slaves in Early Sixteenth-Century Istanbul," *Journal of the Economic and Social History of the Orient* 39, no. 2 (1996): 136–69.

22. On the relationship Selim established with the Khan of Crimea, see Çıpa, *The Making of Selim*, 79–81; Yelçe, "The Making of Sultan Süleyman," 71–73.

23. The letter is TSMA, E. 672/5.

24. Marino Sanuto, *I Diarii di Marino Sanuto*, ed. Rinaldo Fulin et. al. (Venice: F. Visentini, 1879–1903), vol. 12, 508 (hereafter *I Diarii*).

25. The register is TSMA, D. 743. A partial transliteration is provided in Çağatay Uluçay, "Kanunî Sultan Süleyman ve Ailesi ile İlgili Bazı Notlar ve Vesikalar," in *Kanunî Armağanı*, ed. Uluğ İğdemir (Ankara: Türk Tarih Kurumu, 1970), 237–39.

26. TSMA, D. 743, 1b.

27. TSMA, D. 743, 2a–2b.

28. TSMA, D. 743, 3a–5a.

29. For Korkud's life and career up to 1509, see Nabil al-Tikriti, "Şehzade Korkud (ca. 1468-1513) and the Articulation of Early 16th Century Ottoman Religious Identity" (PhD diss., University of Chicago, 2004), 48–89; for Korkud's departure and his time in Cairo, see 235–80.

30. My account of Selim's move to Caffa, his confrontation with Bayezid II, his accession to the throne in April 1512, and his elimination of the remaining heirs to the throne by the end of spring 1513 is based on Çıpa, *The Making of Selim*, 37–61; also see Emecen, *Yavuz Sultan Selim*, 46–91.

31. My interpretation of the rebellion stems from Feridun M. Emecen, "'İhtilalci Bir Mehdilik' Hareketi mi? Şahkulu Baba Tekeli İsyanı Üzerine Yeni Yaklaşımlar," in *Ötekilerin Peşinde: Ahmet Yaşar Ocak'a Armağan*, eds. Mehmet Öz and Fatih Yeşil (Istanbul: Timaş, 2015), 521–34. Cf. Çıpa, *The Making of Selim*, 43–48. About Ottoman repression as a factor that pushed pro-Safavid individuals and communities to rebel, see Fariba Zarinabaf-Shahr, "Qizilbash 'Heresy' and Rebellion in Ottoman Anatolia in the Sixteenth Century," *Anatolia Moderna* 7 (1997): 1–15.

32. For an Ottoman official's letter to Constantinople about the risk of Şehinşah joining the rebels, see TSMA, E. 747/2.

33. Sad b. Abdülmüteal, *Selimname*, 51b–52b; Burhan Keskin, "Selîm-Nâme (İshâk b. İbrâhîm)" (MA thesis, Ege University, 1998), 165–68.

34. For the symbolic aspects of Süleyman's arrival and greeting, also see Yelçe, "The Making of Sultan Süleyman," 77–79.

35. TSMA, E. 754/101, 1.

36. İsmail Hakkı Uzunçarşılı, "Onbeşinci Yüzyılın İlk Yarısiyle Onaltıncı Yüzyılın Başlarında Memlûk Sultanları Yanına İltica Etmiş Olan Osmanlı Hanedanına Mensub Şehzadeler," *Belleten* 17, no. 68 (1953): 530–35.

37. For a critique of this argument, see Yelçe, "The Making of Sultan Süleyman," 58 and throughout.

38. For the House of Saruhan, see Feridun M. Emecen, "Saruhanoğulları," *TDVİA*, vol. 36, 170–73.

39. For an overview of the history, demography, and economy of the town, see Feridun M. Emecen, *XVI. Asırda Manisa Kazâsı* (Ankara: Türk Tarih Kurumu, 1989), 42–86; for the built environment, see 86–109; for a snapshot of the population, see 154–57; for food and animal products, see 239–71.

40. On the question of whether princes had autonomy and to what extent, I agree with Emecen's position, summarized in *XVI. Asırda Manisa Kazâsı*, 40–41.

41. The list is transliterated in Uzunçarşılı, "Sancağa Çıkarılan Osmanlı Şehzadeleri," 684–85. A reproduction of the original is provided in the same article, marked as Res. [Fig.] 17.

42. The register is TSMA, D. 8030.

43. TSMA, D. 8030, 1b.

44. TSMA, D. 8030, 1b.

45. TSMA, D. 8030, 2a–3a, 3b, 7b, 9b–10a, 11a, 11b.

46. TSMA, D. 8030, 2b–3b.

47. TSMA, D. 8030, 4a–6b, 7a, 8a, 8b–9a, 10b.

48. TSMA, D. 4056, 6a, 4a.

49. A similar explanation for this legal text is found in Emecen, *XVI. Asırda Manisa Kazâsı*, 31; Yelçe, "The Making of Sultan Süleyman," 87–88.

50. Only the criminal section of the instructions has survived. For a transliteration, see Enver Ziya Karal, "Yavuz Sultan Selim'in Oğlu Şehzade Süleyman'a Manisa Sancağını İdare Etmesi İçin Gönderdiği Siyasetnâme," *Belleten* 6, nos. 21–22 (January–April 1942): 41–44.

51. The following examples are from Emecen, *XVI. Asırda Manisa Kazâsı*, 186–87.

52. TSMA, E. 581/70.

53. The letter is TSMA, E. 745/26.

54. Şerafettin Turan, *Kanuni Süleyman Dönemi Taht Kavgaları*, second updated edition (Ankara: Bilgi Yayınevi, 1997), 22.

55. Feridun Ahmed, *Mecmua-yı münşeatü's-selatin* (hereafter *Münşeatü's-selatin*), vol. 1 (Istanbul: Daru't-Tıbaati'l-Âmire, 1858–59), 470.

56. Mustafa's approximate date of birth is determined based on Venetian diplomatic reports. According to one from 1526, he was nine years old at the time. See Pietro Bragadin, "Sommario della Relazione," in *Relazioni degli ambasciatori veneti al Senato*, serie III, vol. 3, ed. Eugenio Albèri (Florence: Società editrice fiorentina, 1855), 101; another, from 1534, says he was eighteen when the report was drafted. See Daniello de Ludovisi, "Relazione dell'impero ottomano," in *Relazioni degli ambasciatori veneti al Senato*, serie III, vol. 1, ed. Eugenio Albèri (Florence: Tipografia all'insegna di Clio, 1840), 28–9.

57. Uzunçarşılı, "Sancağa Çıkarılan Osmanlı Şehzadeleri," 669–70.

58. The letter is TSMA, E. 640/56.

59. TSMA, E. 745/22.

60. TSMA, E. 745/90.

61. These letters and Süleyman's replies to his father are in Feridun Ahmed, *Münşeatü's-selatin*, vol. 1, 367–68, and 409–10, respectively.

62. Feridun Ahmed, *Münşeatü's-selatin*, vol. 1, 427–30. For details of Süleyman's two stays in Edirne, see Yelçe, "The Making of Sultan Süleyman," 92–97.

63. Feridun Ahmed, *Münşeatü's-selatin*, vol. 1, 466–68.

64. Kasım was dismissed in early December 1516. See Emecen, *XVI. Asırda Manisa Kazâsı*, 32.

65. For these stories, see Emecen, *Yavuz Sultan* Selim, 375–400; Yelçe, "The Making of Sultan Süleyman," 98–102.

66. On the effectiveness of the Ottomans' gunpowder weapons and battle tactics over their Safavid and Mamluk rivals, see Gábor Ágoston, "War-Winning Weapons? On the Decisiveness of Ottoman Firearms from the Siege of Constantinople (1453) to the Battle of Mohács (1526)," *Journal of Turkish Studies* 39 (2013): 134–40.

67. The most detailed account of Selim's campaigns is in Emecen, *Yavuz Sultan Selim*, 92–340. A shorter treatment is found in Finkel, *Osman's Dream*, 103–12. An edited collection that focuses on multiple aspects of the Ottoman conquest of Egypt is Benjamin Lellouch and Nicholas Michel (eds.), *Conquête ottomane de l'Égypte (1517): Arrière-plan, impact, échos* (Leiden: Brill, 2013). For two different interpretations of Selim's conquests, one emphasizing their global impact, the other instead underlining their regional character, see Andrew C. Hess, "The Ottoman Conquest of Egypt (1517) and the Beginning of the Sixteenth-Century World War," *International Journal of Middle East Studies* 4, no. 1 (January 1973): 55–76; Jean Aubin, "La politique impériale de Selim Ier," *Res Orientales* 6 (1994): 197–216.

68. For the challenges of establishing an Ottoman administration in Mamluk territories, see Michael Winter, "The Ottoman Occupation," in *The Cambridge History of Egypt*, vol. 1, *Islamic Egypt, 640–1517*, ed. Carl Petry (Cambridge: Cambridge University Press, 1998), 504–16.

69. For a discussion of this stance on religion and politics, see Abdurrahman Atçıl, "The Safavid Threat and Juristic Authority in the Ottoman Empire in the Sixteenth Century," *International Journal of Middle East Studies* 49, no. 2 (2017): 295–304.

70. See Kenneth M. Setton, *The Papacy and the Levant (1204-1571)*, vol. 3, *The Sixteenth Century* (Philadelphia: The American Philosophical Society, 1984), 381–482.

71. For Selim's last two years on the throne, see Emecen, *Yavuz Sultan Selim*, 341–58.

72. Selim's final days are described in, among others, Kemalpaşazade Ahmed, *Tevarih-i Âl-i Osman. X. Defter*, ed. Şefaettin Severcan (Ankara: Türk Tarih Kurumu, 1996), 10–14; Sad b. Abdülmüteal, *Selimname*, 103b–106a; Celalzade Mustafa, *Geschichte Sultan Süleymān Kānūnīs von 1520 bis 1557, oder, Ṭabakāt ül-Memālik ve Derecāt ül-Mesālik/von Celālzāde Muṣṭafā genannt Ḳoca Niṣāncı*, ed. Petra Kappert (Wiesbaden: Steiner, 1981; hereafter *Tabakat*), 23b–24a; Emecen, *Yavuz Sultan* Selim, 355–58. References to the inauspicious location are in Kemalpaşazade Ahmed, *Tevarih-i Âl-i Osman. X. Defter*, 12 and Sad b. Abdülmüteal, *Selimname*, 104b. For rumors about a "curse" Bayezid placed on his son after he was dethroned, as a result of which Selim would not live into old age, see Sanuto, *I Diarii*, vol. 29, 359 (the word used is *"maledition"*).

73. Gilles Veinstein and Nicolas Vatin, *Le sérail ébranlé: essai sur les morts, dépositions et avènements des sultans ottomans (XIVe-XIXe siècle)* (Paris: Fayard, 2003), 81–109.

74. Both Kemalpaşazade Ahmed (*Tevarih-i Âl-i Osman. X. Defter*, 21) and Sad b. Abdülmüteal (*Selimname*, 108a) mention a four-day journey to underline the quick pace of Süleyman's travel.

CHAPTER 4

1. Ottoman efforts of resettlement and rebuilding are discussed in Kafescioğlu, *Constantinopolis/Istanbul*, 53–129. For a general survey of the city's history under the Ottomans, see Halil İnalcık, "Istanbul," *Encyclopaedia of Islam*, second edition, http://dx.doi.org/10.1163/1573-3912_islam_COM_0393. For more information on the city in the early modern period, see *A Companion to Early Modern Istanbul*.

2. Rhoads Murphey, "Provisioning Istanbul: The State and Subsistence in the Early Modern Middle East," in *Food and Foodways* 2 (1988): 217–63.

3. For the importance of the city in various formulations of Byzantine and Ottoman imperial identities, see M. Pınar Emiralioğlu, *Geographical Knowledge and Imperial Culture in the Early Modern Ottoman Empire* (Burlington, VT: Ashgate, 2014), 57–88.

4. The expression, *nadire-i dehir*, is in Kemalpaşazade Ahmed, *Tevarih-i Âl-i Osman. X. Defter*, 22. For the image of the city in literature, see Kafescioğlu, *Constantinopolis/Istanbul*, 170–77; İskender Pala, "Divan Edebiyatında İstanbul," *TDVİA*, vol. 23, 284–89.

5. Lâtifî, *Evsâf-ı İstanbul*, ed. Nermin Suner Pekin (Istanbul: Baha Matbaası, 1977). For everyday life in the city in the sixteenth century, also see Robert Mantran, *Istanbul au siècle de Soliman le Magnifique*, second updated edition (Paris: Hachette, 1994); Metin And, *Istanbul in the 16th Century: The City, the Palace, Daily Life* (Istanbul: Akbank, 1994).

6. See Kate Fleet and Ebru Boyar, *A Social History of Ottoman Istanbul* (Cambridge: Cambridge University Press, 2010), 72–121 for the impact of fires and the persistence of crimes and violence; and Nükhet Varlık, *Plague and Empire in the Early Modern Mediterranean World: The Ottoman Experience, 1347-1600* (New York: Cambridge University Press, 2015), 160–84 for the impact of the plague between 1517 and 1570.

7. A concise account of these is in Şahin, "Constantinople and the End Time," 322–28.

8. My account of Süleyman's accession, from his reception of the news to the funeral of his father, is based on Kemalpaşazade Ahmed, *Tevarih-i Âl-i Osman. X. Defter*, 19–25: Sad b. Abdülmüteal, *Selimname*, 108a–113b; Celalzade Mustafa, *Tabakat*, 24a–26a; Matrakçı Nasuh, *Târîh-i Âl-i Osmân (Osmanlı Tarihi 699-968/1299-1561)*, ed. Göker İnan (Istanbul: Türkiye Yazma Eserler Kurumu Başkanlığı, 2019), 332–34; Sanuto, *I Diarii*, vol. 29, 357–58, 368–69.

9. There are a few different versions of the order of events during Süleyman's first days as sultan. The version I follow here is from Celalzade Mustafa's *Tabakat*, a close collaborator of Pirî Mehmed at the time.

10. For the Ottoman practice of *biat*, see Veinstein and Vatin, *Le sérail ébranlé*, 269–86. For *bay'a* in early Islamic history, see Andrew Marsham, *Rituals of Islamic Monarchy: Accession and Succession* (Edinburgh: Edinburgh University Press, 2009).

11. Sanuto, *I Diarii*, vol. 29, 368.

12. For a discussion that brings together contemporary testimonies and anthropological perspectives on death, see Yelçe, "The Making of Sultan Süleyman," 129–44.

13. Celalzade Mustafa, *Tabakat*, 26a.

14. The definitive work for the New Palace, on which this short description is based, is Gülru Necipoğlu, *Architecture, Ceremonial and Power: The Topkapi Palace in the Fifteenth and Sixteenth Centuries* (New York: Architectural History Foundation; Cambridge, MA: MIT Press, 1991).

15. For a discussion of the tasks new sultans faced, see Veinstein and Vatin, *Le sérail ébranlé*, 320–51.

16. These numbers are based on Devlet Arşivleri Başkanlığı, Osmanlı Arşivi, Maliyeden Müdevver (hereafter MAD), D. 23, 29b–30a. The register gives a total of 24,603 individuals who received a stipend from the treasury in return for their services; 985 of those served in Egypt.

17. Ömer Lütfi Barkan, "H. 933-934 (M. 1527-1528) Malî Yılına Ait Bir Bütçe Örneği," *İstanbul Üniversitesi İktisat Fakültesi Mecmuası* 15, nos. 1–4 (1953), table I in 255. The total number Barkan provides is 37,741, divided between 28,088 *sipahi*s and 9,653 who held a *tımar* in return for serving at a fortress. These are valid for 1527–28, but they provide a useful estimate for 1520 as well.

18. I follow the estimate provided in Atçıl, *Scholars and Sultans in the Early Modern Ottoman Empire*, 53.

19. Here, I adopt the number suggested by Sanjay Subrahmanyam, on the basis of Ömer Lütfi Barkan, "Essai sur les données statistiques des registres de recensement dans l'empire ottoman au XVe et XVIe siècles," *Journal of the Economic and Social History of the Orient* 1, no. 1 (1957): 9–36. Subrahmanyam provides the number of seventeen million without the Arab provinces. See his *Empires between Islam and Christianity, 1500-1800* (Albany: State University of New York Press, 2019), 168.

20. Kemalpaşazade Ahmed, *Tevarih-i Âl-i Osman. X. Defter*, 16.

21. For the *Selimname* literature, see Çıpa, *The Making of Selim*, particularly 140–55.

22. Eg. Kemalpaşazade Ahmed, *Tevarih-i Âl-i Osman. X. Defter*, 25–30.

23. Celalzade Mustafa, *Tabakat*, 21a, 24a.

24. Lütfi Paşa, *Tevarih-i Âl-i Osman*, ed. Âlî (Istanbul: Matbaa-yı Âmire, 1925), 291. The translation is from Çıpa, *The Making of Selim*, 3–4.

25. European reactions are discussed in *The Papacy and the Levant*, vol. 3, 193, 198.

26. Paolo Giovio, *Commentario de le cose de' Turchi*, ed. Lara Michelacci (Bologna: CLUEB, 2005), 145.

27. Celalzade Mustafa, *Tabakat*, 26b–27a. Other contemporary sources also underline the sultan's generosity. See, for instance, Kemalpaşazade Ahmed, *Tevarih-i Âl-i Osman. X. Defter*, 31–32; Bostan Çelebi, *Tarih-i Sultan Süleyman*, Österreichische Nationalbibliothek, ms. Cod. H. O. 42a, 7v–8r. However, not everyone must have been satisfied. A letter to Venice from its resident envoy (*bailo*) in Constantinople Tomá Contarini (Sanuto, *I Diarii*, vol. 29, 359) states that the janissaries had wanted five thousand *akçe*s per person.

28. Venetian observers note a total expense of either 507,000 or 607,000 gold ducats (for differing amounts, due probably to a scribal error or transliteration mistake, see Sanuto, *I Diarii*, vol. 29, 359, 369). A Venetian gold ducat contained approximately 3.5 grams of nearly pure gold.

29. For the function of the accession gifts within the relationship between sultans and the elite, see Murphey, *Exploring Ottoman Sovereignty*, 120–23 and later.

30. Three of these letters, together with the replies received, are reproduced in Feridun Ahmed, *Münşeatü's-selatin*, vol. 1, 500–1 (to Mecca; the reply is in 501–2); 502–3 (to Crimea; the reply is in 503), 503–6 (to Egypt; the reply is in 506–7); the Venetian translation of the letter to Venice is in Sanuto, *I Diarii*, vol. 29, 395–96.

31. See Celalzade Mustafa, *Tabakat*, 27a-28b; Kemalpaşazade Ahmed, *Tevarih-i Âl-i Osman. X. Defter*, 36–44; Sad b. Abdülmüteal, *Selimname*, 118a–119a; Bostan Çelebi, *Tarih-i Sultan Süleyman*, 8v–10r, etc.

32. For instance, see Bostan Çelebi, *Tarih-i Sultan Süleyman*, 8r–8v. For a discussion on the notion of justice and its functions under Süleyman, see Halil İnalcık, "State, Sovereignty and Law under the Reign of Süleymân," in *Süleymân the Second and His Time*, 59–67.

33. Kemalpaşazade Ahmed, *Tevarih-i Âl-i Osman. X. Defter*, 37–8.

34. See Benjamin Lellouch, "Hain Ahmed Pasha (m. 1524) et sa famille," *Turcica* 52 (2021): 67–91.

35. Bostan Çelebi, *Tarih-i Sultan Süleyman*, 8r.

36. MAD, D. 23, 29a. The group included six *ağas*, seven physicians, six scribes, three food tasters, twenty pursuivants, nine musicians, four messengers, and sixty-one "notables" (*müteferrika*).

37. Bostan Çelebi, *Tarih-i Sultan Süleyman*, 10r–10v.

38. Sanuto, *I Diarii*, vol. 29, 390–91.

39. See Benjamin Lellouch, "La politique mamelouke de Selīm Ier," in *Conquête ottomane de l'Égypte*, 165–210.

40. For detailed treatments of the rebellion, see Celalzade Mustafa, *Tabakat*, 28b–40a; Kemalpaşazade Ahmed, *Tevarih-i Âl-i Osman. X. Defter*, 36–44; Bostan Çelebi, *Tarih-i Sultan Süleyman*, 10v-15r; Matrakçı Nasuh, *Matla-ı Dasitan-ı Sultan Süleyman Han*, TSMK, ms. Revan 1286, 13a–34b. For the attribution of the *Matla*'s anonymous manuscript to Matrakçı Nasuh, I rely on Davut Erkan, "Matrâkçı Nasûh'un Süleymân-nâmesi (1520-1537)" (MA thesis, Marmara University, 2005).

41. For developments on the Ottoman-Hungarian frontier in the previous decade, see Pálosfalvi, *From Nicopolis to Mohács*, 329–71; for the reasons behind the Hungarian decision not to renew the agreement, see 371–6. Also see Ferenc Szakály, "Nándorfehérvár, 1521: The Beginning of the End of the Medieval Hungarian Kingdom," in *Hungarian-Ottoman Military and Diplomatic Relations in the Age of Süleyman the Magnificent*, eds. Géza Dávid and Pál Fodor (Budapest: Loránd Eötvös University, 1994), 49–51.

42. M. Tayyib Gökbilgin, "Kanunî Sultan Süleyman'ın Macaristan ve Avrupa Siyasetinin Sebep ve Âmilleri, Geçirdiği Safhalar," in *Kanunî Armağanı*, 5–7; Pál Fodor, "Ottoman Policy Towards Hungary, 1520-1541," *Acta Orientalia Academiae Scientiarum Hungaricae* 45, nos. 2–3 (1991): 285–91. For the *ad hoc* aspects of Ottoman policy, see Rhoads Murphey, "Süleyman I and the Conquest of Hungary: Ottoman Manifest Destiny or a Delayed Reaction to Charles V's Universalist Vision," *Journal of Early Modern History* 5, no. 3 (2001): 197–221.

43. Necati Avcı, "Tabib Ramazan'ın Er-Risale El-Fethiyye Es-Süleymaniyyesi" (MA thesis, Ankara University, 1989), 15–20.

44. For a discussion that particularly emphasizes cultural factors, see Yelçe, "The Making of Sultan Süleyman," 195–293.

45. In addition to Ramazan's work, other accounts of the campaign that have been consulted are Celalzade Mustafa, *Tabakat*, 41a–65a; Kemalpaşazade Ahmed, *Tevarih-i Âl-i Osman. X. Defter*, 51–112; Matrakçı Nasuh, *Matla-ı Dasitan-ı Sultan Süleyman Han*, 36b-47a; Bostan Çelebi, *Tarih-i Sultan Süleyman*, 15r–40v. The campaign diary kept by Ottoman scribes during the campaign is in Feridun Ahmed, *Münşeatü's-selatin*, vol. 1, 507–15.

46. For a comprehensive coverage of Ottoman warfare, see Rhoads Murphey, *Ottoman Warfare, 1500-1700* (London: UCL Press, 1999). A concise summary of European warfare, followed by a useful bibliographical essay, is Peter H. Wilson, "Warfare in Europe," in *The Cambridge World History of Violence*, vol. 3, *1500-1800 CE*, eds.

Robert Antony, Stuart Carroll, Caroline Dodds Pennock (Cambridge: Cambridge University Press, 2020), 174–93. A detailed study of the financial aspects of Ottoman and early modern European warfare is Erol Özvar, "Transformation of the Ottoman Empire into a Military-Fiscal State: Reconsidering the Financing of War from a Global Perspective," in *The Battle for Central Europe: The Siege of Szigetvár and the Death of Süleyman the Magnificent and Nicholas Zrínyi (1566)*, ed. Pál Fodor (Leiden: Brill, 2019), 21–64.

47. I rely on Celalzade Mustafa's *Tabakat* for the tensions among the officials. Almost all other chroniclers describe the campaign as an orderly affair conducted under Süleyman's supervision. Mustafa was close to the major protagonists, and his observations, albeit with a pro-Pirî Mehmed bias, sound closer to what must have transpired.

48. For letters to judges as well as the Ottoman officials Şehsüvaroğlu Ali and Ferhad, together with Ali and Ferhad's replies, see Feridun Ahmed, *Münşeatü's-selatin*, vol. 1, 515–22.

49. The loss of Belgrade was indeed "the beginning of the end of the medieval Hungarian kingdom." The expression belongs to Ferenc Szakály. For an assessment of the campaign's strategic importance, see his "Nándorfehérvár, 1521," 47–72; and Pálosfalvi, *From Nicopolis to Mohács*, 395–96.

50. See Marco Minio, "Relazione di Marco Minio oratore alla Porta Ottomana," in *Relazioni degli ambasciatori veneti al Senato*, serie III, vol. 3, 74–77.

51. A succinct summary of the situation in Europe is Setton, *The Papacy and the Levant*, vol. 3, 193–97.

52. See Anthony Luttrell, "The Hospitallers at Rhodes, 1306–1421" and Ettore Rossi, "The Hospitallers at Rhodes, 1421–1523," in *A History of the Crusades*, vol. 3, *The Fourteenth and Fifteenth Centuries*, ed. Harry W. Hazard (Madison: The University of Wisconsin Press, 1975), 278–313 and 314–39; Nicolas Vatin, *Rhodes et l'ordre de Saint-Jean-de-Jérusalem* (Paris: Éditions CNRS, 2000).

53. For the Ottomans and the Order of St. John, see Palmira Brummett, "The Overrated Adversary: Rhodes and Ottoman Naval Power," *The Historical Journal* 36, no. 3 (1993): 517–41; Nicolas Vatin, *L'Ordre de Saint-Jean-de-Jérusalem, l'empire ottoman et la Méditerranée orientale entre les deux sièges de Rhodes (1480–1522)* (Paris: Peeters, 1994); Vatin, "The Hospitallers at Rhodes and the Ottoman Turks," in *Crusading in the Fifteenth Century: Message and Impact*, ed. Norman Housley (Houndmills, Basingstoke, Hampshire: Palgrave Macmillan, 2004), 148–62.

54. TSMA, E. 759/95.

55. Very detailed treatments of the campaign are found in Celalzade Mustafa, *Tabakat*, 65a–104a; Matrakçı Nasuh, *Matla-ı Dasitan-ı Sultan Süleyman Han*, 54a–88a; Kemalpaşazade Ahmed, *Tevarih-i Âl-i Osman. X. Defter*, 127–88; Bostan Çelebi, *Tarih-i Sultan Süleyman*, 49r–71v. The official campaign diary is in Feridun Ahmed, *Münşeatü's-selatin*, vol. 1, 529–40. Süleyman's physician Ramazan wrote an account of the Rhodes campaign as well: Necati Avcı, "Tabib Ramazan: Er-Risale

el-fethiyye er-radossiye es-Süleymaniyye" (PhD diss., Erciyes University, 1993). A detailed account of European perspectives is found in Setton, *The Papacy and the Levant*, vol. 3, 198–216.

56. Hasan Khalilieh, "Amān," *Encyclopedia of Islam, Three*, http://dx.doi.org.proxy iub.uits.iu.edu/10.1163/1573-3912_ei3_SIM_0048. The term also applied to the granting of safe conducts to non-Muslims for travel and commerce in lands under Muslim control without becoming subjects of a Muslim political power. See Khalilieh's bibliography for further readings.

57. For Ottoman attempts at image-making after Belgrade and Rhodes, and the domestic and foreign reception, see Yelçe, "The Making of Sultan Süleyman," 272–93.

58. What is probably a summary of the Ottoman original is in Sanuto, *I Diarii*, vol. 34, 47–48.

59. The letter is in Feridun Ahmed, *Münşeatü's-selatin*, vol. 1, 522–25.

60. For immediate reactions, see Setton, *The Papacy and the Levant*, vol. 3, 213–20.

61. For an attempt at tabulating and analyzing this new, Ottoman-focused literature, see Carl Göllner, *Turcica: Die Europäische Türkendrucke des XVI. Jahrhunderts*, 3 vols. (Bucharest: Editura Academiei R.P.R., 1961–78). Also see Nancy Bisaha, *Creating East and West: Renaissance Humanists and the Ottoman Turks* (Philadelphia: University of Pennsylvania Press, 2004); Gregory J. Miller, *The Turks and Islam in Reformation Germany* (New York and London: Routledge, 2014); Charlotte Colding Smith, *Images of Islam, 1453-1600: Turks in Germany and Central Europe* (London: Pickering & Chatto, 2014); Noel Malcolm, *Useful Enemies: Islam and the Ottoman Empire in Western Political Thought, 1450-1750* (Oxford: Oxford University Press, 2019). For the problem of early modern Orientalism, which will not be discussed here, see Kaya Şahin and Julia Schleck, "Courtly Connections: Anthony Sherley's *Relation of his Travels into Persia* (1613) in a Global Context," *Renaissance Quarterly* 69, no. 1 (2016): 80–115.

62. Ismail's letter is reproduced in Feridun Ahmed, *Münşeatü's-selatin*, vol. 1, 525–26, with Süleyman's reply in 526–27; the letter from Shirvan is in 527–28.

63. For a discussion of Hürrem's arrival in the harem, the environment she lived in, and the early stages of her relationship with Süleyman, see Leslie Peirce, *Empress of the East: How a European Slave Girl Became Queen of the Ottoman Empire* (New York: Basic Books, 2017), 27–46, 52–64, 69–73.

64. Kemalpaşazade Ahmed, *Tevarih-i Âl-i Osman. X. Defter*, 114–16, 118–20; Bostan Çelebi, *Tarih-i Sultan Süleyman*, 41r–v, 44v–45v.

65. Sanuto, *I Diarii*, vol. 32, 256.

66. See Matrakçı Nasuh, *Târîh-i Âl-i Osmân*, 340, for Mehmed's birth. The campaign diary (Feridun Ahmed, *Münşeatü's-selatin*, vol. 1, 534) gives Zilkade 9, 928 AH (September 30, 1522) as the date when news of the birth reached the army camp. Kemalpaşazade Ahmed, *Tevarih-i Âl-i Osman. X. Defter*, 171, claims that the newborn prince was named Selim. However, Selim's birth on May 30, 1524, is well documented. See, among others, Celalzade Mustafa, *Tabakat*, 117a.

67. Minio, "Relazione," 78.
68. Pietro Zen, "Sommario della Relazione," in *Relazioni degli ambasciatori veneti al Senato*, serie III, vol. 3, 96.
69. TSMA, D. 4056, 3a.
70. For the potential rivalry between Mahidevran and Hürrem, see Peirce, *Empress of the East*, 82–99.
71. M. Çağatay Uluçay, *Haremden Mektuplar I* (Istanbul: Vakit Matbaası, 1956), 79–80.
72. TSMA, E. 759/89.
73. TSMA, E. 969/61.
74. TSMA, E. 759/1.
75. Bostan Çelebi, *Tarih-i Sultan Süleyman*, 73v–74r.
76. For the battle, see András Kubinyi, "The Battle of Szávaszentdemeter-Nagyolazsi (1523): Ottoman Advance and Hungarian Defence on the Eve of Mohács," in *Ottomans, Hungarians, and Habsburgs in Central Europe: The Military Confines in the Era of Ottoman Conquest*, eds. Géza Dávid and Pál Fodor (Leiden: Brill, 2000), 71–115.
77. Most of the details in this story come from the Venetian ambassador Pietro Bragadin, who reported it a year and a half later: Pietro Bragadin, "Sommario della Relazione," 107–8. A contemporary Ottoman source alludes to Ferhad's mistakes and argues that some individuals, such as Ferhad, pay for their sins in this world rather than the next (Celalzade Mustafa, *Tabakat*, 130a–131a).
78. For the endowment and the complex, see İbrahim Hakkı Konyalı, "Kanunî Sultan Süleyman'ın Annesi Hafsa Sultan'ın Vakfiyesi ve Manisa'daki Hayır Eserleri," *Vakıflar Dergisi* 8 (1969): 47–56; Doğan Yavaş, "Hafsa Sultan Külliyesi," *TDVİA*, vol. 15, 123–24.
79. İ. Aydın Yüksel, "Sultan Selim Camii ve Külliyesi," *TDVİA*, vol. 37, 513–16.
80. Imber, *The Ottoman Empire, 1300-1650*, 130–33; Metin Kunt and Zeynep Yelçe, "Divân-ı Hümâyûn: le Conseil imperial ottoman et ses conseillers (1450-1580)," in *Conseils et conseillers dans l'Europe de la Renaissance (v. 1450-v.1550)*, ed. Cédric Michon (Tours: Presses universitaires de Rennes, Presses universitaires François Rabelais, 2012), 309–31.
81. Minio, "Relazione," 78–79.
82. For İbrahim's appointment and the initial reactions to the sultan's decision, see Ebru Turan, "The Sultan's Favorite: İbrahim Pasha and the Making of the Ottoman Universal Sovereignty in the Reign of Süleyman (1516-1526)" (PhD diss., University of Chicago, 2007), 99–105, 179–88; Turan, "Voices of Opposition in the Reign of Sultan Süleyman: The Case of İbrahim Pasha (1523–1536)," in *Studies on Istanbul and Beyond*, ed. Robert G. Ousterhout (Philadelphia: University of Pennsylvania Museum of Archaeology and Anthropology, 2007), 23–35.
83. For various appointments, see Bostan Çelebi, *Tarih-i Sultan Süleyman*, 74v–75r, 78r–79r, 82v–83r.
84. In my account of İbrahim's early life, his entry into Süleyman's service and the subsequent relationship, I primarily rely on Turan, "The Sultan's Favorite," 106–45,

with one important correction. Turan confuses the İskender in question with another Ottoman official of the same name who died in 1504 and who was not related to Selim and Süleyman. For the marriage between İskender and one of Selim's daughters, see Emecen, "Kanuni Sultan Süleyman'ın Şehzadelik Dönemi," 189–91.

85. For advancement in and out from the palace household, see Imber, *The Ottoman Empire 1300-1650*, 119–24; Kunt, *The Sultan's Servants*, 31–56.

86. A detailed study of Ahmed's revolt is Side Emre, "Anatomy of a Rebellion in Sixteenth-Century Egypt: A Case-Study of Ahmed Pasha's Governorship, Revolt, and a Critique of the Ottoman Imperial Enterprise in the Arab Lands," *Journal of Ottoman Studies* 46 (2015): 333–85. For Ahmed's use of the Great Conjunction for his bid to the sultanate, see Lellouch, "Hain Ahmed Pasha," 66–67, 91–96.

87. Lellouch, "Hain Ahmed Pasha," 67–73, 85–91.

88. There is a long debate on the identity of İbrahim's wife: see Turan, "The Sultan's Favorite," 220–33. I follow Emecen's suggestion that the bride was Süleyman's niece. See Emecen, "Kanuni Sultan Süleyman'ın Şehzadelik Dönemi," 190–91.

89. For the celebrations, see Zeynep Yelçe, "Evaluating Three Imperial Festivals: 1524, 1530 and 1539," in *Celebration, Entertainment and Theatre in the Ottoman World*, eds. Suraiya Faroqhi and Arzu Öztürkmen (London: Seagull Books, 2014), 71–109. The political background to the wedding is discussed in Ebru Turan, "The Marriage of İbrahim Pasha (ca. 1495-1536): The Rise of Sultan Süleyman's Favorite to the Grand Vizierate and the Politics of the Elites in the Early Sixteenth-Century Ottoman Empire," *Turcica* 41 (2009): 3–36.

90. Our main source for the inspection is Celalzade Mustafa, *Tabakat*, 121a–130a. Also see Bostan Çelebi, *Tarih-i Sultan Süleyman*, 91r–98v; Matrakçı Nasuh, *Matla-ı Dasitan-ı Sultan Süleyman Han*, 90a–98a; Turan, "The Sultan's Favorite," 223–33.

91. For the Mamluk-Ottoman transition in jurisprudence and the administration of justice, see Reem Meshal, "Antagonistic Sharī'as and the Construction of Orthodoxy in Sixteenth-Century Ottoman Cairo," *Journal of Islamic Studies* 21, no. 2 (2010): 183–212, to be read together with Abdurrahman Atçıl, "Memlükler'den Osmanlılar'a Geçişte Mısır'da Adlî Teşkilât ve Hukuk (922-931/1517-1525)," *İslâm Araştırmaları Dergisi* 38 (2017): 89–121. For the Portuguese dimension, see Casale, *Ottoman Age of Exploration*, 40–41.

92. For the riots, see Celalzade Mustafa, *Tabakat*, 129a–129b; Bostan Çelebi, *Tarih-i Sultan Süleyman*, 100r–101r; Turan, "The Sultan's Favorite," 233–39.

CHAPTER 5

1. The preamble is discussed in detail in Snjezana Buzov, "The Lawgiver and His Lawmakers: The Role of Legal Discourse in the Formation of Ottoman Imperial Culture" (PhD diss., University of Chicago, 2005), 29–45; an English translation of this seminal text is in Buzov, "The Lawgiver and His Lawmakers," 197–232.

2. For the last Abbasid caliph, after whose death a successor was not named, see Mustafa Banister, "The Abbasid Caliphate of Cairo (1261-1517): History and Tradition in the Mamluk Court" (PhD diss., University of Chicago, 2015), 222–34. For a discussion on the question of the transfer of the Abbasid caliphate to the Ottomans, see Faruk Sümer, "Yavuz Selim Halîfeliği Devraldı mı?," *Belleten* 56, no. 217 (December 1992): 675–701. Also see Emecen, "Klasik Dönem Osmanlı Hilafetine Yeni Bir Bakış."

3. See Christopher Markiewicz, *The Crisis of Kingship in Late Medieval Islam: Persian Emigres and the Making of Ottoman Sovereignty* (Cambridge: Cambridge University Press, 2019), 240–71. For Ottoman contributions to the debate about the definition of the caliphate, see Hüseyin Yılmaz, *Caliphate Redefined: The Mystical Turn in Ottoman Political Thought* (Princeton, NJ: Princeton University Press, 2018), throughout.

4. The sentence, which is often repeated in Süleyman's letters as well as many works from the period, is from chapter 38, verse 26: "O David! Truly We have appointed thee as a vicegerent [*khalifa*] upon the earth." God then instructs David to "judge among the people with truth and follow not caprice, lest it lead thee astray from the way of God," a justice-oriented commandment that must have resonated with Süleyman and his audiences. For the debate and the various points of view that must have been included in it, see Feridun M. Emecen, "Sultan Süleyman ve Hilâfet: 1524," in *Kanûnî Sultan Süleyman ve Dönemi: Yeni Kaynaklar, Yeni Yaklaşımlar / Suleyman the Lawgiver and His Reign: New Sources, New Approaches*, eds. M. Fatih Çalışır, Suraiya Faroqhi, M. Şakir Yılmaz (Istanbul: İbn Haldun Üniversitesi Yayınları, 2020), 45–57.

5. See Markiewicz, *Crisis of Kingship in Late Medieval Islam*, 166–71 (for the development of the concept) and 176–91 (for the circulation of ideas across the Islamic world); for Timur, see A. Azfar Moin, "The Lord of Conjunction: Sacrality and Sovereignty in the Age of Timur," chapter 2 in *The Millennial Sovereign: Sacred Kingship and Sainthood in Islam* (New York: Columbia University Press, 2012), 23–55.

6. For the use of the concept by the Ottomans, especially during the reign of Süleyman, see Fleischer, "A Mediterranean Apocalypse"; Barbara Flemming, "Sāhib-kırān und Mahdī: Türkische Endzeiterwartungen im ersten Jahrzehnt der Regierung Süleymāns," in *Between the Danube and the Caucasus*, ed. György Kara (Budapest: Akadémiai Kiadó, 1987), 43–62.

7. Markiewicz, *Crisis of Kingship in Late Medieval Islam*, 171–76.

8. Celalzade Mustafa, *Tabakat*, 134b, 135a, 136a.

9. Kemalpaşazade Ahmed, *Tevarih-i Âl-i Osman. X. Defter*, 191–96.

10. For the all-pervasiveness of apocalyptic sensibilities in Europe, see Ottavia Niccoli, *Prophecy and People in Renaissance Italy*, trans. Lydia G. Cochrane (Princeton, NJ: Princeton University Press, 1990). The best treatment of the circulation of these ideas at this particular time is Fleischer, "A Mediterranean Apocalypse."

11. Sanuto, *I Diarii*, vol. 41, 95.

12. For the variety of factors behind the campaign and the various positions adopted in the scholarship, see Yelçe, "The Making of Sultan Süleyman," 356–77; also see Turan, "The Sultan's Favorite," 240–322. For the weight of eschatological considerations, see Turan, "The Sultan's Favorite," 322–35.

13. For the post-1521 period viewed from the Hungarian side, see Pálosfalvi, *From Nicopolis to Mohács*, 395–423.

14. TSMA, E. 754/61.

15. Lütfi Paşa, *Tevarih-i Âl-i Osman*, 317–20.

16. Kemalpaşazade Ahmed, *Tevarih-i Âl-i Osman. X. Defter*, 201–9, 218–22.

17. For the impact of the Battle of Pavia on European politics and diplomacy, see Setton, *The Papacy and the Levant*, vol. 3, 229–46.

18. Süleyman's letter is preserved at the Bibliothèque nationale de France, ms. supplément turc 1638.

19. See Kemalpaşazade Ahmed, *Tevarih-i Âl-i Osman. X. Defter*, 218–22; Matrakçı Nasuh, *Matla-ı Dasitan-ı Sultan Süleyman Han*, 98a-99a; Celalzade Salih, *Tarih-i Feth-i Budun*, TSMK, ms. Revan 1280, 11b–14a.

20. For a discussion of the Ottoman policy toward Hungary within the context of the deepening Ottoman-Habsburg rivalry, see Murphey, "Süleyman I and the Conquest of Hungary," 197–202 and throughout.

21. The 1526 campaign is treated in detail in the following works, upon which the current summary is based: Celalzade Mustafa, *Tabakat*, 131a–157a; Kemalpaşazade Ahmed, *Tevarih-i Âl-i Osman. X. Defter*, 223–357; Matrakçı Nasuh, *Matla-ı Dasitan-ı Sultan Süleyman Han*, 99b–133b; Bostan Çelebi, *Tarih-i Sultan Süleyman*, 103r–132r. Next to these regnal histories, several works dedicated to the events of the campaign were composed in the following years. Among them, particularly noteworthy is Celalzade Salih, *Tarih-i Feth-i Budun*. The official account of the campaign's progression is in Feridun Ahmed, *Münşeatü's-selatin*, vol. 1, 554–66.

22. For a description of the battle from Ottoman and Hungarian perspectives, respectively, see Feridun M. Emecen, "'Büyük Türk'e Pannonia Düzlüklerini Açan Savaş Mohaç 1526," in *Muhteşem Süleyman*, ed. Özlem Kumrular (Istanbul: Kitap, 2007), 60–80; Pálosfalvi, *From Nicopolis to Mohács*, 424–44.

23. Celalzade Mustafa, *Tabakat*, 150b–152a; Celalzade Salih, *Tarih-i Feth-i Budun*, 60a–62a; Bostan Çelebi, *Tarih-i Sultan Süleyman*, 128v.

24. For Ottoman perceptions of the 1526 campaign, see Yelçe, "The Making of Sultan Süleyman," 424–36; for European perceptions, see 436–41.

25. For the League of Cognac, see Setton, *The Papacy and the Levant*, vol. 3, 241–43, which also offers a concise account of the coronations of Ferdinand and Szapolyai in 249–52; for more details, see Paula Sutter Fichtner, *Ferdinand I of Austria: The Politics of Dynasticism in the Age of the Reformation* (Boulder, CO: East European Monographs, 1982), 27–65. For Szapolyai's diplomatic openings, see Setton, *The Papacy and the Levant*, vol. 3, 251–53, 312–24.

26. For Ottoman diplomacy, see A. Nuri Yurdusev, "The Ottoman Attitude toward Diplomacy"; and Bülent Arı, "Early Ottoman Diplomacy: Ad Hoc Period," in *Ottoman Diplomacy: Conventional or Unconventional?*, ed. A. Nuri Yurdusev (Houndmills, Basingstoke, Hampshire: Palgrave Macmillan, 2004), 5–35 and 36–65.

27. The classical work on the subject is Garrett Mattingly, *Renaissance Diplomacy* (London: Jonathan Cape, 1955). For a recent discussion that is more inclusive geographically and culturally, see Tracey A. Sowerby and Jan Hennings (eds.), *Practices of Diplomacy in the Early Modern World c. 1410-1800* (London: Routledge, 2017).

28. Emrah Safa Gürkan, "Bir Diplomasi Merkezi Olarak Yeni Çağ İstanbul'u," in *Antik Çağ'dan 21. Yüzyıla Büyük İstanbul Tarihi*, vol. 2, *Siyaset ve Yönetim I*, eds. Feridun M. Emecen and Coşkun Yılmaz (Istanbul: İstanbul Büyükşehir Belediyesi Kültür AŞ.; Türkiye Diyanet Vakfı İslâm Araştırmaları Merkezi, 2015), 372–99. Also see Tracey A. Sowerby and Christopher Markiewicz (eds.), *Diplomatic Cultures at the Ottoman Court, c. 1500—1630* (New York: Routledge, 2021).

29. Sanuto, *I Diarii*, vol. 45, 290–91.

30. Marco Minio, "Sommario della Relazione," in *Relazioni degli ambasciatori veneti al Senato*, serie 3, vol. 3, 116; Necipoğlu, *Architecture, Ceremonial and Power*, 24–5.

31. For Łaski's negotiations in Constantinople, see Setton, *The Papacy and the Levant*, vol. 3, 252–53; for Hoberdanecs' report of their mission, see "Bericht Iohann Hoberdanacz's an König Ferdinand I. (Innsbruck, 19. Februar 1529.) [in Latin]," in *Urkunden und Actenstücke zur Geschichte der Verhältnisse zwischen Österreich, Ungern und der Pforte im XVI. und XVII. Jahrhunderte*, ed. Anton von [Antal] Gévay, vol. 1, bk. 2, *Gesandtschaft König Ferdinands I an Sultan Suleiman I.: 1528* (Vienna: Schaumburg und Comp., 1840), 1–28.

32. For accounts of the campaign, see Celalzade Mustafa, *Tabakat*, 182b–194a; Matrakçı Nasuh, *Matla-ı Dasitan-ı Sultan Süleyman Han*, 150b–169a; Bostan Çelebi, *Tarih-i Sultan Süleyman*, 149r–164r; Lütfi Paşa, *Tevarih-i Âl-i Osman*, 333–38. The campaign diary is in Feridun Ahmed, *Münşeatü's-selatin*, vol. 1, 566–77.

33. See Ferenc Szakály, *Lodovico Gritti in Hungary 1529–1534: A Historical Insight into the Beginnings of Turco-Habsburgian Rivalry*, trans. Dániel Székely (Budapest: Akadémiai Kiadó, 1995), 49–55. For more information, see Robert Finlay, "'I am the Servant of the Turkish Sultan:' Venice, the Ottoman Empire, and Christendom, 1523–1534," chap. 10 in *Venice Besieged: Politics and Diplomacy during the Italian Wars, 1494–1534* (Aldershot: Ashgate Variorum, 2008). The most detailed study on this polyglot merchant and powerbroker is Gizella Nemeth Papo and Adriano Papo, *Ludovico Gritti: Un principe-mercante del Rinascimento tra Venezia, i Turchi e la corona d'Ungheria* (Venice: Edizioni della Laguna, 2002).

34. For a snapshot, see Setton, *The Papacy and the Levant*, vol. 3, 325–26.

35. For an account of Szapolyai's restitution to power by the Ottomans, see Zeynep Yelçe, "Ottoman Reception and Perception of János Szapolyai in 1529," in *Türkenkriege und Adelskultur in Ostmitteleuropa vom 16. bis zum 18. Jahrhundert*, eds. Robert Born and Sabine Jagodzinski (Ostfildern: Jan Thorbecke Verlag, 2014), 141–54.

36. The letter is in Sanuto, *I Diarii*, vol. 52, 370–72.
37. For concise descriptions of the rivalry, see John Elliott, "Ottoman-Habsburg Rivalry: The European Perspective," in *Süleymân the Second and His Time*, 153–62; Gábor Ágoston, "Information, Ideology, and Limits of Imperial Policy," in *The Early Modern Ottomans: Remapping the Empire*, eds. Daniel Goffman and Virginia Aksan (Cambridge: Cambridge University Press, 2007); 75–78, 92–100. A study of the rivalry that pays particular attention to Spanish-language sources is Özlem Kumrular, *El Duelo entre Carlos V y Solimán el Magnífico (1520-1535)* (Istanbul: Editorial Isis, 2005). For a discussion of the respective imperial ideologies, see Turan, "The Sultan's Favorite," 254–355. For a discussion of universal monarchy in the period, see Anthony Pagden, "Monarchia Universalis," chapter 3 in *Lords of All the World: Ideologies of Empire in Spain, Britain and France c. 1500–c. 1800* (New Haven, CT: Yale University Press, 1995), 29–62. Ottoman expansion was indeed seen as a sign of the end times by proponents of Habsburg universal monarchy: see Franz Bosbach, "Imperium Turcorum oder Christianorum Monarchia – Die Osmanen in der heilsgeschichtlichen Deutung Mercurino Gattinaras," in *Das Osmanische Reich und die Habsburgermonarchie*, eds. Marlene Kurz et. al. (Vienna: R. Oldenbourg, 2005), 167–80.
38. For the earliest Habsburg attempts at envisioning a Habsburg-led universal monarchy with the Ottoman enemy in mind, see Alexandra Merle, "L'Empereur et le Tyran: La lutte contre le pouvoir ottoman selon Juan Ginés de Sepúlveda," in *Charles Quint et la monarchie universelle*, eds. Annie Molinié-Bertrand and Jean-Paul Duviols (Paris: Presses de l'Université Paris-Sorbonne, 2001), 183–92.
39. For European reactions to the 1529 campaign, see Yelçe, "The Making of Sultan Süleyman," 506–16; Setton, *The Papacy and the Levant*, vol. 3, 327–37. An account of the period from Charles' perspective is Parker, *Emperor*, 181–94. For the symbolic aspects of Charles' coronation, see Konrad Eisenbichler, "Charles V in Bologna: The Self-Fashioning of a Man and a City," *Renaissance Studies* 13, no. 4 (December 1999): 430–39.
40. For the impact of the Ottoman expansion on Lutheranism as a theological and political movement, see Kenneth M. Setton, "Lutheranism and the Turkish Peril," *Balkan Studies* 3 (1962): 133–68; Stephen A. Fischer-Galati, *Ottoman Imperialism and German Protestantism, 1521–1555* (Cambridge, MA: Harvard University Press, 1959), 13–56. For Luther's views of Islam, see Adam S. Francisco, *Martin Luther and Islam: A Study in Sixteenth-Century Polemics and Apologetics* (Leiden: Brill, 2007).
41. Colding Smith, *Images of Islam, 1453-1600*, 41–62.
42. For a somewhat unnuanced yet still useful discussion of Erasmus' views on the Ottomans, see Nathan Ron, *Erasmus and "the Other:" On Turks, Jews, and Indigenous Peoples* (Cham, Switzerland: Palgrave Pivot, 2019), 29–117. For a more nuanced approach to European views of the "Turk" around this time, see Carina L. Johnson, *Cultural Hierarchy in Sixteenth-Century Europe: The Ottomans and Mexicans* (Cambridge: Cambridge University Press, 2011), 60–69.

43. For more details, see Şahin, "Staging an Empire."

44. For the envoys' report, see "Bericht Josephs von Lamberg und Nicolaus Jurischitsch's an König Ferdinand I. 17. October – 22. December 1530 [in Latin]," in *Urkunden und Actenstücke*, vol. 1, bk. 4, *Gesandtschaft König Ferdinands I an Sultan Suleiman I.: 1530* (Vienna: Schaumburg und Comp., 1838), 74–89.

45. For Ottoman accounts of the campaign, see Celalzade Mustafa, *Tabakat*, 206a–237b; Matrakçı Nasuh, *Matla-ı Dasitan-ı Sultan Süleyman Han*, 170a-203a; Bostan Çelebi, *Tarih-i Sultan Süleyman*, 183r–194r; Celalzade Salih, *Tarih-i Sefer-i Zafer-Rehber-i Alaman*, SK, ms. Kadızade Mehmed 557, 35a–82a. The campaign diary is in Feridun Ahmed, *Münşeatü's-selatin*, vol. 1, 577–83. For Charles' perspective, see Parker, *Emperor*, 226–30; for a wider European perspective, see Setton, *The Papacy and the Levant*, vol. 3, 359–67.

46. For the elaborate diplomatic and political strategies of Francis I, see Ernest Charrière (ed.), *Négociations de la France dans le Levant . . .*, vol. 1, *1515–1547* (Paris: Imprimerie nationale, 1848), 176–214.

47. The envoys' report is in "Berichts Leonhard Grafen von Nogarola und Josephs von Lamberg an König Ferdinand I. [in German]," presented in Linz on 11–21 September 1532, in *Urkunden und Actenstücke*, vol. 1, bk. 5, *Gesandtschaft König Ferdinands I an Sultan Suleiman I.: 1531–1532* (Vienna: Schaumburg und Comp., 1838), 25–42; the letter is in 87–88.

48. Sanuto, *I Diarii*, vol. 47, 46.

49. Sanuto, *I Diarii*, vol. 43, 729. For Gattinara's affinity with eschatology, see Rebecca Ard Boone, *Mercurino di Gattinara and the Creation of the Spanish Empire* (London: Pickering and Chatto, 2014), 25–36. For Gattinara, also see John M. Headley, *The Emperor and His Chancellor: A Study of the Imperial Chancellery under Gattinara* (Cambridge: Cambridge University Press, 1983).

50. Parker, *Emperor*, 189.

51. For the campaign's ceremonial aspects, see Gülru Necipoğlu, "Süleymân the Magnificent and the Representation of Power in the Context of Ottoman-Habsburg-Papal Rivalry," *Art Bulletin* 71, no. 3 (1989): 401–427; Özlem Kumrular, "Campaña de Alemania: Rito, arte y demostración," in *L'Empire ottoman dans l'Europe de la Renaissance / El Imperio Otomano en la Europa renacentista*, eds. Alain Servantie and Ramón Puig de la Bellacasa (Leuven: Leuven University Press, 2005), 191–214.

52. For an analysis of the text, a facsimile, and a translation, see Ana Pulido-Rull, "A Pronouncement of Alliance: An Anonymous Illustrated Venetian Manuscript for Sultan Süleyman," *Muqarnas* 29 (2012): 102–50.

53. Concise accounts of the Diet of Regensburg are found in Parker, *Emperor*, 227–29; Setton, *The Papacy and the Levant*, vol. 3, 357–58; Fichtner, *Ferdinand I of Austria*, 96–98.

54. Details of the negotiations, absent in Ottoman sources, are found in the reports submitted by the envoys after their mission: "Bericht des Hieronymus von Zara

und des Cornelius Duplicius Schepper an König Ferdinand I. [in Latin]," in *Urkunden und Actenstücke*, vol. 2, bk. 1, *Gesandtschaft König Ferdinands I an Sultan Suleiman I.: 1533* (Vienna: Schaumburg und Comp., 1838), 2–48.

55. The letters are in *Urkunden und Actenstücke*, vol. 2, bk. 1, 135–40.

56. "Bericht des Hieronymus von Zara und des Cornelius Duplicius Schepper an König Ferdinand I," 9.

57. For the text of the journal, preceded by an analytical study, see Baron de Saint-Genois and G.-A. Yssel de Schepper (eds.), "Missions diplomatiques de Corneille Duplicius de Schepper (1533-34)," *Mémoires de l'Académie royale des sciences, des lettres et des beaux-arts de Belgique* 30 (1857): 1–222.

58. See "Missions diplomatiques de Corneille Duplicius de Schepper," 135–36.

59. For the atmosphere in Constantinople, see Robert Finlay, "Prophecy and Politics in Istanbul: Charles V, Sultan Süleyman, and the Habsburg Embassy of 1533–1534," *Journal of Early Modern History* 2, no. 1 (1998): 1–31.

60. See Barbara Flemming, "Public Opinion under Sultan Süleymân," in *Süleymân the Second and His Time*, 59–67.

61. Celalzade Mustafa, *Tabakat*, 157b–177a.

62. Kaya Şahin, *Empire and Power in the Reign of Süleyman: Narrating the Sixteenth-Century Ottoman World* (Cambridge: Cambridge University Press, 2013), 68–71. These developments attracted the attention of historians other than Celalzade Mustafa, although his is the most detailed treatment. Cf. Kemalpaşazade Ahmed, *Tevarih-i Âl-i Osman. X. Defter*, 342–47; Bostan Çelebi, *Tarih-i Sultan Süleyman*, 139r–147v.

63. Şahin, *Empire and Power in the Reign of Süleyman*, 72–74. For a translation of the section in *Tabakat* where the case is discussed, see Cornell H. Fleischer and Kaya Şahin, "The Trial of a Heretic, 1527," in *The Ottoman World: A Cultural History Reader, 1450-1700*, eds. Hakan T. Karateke and Helga Anetshofer (Oakland: University of California Press, 2021), 61–65.

64. For a discussion on the costs of war, see Murphey, *Ottoman Warfare*, 16–19; for the Ottoman financing of war, see Özvar, "Transformation of the Ottoman Empire into a Military-Fiscal State," 32–62.

65. Murphey, "Süleyman I and the Conquest of Hungary," 207.

66. For the role of justice as an instrument of justification and government in early Ottoman history, see Linda T. Darling, *A History of Social Justice and Political Power in the Middle Eas:. The Circle of Justice from Mesopotamia to Globalization* (New York: Routledge, 2013), 128–38; for the reign of Süleyman, see 138–44.

67. Özvar, "Transformation of the Ottoman Empire into a Military-Fiscal State," 37, table I in 38.

68. Barkan, "H. 933-934 (M. 1527-1528) Malî Yılına Ait Bir Bütçe Örneği," table 7 on 277.

69. For a transliteration of the decree, see Ahmed Akgündüz, *Osmanlı Kanunnâmeleri ve Hukukî Tahlilleri*, vol. 1, *Kanunî Sultân Süleyman Devri Kanunnâmeleri: I. Kısım. Merkezî ve Umumî Kanunnâmeler* (Istanbul: FEY Vakfı, 1992), 563–67; the original is SK, ms. Âtıf Efendi 1734, 1b–8b.

70. Necipoğlu, *Architecture, Ceremonial and Power*, 23.

71. Bragadin, "Sommario della relazione," 105.

72. For an overview of administrative developments under Süleyman, see Şahin, *Empire and Power in the Reign of Süleyman*, 215–20; Şahin, "From Frontier Principality to Early Modern Empire," 328–32.

73. For a survey, see Abdülkadir Özcan, "Historiography in the Reign of Süleyman the Magnificent," in *The Ottoman Empire in the Reign of Süleyman the Magnificent*, ed. Tülay Duran (Istanbul: Historical Research Foundation, Istanbul Research Center, 1988), vol. 2, 165–222. For more analytical approaches, see Cornell H. Fleischer, *Bureaucrat and Intellectual in the Ottoman Empire: The Historian Mustafa Âli (1541–1600)* (Princeton, NJ: Princeton University Press, 1986), 235–45; Şahin, *Empire and Power in the Reign of Süleyman*, 161–66.

74. See Rhoads Murphey, "Polemic, Panegyric, and Pragmatism in Ottoman Historical Writing during the Early Years of Sultan Suleyman's Reign, 1520-1540," in *Kanûnî Sultan Süleyman ve Dönemi: Yeni Kaynaklar, Yeni Yaklaşımlar / Suleyman the Lawgiver and His Reign: New Sources, New Approaches*, 267–97.

75. For the dating of the work, see Hüseyin Gazi Yurdaydın, "Bostan'ın Süleymannâmesi (Ferdî'ye Atfedilen Eser)," *Belleten* 19, no. 74 (1955): 155–59.

76. Sad b. Abdülmüteal, *Selimname*, 174b–176b.

77. Celalzade Salih, *Tarih-i Feth-i Budun*, 4a–5a.

78. For a study of the text, see Ahmet Çolak, "Bahârî, Fetihnâme-yi Üngürüs Adlı Eseri ve Bu Eserden Hareketle Macaristan Fethinin Edebi-Tarihi Üslupla Anlatılışı," *Turkish Studies: International Periodical for the Languages, Literature and History of Turkish or Turkic* 10, no. 4 (Winter 2015): 379–88.

79. Kemalpaşazade Ahmed, *Tevarih-i Âl-i Osman. X. Defter*, 8–9.

80. Matrakçı Nasuh, *Beyān-ı menāzil-i sefer-i 'Irakeyn-i Sulṭān Süleymān Ḫān*, ed. Hüseyin G. Yurdaydın (Ankara: Türk Tarih Kurumu, 1976), 5.

81. Hüseyin b. Hasan, *Letâ'ifü'l-Efkâr: Kâdı Hüseyin b. Hasan'ın Siyâsetnâmesi*, ed. Özgür Kavak (Istanbul: Türkiye Yazma Eserler Kurumu, 2018).

82. A detailed study of İbrahim's patronage is Esma Tezcan, "Pargalı İbrahim Paşa Çevresindeki Edebi Yaşam" (MA thesis, Bilkent University, 2005). For poetic patronage in general, see Halil İnalcık, *Şâir ve Patron: Patrimonyal Devlet ve Sanat Üzerinde Sosyolojik Bir İnceleme* (Ankara: Doğu Batı, 2003).

83. For these developments, see Sooyong Kim, *The Last of an Age: The Making and Unmaking of a Sixteenth-Century Ottoman Poet* (London: Routledge, 2018), 7–31, 45–49.

84. For the earliest known examples of Süleyman's poetry, see TSMK, D. 4056, 1b and 10b.

85. Bragadin, "Sommario della relazione," 101–2.

86. Bayezid was born in November 1526 (Celalzade Mustafa, *Tabakat*, 157a–157b) and Abdullah died around the same time (Kemalpaşazade Ahmed, *Tevarih-i Âl-i Osman. X. Defter*, 350–53).

312 Notes to pages 171–177

87. For the diagnosis, albeit on the basis of limited information, see Ali Ç. Turgut, Yaşar B. Turgut, Mehmet Turgut, "Neurological Disease of Şehzade Cihangir in the [sic] Ottoman History: Spinal Dysraphism," *Child's Nervous System* 32 (2016): 765–67.

88. For Hürrem's growing status as companion to Süleyman and mother to his children, see Peirce, *Empress of the East*, 69–79, 101–110.

89. The translation is by Talat S. Halman, from his *Süleyman the Magnificent Poet* (Istanbul: Dost Yayınları, 1987), 30–31. For a discussion on the textual repercussions of Süleyman and Hürrem's affection, see Christiane Czygan, "Depicting Imperial Love: Songs and Letters between Sultan Süleyman (Muhibbî) and Hürrem," in *Kanûnî Sultan Süleyman ve Dönemi: Yeni Kaynaklar, Yeni Yaklaşımlar / Suleyman the Lawgiver and His Reign: New Sources, New Approaches*, 254–61.

90. For a transliteration and translation of the letters, see Çağatay Uluçay, *Osmanlı Sultanlarına Aşk Mektupları* (Istanbul: Ufuk Kitapları, 2001), 36–50. They are discussed in Peirce, *Empress of the East*, 73–77. I have not been able to locate the original of the first letter. The second one is TSMA, E. 745/9.

91. Halman, *Süleyman the Magnificent Poet*, 78.

92. Bragadin, "Sommario della relazione," 102–3.

93. Bragadin, "Sommario della relazione," 103–4.

94. For such a hunting trip, see Celalzade Salih, *Tarih-i Feth-i Budun*, 78a–80a.

95. Bragadin, "Sommario della relazione," 103.

96. Celalzade Salih, *Tarih-i Feth-i Budun*, 4a–5a.

97. See Bragadin, "Sommario della relazione," 106, for a description of İbrahim's appearance in public.

98. Bragadin, "Sommario della relazione," 103; Minio, "Sommario della relazione," 116.

99. de Ludovisi, "Relazione," 10–12.

100. "Bericht des Hieronymus von Zara und des Cornelius Duplicius Schepper an König Ferdinand I," 28.

CHAPTER 6

1. For the Ottoman-Safavid relationship in the early years of Süleyman, see Jean-Louis Bacqué-Grammont, "The Eastern Policy of Süleymân the Magnificent, 1520-33" in *Süleymân the Second and His Time*, 249–58; Bacqué-Grammont, *Les Ottomans, les Safavides et leurs voisins: contribution à l'histoire des relations internationales dans l'Orient islamique de 1514 à 1524* (Istanbul: Nederlands Historisch-Archaeologisch Instituut te Istanbul, 1987), 275–368.

2. Celalzade Mustafa, *Tabakat*, 247b.

3. For the image of the Safavids in Ottoman histories as well as the cultural affinity between the two sides, see Hüseyin Ongan Arslan, "Varieties of Sectarian Consciousness among the Ottoman Elite: Sunni and Shiite Identities in Ottoman Historiography, 1450s-1580s" (PhD diss., Indiana University, 2020), 40–119.

4. For the impact of environmental conditions on the effectiveness of the Ottoman army, see Murphey, *Ottoman Warfare*, 20–24. For a specific focus on the Ottoman-Safavid frontier, see James Tracy, "Foreign Correspondence: European Accounts of Sultan Süleyman I's Persian Campaigns, 1548 and 1554," *Turkish Historical Review* 6 (2015): 194–219.

5. For a description of the frontier, see Walter Posch, *Osmanisch-safavidische Beziehungen (1545-1550): der Fall Alḳas Mîrzâ* (Vienna: Verlag der Österreichischen Akademie der Wissenschaften, 2013), vol. 1, 45–158. A study on the migration of scholars and artists into the Ottoman realm is Hanna Sohrweide, "Dichter und Gelehrte aus dem Osten im Osmanischen Reich (1453-1600): Ein Beitrag zur türkisch-persischen Kulturgeschichte," *Der Islam* 46 (1970): 263–302. On Kurds as necessary intermediaries and information-brokers, see Mostafa Dehqan and Vural Genç, "Kurds as Spies: Information-Gathering on the 16th-Century Ottoman-Safavid Frontier," *Acta Orientalia Academiae Scientiarum Hungaricae* 71, no. 2 (2018): 197–230.

6. For a description of these events from the perspective of the Safavid dynasty, see Eskandar Beg Monshi, *History of Shah ʿAbbas the Great* (Tārīḵ-e ʿālamārā-ye ʿAbbāsī), trans. Roger M. Savory (Boulder, CO: Westview Press, 1978), vol. 1, 75–109. For a concise treatment, see Roger Savory, *Iran under the Safavids* (Cambridge: Cambridge University Press, 1980), 50–57; for cultural developments, see Colin P. Mitchell, *The Practice of Politics in Safavid Iran: Power, Religion and Rhetoric* (London: I.B. Tauris, 2009), 58–79.

7. The letter is in Feridun Ahmed, *Münşeatü's-selatin*, vol. 1, 541–43.

8. *Muhibbî Dîvânı*, eds. Yavuz and Yavuz, vol. 2, 1208–9 (no. 2358).

9. Ismail's initial followers were called "Red Heads" (*Kızılbaş*) in reference to a distinct red headgear they wore. The Ottomans used *Kızılbaş* as a derogatory term to define anyone who had political and religious affinities with the Safavids. See Ayşe Baltacıoğlu-Brammer, "One Word, Many Implications: The Term 'Kızılbaş' in the Early Modern Ottoman Context," in *Ottoman Sunnism: New Perspectives*, ed. Vefa Erginbaş (Edinburgh: Edinburgh University Press, 2019), 47–70. In the poem in question, Süleyman uses the Persian translation (*surh-ser*) of the Turkish word *kızılbaş*.

10. Beşiktaşlı Yaḥyā Efendi, *Dīvān*, 214.

11. For a discussion of the campaign's potential reasons, from the local to the international, see Rhoads Murphey, "Süleyman's Eastern Policy," in *Süleymân the Second and His Time*, 235–46.

12. For the Safavid experience with gunpowder technology, see Rudi Matthee, "Unwalled Cities and Restless Nomads: Firearms and Artillery in Safavid Iran," in *Safavid Persia: The History and Politics of an Islamic Society*, ed. Charles Melville (London: I.B. Tauris, 1996), 389–416.

13. For Ottoman views on Ulama's activities before the campaign, see Lütfi Paşa, *Tevarih-i Âl-i Osman*, 341–44; Bostan Çelebi, *Tarih-i Sultan Süleyman*, 198r–199v,

200v–202r. For the Safavid side's views on Ulama, see Shah Tahmasb, *Tazkira-i Shah Tahmasb* (Berlin: Kaviani, 1964), 18–22; Eskandar Beg Monshi, *History of Shah 'Abbas the Great*, vol. 1, 109–10.

14. The summary of the events here is based on Celalzade Mustafa, *Tabakat*, 242a–277a; Lütfi Paşa, *Tevarih-i Âl-i Osman*, 344–55; Bostan Çelebi, *Tarih-i Sultan Süleyman*, 205v–242r; Shah Tahmasb, *Tazkira*, 25–42; Hasan Beg Rumlu, *Ahsan al-tavarikh*, ed. Abdulhusayn Navai (Tehran: Asatir, 2005–6), vol. 3, 1215–21, 1226–29; Eskandar Beg Monshi, *History of Shah 'Abbas the Great*, vol. 1, 110–115. For an illustrated history commissioned by Süleyman after the campaign, see Matrakçı Nasuh, *Beyan-ı menazil*. The campaign diary, which only covers Süleyman's movements, is in Feridun Bey, *Münşeatü's-selatin*, vol. 1, 584–98.

15. Some Ottoman sources, most notably Celalzade Mustafa, offer a highly dramatic account of the campaign and hint that a rift between sultan and grand vizier opened up from its early stages onward. The documentary evidence, however, shows that the partners continued to act in unison. See M. Tayyib Gökbilgin, "Arz ve Raporlarına Göre İbrahim Paşa'nın Irakeyn Seferindeki İlk Tedbirleri ve Fütuhatı," *Belleten* 21, no. 83 (1957): 449–82.

16. *Muhibbî Dîvânı*, eds. Yavuz and Yavuz, vol. 2, 1112 (no. 2147). It is possible to date this couplet to 1534 since, at the beginning of the poem, Süleyman states that it is the time of the Eid al-Adha, the "Feast of Sacrifice." In 1534, the Feast started on Zilhicce 10, 940 AH/June 22, 1534 CE, around the time of his departure from Constantinople.

17. Cornell H. Fleischer, "Shadows of Shadows: Prophecy and Politics in 1530s Istanbul," *International Journal of Turkish Studies* 13, nos. 1–2 (2007): 57. This information comes from the historian Mustafa Âli, who wrote his work a few decades after Süleyman's death on the basis of earlier testimonies.

18. For discussions on the Friday prayer in early Safavid Iran, see Rula Jurdi Abisaab, *Converting Persia. Religion and Power in the Safavid Empire* (London: I.B. Tauris, 2004), 20–22; Dewin J. Stewart, "Polemics and Patronage in Safavid Iran: The Debate on Friday Prayer during the Reign of Shah Tahmasb," *Bulletin of the School of Oriental and African Studies* 72, no. 3 (2009): 427–29.

19. For a list of the tombs belonging to these prominent figures, see Matrakçı Nasuh, *Beyan-ı menazil*, 242–49.

20. Celalzade Mustafa, *Tabakat*, 256b–257a.

21. See Derin Terzioğlu, "How to Conceptualize Ottoman Sunnitization: A Historiographical Discussion," *Turcica* 44 (2012–13): 301–38; for the anti-Safavid stance of the Ottoman elite in the sixteenth century, see Şahin, *Empire and Power in the Reign of Süleyman*, 205–13.

22. See, for instance, a chronogram on the capture of Baghdad by the poet Kandî in Celalzade Mustafa, *Tabakat*, 262a.

23. Cornelius de Schepper, "Bericht Cornelius Duplicius Schepper's an König Ferdinand I. (Prag, 2. August 1534.) [in Latin]," in *Urkunden und Actenstücke,*

vol. 2, bk. 2, *Gesandtschaft König Ferdinands I an Sultan Suleiman I.: 1534* (Vienna: Schaumburg und Comp., 1839), 45–46.

24. Guillaume Postel, *De la Republique des Turcs* (Poitiers: Imprimerie d'Enguilbert de Marnes, 1560), bk. 3, 53.

25. Postel, *De la Republique des Turcs*, bk. 3, 54–61.

26. Anonymous, *Tarih-i Âl-i Osman*, Bibliothèque nationale de France, ms. Turc 98, 86b.

27. Anonymous, *Tarih-i Âl-i Osman*, 89a–89b.

28. The English translation is from E. J. W. Gibb, *A History of Ottoman Poetry*, ed. Edward G. Browne (London: Luzac & Co., 1904), vol. 3, 35.

29. İ. Güven Kaya, "Figânî'nin Ölümü ve Taşlıcalı Yahya Bey'in Bir Şiiri," *Atatürk Üniversitesi Türkiyat Araştırmaları Enstitüsü Dergisi* 34 (2007): 47–62.

30. The letter is TSMA, E. 750/35, 1. A transliteration and Turkish translation is in Uluçay, *Osmanlı Sultanlarına Aşk Mektupları*, 106–12.

31. For Hürrem's potential impact on the grand vizier's downfall, se Peirce, *Empress of the East*, 150–54.

32. Bostan Çelebi, *Tarih-i Sultan Süleyman*, 243v–244r.

33. Celalzade Mustafa, *Tabakat*, 277a–278b.

34. For instance, while admitting the grand vizier's fondness for wealth and grandeur, Latifi left behind the portrait of a dedicated patron of poetry. See *Lâtîfî'nin İki Risâlesi: Enîsü'l-Fusahâ ve Evsâf-ı İbrâhim Pâşâ*, ed. Ahmet Sevgi (Konya: Selçuk Üniversitesi Yayınları, 1986).

35. See Peirce, *Empress of the East*, 160–65 for another overview.

36. M. Kemal Özergin, *Sultan Kanunî Süleyman Han Çağına Âit Tarih Kayıtları* (Erzurum: n.p., 1971), 13.

37. This information, including the translations between quotation marks from Arabic and Persian, are in Cornell H. Fleischer, "Seer to the Sultan: Haydar-i Remmal and Sultan Süleyman," in *Cultural Horizons*, vol. 1, *A Festschrift in Honor of Talat S. Halman*, ed. Jayne L. Warner (Syracuse, NY: Syracuse University Press, 2001), 298.

38. Schepper's full report to Ferdinand upon the completion of his mission is in *Urkunden und Actenstücke*, vol. 2, bk. 2, 27–65. For a short summary of the negotiations, see Setton, *The Papacy and the Levant*, vol. 3, 385–87.

39. For this new phase of Ottoman presence in the Mediterranean, see Kate Fleet, "Ottoman Expansion in the Mediterranean," in *The Cambridge History of Turkey*, vol. 2, 155–66.

40. For a study of the region, see Andrew C. Hess, *The Forgotten Frontier: A History of the Sixteenth-Century Ibero-African Frontier* (Chicago: University of Chicago Press, 1978). The relationship between Constantinople and the western Mediterranean and the role of privateers in Ottoman naval policy are described in Emrah Safa Gürkan, "The Centre and the Frontier: Ottoman Cooperation with the North African Corsairs in the Sixteenth Century," *Turkish Historical Review* 1 (2010): 125–63.

41. For Barbarossa's image in Europe, see Gülru Necipoğlu, "The Aesthetics of Empire: Arts, Politics and Commerce in the Construction of Sultan Süleyman's Magnificence," in *The Battle for Central Europe*, 140–49.

42. Barbarossa's accommodation with the Ottomans is predictably presented as a submission to Süleyman in Celalzade Mustafa, *Tabakat*, 245a–246a. For a source sympathetic to Barbarossa, see Mustafa Yıldız "Ġazavāt-ı Ḫayreddīn Paşa (MS 2639 Universitäts Bibliothek Istanbul). Kommentierte Edition mit Deutsche Zusammenfassung" (PhD diss., University of Göttingen, 1991), 201–3. A discussion of this unabashedly pro-Barbarossa source is in Rhoads Murphey, "Seyyid Muradî's Prose Biography on Hızır Ibn Yakub, Alias Hayreddin Barbarossa: Ottoman Folk Narrative as an Under-Exploited Source for Historical Reconstruction," *Acta Orientalia Academiae Scientiarum Hungaricae* 54, no. 4 (2001): 519–32. A detailed treatment of Barbarossa's reception in Constantinople is Nicolas Vatin, "Comment Ḫayr ed-Dîn Barberousse fut reçu à Istanbul en 1533," *Turcica* 49 (2018): 119–51.

43. Yıldız, "Ġazavāt-ı Ḫayreddīn Paşa," 203–19.

44. For the Tunis campaign and its aftermath, see Setton, *The Papacy and the Levant*, vol. 3, 395–400; Parker, *Emperor*, 237–47.

45. For the tapestries, see Hendrick J. Horn, *Jan Cornelisz Vermeyen, Painter of Charles V and His Conquest of Tunis: Paintings, Etchings, Drawings, Cartoons & Tapestries*, 2 vols. (Doornspijk: Davaco, 1989).

46. For the Franco-Ottoman relationship from 1525 to this point, see De Lamar Jensen, "The Ottoman Turks in Sixteenth Century French Diplomacy," *Sixteenth Century Journal* 16, no. 4 (Winter 1985): 451–56; Christine Isom-Verhaaren, *Allies with the Infidel: The Ottoman and French Alliance in the Sixteenth Century* (London: I.B. Tauris, 2011), 34–43.

47. For a study of the major French works on the Ottomans produced in this period, see Frédéric Tinguely, *L'écriture du Levant à la Renaissance: Enquête sur les voyageurs français dans l'empire de Soliman le Magnifique* (Geneva: Droz, 2000). A shorter exploration is in Philip Mansel, "The French Renaissance in Search of the Ottoman Empire," in *Re-Orienting the Renaissance: Cultural Exchanges with the East*, ed. Gerard MacLean (Houndmills, Basingstoke, Hampshire: Palgrave Macmillan, 2005), 96–107; and Isom-Verhaaren, *Allies with the Infidel*, 165–79.

48. For Postel on the Ottomans, see Frank Lestringant, "Guillaume Postel et l'obsession turque," reprinted in *Écrire le monde à la Renaissance: Quinze études sur Rabelais, Postel, Bodin et la littérature géographique* (Caen: Paradigme, 1993), 189–224.

49. *Négociations de la France dans le Levant*, vol. 1, 262.

50. The account of the campaign here is based on Celalzade Mustafa, *Tabakat*, 284b–290b; Matrakçı Nasuh, *Matla-ı Dasitan-ı Sultan Süleyman Han*, 287a–302b; Lütfi Paşa, *Tevarih-i Âl-i Osman*, 358–64; Bostan Çelebi, *Tarih-i Sultan Süleyman*, 257r–269r. The campaign diary is in Feridun Ahmed, *Münşeatü's-selatin*, vol. 1, 598–602.

51. See Pierre Grillon, "La croisière du Baron de Saint-Blancard (1537-1538)," *Revue d'histoire moderne et contemporaine* 15 (1968): 624–62. For naval cooperation

between the Ottomans and the French, see Isom Verhaaren, *Allies with the Infidel*, 116–19.

52. For the repercussions and aftermath of the 1537 campaign in Europe, see Setton, *The Papacy and the Levant*, vol. 3, 422–27, 430–34, 445.

53. For European perceptions of the 1538 campaign, see Setton, *The Papacy and the Levant*, vol. 3, 442–44.

54. For the relationship between the Ottomans and the rulers of Moldavia, see Viorel Panaite, "The Legal and Political Status of Wallachia and Moldavia in Relation to the Ottoman Porte," in *The European Tributary States of the Ottoman Empire in the Sixteenth and Seventeenth Centuries*, 9–42.

55. See Carl M. Kortepeter, "Ottoman Imperial Policy and the Economy of the Black Sea Region in the Sixteenth Century," *Journal of the American Oriental Society* 86, no. 2 (1966): 86–113.

56. Major Ottoman accounts of the campaign are Celalzade Mustafa, *Tabakat*, 301a–326a; Bostan Çelebi, *Tarih-i Sultan Süleyman*, 280r–292r, 294r–302v; Matrakçı Nasuh, *Fethname-yi Karaboğdan*, TSMK, Revan 1284, 105b–122a; Yıldız, "Ġazavāt-ı Ḥayreddīn Paşa," 223–28.

57. For the impact of the 1538 campaign, see Setton, *The Papacy and the Levant*, vol. 3, 444–48.

58. Ottoman descriptions of the festivities are in Celalzade Mustafa, *Tabakat*, 337a–340b; Bostan Çelebi, *Tarih-i Sultan Süleyman*, 316v–331r. A scholarly discussion is Yelçe, "Evaluating Three Imperial Festivals," 71–109.

59. For Rüstem's choice as Süleyman's son-in-law and the marriage, see M. Zahit Atçıl, "State and Government in the Mid-Sixteenth Century Ottoman Empire: The Grand Vizierates of Rüstem Pasha (1544-1561)" (PhD diss., University of Chicago, 2015), 36–43.

60. For the text of the peace treaty (*ahdname*) of 1540, see Hans Theunissen, "Ottoman-Venetian Diplomatics: The 'Ahd-names. The Historical Background and the Development of a Category of Political-Commercial Instruments together with an Annotated Edition of a Corpus of Relevant Documents," *Electronic Journal of Oriental Studies* 1, no. 2 (1998): 437–69. A quick analysis is in Setton, *The Papacy and the Levant*, vol. 3, 448–49.

61. Fichtner, *Ferdinand I of Austria*, 118–23; Setton, *The Papacy and the Levant*, vol. 3, 434–37. The French watched the developments closely, as seen in *Négociations de la France dans le Levant*, vol. 1, 436–74.

62. Fichtner, *Ferdinand I of Austria*, 124–25.

63. Lütfi Paşa, *Tevarih-i Âl-i Osman*, 384–85.

64. *Urkunden und Actenstücke*, vol. 3, bk. 3, *Gesandtschaft König Ferdinands I an Sultan Suleiman I.: 1540–41* (Vienna: Schaumburg und Comp., 1842), 3–65.

65. Bostan Çelebi, *Tarih-i Sultan Süleyman*, 336r.

66. The details of the campaign are found in Celalzade Mustafa, *Tabakat*, 341a–346a; Bostan Çelebi, *Tarih-i Sultan Süleyman*, 338v–356r; Lütfi Paşa, *Tevarih-i Âl-i Osman*, 385–90; Matrakçı Nasuh, *Târîh-i Âl-i Osmân*, 386–90.

67. Two different approaches to the Ottoman takeover of Szapolyai's kingdom in 1541, both of which should be taken into account for a complete picture, are found in Fodor, "Ottoman Policy towards Hungary," 305–33; Murphey, "Süleyman I and the Conquest of Hungary," 218–19.

68. Setton, *The Papacy and the Levant*, vol. 3, 459–66; Fichtner, *Ferdinand I of Austria*, 126–31.

69. An English translation of the letter is in Hani Khafipour (ed.), *The Empires of Near East and India: Source Studies of the Ottoman, Mughal, and Safavid Literate Communities* (New York: Columbia University Press, 2019), 283–86 (trans. Zahit Atçıl).

70. Fichtner, *Ferdinand I of Austria*, 131–32.

71. Ottoman accounts of the events are found in Celalzade Mustafa, *Tabakat*, 346a–374a; Sinan Çavuş [Matrakçı Nasuh], *Tarih-i Feth-i Şikloş, Estergon ve İstol(n)i-Belgrad, or Süleyman-Name*, ed. Tülay Duran (Istanbul: Historical Research Foundation, Istanbul Research Center, 1987), with an English summary in 18–35; Lütfi Paşa, *Tevarih-i Âl-i Osman*, 412–19; Matrakçı Nasuh, *Târîh-i Âl-i Osmân*, 391–408. For the French-Ottoman alliance, see Isom-Verhaeren, *Allies with the Infidel*, 121–40.

72. *Négociations de la France dans le Levant*, vol. 1, 555–77.

73. Fichtner, *Ferdinand I of Austria*, 133.

74. Parker, *Emperor*, 273–307.

75. For the negotiations leading up to the treaty of 1547, see Setton, *The Papacy and the Levant*, vol. 3, 480–86. The French position during the negotiations is in *Négociations de la France dans le Levant*, vol. 1, 580–620; the Ottoman text of the treaty is in Anton C. Schaendlinger and Claudia Römer (eds.), *Die Schreiben Süleymāns des Prächtigen an Karl V., Ferdinand I. und Maximilian II* (Vienna: Verlag der Österreichischen Akademie der Wissenschaften, 1983), vol. 1, 14–16 (transcription), 17–18 (German translation).

76. For the impact of the Ottoman-Habsburg negotiations on the Council of Trent, see Setton, *The Papacy and the Levant*, vol. 3, 486–504.

77. Karl Nehring (ed.), *Austro-Turcica 1541–1552. Diplomatische Akten des habsburgischen Gesandtschaftsverkehrs mit der Hohen Pforte im Zeitalter Süleymans des Prächtigen* (Munich: R. Oldenbourg, 1995), 87–96. For Veltwyck's role in the negotiations, see Bart Severi, "'Denari in Loco delle Terre . . . ' Imperial Envoy Gerard Veltwyjck and Habsburg Policy towards the Ottoman Empire, 1545–1547," *Acta Orientalia Academiae Scientiarum Hungaricae* 54, nos. 2–3 (2001): 211–56.

78. Parker, *Emperor*, 288–93.

79. For the bureaucratic and cultural transformations, see Mitchell, *The Practice of Politics*, 68–78, 88–103; Abisaab, *Converting Persia*, 7–53. For the political developments to 1547, see Hasan Beg Rumlu, *Ahsan al-tavarikh*, vol. 3, 1230–98.

80. Hasan Beg Rumlu, *Ahsan al-tavarikh*, vol. 3, 1230–33.

81. For the Safavid position on Alqas' defection, which was interpreted as a betrayal, see Eskandar Beg Monshi, *History of Shah 'Abbas the Great*, vol. 1, 115–17; Shah

Tahmasb, *Tazkira*, 42–47. For Alqas' biography, see Cornell H. Fleischer, "ALQĀS MĪRZA," *Encyclopædia Iranica*, I/9, pp. 907–909, available online at https://www.iranicaonline.org/articles/alqas-alqasb-alqas-mirza-safawi. A short treatment of Alqas' defection and the subsequent campaign is in Şahin, *Empire and Power in the Reign of Süleyman*, 116–21. The definitive study of the Alqas affair is Posch, *Osmanisch-safavidische Beziehungen (1545-1550)*, 2 vols.

82. The contents of the letter are discussed in Mitchell, "The Pen and the Sword," 314–19.

83. For a discussion on the meaning of these gifts, see Christopher Markiewicz and Tracey A. Sowerby, "Languages of Diplomatic Gift-Giving at the Ottoman Court," in *Diplomatic Cultures at the Ottoman Court, c.1500-1630*, 57–58.

84. Peirce, *Empress of the East*, 255.

85. Ömer Lütfi Barkan, "954-955 (1547-1548) Mali Yılına Ait Bir Osmanlı Bütçesi," *İstanbul Üniversitesi İktisat Fakültesi Mecmuası* 19, nos. 1–4 (1957): 262–63.

86. For Alqas' speech in front of Süleyman and the imperial council, see Celalzade Mustafa, *Tabakat*, 383a-383b. Details of Alqas' reception in Constantinople are in Matrakçı Nasuh, *Târîh-i Âl-i Osmân*, 424–27.

87. Barkan, "954-955 (1547-1548) Mali Yılına Ait Bir Osmanlı Bütçesi," 264.

88. Boyar and Fleet, *A Social History of Istanbul*, 43.

89. For the translations of the *fetvas*, see Abdurrahman Atçıl, "Ottoman Religious Rulings Concerning the Safavids: Ebussuud Efendi's Fatwas," in *The Empires of Near East and India*, 101–3. A discussion of Ebussuud and his legal opinions against the Safavids is in Atçıl, "The Safavid Threat and Juristic Authority," 306–9.

90. The Ottoman version of the campaign is narrated in great detail in Celalzade Mustafa, *Tabakat*, 385a–411a. For the Safavid perspective, see Eskandar Beg Monshi, *History of Shah 'Abbas the Great*, vol. 1, 117–24; Hasan Beg Rumlu, *Ahsan al-tavarikh*, vol. 3, 1315–25, 1330–31. Also see James Tracy, "Foreign Correspondence," 203-7 and throughout.

91. For more details about Süleyman's stay in Aleppo, see Leslie Peirce, "Süleyman in Aleppo," in *Turkish Language, Literature, and History: Travelers' Tales, Sultans, and Scholars since the Eighth Century*, eds. Bill Hickman and Gary Leiser (Milton Park, Abingdon, Oxon: Routledge, 2016), 311–16.

92. Hasan Beg Rumlu, *Ahsan al-tavarikh*, vol. 3, 1331.

93. Alvise Renier, "Relazione," in *Relazioni di ambasciatori veneti al Senato*, vol. 14, 71–72.

94. The tone of regret is particularly strident in Celalzade Mustafa, *Tabakat*, 379b–385a. Alqas' supposed reversion to Shiism is in *Tabakat*, 399b.

95. Vladimir Minorsky, "Shaykh Bālī-efendi on the Safavids," *Bulletin of the School of Oriental and African Studies* 20, nos. 1–3 (1957): 441–48.

96. Celalzade Mustafa, *Tabakat*, 406a–407a.

97. *Négociations de la France dans le Levant*, vol. 2, 103.

98. See W. S. Copeman, "Historical Aspects of Gout," *Clinical Orthopaedics and Related Research* 71 (July-August 1970): 14–22. For the specifics of Süleyman's illness and treatment, see Vural Genç, "Kanuni Sultan Süleyman'ın Nikris Hastalığına Atfedilen Farsça Bir Reçete," *Belleten* 80, no. 287 (April 2016): 41–58.

99. Matrakçı Nasuh, *Târîh-i Âl-i Osmân*, 384.

100. Bernardo Navagero, "Relazione," in *Relazioni degli ambasciatori veneti al Senato*, serie III, vol. 1, 72–73.

101. Genç, "Kanuni Sultan Süleyman'ın Nikris Hastalığına Atfedilen Farsça Bir Reçete," 47–54.

102. For more details, see Setton, *The Papacy and the Levant*, vol. 4, 656–86; Fodor, *Unbearable Weight of Empire*, 103–21.

103. For a map that shows the extent of imperial engagements, see Fodor, *Unbearable Weight of Empire*, 120.

104. For the text, see Dariusz Kołodziejczyk, *Ottoman-Polish Diplomatic Relations (15th–18th Century): An Annotated Edition of ʿAhdnames and Other Documents* (Leiden: Brill, 2000), 234–38 (transliteration), 239–42 (English translation).

105. For a summary of his activities as chancellor, see Şahin, *Empire and Power in the Reign of Süleyman*, 220–30; Halil İnalcık, "State and Ideology under Sultan Süleyman I," in *The Middle East and the Balkans under the Ottoman Empire*, 87.

106. For a comprehensive study of this important figure, see Imber, *Ebu's-suʿud*.

107. Douglas Howard, "The Historical Development of the Ottoman Imperial Registry (Defter-i Hakanî): mid-Fifteenth to mid-Seventeenth Centuries," *Archivum Ottomanicum* 11 (1986): 214–17; Linda T. Darling, *Revenue-Raising and Legitimacy: Tax Collection and Finance Administration in the Ottoman Empire, 1560–1660* (Leiden: Brill, 1996), 53–67.

108. For a quick overview of Rüstem's financial policies, see Atçıl, "State and Government in the Mid-Sixteenth Century Ottoman Empire," 257–69. A detailed study is Hacı Ahmet Arslantürk, "Bir Bürokrat ve Yatırımcı Olarak Kanuni Sultan Süleyman'ın Veziriazamı Rüstem Paşa" (PhD diss., Marmara University, 2011).

109. Celalzade Mustafa, *Tabakat*, 335a.

110. For these new notions of the caliphate, see İnalcık, "State and Ideology under Sultan Süleyman I," 78–81; Imber, *Ebu's-suʿud*, 103–11.

111. For Hadım Süleyman's expedition of 1538, see Casale, *The Ottoman Age of Exploration*, 53–63. For Ottoman-Portuguese relations, see Salih Özbaran, "Ottoman Naval Policy in the South," in *Süleyman the Magnificent and His Age: The Ottoman Empire in the Early Modern World*, eds. Metin Kunt and Christine Woodhead (London: Longman, 1995), 55–70; Özbaran, "The Ottoman Turks and the Portuguese in the Persian Gulf 1534–1581," *Journal of Asian History* 6, no. 1 (1972): 45–87.

112. For an analysis of Ottoman expansion and its costs, see Rhoads Murphey, "Ottoman Expansion, 1451–1556 II. Dynastic Interest and International Power Status," in

*Early Modern Military History, 1450–1815*, ed. Geoff Mortimer (Houndmills, Basingstoke, Hampshire: Palgrave Macmillan, 2004), 60–80, particularly 70.

113. On Ottoman war-weariness, see Atçıl, "State and Government in the Mid-Sixteenth Century Ottoman Empire," 176–84.

114. For the interface between *kanun* and Sharia, see Imber, *Ebu's-su'ud*, 24–65.

115. See Fleischer, *Bureaucrat and Intellectual in the Ottoman Empire*, 191–200.

116. See Celalzade Mustafa, *Tabakat*, 239b, for the date of Hafsa's death; Özergin, *Sultan Kanunî Süleyman Han Çağına Âit Tarih Kayıtları*, 15, for Hayreddin's.

117. For an evaluation of Kemalpaşazade's scholarship, see Şamil Öçal, *Kışladan Medreseye: Osmanlı Bilgini Kemalpaşazade'nin Düşünce Dünyası* (Istanbul: İz Yayıncılık, 2013).

118. Celalzade Mustafa, *Tabakat*, 238b–240a. For Hafsa's death and a discussion of her career, see Peirce, *Empress of the East*, 113–14.

119. The date and conditions of the prince's death are recorded in a local court register, quoted in Uluçay, "Kanunî Sultan ve Süleyman ve Ailesi ile İlgili Bazı Notlar ve Vesikalar," 250.

120. For the impact of Mehmed's death, the funeral, and the details of the complex built in his honor, see Celalzade Mustafa, *Tabakat*, 374a–379a. For a detailed analysis of the complex, see Gülru Necipoğlu, *The Age of Sinan: Architectural Culture in the Ottoman Empire* (London: Reaktion Books, 2005), 191–207.

121. The Turkish chronogram forms the last line in each quatrain of a recently discovered six-quatrain elegy. See Benedek Péri, "The Persian Imitation Gazels (Nazires) of Sultan Süleyman 'Muhibbi' (1520-1566) as They Are Preserved in a Hitherto Unnoticed Copy of His Divan," *Amasya Üniversitesi Sosyal Bilimler Dergisi* 5 (June 2019): 99; a transliteration of the elegy is in 118.

122. Bekir Kütükoğlu, "Ayas Paşa," *TDVİA*, vol. 4, 202–3.

123. Mehmet İpşirli, "Lutfi Paşa," *TDVİA*, vol. 27, 234–36. For Lütfi as a scholar, see Asım Cüneyd Köksal, "Bir İslam Âlimi olarak Lutfi Paşa," *Journal of Ottoman Studies* 50 (2017): 29–72.

124. Erhan Afyoncu, "Süleyman Paşa, Hadım," *TDVİA*, vol. 38, 96–98.

125. Navagero, "Relazione," 98.

126. For Rüstem's rise from *devşirme* recruit to grand vizier and his perception by contemporaries, see Atçıl, "State and Government in the Mid-Sixteenth Century Ottoman Empire," 16–47.

127. Navagero, "Relazione," 89, 90.

128. For the marriage and its aftermath in terms of Hürrem's new status, see Peirce, *Empress of the East*, 114–38. The celebrations are mentioned in 145–47, and the rumors in 147–50.

129. *Muhibbî Dîvânı*, eds. Yavuz and Yavuz, vol. 2, 1256–57 (no. 2466).

130. TSMA E. 714/13, 2.

131. TSMA E. 753/36.

132. For the letters to Isabella and to Poland, see Peirce, *Empress of the East*, 223–25, 251–54.

133. For a discussion of the complex and its significance, see Peirce, *Empress of the East*, 170–94; a concise treatment of Hürrem's personality and her complex in Constantinople is in Necipoğlu, *The Age of Sinan*, 268–76.

134. Peirce, *Empress of the East*, 288–94; Necipoğlu, *The Age of Sinan*, 276–78. For more information on the soup kitchen, see Amy Singer, *Constructing Ottoman Beneficence: An Imperial Soup Kitchen in Jerusalem* (Albany: State University of New York Press, 2002).

135. For the significance of Jerusalem for Süleyman as a site of architectural patronage and a holy city with eschatological connotations, see Gülru Necipoğlu, "The Dome of the Rock as Palimpsest: 'Abd al-Malik's Grand Narrative and Sultan Süleyman's Glosses," *Muqarnas* 25 (2008): 57–81. Also see Amy Singer, "Making Jerusalem Ottoman," in *Living in the Ottoman Realm: Empire and Identity, 13th to 20th Centuries*, eds. Christine Isom-Verhaaren and Kent F. Schull (Bloomington: Indiana University Press, 2016), 128–35.

136. For Mihrümah and her complex in Üsküdar, see Necipoğlu, *The Age of Sinan*, 296–305.

137. Renier, "Relazione," 51–52.

138. The translation is from Gibb, *A History of Ottoman Poetry*, vol. 3, 10; a transliteration is in *Muhibbî Dîvânı*, eds. Yavuz and Yavuz, vol. 2, 1676 (no. 3406).

139. On Haydar, see Fleischer, "Seer to the Sultan," 290–304. The text in question, for which I adopt the author and title proposed by Cornell H. Fleischer, is Haydar-ı Remmal, *Remil Risalesi*, TSMK, ms. Hazine 1697. For a discussion of the text, with a focus on its eschatological passages, see Fleischer, "A Mediterranean Apocalypse," 69–76. I prefer a slightly later completion/submission date for the work than the one Fleischer proposes. I thank him for sharing his reading notes with me.

140. Haydar-ı Remmal, *Remil Risalesi*, 39b–42a, 47b–48a, 53a.

CHAPTER 7

1. For a comprehensive study of Mustafa's execution, see Zahit Atçıl, "Why Did Sultan Süleyman Execute His Son Şehzade Mustafa in 1553?," *Osmanlı Araştırmaları/The Journal of Ottoman Studies* 48 (2016): 67–103. For an approach that gives more weight to social and economic problems, see Şerafettin Turan, *Kanuni Süleyman Dönemi Taht Kavgaları*, revised second edition (Ankara: Bilgi, 1997), 18–43.

2. Renier, "Relazione," 74–75.

3. Navagero, "Relazione," 77–78.

4. *Négociations de la France dans le Levant*, vol. 2, 103–5.

5. Uluçay, "Kanunî Sultan Süleyman ve Ailesi ile İlgili Bazı Notlar ve Vesikalar," 250; Peirce, *Empress of the East*, 225–27.

6. For rumors about Rüstem and Hürrem's activities against Mustafa, see Ogier Ghiselin de Busbecq, *Les lettres turques*, ed. and trans. Dominique Arrighi (Paris: Honoré Champion, 2010), 73–75; for a discussion of anti-Hürrem sentiments, see Peirce, *Empress of the East*, 272–79.

7. The increase of half a million *akçe*s is mentioned in Bostan Çelebi, *Tarih-i Sultan Süleyman*, 344r.

8. See Emecen, *XVI. Asırda Manisa Kazâsı*, 34–35.

9. The untitled text, today kept at Staatsbibliotek zu Berlin as ms. Hs. or. 955, is part of Matrakçı Nasuh's history of the reign of Süleyman. The relevant section is 29b–33a. The section is either missing from or has been blackened in other copies of the same text. Cf. Sinan Çukuryurt, "Matrakçı Nasuh: Süleymannâme (1a-95b) (Eserin Transkripsiyonu ve Değerlendirmesi)" (MA thesis, Marmara University, 2003), 93.

10. Fethullah Ârif, *Sulaymannama*, 478a–480a.

11. For the relationship between social and economic problems and succession struggles, see Ş. Turan, *Kanuni Süleyman Dönemi Taht Kavgaları*, 18–22.

12. Mustafa's letter is in *Mecmua-yı Münşeat*, aka *Dizfulî Mecmuası*, SK, ms. Veliyüddin Efendi 2735, 100a–100b; the official's reply is in 100b–101b. A transliteration of Mustafa's letter is in Ş. Turan, *Kanuni Süleyman Dönemi Taht Kavgaları*, 157–58.

13. Atçıl, "Why Did Sultan Süleyman Execute His Son?," 78–79; "Relazione anonima della guerra di Persia dell'anno 1553, e di molti altri particolari, relative alle cose di Solimano in quell'epoca," in *Relazioni degli ambasciatori veneti al Senato*, serie III, vol. 1, 240–41.

14. Celalzade Mustafa, *Tabakat*, 426b–433b. Safavid sources treat these events in greater detail: see Eskandar Beg Monshi, *History of Shah 'Abbas the Great*, vol. 1, 124–29; Hasan Beg Rumlu, *Ahsan al-tavarikh*, vol. 3, 1349–72. Also see "Relazione anonima," 199–203.

15. "Relazione anonima," 203–4; the translation of the relevant passage is in Atçıl, "Why Did Sultan Süleyman Execute His Son?," 85–86.

16. The letter is TSMA, E. 715/17. For a transliteration, see M. Tayyib Gökbilgin, "Rüstem Paşa ve Hakkındaki İthamlar," *Tarih Dergisi* 8, nos. 11–12 (1956): 38–43.

17. Celalzade Mustafa, *Tabakat*, 436b–438b; a discussion of the passage is in Şahin, *Empire and Power in the Reign of Süleyman*, 125–27.

18. The execution is described in Fethullah Ârif, *Sulaymannama*, 571b–573b.

19. Even a typically pro-Süleyman and pro-Rüstem historian like Matrakçı Nasuh admits Rüstem's role in the affair in his *Târîh-i Âl-i Osmân*, 468–69.

20. Mehmed Çavuşoğlu, "Şehzâde Mustafa Mersiyeleri," *İstanbul Üniversitesi Edebiyat Fakültesi Tarih Enstitüsü Dergisi* 12 (1982): 654-86.

21. Gibb, *A History of Ottoman Poetry*, vol. 3, 131. For an in-depth analysis of the Mustafa affair and this particular elegy, see Ahmet Atillâ Şentürk, *Şehzâde Mustafa Mersiyesi yahut Kanunî Hicviyesi* (Istanbul: Enderun, 1998).

22. While a *fetva* is not mentioned in the majority of the sources, it is referred to by Busbecq and by an Ottoman poet writing under the penname Nisayî. They may

have assumed that such a major act as the execution would have necessitated justification. See Busbecq, *Les lettres turques*, 77; Çavuşoğlu, "Şehzâde Mustafa Mersiyeleri," 675.

23. Hasan Beg Rumlu, *Ahsan al-tavarikh*, vol. 3, 1368.

24. The account of Süleyman's final campaign against the Safavids is based on Celalzade Mustafa, *Tabakat*, 433b–436a, 438b–476a, including the critical diplomatic correspondence between the two sides. The level of detail in Celalzade Mustafa is matched by the long section on the campaign in "Relazione anonima," 213–63. Safavid sources, on the other hand, downplay the importance of the campaign. See Hasan Beg Rumlu, *Ahsan al-tavarikh*, vol. 3, 1372–75; cf. Eskandar Beg Monshi, *History of Shah 'Abbas the Great*, vol. 1, 129–30.

25. An analysis and transliteration of the work is Kadri Hüsnü Yılmaz, "Türk Edebiyatında Süleymân-Nâmeler ve Hâkî Efendi'nin Süleymân-Nâmesi" (PhD diss., Gazi University, 2017).

26. While contemporary Ottoman observers refrain from this position or claim that the Safavids sued for peace, the events of the campaign as well as Süleyman and his officials' overall approach to foreign policy during this period support such an interpretation. See Şahin, *Empire and Power in the Reign of Süleyman*, 127–31; Zahit Atçıl, "Warfare as a Tool of Diplomacy: Background of the First Ottoman-Safavid Treaty in 1555," *Turkish Historical Review* 10, no. 1 (June 2019): 3–24.

27. E. Delmar Morgan and C.H. Coote (eds.), *Early Voyages to Russia and Persia: Anthony Jenkinson and Other Englishmen* (New York: Burt Franklin, 1886), 1–5; more details are provided in "Relazione anonima," 224–33.

28. I am grateful to Halil Dilek MD, a specialist of orthopedics and traumatology, for discussing Cihangir's condition with me.

29. For a discussion of this correspondence, see Vural Genç, "16. Yüzyılın İlk Yarısında Osmanlılar ile Safeviler Arasında Yaşanan Dini ve Siyasi Polemikler," *Osmanlı Araştırmaları/The Journal of Ottoman Studies* 57 (2021): 90–98.

30. For a letter by Tahmasb that reflects a strong sense of Safavid self-confidence, in addition to Genç, see Mitchell, *The Practice of Politics*, 81–87.

31. For a discussion of the shah's letter, see Colin Paul Mitchell, "The Sword and the Pen: Diplomacy in Early Safavid Iran, 1501–1555" (PhD diss., University of Toronto, 2002), 354–59.

32. The chancellor's account of the negotiations as well as his anti-Safavid and anti-Shiite diatribes are found in Celalzade Mustafa, *Tabakat*, 483b–497a. For a Venetian perspective, see "Relazione anonima," 263–68; Busbecq, *Les lettres turques*, 120–23.

33. For the creation and transformation of different images for Süleyman, see Cornell H. Fleischer, "The Lawgiver as Messiah: The Making of the Imperial Image in the Reign of Süleymân," in *Soliman le magnifique et son temps*, ed. Gilles Veinstein (Paris: La Documentation Française, 1992), 159–77; Christine Woodhead,

"Perspectives on Süleyman," in *Süleyman the Magnificent and His Age*, 164–81; Şahin, *Empire and Power in the Reign of Süleyman*, 187–93.

34. For this transition, in addition to Fleischer, "The Lawgiver as Messiah," 167–69, 171–74, see Gülru Necipoğlu, "A Kânûn for the State, a Canon for the Arts: Conceptualizing the Classical Synthesis of Ottoman Arts and Architecture," in *Soliman le magnifique et son temps*, 195–216.

35. For the construction of the complex, its architectural features, and its cultural and political significance, see Necipoğlu, *Age of Sinan*, 207–22.

36. For a concise study, supported by impressive photography, see Cyril A. Mango (essay) and Ahmet Ertuğ (photography), *Hagia Sophia* ([Istanbul]: Ertuğ & Kocabıyık, 1987).

37. See Stéphane Yerasimos, *Légendes d'Empire: La fondation de Constantinople et de Sainte-Sophie dans les traditions turques* (Paris: Institut français d'études anatoliennes–Jean Maisonneuve, 1990), 111–59.

38. Celalzade Mustafa, *Tabakat*, 518a–519a.

39. For the life and work of Sinan, the most comprehensive study to date is Necipoğlu, *Age of Sinan*. For English translations of Sinan's autobiographical writings, see *Sinan's Autobiographies: Five Sixteenth-Century Texts*, trans. and ed. Howard Crane and Esra Akın, with notes and a preface by Gülru Necipoğlu (Leiden: Brill, 2006).

40. *Sinan's Autobiographies*, 124–26.

41. The number and specializations of those employed in the construction fluctuated throughout, as can be expected in any major project. More details are found in a comprehensive study of the technical details of the construction: Serpil Çelik, "Mevcut Belgeler Işığında Süleymaniye Külliyesinin Yapım Süreci" (PhD diss., Istanbul Technical University, 2001), 201–15; for the cost of the project, see 221–23.

42. This is how Celalzade Mustafa presented the complex in *Tabakat*, 521a–527a. A discussion of the complex's function and significance is in Gülru Necipoğlu-Kafadar, "The Süleymaniye Complex: An Interpretation," *Muqarnas* 3 (1985): 92–117.

43. These numbers are provided, on the basis of the complex' endowment deed, in Kemal Edib Kürkçüoğlu, *Süleymaniye Vakfiyesi* (Ankara: Vakıflar Umum Müdürlüğü, 1962), 8–11.

44. For an analysis of the mosque as building and prayer space, see Necipoğlu, *Age of Sinan*, 210–18.

45. See Nina Ergin, "The Soundscape of Sixteenth-Century Istanbul Mosques: Architecture and Qur'an Recital," *Journal of the Society of Architectural Historians* 67, no. 2 (2008): 204–8, 213–16.

46. For the inscription, see Cevdet Çulpan, "İstanbul Süleymaniye Camii Kitabesi," in *Kanuni Armağanı*, 291–99.

47. For a detailed analysis of the *Sulaymannama*, see Fatma Sinem Eryılmaz Arenas-Vives, "The *Shehnameci*s of Sultan Süleyman: 'Arif and Eflatun and Their Dynastic Project" (PhD diss., University of Chicago, 2010), 166–209.

48. For this seminal text's reception in the Ottoman realm, see Schmidt, "The Reception of Firdausi's *Shahnama* among the Ottomans"; Uluç, "The *Shahnama* of Firdausi in the Lands of Rum."

49. See Murat Umut İnan, "Imperial Ambitions, Mystical Aspirations: Persian Learning in the Ottoman World," in *The Persianate World: The Frontiers of a Eurasian Lingua Franca*, ed. Nile Green (Berkeley: University of California Press, 2019), 75–92.

50. On the rise and slow decline of Persian in the Ottoman lands, see Sara Nur Yıldız, "Ottoman Historical Writing in Persian, 1400-1600," in *A History of Persian Literature,* ed. Ehsan Yarshater, vol. 10, *Persian Historiography*, ed. Charles Melville (London: I.B. Tauris, 2012), 436–502.

51. For details, see Atıl, *Süleymanname,* 57–61; Eryılmaz, "The Shehnamecis of Sultan Süleyman," 76–165.

52. For Fethullah Arif's biography and works, see Eryılmaz, "The Shehnamecis of Sultan Süleyman," 24–75.

53. For the role of the *şehnameci*, see Christine Woodhead, "An Experiment in Official Historiography: The Post of Şehnameci in the Ottoman Empire, c.1555–1605," *Wiener Zeitschrift für die Kunde des Morgenlandes* 75 (1983): 157–82; a more nuanced interpretation of the notion of "official historiography" is offered in Emine Fetvacı, "The Office of the Ottoman Court Historian," In *Studies on Istanbul and Beyond,* 7–21.

54. My interpretation of the work is based on Eryılmaz, "The Shehnamecis of Sultan Süleyman," 166–209.

55. For a reading of the work as a history, see Fatma Sinem Eryılmaz, "The *Sulaiman-nama (Süleyman-name)* as a Historical Source," in *Shahnama Studies III: The Reception of the* Shahnama, eds. Gabrielle van den Berg and Charles Melville (Leiden: Brill, 2018), 173–98.

56. For a contemporary, pro-Süleyman account, see Celalzade Mustafa, *Tabakat,* 497b–500a; an analysis that puts emphasis on social questions is in Ş. Turan, *Kanuni Süleyman Dönemi Taht Kavgaları,* 44–49.

57. For Ottoman settlement in the region in the fifteenth and sixteenth centuries, see Antov, *The Ottoman "Wild West"*, 89–157.

58. For a reproduction of the painting, see Atıl, *Süleymanname,* 232.

59. Busbecq, *Les Lettres turques,* 142–150.

60. Antonio Erizzo, "Sommario della Relazione," in *Relazioni degli ambasciatori veneti al Senato,* serie III, vol. 3, 135.

61. For these assessments, see Erizzo, "Sommario della Relazione," 134–35; Antonio Barbarigo, "Sommario della Relazione," in *Relazioni degli ambasciatori veneti al Senato,* serie III, vol. 3, 148–49.

62. *Négociations de la France dans le Levant,* vol. 2, 394–95.

63. For the next stages of the struggle between Selim and Bayezid, near-contemporary accounts are found in Busbecq, *Les lettres turques,* 228–74; Matrakçı Nasuh,

*Târîh-i Âl-i Osmân*, 474–84; Derviş Mehmed, *İtaatname*, transcribed in Pınar Tarlak, "Klasik Dönem Taht Mücadeleleri: Kanuni ve Oğulları" (MA thesis, Bahçeşehir University, 2016), 92–155. The most detailed scholarly treatment of the events is in Ş. Turan, *Kanuni Süleyman Dönemi Taht Kavgaları*, 56–113.

64. Ş. Turan, *Kanuni Süleyman Dönemi Taht Kavgaları*, 50–75; an example of Bayezid's letters to his father is in 170–72.

65. Ş. Turan, *Kanuni Süleyman Dönemi Taht Kavgaları*, 176–77.

66. Süleyman's attempts at appeasing Bayezid are discussed in Ş. Turan, *Kanuni Süleyman Dönemi Taht Kavgaları*, 66–75; the princes' move to their new governorates, war preparations, and Süleyman's increasing support for Selim are in 75–96.

67. The texts of the *fetva*s are in Ş. Turan, *Kanuni Süleyman Dönemi Taht Kavgaları*, 180–82.

68. The zeal of Bayezid's forces is described in Matrakçı Nasuh, *Târîh-i Âl-i Osmân*, 477–79. *İtaatname* reproduces a letter from Selim to his father where the emphasis is on the victory of Selim and the Ottoman officials who supported him (Tarlak, "Klasik Dönem Taht Mücadeleleri," 143–51).

69. Many of these orders are found in *3 Numaralı Mühimme Defteri* (Ankara: Başbakanlık Devlet Arşivleri Genel Müdürlüğü, 1993).

70. Shah Tahmasb, *Tazkira*, 72–79. These passages have a defensive tone, as Tahmasb assures his readers, who would have known about the prince and his sons' eventual demise, that it was not his intention to place them in harm's way.

71. Safavid historians offer more information than their Ottoman counterparts about Bayezid's stay in Iran. See Eskandar Beg Monshi, *History of Shah 'Abbas the Great*, vol. 1, 166–73; Hasan Beg Rumlu, *Ahsan al-tavarikh*, vol. 3, 1410–13, 1415–17, 1420–21, 1424–25. A modern study that reflects the Safavid perspective is Colin P. Mitchell, "Am I My Brother's Keeper? Negotiating Corporate Sovereignty and Divine Absolutism in Sixteenth-Century Turco-Iranian Politics," in *New Perspectives on Safavid Iran: Empire and Society*, ed. Mitchell (New York: Routledge, 2011), 41–58. This article should be read together with Ş. Turan, *Kanuni Süleyman Dönemi Taht Kavgaları*, 113–36, which skillfully uses Ottoman archival records about the Bayezid affair.

72. The correspondence between the sides is preserved, among other places, in an Ottoman collection of letters. A transliteration is in İsa Şevik, "Şah Tahmasb (1524–1576) ile Osmanlı Sarayı Arasında Teati Edilen Mektupları İçeren 'Münşe'āt-ı 'Atīk'in Edisyon Kritiği ve Değerlendirilmesi" (MA thesis, Dokuz Eylül Üniversitesi, 2008), 100–223.

73. The repercussions of the Bayezid affair are discussed in Ş. Turan, *Kanuni Süleyman Dönemi Taht Kavgaları*, 137–54.

74. Yaşar Yücel (ed.), *Osmanlı Devlet Düzenine Ait Metinler III: Kitâbu Mesâlihi'l-Müslimîn ve Menâfi'i'l-Mü'minîn* (Ankara: Dil Tarih Coğrafya Fakültesi Yayınları, 1980).

75. Mübahat S. Kütükoğlu (ed.), *Lütfi Paşa Âsafnâmesi (Yeni Bir Metin Tesisi Denemesi)* (Istanbul: Edebiyat Fakültesi Basımevi, 1991).

76. This monumental work of politics and ethics, composed at the very end of Süleyman's reign, is Kınalızâde Ali Çelebi, *Ahlâk-ı Alâ'î: Kınalızâde Ali Çelebi'nin Ahlâk Kitabı*, ed. Mustafa Koç (Istanbul: Türkiye Yazma Eserler Kurumu, 2014).

77. Yılmaz, *Beşiktaşlı Yahyâ Efendi*, 22.

78. The Meccan envoy visited Yahya at his dervish lodge. See Richard Blackburn (ed. and trans.), *Journey to the Sublime Porte: The Arabic Memoir of a Sharifian Agent's Diplomatic Mission to the Imperial Court in the Era of Süleyman the Magnificent* (Beirut-Würzburg: Orient-Institut Berlin, Ergon Verlag, 2005), 197–99.

79. Blackburn (ed.), *Journey to the Sublime Porte*, 200–2; Matrakçı Nasuh, *Târîh-i Âl-i Osmân*, 372–73; for the last years of Hürrem, also see Peirce, *Empress of the East*, 299–303.

80. Marcantonio Donini, "Relazione dell'impero ottomano di Marcantonio Donini, segretario del bailo Girolamo Ferro," in *Relazioni degli ambasciatori veneti al Senato*, serie III, vol. 3, 178–9.

81. Halman, *Süleyman the Magnificent Poet*, 76–77.

82. Erizzo, "Relazione," 138.

83. The letter is in Feridun Ahmed, *Münşeatü's-selatin*, vol. 2, 11–14.

84. Hilal Kazan, *XVI. Asırda Sarayın Sanatı Himayesi* (Istanbul: İSAR Vakfı, 2010), 103.

85. Necipoğlu, *Age of Sinan*, 222–30 (for the mosque and hospice in Damascus), 72–73.

86. For the aqueducts, see Necipoğlu, *Age of Sinan*, 141–42, 305–6; the expenses for construction projects are in 562.

87. For the new complex, see Necipoğlu, *Age of Sinan*, 305–15.

88. For this transition from a Spanish perspective, see M. J. Rodríguez-Salgado, *The Changing Face of Empire: Charles V, Philip II and Habsburg Authority, 1551–1559* (Cambridge: Cambridge University Press, 1988).

89. For the Ottomans' inability to help the French during the war of 1551–59 and the conditions of the treaty, see Setton, *The Papacy and the Levant*, vol. 4, 704–9.

90. For detailed information on these developments, see Setton, *The Papacy and the Levant*, vol. 4, 758–66 (Djerba), 853–78 (Malta), 893–99 (Chios).

91. Setton, *The Papacy and the Levant*, vol. 4, 771. For the text, see Schaendlinger and Römer (eds.) *Die Schreiben Süleymāns des Prächtigen*, vol. 1, 67–70 (transcription), 70–74 (German translation).

92. A detailed Ottoman account of the campaign is H. Ahmet Arslantürk and Günhan Börekçi (eds.), *Nüzhet-i esrârü'l-ahyâr der-ahbâr-ı sefer-i Sigetvar: Sultan Süleyman'ın Son Seferi* (Istanbul: Zeytinburnu Belediyesi, 2012). My account here is also based on the following articles from *The Battle for Central Europe*: Claudia Römer and Nicolas Vatin, "The Hungarian Frontier and Süleyman's Way to Szigetvár according to Ottoman Sources," 341–58; James D. Tracy, "Tokaj, 1565: A Habsburg Prize of War, and an Ottoman *Casus Belli*," 359–76; Szabolcs Varga, "Miklós Zrínyi, Captain-General of Szigetvár (1561–1566) – His Organisational

Activity and Death," 377–95; József Kelenik, "The Sieges of Szigetvár and Gyula, 1566," 399–410.

93. TSMA, E. 750/67.

94. An analysis and transliteration are found in Kübra Naç, "Âgehî'nin Fetih-nâme-i Kal'a-i Sigetvar'ı (İnceleme–Tenkitli Metin)" (MA thesis, Fatih University, 2013).

95. See Nicolas Vatin, "On Süleyman the Magnificent's Death and Burials," in *The Battle for Central Europe*, 427–43.

96. See Kunt, "A Prince Goes Forth," 67–70 for Selim's succession.

97. Gibb, *A History of Ottoman Poetry*, vol. 3, 152. The full translation of the elegy is in 151–55.

### CONCLUSION: LEGACIES

1. "Kadd-i yâri kimi halkun serv okur kimi elif / Cümlenün maksudı bir amma rivayet muhtelif" (*Muhibbî Dîvânı*, ed. Ak, 4).

2. For positive reassessments of Süleyman's reign, see Woodhead, "Perspectives on Süleyman," 181–87; Günhan Börekçi, "The Memory of Szigetvár and Sultan Süleyman in Ottoman/Turkish Culture," in *The Battle for Central Europe*, 532–35. For negative evaluations, see Cemal Kafadar, "The Myth of the Golden Age: Ottoman Historical Consciousness in the Post-Süleymânic Era," in *Süleymân the Second and His Time*, 37–48.

3. For D'Ohsson and his work, see Carter Vaughn Findley, *Enlightening Europe on Islam and the Ottomans: Mouradgea d'Ohsson and His Masterpiece* (Leiden: Brill, 2019).

4. https://www.aoc.gov/explore-capitol-campus/art/suleiman-relief-portrait.

5. For a comparison of the images of Süleyman in his *Sulaymannama* and *Hünername*, see Emine Fetvacı, *Picturing History at the Ottoman Court* (Bloomington: Indiana University Press, 2013), 269–82.

6. For an exhibition catalogue, see Esin Atıl, *The Age of Sultan Süleyman the Magnificent* (Washington, DC; New York: National Gallery of Art; Harry N. Abrams, 1987).

7. For a concise evaluation of recent scholarship, see Kaya Şahin, "The Ottoman Empire in the Long Sixteenth Century," *Renaissance Quarterly* 70, no. 1 (2017): 220–34.

8. For a comprehensive analysis of the series, see Josh Carney, "A Dizi-ying Past: *Magnificent Century* and the Motivated Uses of History in Contemporary Turkey" (PhD diss., Indiana University, 2015).

# Bibliography

## PRIMARY SOURCES

*3 Numaralı Mühimme Defteri.* Ankara: Başbakanlık Devlet Arşivleri Genel Müdürlüğü, 1993.

Ahmed Bican Yazıcıoğlu [attributed]. *Dürr-i Meknun: kritische Edition mit Kommentar.* Edited by Laban Kaptein. Asch: self-publication, 2007.

Ak, Coşkun, ed. *Muhibbî Dîvânı. İzahlı Metin.* Ankara: Kültür ve Turizm Bakanlığı, 1987.

Albèri, Eugenio, ed. *Relazioni degli ambasciatori veneti al Senato.* Serie III, vol. 1. Florence: Tipografia all'insegna di Clio, 1840.

———. *Relazioni degli ambasciatori veneti al Senato.* Serie III, vol. 3. Florence: Società editrice fiorentina, 1855.

Arslantürk, H. Ahmet, and Günhan Börekçi, eds. *Nüzhet-i esrârü'l-ahyâr der-ahbâr-ı sefer-i Sigetvar: Sultan Süleyman'ın Son Seferi.* Istanbul: Zeytinburnu Belediyesi, 2012.

Âşık Mehmed. *Menâzırü'l-Avâlim.* Edited and transliterated by Mahmut Ak. 3 volumes. Ankara: Türk Tarih Kurumu, 2007.

ʿÂşıkpaşazāde Aḥmed. *Tevārīḫ-i Āl-i ʿOsmān.* Edited by Âlî. Istanbul: Matbaa-yı Âmire, 1914.

Atıl, Esin. *Süleymanname: The Illustrated History of Süleyman the Magnificent.* Washington, DC; New York: National Gallery of Art; Harry N. Abrams, 1986.

———. *The Age of Sultan Süleyman the Magnificent.* Washington, DC; New York: National Gallery of Art; Harry N. Abrams, 1987.

Avcı, Necati. "Tabib Ramazan'ın Er-Risale El-Fethiyye Es-Süleymaniyyesi." MA thesis, Ankara University, 1989.

———. "Tabib Ramazan: Er-Risale el-fethiyye er-radossiye es-Süleymaniyye." PhD dissertation, Erciyes University, 1993.

Bessarion. *Encomium on Trebizond.* In *Two Works on Trebizond: Michael Panaretos, Bessarion,* edited and translated by Scott Kennedy, 59–215. Cambridge, MA: Harvard University Press, 2019.

Beşiktaşlı Yaḥyā Efendi. *Dīvān: Analysis – Critical Text – Dictionary – Facsimile.* Edited by Enis Tombul. Cambridge, MA: Department of Near Eastern Languages and Civilizations, Harvard University, 2018.

Blackburn, Richard, ed. and trans. *Journey to the Sublime Porte: The Arabic Memoir of a Sharifian Agent's Diplomatic Mission to the Imperial Court in the Era of Süleyman the Magnificent*. Beirut-Würzburg: Orient-Institut Berlin, Ergon Verlag, 2005.

Bostān Çelebi. *Tārīḫ-i Sulṭān Süleymān*. Österreichische Nationalbibliothek, ms. Cod. H. O. 42a.

Busbecq, Ogier Ghiselin de. *Les lettres turques*. Edited and translated by Dominique Arrighi. Paris: Honoré Champion, 2010.

Celalzāde Muṣṭafā. *Tārīḫ-i Sulṭān Selīm*. British Museum, ms. Add. 7848.

_____. *Geschichte Sultan Süleymān Ḳānūnīs von 1520 bis 1557, oder, Ṭabaḳāt ül-Memālik ve Derecāt ül-Mesālik/von Celālzāde Muṣṭafā genannt Ḳoca Nişāncı*. Edited by Petra Kappert. Wiesbaden: Steiner, 1981.

Celalzāde Ṣāliḥ. *Tārīḫ-i Fetḥ-i Budun*. TSMK, ms. Revan 1280.

Charrière, Ernest, ed. *Négociations de la France dans le Levant, ou, Correspondances, mémoires et actes diplomatiques des ambassadeurs de France à Constantinople et des ambassadeurs, envoyés ou résidents à divers titres à Venise, Raguse, Rome, Malte et Jérusalem, en Turquie, Perse, Géorgie, Crimée, Syrie, Egypte, etc., et dans les états de Tunis, d'Alger et de Maroc*. Vol. 1: *1515-1547*. Paris: Imprimerie nationale, 1848. Vol. 2: *1547-1566*. Paris: Imprimerie nationale, 1850.

Clavijo, Ruy Gonzalez de. *Narrative of the Embassy of Ruy Gonzalez de Clavijo to the Court of Timour, at Samarcand, A.D. 1403-6*. Translated by Clements R. Markham. London: The Hakluyt Society, 1869.

Çavuşoğlu, Mehmed. "Şehzâde Mustafa Mersiyeleri." *İstanbul Üniversitesi Edebiyat Fakültesi Tarih Enstitüsü Dergisi* 12 (1982): 641–86.

Çukuryurt, Sinan. "Matrakçı Nasuh: Süleymannâme (1a-95b) (Eserin Transkripsiyonu ve Değerlendirmesi)." MA thesis, Marmara University, 2003.

*Defter-i Müsveddāt-ı İnʿāmāt ve Taṣaddukāt ve Teşrīfāt ve İrsāliyāt ve ʿĀdet ve Nökeriye ve Gayrıhu*. Istanbul Atatürk Library, ms. Muallim Cevdet O. 71.

Derviş Mehmed. *İtaatname*. Transcribed in Pınar Tarlak, "Klasik Dönem Taht Mücadeleleri: Kanuni ve Oğulları," 92–155. MA thesis, Bahçeşehir University, 2016.

Erkan, Davut. "Matrâkçı Nasûh'un Süleymân-nâmesi (1520-1537)." MA thesis, Marmara University, 2005.

Eskandar Beg Monshi. *History of Shah ʿAbbas the Great* (Tārīḫ-e ʿālamārā-ye ʿAbbāsī). Translated by Roger M. Savory. 2 volumes. Boulder, CO: Westview Press, 1978.

Evliyâ Çelebi b. Derviş Mehemmed Zıllî. *Evliyâ Çelebi Seyahatnâmesi. 2. Kitap*. Edited by Zekeriya Kurşun, Seyit Ali Kahraman, Yücel Dağlı. Istanbul: Yapı Kredi, 2011.

Ferīdūn Aḥmed. *Mecmūʿa-yı Münşeʾātüʾs-selāṭīn*. 2 volumes. Istanbul: Daruʾt-Tıbaatiʾl-Âmire, 1858-59.

Fetḥullah ʿĀrif. *Sulaymānnāma*. TSMK, ms. Hazine 1517.

Firdevsī-i Rūmī. *Süleymānnāme*. Chester Beatty Library, ms. T 406.

Foscolo, Andrea. "Relazione." In *Relazioni di ambasciatori veneti al Senato*. Vol. 14: *Costantinopoli: Relazioni inedite (1512-1789)*, edited by Maria Pia Pedani Fabris, 3–32. Padua: Aldo Ausilio-Bottega d'Erasmo, 1996.

Gelen, Kasım. "Kânûnî Sultan Süleymân'ın Farsça Dîvanı." MA thesis, Istanbul University, 1989.

Gévay, Anton von [Antal], ed. *Urkunden und Actenstücke zur Geschichte der Verhältnisse zwischen Österreich, Ungern und der Pforte im XVI. und XVII. Jahrhunderte.* Vol. 1, bk. 2, *Gesandtschaft König Ferdinands I an Sultan Suleiman I.: 1528* (Vienna: Schaumburg und Comp., 1840); vol. 1, bk. 4, *Gesandtschaft König Ferdinands I an Sultan Suleiman I.: 1530* (Vienna: Schaumburg und Comp., 1838); vol. 1, bk. 5, *Gesandtschaft König Ferdinands I an Sultan Suleiman I.: 1531–1532* (Vienna: Schaumburg und Comp., 1838); vol. 2, bk. 1, *Gesandtschaft König Ferdinands I an Sultan Suleiman I.: 1533* (Vienna: Schaumburg und Comp., 1838); vol. 2, bk. 2, *Gesandtschaft König Ferdinands I an Sultan Suleiman I.: 1534* (Vienna: Schaumburg und Comp., 1839); vol. 3, bk. 3, *Gesandtschaft König Ferdinands I an Sultan Suleiman I.: 1540–41* (Vienna: Schaumburg und Comp., 1842).

Giovio, Paolo. *Commentario de le cose de' Turchi.* Edited by Lara Michelacci. Bologna: CLUEB, 2005.

Ḥasan Beg Rūmlū. *Aḥsan al-tavarikh.* Edited by ʿAbdulḥusayn Navāī. 3 volumes. Tehran: Asatir, 2005–6.

Ḥaydar-ı Remmāl. *Remil Risālesi.* TSMK, ms. Hazine 1697.

Hoca Sadeddin Efendi. *Prognostic Dreams, Otherworldly Saints, and Caliphal Ghosts: A Critical Edition of Saʿdeddin Efendi's (d. 1599) Selimname.* Edited and translated by H. Erdem Çıpa. Leiden: Brill, 2022.

Hüseyin b. Hasan. *Letâ'ifü'l-Efkâr: Kâdı Hüseyin b. Hasan'ın Siyâsetnâmesi.* Edited by Özgür Kavak. Istanbul: Türkiye Yazma Eserler Kurumu, 2018.

İbn Kemal. *Tevârih-i Âl-i Osman. VII. Defter.* Edited by Şerafettin Turan. Ankara: Türk Tarih Kurumu, 1991.

_____. [as Kemalpaşazade Ahmed]. *Tevarih-i Âl-i Osman. X. Defter.* Edited by Şefaettin Severcan. Ankara: Türk Tarih Kurumu, 1996.

_____. *Tevârîḫ-i Âl-i Osmân. VIII. Defter.* Edited by Ahmet Uğur. Ankara: Türk Tarih Kurumu, 1997.

Kânûnî Sultan Süleyman. *Muhibbî Dîvânı. Bütün Şiirleri.* Edited by Kemal Yavuz and Orhan Yavuz. 2 volumes. Istanbul: Türkiye Yazma Eserler Kurumu Başkanlığı, 2016.

_____. *Süleyman the Magnificent Poet.* Translated by Talat S. Halman. Istanbul: Dost Yayınları, 1987.

*Ḳānûnnāme.* SK, ms. Âtıf Efendi 1734, 1b-8b.

*Kânûnnâme-i Âl-i Osman (Tahlil ve Karşılaştırmalı Metin).* Revised second edition. Edited by Abdülkadir Özcan. Istanbul: Kitabevi, 2003.

Keskin, Burhan. "Selîm-Nâme (İshâk b. İbrâhîm)." MA thesis, Ege University, 1998.

Kınalızâde Ali Çelebi. *Ahlâk-ı Alâ'î: Kınalızâde Ali Çelebi'nin Ahlâk Kitabı.* Edited by Mustafa Koç. Istanbul: Türkiye Yazma Eserler Kurumu, 2014.

Kütükoğlu, Mübahat S., ed. *Lütfi Paşa Âsafnâmesi (Yeni Bir Metin Tesisi Denemesi).* Istanbul: Edebiyat Fakültesi Basımevi, 1991.

Lâtifî. *Evsâf-ı İstanbul.* Edited by Nermin Suner Pekin. Istanbul: Baha Matbaası, 1977.

_____. *Lâtîfî'nin İki Risâlesi: Enîsü'l-Fusahâ ve Evsâf-ı İbrâhim Pâşâ*. Edited by Ahmet Sevgi. Konya: Selçuk Üniversitesi Yayınları, 1986.

Lütfi Paşa. *Tevârīḫ-i Āl-i ʿOsmān*. Edited by Âlî. Istanbul: Matbaa-yı Âmire, 1925.

Maliyeden Müdevver, D. 23. Devlet Arşivleri Başkanlığı, Osmanlı Arşivi.

Maṭrāḳcı Naṣūḫ. *Maṭlaʿ-ı Dāsitān-ı Sulṭān Süleymān Ḫān*. TSMK, ms. Revan 1286.

_____. Untitled [part of his history of Süleyman's reign]. Staatsbibliotek zu Berlin, ms. Hs. or. 955.

_____. *Beyān-ı menāzil-i sefer-i ʿIrakeyn-i Sulṭān Süleymān Ḫān*. Edited by Hüseyin G. Yurdaydın. Ankara: Türk Tarih Kurumu, 1976.

_____. *Tārîh-i Āl-i Osmān (Osmanlı Tarihi 699-968/1299-1561)*. Edited by Göker İnan. Istanbul: Türkiye Yazma Eserler Kurumu Başkanlığı, 2019.

[Matrakçı Nasuh] Sinan Çavuş. *Tarih-i Feth-i Şikloş, Estergon ve İstol(n)i-Belgrad, or Süleyman-Name*. Edited by Tülay Duran. Facsimile edition with English summary. Istanbul: Historical Research Foundation, Istanbul Research Center, 1987.

Mecdī Efendi. *Terceme-yi Şaḳāʾiḳ*. Istanbul: Daru't-Tıbaati'l-Âmire, 1853-54.

*Mecmūʿa-yı Münşeʾāt*. SK, ms. Veliyüddin Efendi 2735.

Meḥmed Dāʾī. *Menāḳıb-ı Şeyḫ Yaḥyā Beşikṭaşī*. SK, ms. Hacı Mahmud Efendi 4604.

Mimar Sinan. *Sinan's Autobiographies: Five Sixteenth-Century Texts*. Translated and edited by Howard Crane and Esra Akın, with notes and a preface by Gülru Necipoğlu. Leiden: Brill, 2006.

Muṣṭafā ʿĀlī. *Künhü'l-aḫbār*. Istanbul University Library, ms. TY 5959.

Naç, Kübra. "Âgehî'nin Fetih-nâme-i Kalʿa-i Sigetvar'ı (İnceleme–Tenkitli Metin)." MA thesis, Fatih University, 2013.

Özergin, M. Kemal. *Sultan Kanunî Süleyman Han Çağına Âit Tarih Kayıtları*. Erzurum: n.p., 1971.

Péri, Benedek. *The Persian Dīvān of Yavuz Sulṭān Selīm: A Critical Edition*. Budapest: Research Center for the Humanities, 2021.

Postel, Guillaume. *De la Republique des Turcs*. Poitiers: Imprimerie d'Enguilbert de Marnes, 1560.

Saʿd b. ʿAbdü'l-müʿteāl. *Selīmnāme*. TSMK, ms. Revan 1277.

Sanuto, Marino. *I Diarii di Marino Sanuto*. Edited by Rinaldo Fulin et al. Venice: F. Visentini, 1879–1903. Vols. 12, 29, 32, 41, 43, 45, 47, 52.

Schepper, Baron de Saint-Genois de and G.-A. Yssel, eds. "Missions diplomatiques de Corneille Duplicius de Schepper (1533-34)." *Mémoires de l'Académie royale des sciences, des lettres et des beaux-arts de Belgique* 30 (1857): 1–222.

Seyyid Loḳmān. *Hünernâme*. Vol. 2. TSMK, ms. Hazine 1524.

Shāh Tahmāsb. *Tazkira-i Shāh Tahmāsb*. Berlin: Kaviani, 1964.

Süleymān. Letter to Francis I, 1526. Bibliothèque nationale de France, ms. supplément turc 1638.

Şevik, İsa. "Şah Tahmasb (1524–1576) ile Osmanlı Sarayı Arasında Teati Edilen Mektupları İçeren 'Münşeʾāt-ı ʿAtīk'in Edisyon Kritiği ve Değerlendirilmesi." MA thesis, Dokuz Eylül University, 2008.

Spandounes, Theodore. *On the Origin of the Ottoman Emperors*. Translated and edited by Donald M. Nicol. Cambridge: Cambridge University Press, 1997.

*Tārīḫ-i Āl-i ʿOsmān*. Bibliothèque nationale de France, ms. Turc 98.

Theunissen, Hans. "Ottoman-Venetian Diplomatics: The ʿAhd-names. The Historical Background and the Development of a Category of Political-Commercial Instruments together with an Annotated Edition of a Corpus of Relevant Documents." *Electronic Journal of Oriental Studies* 1, no. 2 (1998): 1–698.

TSMA. D. 743; D. 4056; D. 8030.

TSMA. E. 581/70; E. 640/56; E. 672/5; E. 714/13; E. 715/17; E. 745/21; E. 745/22; E. 745/26; E. 745/9; E. 745/90; E. 747/2; E. 750/35; E. 750/67; E. 752/18; E. 753/36; E. 754/61; E. 754/101; E. 759/1; E. 759/89; E. 759/94; E. 759/95; E. 760/17; E. 850/38; E. 969/61.

Tursun Beg. *Tārīḫ-i Ebü'l-fetḥ*. SK, ms. Ayasofya 3032.

Yıldız, Mustafa. "Ġazavāt-ı Ḫayreddīn Paşa (MS 2639 Universitäts Bibliothek Istanbul). Kommentierte Edition mit Deutscher Zusammenfassung." PhD diss., University of Göttingen, 1991.

Yılmaz, Kadri Hüsnü. "Türk Edebiyatında Süleymân-Nâmeler ve Hâkî Efendi'nin Süleymân-Nâmesi." PhD diss., Gazi University, 2017.

Yücel, Yaşar, ed. *Osmanlı Devlet Düzenine Ait Metinler III: Kitâbu Mesâlihi'l-Müslimîn ve Menâfi'i'l-Mü'minîn*. Ankara: Dil Tarih Coğrafya Fakültesi Yayınları, 1980.

SECONDARY SOURCES

Abdulkadiroğlu, Abdulkerim. "Halîmî Çelebi." *TDVİA*. Vol. 15, 343–44. Ankara: Türkiye Diyanet Vakfı, 1988–2013, 2016.

Abisaab, Rula Jurdi. *Converting Persia. Religion and Power in the Safavid Empire*. London: I. B. Tauris, 2004.

Ágoston, Gábor. "A Flexible Empire: Authority and its Limits on the Ottoman Frontiers." *International Journal of Turkish Studies* 9 (2003): 15–31.

———. *Guns for the Sultan: Military Power and the Weapons Industry in the Ottoman Empire*. Cambridge: Cambridge University Press, 2005.

———. "Information, Ideology, and Limits of Imperial Policy." In *The Early Modern Ottomans: Remapping the Empire*, edited by Daniel Goffman and Virginia Aksan, 75–103. Cambridge: Cambridge University Press, 2007.

———. "War-Winning Weapons? On the Decisiveness of Ottoman Firearms from the Siege of Constantinople (1453) to the Battle of Mohács (1526)." *Journal of Turkish Studies* 39 (2013): 129–43.

———. "Ottoman Expansion and Military Power, 1300-1453." In *The Cambridge History of War*. Vol. 2, *War and the Medieval World*, edited by Anne Curry and David A. Graf, 449–69. Cambridge: Cambridge University Press, 2020.

Akdağ, Mustafa, *Celâlî İsyanları (1550-1603)*. Ankara: Ankara Üniversitesi Basımevi, 1963.

Akgündüz, Ahmed. *Osmanlı Kanunnâmeleri ve Hukukî Tahlilleri*. Vol. 1, *Kanunî Sultân Süleyman Devri Kanunnâmeleri: I. Kısım. Merkezî ve Umumî Kanunnâmeler*. Istanbul: FEY Vakfı, 1992.

Akışık-Karakullukçu, Aslıhan. "The Empire of Trebizond in the World Trade System: Economy and Culture." In *Trade in Byzantium: Papers from the Third International Sevgi Gönül Byzantine Studies Symposium*, edited by Paul Magdalino and Nevra Necipoğlu, 323–36. Istanbul: Koç University Research Center for Anatolian Civilizations, 2016.

Albayrak, Hüseyin. *Trabzon Orta Hisâr ve Çevresi*. Ankara: Kozan Ofset, 1998.

Ali, Kecia. *Marriage and Slavery in Early Islam*. Cambridge, MA: Harvard University Press, 2010.

Allsen, Thomas T. *The Hunt in Eurasian History*. Philadelphia: University of Pennsylvania Press, 2006.

And, Metin. *Istanbul in the 16th Century: The City, the Palace, Daily Life*. Istanbul: Akbank, 1994.

Andrews, Walter G. *Poetry's Voice, Society's Song: Ottoman Lyric Poetry*. Seattle: University of Washington Press, 1985.

Angelov, Dimiter G. "Emperors and Patriarchs as Ideal Children and Adolescents: Literary Conventions and Cultural Expectations." In *Becoming Byzantine: Children and Childhood in Byzantium*, edited by Arietta Papaconstantinou and Alice-Mary Talbot, 85–116. Washington, DC: Dumbarton Oaks Research Library and Collection, distributed by Harvard University Press, 2009.

Antov, Nikolay. "Crusading in the Fifteenth Century and Its Relation to the Development of Ottoman Dynastic Legitimacy, Self-Image and the Ottoman Consolidation of Authority." In *The Crusade in the Fifteenth Century: Converging and Competing Cultures*, edited by Norman Housley, 15–33. London: Routledge, 2016.

———. *The Ottoman "Wild West:" The Balkan Frontier in the Fifteenth and Sixteenth Centuries*. Cambridge: Cambridge University Press, 2017.

Araz, Yahya. *16. Yüzyıldan 19. Yüzyıl Başlarına Osmanlı Toplumunda Çocuk Olmak*. Istanbul: Kitap, 2013.

Arı, Bülent. "Early Ottoman Diplomacy: Ad Hoc Period." In *Ottoman Diplomacy: Conventional or Unconventional?*, edited by A. Nuri Yurdusev, 36–65. Houndmills, Basingstoke, Hampshire: Palgrave Macmillan, 2004.

Arslan, Hüseyin Ongan. "Varieties of Sectarian Consciousness among the Ottoman Elite: Sunni and Shiite Identities in Ottoman Historiography, 1450s-1580s." PhD diss., Indiana University, 2020.

Arslantürk, Hacı Ahmet. "Bir Bürokrat ve Yatırımcı Olarak Kanuni Sultan Süleyman'ın Veziriazamı Rüstem Paşa." PhD diss., Marmara University, 2011.

Atçıl, Abdurrahman. *Scholars and Sultans in the Early Modern Ottoman Empire*. Cambridge: Cambridge University Press, 2017.

———. "The Safavid Threat and Juristic Authority in the Ottoman Empire in the Sixteenth Century." *International Journal of Middle East Studies* 49, no. 2 (2017): 295–304.

_____. "Memlükler'den Osmanlılar'a Geçişte Mısır'da Adlî Teşkilât ve Hukuk (922-931/1517-1525)." *İslâm Araştırmaları Dergisi* 38 (2017): 89–121.

Atçıl, M. Zahit. "State and Government in the Mid-Sixteenth Century Ottoman Empire: The Grand Vizierates of Rüstem Pasha (1544-1561)." PhD diss., University of Chicago, 2015.

_____. "Why Did Sultan Süleyman Execute His Son Şehzade Mustafa in 1553?" *Osmanlı Araştırmaları/The Journal of Ottoman Studies* 48 (2016): 67–103.

_____. "Warfare as a Tool of Diplomacy: Background of the First Ottoman-Safavid Treaty in 1555." *Turkish Historical Review* 10, no. 1 (June 2019): 3–24.

Aubin, Jean. "L'avènement des safavides reconsidéré." *Moyen Orient & Océan Indien* 5 (1988): 1–130.

_____. "La politique impériale de Selim Ier." *Res Orientales* 6 (1994): 197–216.

Bacqué-Grammont, Jean-Louis. *Les Ottomans, les Safavides et leurs voisins: contribution à l'histoire des relations internationales dans l'Orient islamique de 1514 à 1524.* Istanbul: Nederlands Historisch-Archaeologisch Instituut te Istanbul, 1987.

_____. "The Eastern Policy of Süleymân the Magnificent, 1520-33." In *Süleymân the Second and His Time*, edited by Halil İnalcık and Cemal Kafadar, 249–58. Istanbul: Isis Press, 1993.

Baltacıoğlu-Brammer, Ayşe. "One Word, Many Implications: The Term 'Kızılbaş' in the Early Modern Ottoman Context." In *Ottoman Sunnism: New Perspectives*, edited by Vefa Erginbaş, 47–70. Edinburgh: Edinburgh University Press, 2019.

_____. "Neither Victim Nor Accomplice: The Kızılbaş as Borderland Actors in the Early Modern Ottoman Realm." In *Historicizing Sunni Islam in the Ottoman Empire, c.1450-c.1750*, edited by Tijana Krstić and Derin Terzioğlu, 423–50. Leiden: Brill, 2021.

Banister, Mustafa. "The Abbasid Caliphate of Cairo (1261-1517): History and Tradition in the Mamluk Court." PhD diss., University of Chicago, 2015.

Barkan, Ömer Lütfi. "H. 933-934 (M. 1527-1528) Malî Yılına Ait Bir Bütçe Örneği." *İstanbul Üniversitesi İktisat Fakültesi Mecmuası* 15, nos. 1–4 (1953): 251–329.

_____. "Essai sur les données statistiques des registres de recensement dans l'empire ottoman au XVe et XVIe siècles." *Journal of the Economic and Social History of the Orient* 1, no. 1 (1957): 9–36.

_____. "954-955 (1547-1548) Mali Yılına Ait Bir Osmanlı Bütçesi." *İstanbul Üniversitesi İktisat Fakültesi Mecmuası* 19, nos. 1–4 (1957): 219–76.

Beldiceanu, Nicoara. *Le timar dans l'État ottoman (début XIVe-début XVIe siècle).* Wiesbaden: Otto Harrassowitz, 1980.

Beldiceanu-Steinherr, Irène. "Analyse de la titulature d'Orḥan sur deux inscriptions de Brousse." *Turcica* 34 (2002): 223–40.

Bentley, Jerry H., Sanjay Subrahmanyam, and Merry Wiesner-Hanks, eds. *The Cambridge World History.* Vol. 6, *The Construction of a Global World, 1400-1800 CE.* 2 volumes. Cambridge: Cambridge University Press, 2015.

Bercé, Yves-Marie. *History of Peasant Revolts: The Social Origins of Rebellion in Early Modern France.* Translated by Amanda Whitmore. Ithaca, NY: Cornell University Press, 1990.

Bilge, Mustafa. *İlk Osmanlı Medreseleri*. Istanbul: Edebiyat Fakültesi Basımevi, 1984.

Binbaş, İlker Evrim. "Oguz Khan Narratives." *Encyclopædia Iranica* (https://www. iranicaonline.org/articles/oguz-khan-narratives), last updated April 15, 2010.

Bisaha, Nancy. *Creating East and West: Renaissance Humanists and the Ottoman Turks*. Philadelphia: University of Pennsylvania Press, 2004.

Bonney, Richard. *The European Dynastic States 1494-1660*. Oxford: Oxford University Press, 1991.

Boone, Rebecca Ard. *Mercurino di Gattinara and the Creation of the Spanish Empire*. London: Pickering and Chatto, 2014.

Bosbach, Franz. "Imperium Turcorum oder Christianorum Monarchia – Die Osmanen in der heilsgeschichtlichen Deutung Mercurino Gattinaras." In *Das Osmanische Reich und die Habsburgermonarchie*, edited by Marlene Kurz, Martin Scheutz, Karl Vocelka, and Thomas Winkelbauer, 167–80. Vienna: R. Oldenbourg, 2005.

Bostan, M. Hanefi. *XV–XVI. Asırlarda Trabzon Sancağında Sosyal ve İktisadi Hayat*. Ankara: Türk Tarih Kurumu, 2002.

———. "Yavuz Sultan Selim'in Şehzâdelik Dönemi (1487-1512)." *Türk Kültürü İncelemeleri Dergisi* 40 (Spring 2019): 1–86.

Börekçi, Günhan. "The Memory of Szigetvár and Sultan Süleyman in Ottoman/ Turkish Culture." In *The Battle for Central Europe: The Siege of Szigetvár and the Death of Süleyman the Magnificent and Nicholas Zrínyi (1566)*, edited by Pál Fodor, 523–38. Leiden: Brill, 2019.

Brack, Jonathan. "A Mongol Mahdi in Medieval Anatolia: Rebellion, Reform, and Divine Right in the Post-Mongol Islamic World." *Journal of the American Oriental Society* 139, no. 3 (2019): 611–29.

Bridge, Antony. *Suleiman the Magnificent, Scourge of Heaven*. London and New York: Granada, 1983.

Brummett, Palmira. "The Overrated Adversary: Rhodes and Ottoman Naval Power." *The Historical Journal* 36, no. 3 (1993): 517–41.

Bryer, Anthony, and David Winfield. *The Byzantine Monuments and Topography of the Pontos*. 2 volumes. Washington, DC: Dumbarton Oaks Research Library and Collection, 1985.

Buzov, Snjezana. "The Lawgiver and His Lawmakers: The Role of Legal Discourse in the Formation of Ottoman Imperial Culture." PhD diss., University of Chicago, 2005.

Carney, Josh. "A Dizi-ying Past: *Magnificent Century* and the Motivated Uses of History in Contemporary Turkey." PhD diss., Indiana University, 2015.

Casale, Giancarlo. *The Ottoman Age of Exploration*. New York: Oxford University Press, 2010.

Chebel, Malek. *Histoire de la circoncision, des origines à nos jours*. Paris: Éditions Balland, 1992.

Clot, André. *Suleiman the Magnificent*. New York: New Amsterdam, 1992.

Colding Smith, Charlotte. *Images of Islam, 1453-1600: Turks in Germany and Central Europe*. London: Pickering & Chatto, 2014.

Copeman, W. S. "Historical Aspects of Gout." *Clinical Orthopaedics and Related Research* 71 (July-August 1970): 14–22.

Creswell, Tim. *Place: An Introduction.* Second edition. Malden, MA: Wiley Blackwell, 2015.

Crouzet, Denis. *Charles V: empereur d'une fin des temps.* Paris: Odile Jacob, 2016.

Csirkés, Ferenc. "Turkish/Turkic Books of Poetry, Turkish and Persian Lexicography: The Politics of Language Under Bayezid II." In *Treasures of Knowledge: An Inventory of the Ottoman Palace Library (1502/3-1503/4).* Vol. 1, *Essays*, edited by Gülru Necipoğlu, Cemal Kafadar and Cornell H. Fleischer, 673–734. Leiden: Brill, 2019.

Czygan, Christiane. "Depicting Imperial Love: Songs and Letters between Sultan Süleyman (Muhibbî) and Hürrem." In *Kanûnî Sultan Süleyman ve Dönemi: Yeni Kaynaklar, Yeni Yaklaşımlar / Suleyman the Lawgiver and His Reign: New Sources, New Approaches*, edited by M. Fatih Çalışır, Suraiya Faroqhi, M. Şakir Yılmaz, 247–65. Istanbul: İbn Haldun Üniversitesi Yayınları, 2020.

Çağaptay, Suna. *The First Capital of the Ottoman Empire: The Religious, Architectural, and Social History of Bursa.* London: I.B. Tauris, 2021.

Çelik, Serpil. "Mevcut Belgeler Işığında Süleymaniye Külliyesinin Yapım Süreci." PhD diss., Istanbul Technical University, 2001.

Çıpa, H. Erdem. *The Making of Selim: Succession, Legitimacy, and Memory in the Early Modern Ottoman World.* Bloomington: Indiana University Press, 2017.

Çolak, Ahmet. "Bahârî, Fetihnâme-yi Üngürüs Adlı Eseri ve Bu Eserden Hareketle Macaristan Fethinin Edebi-Tarihi Üslupla Anlatılışı." *Turkish Studies: International Periodical for the Languages, Literature and History of Turkish or Turkic* 10, no. 4 (Winter 2015): 373–408.

Çulpan, Cevdet. "'İstanbul Süleymaniye Camii Kitabesi." In *Kanunî Armağanı*, edited by Uluğ İğdemir, 291–99. Ankara: Türk Tarih Kurumu, 1970.

Dağlı, Murat. "The Limits of Ottoman Pragmatism." *History and Theory* 52 (May 2013): 194–213.

Darling, Linda T. *Revenue-Raising and Legitimacy: Tax Collection and Finance Administration in the Ottoman Empire, 1560–1660.* Leiden: Brill, 1996.

———. "Rethinking Europe and the Islamic World in the Age of Exploration." *Journal of Early Modern History* 2, no. 3 (1998): 221–46.

———. "Contested Territory: Ottoman Holy War in Comparative Context." *Studia Islamica* 91 (2000): 133–63.

———. *A History of Social Justice and Political Power in the Middle East: The Circle of Justice from Mesopotamia to Globalization.* New York: Routledge, 2013.

———. "Historicizing the Ottoman *Timar* System: Identities of *Timar*-Holders, Fourteenth to Seventeenth Centuries." *Turkish Historical Review* 8, no. 2 (2017): 145–73.

Darwin, John. *After Tamerlane: The Global History of Empire since 1405.* London: Allen Lane, 2007.

Dehqan, Mostafa and Vural Genç. "Kurds as Spies: Information-Gathering on the 16ᵗʰ-Century Ottoman-Safavid Frontier." *Acta Orientalia Academiae Scientiarum Hungaricae* 71, no. 2 (2018): 197–230.

Dumas, Juliette. "Des esclaves pour époux. . . Stratégies matrimoniales dans la dynastie ottoman (mi-XIVe- début XVIe siècle)." *Clio. Femmes, Genre, Histoire* 34 (2011): 255–75.

Eisenbichler, Konrad. "Charles V in Bologna: The Self-Fashioning of a Man and a City." *Renaissance Studies* 13, no. 4 (December 1999): 430–39.

Elliott, John. "Ottoman-Habsburg Rivalry: The European Perspective." In *Süleymân the Second and His Time*, 153–62.

Emecen, Feridun M. "Saruhanoğulları." *TDVİA*. Vol. 36, 170–73.

_____. *XVI. Asırda Manisa Kazâsı*. Ankara: Türk Tarih Kurumu, 1989.

_____. *İlk Osmanlılar ve Anadolu Beylikler Dünyası*. Istanbul: Kitabevi, 2001.

_____. "'Büyük Türk'e Pannonia Düzlüklerini Açan Savaş Mohaç 1526.'" In *Muhteşem Süleyman*, ed. Özlem Kumrular, 60–80. Istanbul: Kitap, 2007.

_____. "'İhtilalci Bir Mehdilik' Hareketi mi? Şahkulu Baba Tekeli İsyanı Üzerine Yeni Yaklaşımlar." In *Ötekilerin Peşinde: Ahmet Yaşar Ocak'a Armağan*, edited by Mehmet Öz and Fatih Yeşil, 521–34. Istanbul: Timaş, 2015.

_____. *Yavuz Sultan Selim*. Revised edition. Istanbul: Kapı, 2016.

_____. "Osmanlı Şehzadeleri ve Taşra İdaresi." Reprinted in Emecen, *Osmanlı Klasik Çağında Hanedan Devlet ve Toplum*, 63–84. Istanbul: Kapı Yayınları, 2018.

_____. "Kanuni Sultan Süleyman'ın Şehzadelik Dönemine Ait Bazı Yeni Tespitler ve Notlar." Reprinted in Emecen, *Osmanlı Klasik Çağında Hilafet ve Saltanat*, 177–95. Istanbul: Kapı Yayınları, 2020.

_____. "Sultan Süleyman ve Hilâfet: 1524." In *Kanûnî Sultan Süleyman ve Dönemi: Yeni Kaynaklar, Yeni Yaklaşımlar / Suleyman the Lawgiver and His Reign: New Sources, New Approaches*, 45–57.

Emiralioğlu, M. Pınar. *Geographical Knowledge and Imperial Culture in the Early Modern Ottoman Empire*. Burlington, VT: Ashgate, 2014.

Emon, Anver M. *Religious Pluralism and Islamic Law: Dhimmis and Others in the Empire of Law*. Oxford: Oxford University Press, 2012.

Emre, Side. "Anatomy of a Rebellion in Sixteenth-Century Egypt: A Case-Study of Ahmed Pasha's Governorship, Revolt, and a Critique of the Ottoman Imperial Enterprise in the Arab Lands." *Journal of Ottoman Studies* 46 (2015): 333–85.

Engel, Pál. *The Realm of St. Stephen: A History of Medieval Hungary, 895-1526*. Translated by Tamás Pálosfalvi. London: I.B. Tauris, 2001.

Ergin, Nina. "The Soundscape of Sixteenth-Century Istanbul Mosques: Architecture and Qur'an Recital." *Journal of the Society of Architectural Historians* 67, no. 2 (2008): 204–21.

Eroğlu, Haldun. *Osmanlı Devletinde Şehzadelik Kurumu*. Ankara: Akçağ, 2004.

Ertuğrul, Özkan. "Gülbahar Hatun Camii ve Türbesi." *TDVİA*. Vol. 14, 231–32.

Eryılmaz Arenas-Vives, Fatma Sinem. "The *Shehnameci*s of Sultan Süleyman: 'Arif and Eflatun and Their Dynastic Project." PhD diss., University of Chicago, 2010.

———. "The *Sulaiman-nama (Süleyman-name)* as a Historical Source." In *Shahnama Studies III: The Reception of the* Shahnama, edited by Gabrielle van den Berg and Charles Melville, 173–98. Leiden: Brill, 2018.

Fetvacı, Emine. "The Office of the Ottoman Court Historian." In *Studies on Istanbul and Beyond*, ed. Robert G. Ousterhout, 7–21. Philadelphia: University of Pennsylvania Museum of Archaeology and Anthropology, 2007.

———. *Picturing History at the Ottoman Court*. Bloomington: Indiana University Press, 2013.

Fichtner, Paula Sutter. *Ferdinand I of Austria: The Politics of Dynasticism in the Age of the Reformation*. Boulder, CO: East European Monographs, 1982.

Findley, Carter Vaughn. *Enlightening Europe on Islam and the Ottomans: Mouradgea d'Ohsson and His Masterpiece*. Leiden: Brill, 2019.

Finkel, Caroline. *Osman's Dream: The Story of the Ottoman Empire, 1300-1923*. New York: Basic Books, 2007.

Finlay, Robert. "Prophecy and Politics in Istanbul: Charles V, Sultan Süleyman, and the Habsburg Embassy of 1533–1534." *Journal of Early Modern History* 2, no. 1 (1998): 1–31.

———. "'I Am the Servant of the Turkish Sultan:' Venice, the Ottoman Empire, and Christendom, 1523–1534." Chapter 10 in Finlay, *Venice Besieged: Politics and Diplomacy during the Italian Wars, 1494–1534*. Aldershot: Ashgate Variorum, 2008.

Fischer-Galati, Stephen A. *Ottoman Imperialism and German Protestantism, 1521–1555*. Cambridge, MA: Harvard University Press, 1959.

Fleet, Kate. "Ottoman Expansion in the Mediterranean." In *The Cambridge History of Turkey*. Vol. 2, *The Ottoman Empire as a World Power, 1453–1603*, edited by Suraiya N. Faroqhi and Kate Fleet, 141–72. Cambridge: Cambridge University Press, 2009.

——— and Ebru Boyar. *A Social History of Ottoman Istanbul*. Cambridge: Cambridge University Press, 2010.

Fleischer, Cornell H. *Bureaucrat and Intellectual in the Ottoman Empire: The Historian Mustafa Âli (1541-1600)*. Princeton, NJ: Princeton University Press, 1986.

———. "The Lawgiver as Messiah: The Making of the Imperial Image in the Reign of Süleymân." In *Soliman le magnifique et son temps*, ed. Gilles Veinstein, 159–77. Paris: La Documentation Française, 1992.

———. "Seer to the Sultan: Haydar-i Remmal and Sultan Süleyman." In *Cultural Horizons*. Vol. 1, *A Festschrift in Honor of Talat S. Halman*, edited by Jayne L. Warner, 290–304. Syracuse, NY: Syracuse University Press, 2001.

———. "Shadows of Shadows: Prophecy and Politics in 1530s Istanbul." *International Journal of Turkish Studies* 13, nos. 1–2 (2007): 51–62.

———. "A Mediterranean Apocalypse: Prophecies of Empire in the Fifteenth and Sixteenth Centuries." *Journal of the Social and Economic History of the Orient* 61, nos. 1-2 (2018): 18–90.

_____ and Kaya Şahin. "On the Works of a Historical Nature in the Bayezid II Library Inventory" and "List of Entries." In *Treasures of Knowledge*, vol. 1, 569–96.

_____ and Kaya Şahin. "The Trial of a Heretic, 1527." In *The Ottoman World: A Cultural History Reader, 1450-1700*, edited by Hakan T. Karateke and Helga Anetshofer, 61–65. Oakland: University of California Press, 2021.

Flemming, Barbara. "Sāhib-kırān und Mahdī: Türkische Endzeiterwartungen im ersten Jahrzehnt der Regierung Süleymāns." In *Between the Danube and the Caucasus*, edited by György Kara, 43–62. Budapest: Akadémiai Kiadó, 1987.

_____. "Public Opinion under Sultan Süleymân." In *Süleymân the Second and His Time*, 59–67.

Fletcher, Joseph. "Turco-Mongolian Monarchic Tradition in the Ottoman Empire." *Harvard Ukrainian Studies* 3–4 (1979–1980): 236–51.

Fodor, Pál. "Ottoman Policy Towards Hungary, 1520-1541." *Acta Orientalia Academiae Scientiarum Hungaricae* 45, nos. 2–3 (1991): 285–91.

_____. "The View of the Turk in Hungary: The Apocalyptic Tradition and the Legend of the Red Apple in Ottoman-Hungarian Context." In *Les traditions apocalyptiques au tournant de la chute de Constantinople*, edited by Benjamin Lellouch and Stéphane Yerasimos, 99–131. Paris: Harmattan; Istanbul: Institut français d'études anatoliennes Georges-Dumézil, 2000.

_____. "Ottoman Warfare, 1300-1453." In *The Cambridge History of Turkey*. Vol. 1, *Byzantium to Turkey, 1071-1453*, edited by Kate Fleet, 192–226. Cambridge: Cambridge University Press, 2009.

Francisco, Adam S. *Martin Luther and Islam: A Study in Sixteenth-Century Polemics and Apologetics*. Leiden: Brill, 2007.

Freamon, Bernard K. *Possessed by the Right Hand: The Problem of Slavery in Islamic Law and Muslim Cultures*. Leiden: Brill, 2019.

Gara, Eleni. "Conceptualizing Interreligious Relations in the Ottoman Empire: The Early Modern Centuries." *Acta Poloniae Historica* 116 (2017): 57–91.

Genç, Vural. "Kanuni Sultan Süleyman'ın Nikris Hastalığına Atfedilen Farsça Bir Reçete." *Belleten* 80, no. 287 (April 2016): 41–58.

_____. "16. Yüzyılın İlk Yarısında Osmanlılar ile Safeviler Arasında Yaşanan Dini ve Siyasi Polemikler." *Osmanlı Araştırmaları / The Journal of Ottoman Studies* 57 (2021): 81–130.

Gibb, E. J. W. *A History of Ottoman Poetry*. Vol. 3. Edited by Edward G. Browne. London: Luzac & Co., 1904.

Giladi, Avner. *Children of Islam: Concepts of Childhood in Medieval Muslim Society*. Houndmills, Basingstoke, Hampshire: Palgrave Macmillan, 1992.

Glick, Leonard B. *Marked in Your Flesh: Circumcision from Ancient Judea to Modern America*. New York: Oxford University Press, 2005.

Gordon, Matthew S., and Kathryn A. Hain, eds. *Concubines and Courtesans: Women and Slavery in Islamic History*. New York: Oxford University Press, 2017.

Gök, İlhan. "Atatürk Kitaplığı M.C. O.71 Numaralı 909-933/1503-1527 Tarihli İn'âmât Defteri (Transkripsiyon-Değerlendirme)." PhD diss., Marmara University, 2014.

Gökbilgin, M. Tayyib. "Rüstem Paşa ve Hakkındaki İthamlar." *Tarih Dergisi* 8, nos. 11-12 (1956): 11–50.

———. "Arz ve Raporlarına Göre İbrahim Paşa'nın Irakeyn Seferindeki İlk Tedbirleri ve Fütuhatı." *Belleten* 21, no. 83 (1957): 449–82.

———. "Kanunî Sultan Süleyman'ın Macaristan ve Avrupa Siyasetinin Sebep ve Âmilleri, Geçirdiği Safhalar." In *Kanunî Armağanı*, 5–39.

Göllner, Carl. *Turcica: Die Europäische Türkendrucke des XVI. Jahrhunderts.* 3 volumes. Bucharest: Editura Academiei R.P.R., 1961–78.

Grillon, Pierre. "La croisière du Baron de Saint-Blancard (1537-1538)." *Revue d'histoire moderne et contemporaine* 15 (1968): 624–62.

Griswold, William J. *The Great Anatolian Rebellion, 1000-1020/1591-1611.* Berlin: Klaus Schwarz, 1983.

Gürkan, Emrah Safa. "The Centre and the Frontier: Ottoman Cooperation with the North African Corsairs in the Sixteenth Century." *Turkish Historical Review* 1 (2010): 125–63.

———. "Bir Diplomasi Merkezi Olarak Yeni Çağ İstanbul'u." In *Antik Çağ'dan 21. Yüzyıla Büyük İstanbul Tarihi.* Vol. 2, *Siyaset ve Yönetim I*, edited by Feridun M. Emecen and Coşkun Yılmaz, 372–99. Istanbul: İstanbul Büyükşehir Belediyesi Kültür AŞ.; Türkiye Diyanet Vakfı İslâm Araştırmaları Merkezi, 2015.

Hagen, Gottfried. "Legitimacy and World Order." In *Legitimizing the Order: The Ottoman Rhetoric of State Power*, edited byHakan Karateke and Maurus Reinkowski, 55–83. Leiden: Brill, 2005.

———. "The Order of Knowledge, the Knowledge of Order: Intellectual Life." In *The Cambridge History of Turkey.* Vol. 2, 407–56.

Har-El, Shai. *Struggle for Domination in the Middle East: The Ottoman-Mamluk War, 1485-1491.* Leiden: Brill, 1995.

Havlioğlu, Didem Z. *Mihrî Hatun: Performance, Gender-Bending, and Subversion in Ottoman Intellectual History.* Syracuse, NY: Syracuse University Press, 2017.

Headley, John M. *The Emperor and His Chancellor: A Study of the Imperial Chancellery under Gattinara.* Cambridge: Cambridge University Press, 1983.

Hess, Andrew C. "The Ottoman Conquest of Egypt (1517) and the Beginning of the Sixteenth-Century World War." *International Journal of Middle East Studies* 4, no. 1 (January 1973): 55–76.

———. *The Forgotten Frontier: A History of the Sixteenth-Century Ibero-African Frontier.* Chicago: University of Chicago Press, 1978.

Hirschler, Konrad. *The Written Word in the Medieval Arabic Lands: A Social and Cultural History of Reading Practices.* Edinburgh: Edinburgh University Press, 2012.

Horn, Hendrick J. *Jan Cornelisz Vermeyen, Painter of Charles V and His Conquest of Tunis: Paintings, Etchings, Drawings, Cartoons & Tapestries.* 2 volumes. Doornspijk: Davaco, 1989.

Horuluoğlu, Şâmil. *Trabzon ve Çevresinin Tarihi Eserleri.* Ankara: Er Ofset Matbaacılık, 1983.

Howard, Douglas. "The Historical Development of the Ottoman Imperial Registry (Defter-i Hakanî): mid-Fifteenth to mid-Seventeenth Centuries." *Archivum Ottomanicum* 11 (1986): 213–30.

Hupchick, Dennis P. *The Balkans: From Constantinople to Communism.* New York: Palgrave Macmillan, 2004.

Imber, Colin. "The Ottoman Dynastic Myth." *Turcica* 19 (1987): 7–27.

_____. "The Legend of Osman Gazi." In *The Ottoman Emirate (1300-1389)*, edited by Elizabeth Zachariadou, 67–75. Rethymnon: Crete University Press, 1993.

_____. *Ebu's-su'ud: The Islamic Legal Tradition.* Stanford, CA: Stanford University Press, 1997.

_____. *The Ottoman Empire, 1300-1650: The Structure of Power.* Third edition. London: Red Globe Press, 2019.

İnalcık, Halil. "Ottoman Methods of Conquest." *Studia Islamica* 2 (1954): 103–29.

_____. "The Question of the Emergence of the Ottoman State." *International Journal of Turkish Studies* 2 (1980): 71–79.

_____. "Turkish Settlement and Christian Reaction, 1329-1361"; "Ottoman Conquests and the Crusade, 1361-1421"; "The Struggle for the Balkans, 1421-1451"; "The Ottomans, the Crusade, and Renaissance Diplomacy, 1481-1522." In *A History of the Crusades*, edited by Kenneth M. Setton. Vol. 6, *The Impact of the Crusades on Europe*, edited by Harry W. Hazard and Norman P. Zacour, 222–38, 239–54, 254–75, 331–53. Madison: University of Wisconsin Press, 1989.

_____. "The Ottoman Succession and Its Relation to the Turkish Concept of Sovereignty." In İnalcık, *The Middle East and the Balkans under the Ottoman Empire: Essays on Economy and Society*, 37–69. Bloomington: Indiana University Turkish Studies, 1993.

_____. "State and Ideology under Sultan Süleyman I." In *The Middle East and the Balkans under the Ottoman Empire: Essays on Economy and Society*, 70–94.

_____. *1300-1600*. Vol. 1 of *An Economic and Social History of the Ottoman Empire*, edited by Halil İnalcık and Donald Quataert. Cambridge: Cambridge University Press, 1994.

_____. "State, Sovereignty and Law under the Reign of Süleymân." In *Süleymân the Second and His Time*, 59–67.

_____. "Harem Bir Fuhuş Yuvası Değil, Bir Okuldu." Preface to M. Çağatay Uluçay, *Osmanlı Sultanlarına Aşk Mektupları*, 7–15. Istanbul: Ufuk Yayınları, 2001.

_____. *Şâir ve Patron: Patrimonyal Devlet ve Sanat Üzerinde Sosyolojik Bir İnceleme.* Ankara: Doğu Batı, 2003.

İnan, Murat Umut. "Rethinking the Ottoman Imitation of Persian Poetry." *Iranian Studies* 50, no. 5 (2017): 671–89.

_____. "Imperial Ambitions, Mystical Aspirations: Persian Learning in the Ottoman World." In *The Persianate World: The Frontiers of a Eurasian Lingua Franca*, ed. Nile Green, 75–92. Berkeley: University of California Press, 2019.

İpşirli, Mehmet. "Lutfi Paşa." *TDVİA*. Vol. 27, 234–36.

Isom-Verhaaren, Christine. *Allies with the Infidel: The Ottoman and French Alliance in the Sixteenth Century.* London: I.B. Tauris, 2011.

Ivanics, Mária, "The Military Co-operation of the Crimean Khanate with the Ottoman Empire in the Sixteenth and Seventeenth Centuries." In *The European Tributary States of the Ottoman Empire in the Sixteenth and Seventeenth Centuries,* edited by Gábor Kármán and Lovro Kunčević, 43–65. Leiden: Brill, 2013.

Janssens, Émile. *Trébizonde en Colchide.* Brussels: Presses universitaires de Bruxelles, 1969.

Jensen, De Lamar. "The Ottoman Turks in Sixteenth Century French Diplomacy." *Sixteenth Century Journal* 16, no. 4 (Winter 1985): 451–70.

Johnson, Carina L. *Cultural Hierarchy in Sixteenth-Century Europe: The Ottomans and Mexicans.* Cambridge: Cambridge University Press, 2011.

Kafadar, Cemal. *Between Two Worlds: The Construction of the Ottoman State.* Berkeley: University of California Press, 1995.

———. "The Myth of the Golden Age: Ottoman Historical Consciousness in the Post-Süleymânic Era." In *Süleymân the Second and His Time,* 37–48.

———. "A Rome of One's Own: Reflections on Cultural Geography and Identity in the Lands of Rum." *Muqarnas* 24 (2007): 7–25.

Kafescioğlu, Çiğdem. *Constantinopolis/Istanbul: Cultural Encounter, Imperial Vision, and the Construction of the Ottoman Capital.* University Park: Pennsylvania State University Press, 2009.

Karal, Enver Ziya. "Yavuz Sultan Selim'in Oğlu Şehzade Süleyman'a Manisa Sancağını İdare Etmesi İçin Gönderdiği Siyasetnâme." *Belleten* 6, nos. 21–22 (January-April 1942): 37–44.

Karateke, Hakan T. "Legitimizing the Ottoman Sultanate: A Framework for Historical Analysis." In *Legitimizing the Order,* 13–52.

Kaya, İ. Güven. "Figânî'nin Ölümü ve Taşlıcalı Yahya Bey'in Bir Şiiri." *Atatürk Üniversitesi Türkiyat Araştırmaları Enstitüsü Dergisi* 34 (2007): 47–62.

Kazan, Hilal. *XVI. Asırda Sarayın Sanatı Himayesi.* Istanbul: İSAR Vakfı, 2010.

Kelenik, József. "The Sieges of Szigetvár and Gyula, 1566." In *The Battle for Central Europe,* 399–410.

Khafipour, Hani, ed. *The Empires of Near East and India: Source Studies of the Ottoman, Mughal, and Safavid Literate Communities.* New York: Columbia University Press, 2019.

Kiel, Machiel. "The Incorporation of the Balkans into the Ottoman Empire, 1353-1453." In *The Cambridge History of Turkey.* Vol. 1, 138–91.

Kim, Sooyong. *The Last of an Age: The Making and Unmaking of a Sixteenth-Century Ottoman Poet.* London: Routledge, 2018.

———. "An Ottoman Order of Persian Verse." In *Treasures of Knowledge.* Vol. 1, 635–56.

Köksal, Asım Cüneyd. "Bir İslam Âlimi olarak Lutfi Paşa." *Journal of Ottoman Studies* 50 (2017): 29–72.

Kołodziejczyk, Dariusz. *Ottoman-Polish Diplomatic Relations (15th–18th Century): An Annotated Edition of 'Ahdnames and Other Documents.* Leiden: Brill, 2000.

Konyalı, İbrahim Hakkı. "Kanunî Sultan Süleyman'ın Annesi Hafsa Sultan'ın Vakfiyesi ve Manisa'daki Hayır Eserleri." *Vakıflar Dergisi* 8 (1969): 47–56.

Królikowska, Natalia. "Sovereignty and Subordination in Ottoman-Crimean Relations (Sixteenth-Eighteenth Centuries)." In *The European Tributary States of the Ottoman Empire in the Sixteenth and Seventeenth Centuries*, 275–99.

Kortepeter, Carl M. "Ottoman Imperial Policy and the Economy of the Black Sea Region in the Sixteenth Century." *Journal of the American Oriental Society* 86, no. 2 (1966): 86–113.

Kubinyi, András. "The Battle of Szávaszentdemeter-Nagyolazsi (1523): Ottoman Advance and Hungarian Defence on the Eve of Mohács." In *Ottomans, Hungarians, and Habsburgs in Central Europe: The Military Confines in the Era of Ottoman Conquest*, edited by Géza Dávid and Pál Fodor, 71–115. Leiden: Brill, 2000.

Kumrular, Özlem. "Campaña de Alemania: Rito, arte y demostración." In *L'Empire ottoman dans l'Europe de la Renaissance / El Imperio Otomano en la Europa renacentista*, eds. Alain Servantie and Ramón Puig de la Bellacasa, 191–214. Leuven: Leuven University Press, 2005.

———. *El Duelo entre Carlos V y Solimán el Magnífico (1520-1535)*. Istanbul: Editorial Isis, 2005.

Kunt, İ. Metin. *The Sultan's Servants: The Transformation of Ottoman Provincial Government, 1550-1650*. New York: Columbia University Press, 1983.

———. "Ottoman Names and Ottoman Ages." *Journal of Turkish Studies* 10 (1986): 229–34.

———. "The Rise of the Ottomans." In *The New Cambridge Medieval History*. Vol. 6, *c. 1300-c. 1415*, edited by Michael Jones, 839–63. Cambridge: Cambridge University Press, 2000.

———. "A Prince Goes Forth (Perchance to Return)." In *Identity and Identity Formation in the Ottoman World: A Volume of Essays in Honor of Norman Itzkowitz*, edited by Baki Tezcan and Karl K. Barbir, 63–71. Madison: University of Wisconsin Press, 2007.

———. "Royal and Other Households." In *The Ottoman World*, edited by Christine Woodhead, 103–15. London: Routledge, 2012.

——— and Zeynep Yelçe. "Divân-ı Hümâyûn: le Conseil imperial ottoman et ses conseillers (1450-1580)." In *Conseils et conseillers dans l'Europe de la Renaissance (v. 1450-v.1550)*, edited by Cédric Michon, 309–31. Tours: Presses universitaires de Rennes, Presses universitaires François Rabelais, 2012.

Kürkçüoğlu, Kemal Edib. *Süleymaniye Vakfiyesi*. Ankara: Vakıflar Umum Müdürlüğü, 1962.

Kuru, Selim S. "The Literature of Rum: The Making of a Literary Tradition (1450–1600)." In *The Cambridge History of Turkey*. Vol. 2, 548–92.

Kütükoğlu, Bekir. "Ayas Paşa." *TDVİA*. Vol. 4, 202–3.

Lamb, Harold. *Suleiman the Magnificent, Sultan of the East*. Garden City, NY: Doubleday, 1951.

Lellouch, Benjamin. "La politique mamelouke de Selīm Ier." In *Conquête ottomane de l'Égypte (1517): Arrière-plan, impact, échos,* edited by Benjamin Lellouch and Nicholas Michel, 165–210. Leiden: Brill, 2013.

———. "Hain Ahmed Pasha (m. 1524) et sa famille." *Turcica* 52 (2021): 63–102.

Lestringant, Frank. "Guillaume Postel et l'"obsession turque."" Reprinted in *Écrire le monde à la Renaissance: Quinze études sur Rabelais, Postel, Bodin et la littérature géographique,* 189–224. Caen: Paradigme, 1993.

Lindner, Rudi Paul. "Anatolia, 1300-1451." In *The Cambridge History of Turkey.* Vol. 1, 102–37.

Lowry, Heath W. "From Trabzon to Istanbul: The Relationship between Süleyman the Lawgiver and His Foster Brother (*Süt Karındaşı*) Yahya Efendi." *Osmanlı Araştırmaları* 10 (1990): 39–48

———. "Süleymân's Formative Years in the City of Trabzon: Their Impact on the Future Sultan and the City." In *Süleymân the Second and His Time,* 29–44.

———. *The Islamization and Turkification of the City of Trabzon (Trebizond), 1461-1583.* Istanbul: Isis Press, 2009.

Luttrell, Anthony. "The Hospitallers at Rhodes, 1306–1421." In *A History of the Crusades.* Vol. 3, *The Fourteenth and Fifteenth Centuries,* edited by Harry W. Hazard, 278–313. Madison: University of Wisconsin Press, 1975.

Malcolm, Noel. *Useful Enemies: Islam and the Ottoman Empire in Western Political Thought, 1450-1750.* Oxford: Oxford University Press, 2019.

Mango, Cyril A., and Ahmet Ertuğ. *Hagia Sophia.* [Istanbul]: Ertuğ & Kocabıyık, 1987.

Mansel, Philip. "The French Renaissance in Search of the Ottoman Empire." In *Re-Orienting the Renaissance: Cultural Exchanges with the East,* edited by Gerard MacLean, 96–107. Houndmills, Basingstoke, Hampshire: Palgrave Macmillan, 2005.

Mantran, Robert. *Istanbul au siècle de Soliman le Magnifique.* Second updated edition. Paris: Hachette, 1994.

Manz, Beatrice Forbes. *The Rise and Rule of Tamerlane.* Cambridge: Cambridge University Press, 1999.

Markiewicz, Christopher. *The Crisis of Kingship in Late Medieval Islam: Persian Emigres and the Making of Ottoman Sovereignty.* Cambridge: Cambridge University Press, 2019.

——— and Tracey A. Sowerby. "Languages of Diplomatic Gift-Giving at the Ottoman Court." In *Diplomatic Cultures at the Ottoman Court, c.1500-1630,* edited by Sowerby and Markiewicz, 53–84. New York: Routledge, 2021.

Marsham, Andrew. *Rituals of Islamic Monarchy: Accession and Succession.* Edinburgh: Edinburgh University Press, 2009.

Matthee, Rudi. "Unwalled Cities and Restless Nomads: Firearms and Artillery in Safavid Iran." In *Safavid Persia: The History and Politics of an Islamic Society,* edited by Charles Melville, 389–416. London: I.B. Tauris, 1996.

Mattingly, Garrett. *Renaissance Diplomacy.* London: Jonathan Cape, 1955.

Mazzaoui, Michel M. *The Origins of the Ṣafawids; Šīʿism, Ṣūfism, and the Ġulāt.* Wiesbaden: F. Steiner, 1972.

Merle, Alexandra. "L'Empereur et le Tyran: La lutte contre le pouvoir ottoman selon Juan Ginés de Sepúlveda." In *Charles Quint et la monarchie universelle*, edited by Annie Molinié-Bertrand and Jean-Paul Duviols, 183–92. Paris: Presses de l'Université Paris-Sorbonne, 2001.

Merriman, Roger Bigelow. *Suleiman the Magnificent, 1520-1566*. Cambridge, MA: Harvard University Press, 1944.

Meshal, Reem. "Antagonistic Sharīʿas and the Construction of Orthodoxy in Sixteenth-Century Ottoman Cairo." *Journal of Islamic Studies* 21, no. 2 (2010): 183–212.

Miller, Gregory J. *The Turks and Islam in Reformation Germany*. New York: Routledge, 2014.

Minkov, Anton. *Conversion to Islam in the Balkans:* Kisve Bahası *Petitions and Ottoman Social Life, 1670-1730*. Leiden: Brill, 2004.

Minorsky, Vladimir. "Shaykh Bālī-efendi on the Safavids." *Bulletin of the School of Oriental and African Studies* 20, nos. 1–3 (1957): 437–50.

Mitchell, Colin P. "The Sword and the Pen: Diplomacy in Early Safavid Iran, 1501–1555." PhD diss., University of Toronto, 2002.

———. *The Practice of Politics in Safavid Iran: Power, Religion and Rhetoric*. London: I.B. Tauris, 2009.

———. "Am I My Brother's Keeper? Negotiating Corporate Sovereignty and Divine Absolutism in Sixteenth-Century Turco-Iranian Politics." In *New Perspectives on Safavid Iran: Empire and Society*, edited by Mitchell, 33–58. New York: Routledge, 2011.

Moin, A. Azfar. *The Millennial Sovereign: Sacred Kingship and Sainthood in Islam*. New York: Columbia University Press.

Morgan, E. Delmar, and C. H. Coote, eds. *Early Voyages to Russia and Persia: Anthony Jenkinson and Other Englishmen*. New York: Burt Franklin, 1886.

Morris, Ian, and Walter Scheidel, eds. *The Dynamics of Ancient Empires: State Power from Assyria to Byzantium*. Oxford: Oxford University Press, 2009.

Murphey, Rhoads. "Provisioning Istanbul: The State and Subsistence in the Early Modern Middle East." *Food and Foodways* 2 (1988): 217–63.

———. "Süleyman's Eastern Policy." In *Süleymân the Second and His Time*, 235–46.

———. "Seyyid Muradî's Prose Biography on Hızır Ibn Yakub, Alias Hayreddin Barbarossa: Ottoman Folk Narrative as an Under-Exploited Source for Historical Reconstruction." *Acta Orientalia Academiae Scientiarum Hungaricae* 54, no. 4 (2001): 519–32.

———. "Süleyman I and the Conquest of Hungary: Ottoman Manifest Destiny or a Delayed Reaction to Charles V's Universalist Vision." *Journal of Early Modern History* 5, no. 3 (2001): 197–221.

———. "Ottoman Expansion, 1451–1556 II. Dynastic Interest and International Power Status." In *Early Modern Military History, 1450–1815*, ed. Geoff Mortimer, 60–80. Houndmills, Basingstoke, Hampshire: Palgrave Macmillan, 2004.

———. *Exploring Ottoman Sovereignty: Tradition, Image and Practice in the Ottoman Imperial Household, 1400-1800*. London: Continuum, 2008.

_____. "Polemic, Panegyric, and Pragmatism in Ottoman Historical Writing during the Early Years of Sultan Suleyman's Reign, 1520-1540." In *Kanûnî Sultan Süleyman ve Dönemi: Yeni Kaynaklar, Yeni Yaklaşımlar / Suleyman the Lawgiver and His Reign: New Sources, New Approaches*, 267–97.

Nasr, Seyyed Hossein, et al., eds. *The Study Quran. A New Translation and Commentary*. New York: HarperOne, 2015.

Necipoğlu, Gülru. "The Süleymaniye Complex: An Interpretation." *Muqarnas* 3 (1985): 92–117.

_____. "Süleymân the Magnificent and the Representation of Power in the Context of Ottoman-Habsburg-Papal Rivalry." *Art Bulletin* 71, no. 3 (1989): 401–427.

_____. *Architecture, Ceremonial and Power: The Topkapi Palace in the Fifteenth and Sixteenth Centuries*. New York: Architectural History Foundation; Cambridge, MA: MIT Press, 1991.

_____. "A Kânûn for the State, a Canon for the Arts: Conceptualizing the Classical Synthesis of Ottoman Arts and Architecture." In *Soliman le magnifique et son temps*, 195–216.

_____. *The Age of Sinan: Architectural Culture in the Ottoman Empire*. London: Reaktion Books, 2005.

_____. "The Dome of the Rock as Palimpsest: 'Abd al-Malik's Grand Narrative and Sultan Süleyman's Glosses." *Muqarnas* 25 (2008): 57–81.

_____. "Visual Cosmopolitanism and Creative Translation: Artistic Conversations with Renaissance Italy in Mehmed II's Constantinople." *Muqarnas* 29 (2012): 1–81.

_____. "The Aesthetics of Empire: Arts, Politics and Commerce in the Construction of Sultan Süleyman's Magnificence." In *The Battle for Central Europe*, 115–59.

Nehring, Karl, ed. *Austro-Turcica 1541–1552. Diplomatische Akten des habsburgischen Gesandtschaftsverkehrs mit der Hohen Pforte im Zeitalter Süleymans des Prächtigen*. Munich: R. Oldenbourg, 1995.

Nicol, Donald M. *The Last Centuries of Byzantium, 1261-1453*. Second edition. Cambridge: Cambridge University Press, 1993.

Norwich, John Julius. *Four Princes: Henry VIII, Francis I, Charles V, Suleiman the Magnificent and the Obsessions That Forged Modern Europe*. London: John Murray, 2016.

Ocak, Ahmet Yaşar. "Social, Cultural and Intellectual Life, 1071–1453." In *The Cambridge History of Turkey*. Vol. 1, 353–422.

Öçal, Şamil. *Kışladan Medreseye: Osmanlı Bilgini Kemalpaşazade'nin Düşünce Dünyası*. Istanbul: İz Yayıncılık, 2013.

Özbaran, Salih. "The Ottoman Turks and the Portuguese in the Persian Gulf 1534–1581." *Journal of Asian History* 6, no. 1 (1972): 45–87.

_____. "Ottoman Naval Policy in the South." In *Süleyman the Magnificent and His Age: The Ottoman Empire in the Early Modern World*, edited by Metin Kunt and Christine Woodhead, 55–70. London: Longman, 1995.

Özcan, Abdülkadir. "Historiography in the Reign of Süleyman the Magnificent." In *The Ottoman Empire in the Reign of Süleyman the Magnificent*. Vol. 2, edited by Tülay

Duran, 165–222. Istanbul: Historical Research Foundation, Istanbul Research Center, 1988.

Öztürk, Yücel. *Osmanlı Hakimiyetinde Kefe (1475–1600)*. Ankara: Kültür Bakanlığı Yayınları, 2000.

Özvar, Erol. "Transformation of the Ottoman Empire into a Military-Fiscal State: Reconsidering the Financing of War from a Global Perspective." In *The Battle for Central Europe*, 21–64.

Pagden, Anthony. *Lords of All the World: Ideologies of Empire in Spain, Britain and France c. 1500–c. 1800*. New Haven, CT: Yale University Press, 1995.

Pala, İskender. "Divan Edebiyatında İstanbul." *TDVİA*. Vol. 23, 284–89.

Pálosfalvi, Tamás. *From Nicopolis to Mohács: A History of Ottoman-Hungarian Warfare, 1389-1526*. Leiden: Brill, 2008.

Panaite, Viorel. "The Legal and Political Status of Wallachia and Moldavia in Relation to the Ottoman Porte." In *The European Tributary States of the Ottoman Empire in the Sixteenth and Seventeenth Centuries*, 9–42.

Papo, Gizella Nemeth, and Adriano Papo. *Ludovico Gritti: Un principe-mercante del Rinascimento tra Venezia, i Turchi e la corona d'Ungheria*. Venice: Edizioni della Laguna, 2002.

Parker, Charles H. *Global Interactions in the Early Modern Age, 1400–1800*. Cambridge: Cambridge University Press, 2010.

Parker, Geoffrey. *Emperor: A New Life of Charles V*. New Haven, CT: Yale University Press, 2019.

Peacock, A. C. S. *Islam, Literature and Society in Mongol Anatolia*. Cambridge: Cambridge University Press, 2019.

Peirce, Leslie. *The Imperial Harem: Women and Sovereignty in the Ottoman Empire*. New York: Oxford University Press, 1993.

———. "Süleyman in Aleppo." In *Turkish Language, Literature, and History: Travelers' Tales, Sultans, and Scholars since the Eighth Century*, edited by Bill Hickman and Gary Leiser, 308–22. Milton Park, Abingdon, Oxon: Routledge, 2016.

———. *Empress of the East: How a European Slave Girl Became Queen of the Ottoman Empire*. New York: Basic Books, 2017.

Péri, Benedek. "The Persian Imitation Gazels (Nazires) of Kanuni Sultan Süleyman 'Muhibbi' (1520–1566) as They Are Preserved in a Hitherto Unnoticed Early Copy of his Divan." *Amasya Üniversitesi Sosyal Bilimler Dergisi* 5 (June 2019): 95–120.

Posch, Walter. *Osmanisch-safavidische Beziehungen (1545-1550): der Fall Alkas Mîrzâ*. 2 volumes. Vienna: Verlag der Österreichischen Akademie der Wissenschaften, 2013.

Pulido-Rull, Ana. "A Pronouncement of Alliance: An Anonymous Illustrated Venetian Manuscript for Sultan Süleyman." *Muqarnas* 29 (2012): 102–50.

Rodríguez-Salgado, M.J. *The Changing Face of Empire: Charles V, Philip II and Habsburg Authority, 1551–1559*. Cambridge: Cambridge University Press, 1988.

Römer, Claudia, and Nicolas Vatin. "The Hungarian Frontier and Süleyman's Way to Szigetvár according to Ottoman Sources." In *The Battle for Central Europe*, 341–58.

Ron, Nathan. *Erasmus and "the Other": On Turks, Jews, and Indigenous Peoples*. Cham, Switzerland: Palgrave Pivot, 2019.

Rossi, Ettore. "The Hospitallers at Rhodes, 1421–1523." In *A History of the Crusades*. Vol. 3, *The Fourteenth and Fifteenth Centuries*, 314–39.

Savory, Roger M. *Iran under the Safavids*. Cambridge: Cambridge University Press, 1980.

_____ and Ahmet T. Karamustafa. "ESMĀʿĪL I ṢAFAWĪ." *Encyclopaedia Iranica*, VIII/6, 628–636.

Schaendlinger, Anton C., and Claudia Römer, eds. *Die Schreiben Süleymāns des Prächtigen an Karl V., Ferdinand I. und Maximilian II*. Vol. 1. Vienna: Verlag der Österreichischen Akademie der Wissenschaften, 1983.

Schick, Irvin Cemil. *The Erotic Margin: Sexuality and Spatiality in Alterist Discourse*. London: Verso, 1999.

Schmidt, Jan. "The Reception of Firdausi's *Shahnama* among the Ottomans." In *Shahnama Studies II: The Reception of Firdausi's* Shahnama, edited by Charles Melville and Gabrielle van den Berg, 121–39. Leiden: Brill, 2012.

Schmitt, Oliver Jens, ed. *The Ottoman Conquest of the Balkans: Interpretations and Research Debates*. Vienna: Verlag der Österreichischen Akademie der Wissenschaften, 2016.

Seng, Yvonne J. "Fugitives and Factotums: Slaves in Early Sixteenth-Century Istanbul." *Journal of the Economic and Social History of the Orient* 39, no. 2 (1996): 136–69.

Setton, Kenneth M. "Lutheranism and the Turkish Peril." *Balkan Studies* 3 (1962): 133–68.

_____. *The Papacy and the Levant (1204-1571)*. Vol. 2, *The Fifteenth Century*. Philadelphia: The American Philosophical Society, 1978; Vol. 3, *The Sixteenth Century*. Philadelphia: The American Philosophical Society, 1984; Vol. 4, *The Sixteenth Century from Julius III to Pius V*. Philadelphia: The American Philosophical Society, 1984.

Severi, Bart. "'Denari in Loco delle Terre . . . ' Imperial Envoy Gerard Veltwyjck and Habsburg Policy towards the Ottoman Empire, 1545–1547." *Acta Orientalia Academiae Scientiarum Hungaricae* 54, nos. 2–3 (2001): 211–56.

Singer, Amy. *Constructing Ottoman Beneficence: An Imperial Soup Kitchen in Jerusalem*. Albany: State University of New York Press, 2002.

_____. "Making Jerusalem Ottoman." In *Living in the Ottoman Realm: Empire and Identity, 13th to 20th Centuries*, edited by Christine Isom-Verhaaren and Kent F. Schull, 123–36. Bloomington: Indiana University Press, 2016.

Sohrweide, Hanna. "Dichter und Gelehrte aus dem Osten im Osmanischen Reich (1453-1600): Ein Beitrag zur türkisch-persischen Kulturgeschichte." *Der Islam* 46 (1970): 263–302.

Sowerby, Tracey A., and Jan Hennings, eds. *Practices of Diplomacy in the Early Modern World c. 1410-1800*. London: Routledge, 2017.

Stetkevych, Suzanne P. "Solomon and Mythic Kingship in the Arab-Islamic Tradition: Qaṣīdah, Qurʾān and Qiṣaṣ al-anbiyāʾ." *Journal of Arabic Literature* 48, no. 1 (June 2017): 1–37.

Stewart, Dewin J. "Polemics and Patronage in Safavid Iran: The Debate on Friday Prayer during the Reign of Shah Tahmasb." *Bulletin of the School of Oriental and African Studies* 72, no. 3 (2009): 425–57.

Subrahmanyam, Sanjay. "Turning the Stones Over: Sixteenth-century Millenarianism from the Tagus to the Ganges." *Indian Economic and Social History Review* 40, no. 3 (2003): 131–63.

_____. *Empires between Islam and Christianity, 1500-1800*. Albany: State University of New York Press, 2019.

Sümer, Faruk. "Yavuz Selim Halîfeliği Devraldı mı?" *Belleten* 56, no. 217 (December 1992): 675–701.

Szakály, Ferenc. "Nándorfehérvár, 1521: The Beginning of the End of the Medieval Hungarian Kingdom." In *Hungarian-Ottoman Military and Diplomatic Relations in the Age of Süleyman the Magnificent*, edited by Géza Dávid and Pál Fodor, 47–76. Budapest: Loránd Eötvös University, 1994.

_____. *Lodovico Gritti in Hungary 1529–1534: A Historical Insight into the Beginnings of Turco-Habsburgian Rivalry*. Translated by Dániel Székely. Budapest: Akadémiai Kiadó, 1995.

Şahin, İlhan, and Feridun M. Emecen, eds. *Osmanlılarda Divân-Bürokrasi-Ahkâm: II. Bâyezid Dönemine Ait 906/1501 Tarihli Ahkâm Defteri*. Istanbul: Türk Dünyası Araştırmaları Vakfı, 1994.

Şahin, Kaya. "Constantinople and the End Time: The Ottoman Conquest as a Portent of the Last Hour." *Journal of Early Modern History* 14, no. 4 (2010): 317–54.

_____. "From Frontier Principality to Early Modern Empire: Limitations and Capabilities of Ottoman Governance." In *The Routledge History of the Renaissance*, edited by William Caferro, 321–36. London: Routledge, 2017.

_____. "The Ottoman Empire in the Long Sixteenth Century." *Renaissance Quarterly* 70, no. 1 (2017): 220–34.

_____. "Staging an Empire: An Ottoman Circumcision Ceremony as Cultural Performance." *American Historical Review* 123, no. 2 (April 2018): 463–92.

_____ and Julia Schleck. "Courtly Connections: Anthony Sherley's *Relation of his Trauels into Persia* (1613) in a Global Context." *Renaissance Quarterly* 69, no. 1 (2016): 80–115.

Şentürk, Ahmet Atillâ. *Şehzâde Mustafa Mersiyesi yahut Kanunî Hicviyesi*. Istanbul: Enderun, 1998.

Terzioğlu, Derin. "Sufis in the Age of State Building and Confessionalization." In *The Ottoman World*, 86–99.

_____. "How to Conceptualize Ottoman Sunnitization: A Historiographical Discussion." *Turcica* 44 (2012–13): 301–338.

Tezcan, Esma. "Pargalı İbrahim Paşa Çevresindeki Edebi Yaşam." MA thesis, Bilkent University, 2005.

al-Tikriti, Nabil. "Şehzade Korkud (ca. 1468-1513) and the Articulation of Early 16th Century Ottoman Religious Identity." PhD diss., University of Chicago, 2004.

Tinguely, Frédéric. *L'écriture du Levant à la Renaissance: Enquête sur les voyageurs français dans l'empire de Soliman le Magnifique.* Geneva: Droz, 2000.

Toledano, Ehud R. "Enslavement in the Ottoman Empire in the Early Modern Period." In *The Cambridge World History of Slavery.* Vol. 3, *AD 1420-AD 1804,* edited by David Eltis and Stanley L. Engerman, 25–46. New York: Cambridge University Press, 2011.

Tracy, James. "Foreign Correspondence: European Accounts of Sultan Süleyman I's Persian Campaigns, 1548 and 1554." *Turkish Historical Review* 6 (2015): 194–219.

————. "Tokaj, 1565: A Habsburg Prize of War, and an Ottoman *Casus Belli.*" In *The Battle for Central Europe,* 359–76.

Turan, Ebru. "The Sultan's Favorite: İbrahim Pasha and the Making of the Ottoman Universal Sovereignty in the Reign of Süleyman (1516-1526)." PhD dissertation, University of Chicago, 2007.

————. "Voices of Opposition in the Reign of Sultan Süleyman: The Case of İbrahim Pasha (1523–1536)." In *Studies on Istanbul and Beyond,* 23–35.

————. "The Marriage of İbrahim Pasha (ca. 1495-1536): The Rise of Sultan Süleyman's Favorite to the Grand Vizierate and the Politics of the Elites in the Early Sixteenth-Century Ottoman Empire." *Turcica* 41 (2009): 3–36.

Turan, Şerafettin. *Kanuni Süleyman Dönemi Taht Kavgaları.* Revised second edition. Ankara: Bilgi Yayınevi, 1997.

Turgut, Ali Ç., Yaşar B. Turgut, Mehmet Turgut. "Neurological Disease of Şehzade Cihangir in the [sic] Ottoman History: Spinal Dysraphism." *Child's Nervous System* 32 (2016): 765–67.

Uluç, Lâle. "The *Shahnama* of Firdausi in the Lands of Rum." In *Shahnama Studies II,* 159–80.

Uluçay, M. Çağatay. *Haremden Mektuplar I.* Istanbul: Vakit Matbaası, 1956.

————. "Bayazıd [sic] II. in Âilesi." *Tarih Dergisi* 10, no. 14 (September 1959): 105–24.

————. "Kanunî Sultan Süleyman ve Ailesi ile İlgili Bazı Notlar ve Vesikalar." In *Kanunî Armağanı,* 227–57.

————. *Padişahların Kadınları ve Kızları.* Ankara: Türk Tarih Kurumu, 1980.

————. *Osmanlı Sultanlarına Aşk Mektupları.* Istanbul: Ufuk Kitapları, 2001.

Usta, Veysel. "Şehzade Süleyman'ın (Kanuni) Trabzon'da Doğduğu Ev Meselesi." *Karadeniz Araştırmaları Dergisi* 26 (Spring 2019): 397–414.

Uzunçarşılı, İsmail Hakkı. "Onbeşinci Yüzyılın İlk Yarısiyle Onaltıncı Yüzyılın Başlarında Memlûk Sultanları Yanına İltica Etmiş Olan Osmanlı Hanedanına Mensub Şehzadeler." *Belleten* 17, no. 68 (1953): 519–35.

Van Steenbergen, Jo, ed. *Trajectories of State-Formation across Fifteenth-Century Western Asia: Eurasian Parallels, Connections and Divergences.* Leiden: Brill, 2020.

Varga, Szabolcs. "Miklós Zrínyi, Captain-General of Szigetvár (1561–1566) – His Organisational Activity and Death." In *The Battle for Central Europe,* 377–95.

Varlık, Nükhet. *Plague and Empire in the Early Modern Mediterranean World: The Ottoman Experience, 1347-1600.* New York: Cambridge University Press, 2015.

Vasiliev, A. A. "The Foundation of the Empire of Trebizond (1204-1222)." *Speculum* 11, no. 1 (January 1936): 3–37.

Vatin, Nicolas. *L'Ordre de Saint-Jean-de-Jérusalem, l'empire ottoman et la Méditerranée orientale entre les deux sièges de Rhodes (1480–1522)*. Paris: Peeters, 1994.

_____. *Rhodes et l'ordre de Saint-Jean-de-Jérusalem*. Paris: Éditions CNRS, 2000.

_____. "The Hospitallers at Rhodes and the Ottoman Turks." In *Crusading in the Fifteenth Century: Message and Impact*, ed. Norman Housley, 148–62. Houndmills, Basingstoke, Hampshire: Palgrave Macmillan, 2004.

_____. "Comment Hayr ed-Dîn Barberousse fut reçu à Istanbul en 1533." *Turcica* 49 (2018): 119–51.

_____. "On Süleyman the Magnificent's Death and Burials." In *The Battle for Central Europe*, 427–43.

Veinstein, Gilles and Nicolas Vatin. *Le sérail ébranlé: essai sur les morts, dépositions et avènements des sultans ottomans (XIVe-XIXe siècle)*. Paris: Fayard, 2003.

Wehr, Hans. *A Dictionary of Modern Written Arabic*. Edited by J. Milton Cowan. Ithaca, NY: Spoken Word Services Inc., 1976.

White, Sam. *The Climate of Rebellion in the Early Modern Ottoman Empire*. New York: Cambridge University Press, 2011.

Wilson, Peter H. "Warfare in Europe." In *The Cambridge World History of Violence*. Vol. 3, *1500-1800 CE*, edited by Robert Antony, Stuart Carroll, and Caroline Dodds Pennock, 174–93. Cambridge: Cambridge University Press, 2020.

Winter, Michael. "The Ottoman Occupation." In *The Cambridge History of Egypt*. Vol. 1, *Islamic Egypt, 640-1517*, edited by Carl Petry, 490–516. Cambridge: Cambridge University Press, 1998.

Woodhead, Christine. "An Experiment in Official Historiography: The Post of Şehnameci in the Ottoman Empire, c.1555–1605." *Wiener Zeitschrift für die Kunde des Morgenlandes* 75 (1983): 157–82.

_____. "Perspectives on Süleyman." In *Süleyman the Magnificent and His Age*, 164–81.

Woods, John E. *The Aqquyunlu: Clan, Confederation, Empire*. Revised and expanded edition. Salt Lake City: University of Utah Press, 1999.

Yavaş, Doğan. "Hafsa Sultan Külliyesi." *TDVİA*. Vol. 15, 123–4.

Yelçe, Nevin Zeynep. "The Making of Sultan Süleyman: A Study of Process/es of Image-Making and Reputation Management." PhD diss., Sabancı University, 2009.

_____. "Evaluating Three Imperial Festivals: 1524, 1530 and 1539." In *Celebration, Entertainment and Theatre in the Ottoman World*, edited by Suraiya Faroqhi and Arzu Öztürkmen, 71–109. London: Seagull Books, 2014.

_____. "Ottoman Reception and Perception of János Szapolyai in 1529." In *Türkenkriege und Adelskultur in Ostmitteleuropa vom 16. bis zum 18. Jahrhundert*, edited by Robert Born and Sabine Jagodzinski, 141–54. Ostfildern: Jan Thorbecke Verlag, 2014.

Yerasimos, Stéphane. *Légendes d'Empire: La fondation de Constantinople et de Sainte-Sophie dans les traditions turques*. Paris: Institut français d'études anatoliennes -Jean Maisonneuve, 1990.

Yılmaz, Gülay. "Urban Protests, Rebellions, and Revolts." In *A Companion to Early Modern Istanbul*, edited by Shirine Hamadeh and Çiğdem Kafescioğlu, 555–80. Leiden: Brill, 2021.

Yıldız, Sara Nur. "Ottoman Historical Writing in Persian, 1400-1600." In *A History of Persian Literature*, edited by Ehsan Yarshater. Vol. 10, *Persian Historiography*, edited by Charles Melville, 436–502. London: I.B. Tauris, 2012.

Yılmaz, Hüseyin. *Caliphate Redefined: The Mystical Turn in Ottoman Political Thought.* Princeton, NJ: Princeton University Press, 2018.

Yılmaz, Müslüm. *Beşiktaşlı Yahyâ Efendi: Hayatı Tasavvufi Şahsiyeti ve Dîvânı.* Istanbul: Dergâh Yayınları, 2014.

Yurdaydın, Hüseyin Gazi. "Bostan'ın Süleymannâmesi (Ferdî'ye Atfedilen Eser)." *Belleten* 19, no. 74 (1955): 137–202.

Yurdusev, A. Nuri. "The Ottoman Attitude Toward Diplomacy." In *Ottoman Diplomacy: Conventional or Unconventional?*, 5–35.

Yücel, Yaşar. "Fatih'in Trabzon'u Fethi Öncesinde Osmanlı-Trabzon-Akkoyunlu İlişkileri." *Belleten* 49, no. 194 (1984): 287–311.

Yüksel, İ. Aydın. "Sultan Selim Camii ve Külliyesi." *TDVİA.* Vol. 37, 513–16.

Yüksel Muslu, Cihan. *The Ottomans and the Mamluks: Imperial Diplomacy and Warfare in the Islamic World.* London: I.B. Tauris, 2014.

Zarinabaf-Shahr, Fariba. "Qizilbash 'Heresy' and Rebellion in Ottoman Anatolia in the Sixteenth Century." *Anatolia Moderna* 7 (1997): 1–15.

# Index

accession to the throne, 2, 99–102, 107–10, 116
  gifts to janissaries and household troops, 106
  letters sent on the occasion, 106–107, 111
Adrianopolis. *See* Edirne
Ahmed (uncle), 40, 53, 56, 61, 117
  during Anatolian rebellion of 1511, 77
  favorable treatment by Bayezid II, 76
  succession struggle with Selim I, 74, 78–81
  and Süleyman's first district governorship, 64, 66–67
Ahmed "the Traitor," 108, 112, 113, 124, 126–27, 129–31
Aleppo, 93*f*, 94, 175, 181, 185*f*, 192, 230, 234
  disturbances in, 164–65
  siege by al-Ghazali, 110
  Süleyman's stays in, 211–13, 238–39
  wealth, 216
Alexander the Great, 42, 53, 174, 209, 271
  in Ottoman imperial ideology, 62, 135, 159, 204
Alqas (Safavid prince), 208–13, 237, 257
Anatolian Seljuk Sultanate, 8, 12, 14, 22, 31, 48, 181

apocalyptic beliefs, 162–63, 196, 201, 242, 249. *See also* messianic beliefs; prophecy and prognostication
  about Constantinople, 99, 242
  and criticism of Ottoman imperial project, 39
  and imperial agendas, 136–37, 152, 226
  and Ottoman–Habsburg rivalry, 158
  and Safavid ideology, 76
*askerî*, 31, 45–46, 59, 86–87, 100, 154, 166, 177
  enrichment through warfare, 112, 138, 165, 201
  identity and status, 18–19, 24, 31, 34, 57
  intermarriage with Ottoman dynasty members, 49
  role in factional and succession struggles, 67, 74, 80, 129, 140, 230–32, 250
  stipendiary soldiers and, 259
  sultans' management of, 55, 59, 104–5, 107–8, 164–65, 215, 218
astrology, 7, 104, 129, 135, 140, 244
Ayas, Grand Vizier, 111, 124, 132, 162, 187
  appointment, 190
  death, 219
  diplomatic efforts, 190–91

Baghdad, 134, 185*f*, 202, 214, 222
 capture by Süleyman (1534), 183–86
 in Süleyman's poetry, 172
Barbarossa (a.k.a. Hızır Hayreddin), 191,
  194, 205, 207
 naval expeditions, 193, 197–98, 203
Battle of Mohács (1526), 141–44, 162,
  172, 273
Bayezid (son), 171–72, 204, 222, 225, 229,
  234, 237
 circumcision, 198
 death, 258
 district governorships, 211, 228, 230
 refuge in Safavid territory, 256–57
 struggle with Süleyman and brother
  Selim, 250–58
Bayezid I, 12, 14, 22–23
Bayezid II (grandfather), 13, 19, 21, 28,
  31–33, 53–54, 64, 67, 74–77, 80, 105
 abdication, 78–79, 228
 accession, 28, 116
 death, 79
 gifts, 34, 49–50, 60
 legal reforms, 30
 military campaigns, 29
 mosque, 100*f*, 115, 219, 261
 relationship with Selim I, 60–61, 66,
  70, 91
Belgrade, 118, 121, 126, 140, 140*f*, 142–43,
  151, 156–57, 206*f*, 268–69
 capture by Süleyman (1521), 113–15,
  138, 168–69
 Süleyman's death announcement in,
  271
Black Sea, 12, 23, 36, 40–42, 67, 256, 275
 importance for Ottoman economy, 29,
  70–71, 196–97
Bragadin, Pietro, 137, 171, 173–75
Buda, 13*f*, 111, 113–14, 137, 140*f*, 150–51,
  175, 206*f*, 269
 as Ottoman governorate-general,
  202–5, 211, 214, 216

 capture by Ferdinand, 145, 148–49
 sieges by Ferdinand, 155, 199–201
 Süleyman's stay in, 142–43
Byzantine Empire, 14, 31, 40, 116, 126
 in apocalyptic prophecies, 27, 39
 collapse, 12
 cultural legacy in Ottoman lands, 47–48,
  82, 98, 125, 152, 223, 242, 247
 Ottomans as symbolic successors of, 22
 struggle with Ottomans, 8–10

Caffa, 40, 41*f*, 68*f*, 77, 79, 81, 97, 99
 Süleyman's governorship in, 66–67,
  69–73, 75, 78, 82–86, 89, 103
caliphate, 107, 131, 134–36, 185, 216, 264
charity, 46, 189, 218–27, 260
 of Hafsa, 125
 of Hürrem, 223
 of Mihrümah, 264
 of Süleyman, 2, 5, 87, 125, 244, 246,
  268, 273, 275
Celalzade Mustafa, 112, 131, 133, 163, 159,
  176, 218, 241
 as author of preamble to law code of
  Egypt, 136
 as chancellor, 214–15, 243, 276
 as historian of Süleyman's reign, 163–64,
  177, 181, 189, 216, 235, 243
Charles V, Holy Roman Emperor, 4–5,
  115–16, 137, 187, 192–94, 265
 abdication as Holy Roman Emperor,
  241
 claim to universal rule, 137, 140, 150,
  196
 Ottoman portrayal as "king of Spain,"
  151, 160, 207
 rivalry with Francis I of France, 116,
  140, 143, 152, 193–94
 rivalry with Ottomans, 152–63, 190–91,
  200
 support of Ferdinand, 144–45, 147–48,
  205

treaty with Ottomans in 1547, 206–8, 243

children, 6, 82, 89, 120, 122. *See also* Bayezid (son); Cihangir (son); Mehmed (son); Mihrümah (daughter); Mustafa (son); Selim II (son)

    circumcision of sons, 154, 198

    with Hürrem, 121, 171, 173, 221, 229

    with Mahidevran, 120

Christians, 4, 7, 9, 11, 17, 27, 37, 43, 115

    in Caffa, 70

    in Constantinople, 97

    in Manisa, 83

    in Ottoman service, 16, 34, 108, 164, 175, 219, 250, 259

    as Ottoman subjects, 15, 18, 105, 164, 176

    in Trabzon, 45–47

*cihad*. See *gaza*

Cihangir (son), 237

    circumcision, 198

    death and burial, 238, 258, 260

    health, 171, 222, 228

    memorial mosque, 263

    relationship with Süleyman, 211, 230, 234

circumcision, 49–52

Clement VII, Pope, 152, 155–56, 162

concubinage, 34–35, 71. *See also* harem; slavery

Constantinople, 13f, 21, 28, 40, 41f, 47–49, 52, 54, 71–72, 98f, 100f, 140f, 185f, 198f, 256f

    capture by Ottomans in 1453, 8, 12, 23, 27, 32, 44, 70, 94, 223, 242

    cultural image, 98

    earthquakes, 31, 77, 99

    population, 97

    prophecies about, 27, 162–63, 242

    redevelopment by Ottomans, 31, 97–98, 223, 243

    riots in, 132

    Süleyman's first trip to, 79–80

conversion to Islam, 48, 97, 120, 175

conversion of churches to mosques, 47, 52, 115, 118, 142, 202, 204, 242

    as part of Ottoman recruitment practices, 7, 16–17, 34, 57, 126

    social benefits, 45

    of Süleyman's ancestors, 8

Crimean Khanate, 12, 13f, 41f, 71–72, 75, 106, 156, 197, 256, 269

*devşirme*, 16–17, 34, 44, 104, 130

    prominent officials recruited through, 111, 126, 127–28, 220

diplomacy, 2, 30, 39, 81, 91, 95, 135, 144–45, 155–56, 160–63, 174–76, 191–92, 210, 219, 226, 267, 273

    between Ottomans and European states, 25, 29, 106, 110, 119, 126, 149, 151, 154, 189, 194, 196, 200, 202–3, 205–8, 222

    between Ottomans and Muslim states, 106, 239–42, 257–58

    new protocols under Süleyman, 146

    symbolic aspects, 207

district governorships, 6, 14–16, 68f, 70, 84

    activities of governors, 15, 59–60

    of Ottoman princes, 6, 15, 32–33, 35, 70, 82

    role in viziers' careers, 128

*sancak* (district), 14–15, 66

*divan* (imperial council), 5, 80, 91, 103, 127, 132, 176, 197, 214, 256

    in earlier Ottoman administrations, 19, 167

    expanded role under Süleyman, 30–31, 167

    notable meetings, 80, 164, 197, 209–10, 220, 241

    in *Sulaymannama*, 20f, 249–50

    Rüstem (Grand Vizier) and, 215

Doria, Andrea, 162, 197

Ebussuud Mehmed, 243, 244, 245, 261, 271, 276
  *fetvas*, 210–11, 236
  friendship with Süleyman, 263
  as legal scholar, 215, 218
Edirne, 10, 13*f*, 77–78, 89, 94–95, 124, 206, 242
  as Ottoman army's campaign stop, 140, 156, 203, 229
  sons' postings to, 229–30, 234, 237, 251
  Süleyman's stays in, 90–92, 100, 128, 132, 209, 213, 226, 253
education, 5, 51–57, 61–63
Egypt, 75, 106–7, 111, 166, 169, 220, 248
  Ottoman conquest, 81, 90, 94, 110, 116
  preamble to the law code of, 133–36, 147, 179
  and rebellion of Ahmed "the Traitor," 127, 129, 131–32

Ferdinand I, Archduke of Austria, Holy Roman Emperor, 142, 146–47, 149, 196, 198, 200–4, 266
  accession as Holy Roman Emperor, 241, 265
  allies in Hungary, 150
  claim to Hungarian crown, 144–45, 148, 154, 156, 199, 214
  correspondence with Süleyman, 151
  negotiations with Ottomans, 154–56, 160–62, 181, 190–91, 205–7, 214, 241, 243, 267
France, Kingdom of, 4, 10, 116, 139, 146, 159, 161, 192, 198*f*, 240
  Holy League membership, 144
  invasions by Charles V, 116, 205
  Prince Cem's sojourn in, 29
Francis I, King of France, 4, 115, 137, 156, 190, 207
  alliance with Ottomans, 193–94, 203
  capture by Habsburgs, 139, 155

rivalry with Charles V, 116, 140, 143, 152, 193–94
fratricide, 5, 33

*gaza*, 9–11, 19, 23, 26, 139
Genghis Khan, 12, 22, 71, 135, 152
Genoa, 24, 41, 46–47, 70–71, 97, 266
grand vizier, 16, 19, 126, 131, 133, 167–68.
  *See also* Ayas; Hadım Süleyman; İbrahim; Lütfi; Piri Mehmed; Rüstem; Sokullu Mehmed.
Gritti, Alvise, 149–50, 159–60, 162–63, 190–91
  assassination, 196, 199
Gülfem (concubine), 120–21, 173, 262

Habsburgs, 1, 25, 113, 116, 156–57, 161, 165, 191–93, 198*f*, 200–201, 265–68
  dynastic marriages, 144
  pro- and anti-Habsburg factions in Hungary, 143, 145, 199
  rivalry with Ottomans, 140, 146, 152, 177, 196, 214, 222, 243
Hadım Süleyman, Grand Vizier, 216, 219–20
Hafsa (mother), 36, 38, 50, 53, 70, 174
  charitable works, 124–25, 224
  death, 181, 188, 218, 221
  influence in politics, 122–24
  letters to Süleyman, 123
  name, 38
  origins, 34–35
  as Süleyman's companion in adult life, 72, 84–85, 88, 108, 218
Hagia Sophia, 100*f*, 142, 242–43
Hanafi legal school, 52, 184
harem
  in Ottoman practice, 34–35, 102
  Selim I's, 39, 48–49
  Süleyman's, 72–73, 85, 88, 108, 120–23, 126, 171, 173, 175, 261
Hayreddin (tutor), 54–56, 90, 113

education and background, 53
illness and death, 218, 222
other notable students, 169
as Süleyman's companion in adult life,
1, 73, 84–85, 108
health, 85, 88, 272
death, 270–71
decline after Hürrem's death, 261
during the final campaign, 268–69
in later years, 1, 6, 208, 213, 225–26,
234, 253
history writing, 22, 105, 112, 168–70, 272.
*See also* Sulaymannama
Holy League, 196–98
holy war, 60, 112, 119, 138–39, 168, 209–
10. *See also* gaza
household, 6, 50, 65–66, 115, 127–28, 165,
167, 174, 204, 218–19, 272
in Caffa, 72–74, 80, 103,
in Constantinople, 101–4, 106–8, 123,
125, 170, 195, 198
in Manisa, 82–89, 103, 106
Hungary, Kingdom of, 4, 11, 13*f*, 25, 27,
29, 110–11, 140*f*, 149, 152, 157–59,
190, 243
claims to throne of, 144–48, 151, 154–
56, 160–62, 199–200, 214
division of the 1540s, 200–202, 206*f*,
206–7
Ottoman campaigns in, 112–16, 136–
45, 148–51, 200–205, 217, 265–70
Hürrem (wife), 6, 121–22, 174–75, 209,
218, 220, 221*f*, 225–26, 228–30, 233,
235, 237–38, 260, 262, 264
charitable works, 223–24
correspondence with Süleyman, 171–
73, 175, 222
death, 1, 253, 261
detractors of, 236
marriage to Süleyman, 221
origins, 71, 120
resting place, 271

role in politics, 188–89, 222–23, 251–
52, 268

İbrahim, Grand Vizier, 125, 129–30, 137–
38, 152, 154, 158–59, 163, 165–70,
178–79, 192, 199, 243
diplomatic efforts, 145–49, 155–57,
160–61, 190–91
execution, 186–90, 218, 221, 249, 275
inspection tour of Egypt, 131–33
on campaign with Süleyman, 140–44,
149, 156, 180–86
origins, 127–28
personal friendship with Süleyman,
171, 174–76, 220, 260
representation in preamble to law code
of Egypt, 134
use of prophecies, 152, 157–58
image of Süleyman, 2, 5, 20, 55, 102, 107,
120, 126–27, 166, 170–71, 242–43,
246, 249, 272
after his death, 273–77
depictions, 3*f*, 153*f*, 158*f*, 159, 221*f*, 232*f*, 261*f*
in European writings, 108–9, 119–20,
171, 272
institution-building, 7, 13–21, 148, 217,
244, 274
growth of bureaucracy, 4, 215
shortcomings, 225, 238
Isabella, Queen of Hungary, 199–201,
204, 214, 222
Ismail I, Safavid Shah, 4, 60, 65, 67, 74,
94, 117, 137, 182, 240
battle against Selim I, 90, 92
correspondence with Ottomans, 120,
178–79
death, 147, 178, 180
influence on rebellions in Ottoman
lands, 76–77, 110, 112
leadership of Safavid movement, 26–27,
30, 59, 62
sons, 208

Italian Peninsula, 97, 137, 140, 152, 155–56, 162
  Barbarossa's raids against, 193, 203
  French invasion in 1494, 25–26, 29
  Süleyman's attempted campaign against, 194–96

janissaries, 7, 17, 19, 57, 59, 101, 104, 110, 113, 130, 142, 149, 156, 244, 251, 255
  in ceremonies, 149, 156, 198, 209, 238
  formation of corps, 16
  in riots, 95, 132
  on campaigns, 91, 115, 201, 203, 223
  payments to, 99, 106, 150, 271
  role in succession struggles, 78–79, 95, 173, 228, 233, 253
Jerusalem, 27–28, 116, 160, 162, 224*f*
  Süleyman and Hürrem's patronage in, 39, 223–24, 276
Jews, 18, 37, 50, 57, 142
  in Caffa, 70
  in Constantinople, 97, 132
  in Manisa, 83
John Sigismund, King of Hungary, 207, 214, 222
  Ottoman support for, 199–204, 266–69
  conflict with Maximilian II, 266–69

*Kanun* (dynastic law), 18, 119, 134, 187, 189, 215, 245
  applications, 14, 217–18
  Süleyman's role in development of, 4, 20, 24, 217, 274
Kasım (overseer), 72, 81, 86, 89–91, 108, 125
Kemalpaşazade Ahmed, 112, 164, 169, 181, 276
  death, 215, 218
  on Hungarian campaign of 1526, 136, 139–40
  view of Selim I, 105

Korkud (uncle), 37, 67, 77
  in succession struggles, 74–75, 79–80, 82

*lala* (overseers), 15, 34, 57, 60, 87–88. *See also* Kasım
Łaski, Hieronymus, 146, 160, 200
Louis II, King of Hungary, 138, 141–45, 151
Lütfi, Grand Vizier, 105, 139, 143, 276
  dismissal, 219–20
  writings in retirement, 260

Mahidevran (concubine), 89, 120, 174, 225, 230
  life after son Mustafa's execution, 235, 260
  position in Süleyman's household, 122, 173
Mamluks, 12, 13*f*, 29–31, 52, 110–11, 116, 123, 129–31, 134, 135, 139, 248
  role in Ottoman dynastic struggles, 28, 75
  rule in Egypt, 12–13
  war with Ottomans, 29–30, 90–92, 94, 105
Manisa, 67, 68*f*, 77, 81, 90, 92, 96, 120, 123, 128, 218–19, 229, 252, 254
  Hafsa's complex in, 124–25, 224
  Süleyman's district governorship in, 82–89
Maximilian II, Holy Roman Emperor, 266–69
Mediterranean Sea
  and the Order of St. John, 116, 119
  and Ottoman competition with Habsburgs, 25, 152, 161, 190–99, 266
  and Ottoman competition with Venetians, 29, 198
  Ottoman presence in, 4, 94, 190–99, 203, 208, 216–17
Mehmed (son), 1, 121–22, 171, 197, 235, 238, 258, 264, 269

circumcision, 154

death and funeral, 218–19, 230

district governorship, 204, 229

memorial mosque complex, 244

on campaign with Süleyman, 195, 201, 222, 230

Mehmed II, 23–24, 28, 31, 48, 56, 100, 114, 126, 142, 242, 265, 273, 275

capture of Constantinople, 27, 44, 94, 115

capture of Trabzon, 40, 42–44

construction of New Palace, 102

mosque complex, 100*f*, 101

naval expeditions, 116–117

Mengli Giray, Khan of Crimea, 72, 75

messianic beliefs, 27, 30, 76, 77, 136–37, 152, 157, 192, 197, 226, 249. *See also* apocalyptic beliefs; prophecy and prognostication

Mihrümah (daughter), 121, 171, 230

charitable works, 224–25, 264

marriage to Rüstem, 198, 220, 229

role in politics, 222–25, 253, 256, 262, 264

military campaigns

first campaign against Safavids (1533–1536), 180–84, 185*f*, 185–86

"German" campaign (1532), 155–61

Hungary (1521), 112–16

Hungary (1526), 136–45

Hungary (1529), 148–51

Hungary (1541–44), 200–205

Hungary (1566), 265–270

Karaboğdan (1538), 196–98

*Pulya* campaign (1537), 195–96

Rhodes campaign (1522), 116–20

second campaign against Safavids (1548–49), 211–13

third campaign against Safavids (1554–55), 237–40

Minio, Marco, 115–16, 121–22, 146, 175

Mongols, 12, 23, 27, 31, 71

influence on Ottoman dynastic practices, 23, 33

as inspiration for Ottomans, 31, 247

invasions, 8, 27, 134, 136

Moldavia, 13*f*, 29, 140*f*, 196–97, 206*f*, 202

Murad I, 23

Murad II, 23, 83

Mustafa (son), 89, 120–22, 187, 225, 249–50, 264

as candidate for the throne, 228, 230, 232–33, 254

circumcision, 154

district governorship, 173

execution, 228–39, 252, 260, 273, 275

meeting with Süleyman (1548), 231

naming of children, 37–40

of Süleyman, 38–39

New Palace, 99–100, 100*f*, 103*f*, 115, 122, 126, 132, 174, 186, 221

administrative functions, 167

construction by Mehmed II, 23–24

as home to Süleyman, 102–3, 108

in literature, 98

Süleyman's first trip to, 80

nomads, 12, 26–27, 30, 45, 71, 86, 116, 178, 217, 254

as Ottoman progenitors, 8–9, 11, 13, 20, 22, 37

Ottoman sedentarization of, 21, 76, 83, 250

Old Palace, 100*f*, 102, 108, 120, 122

Order of St. John (a.k.a. Knights Hospitaller), 28–29, 95, 142, 179, 196

defense of Malta, 266

loss of Rhodes, 116–19, 139

Orhan I (son of Osman I), 9, 23

Osman I (founder of dynasty), 9–10, 16, 21, 26, 82

in later Ottoman histories, 19, 23, 31, 248

in Ottoman dynastic myth, 22, 48

Ottomans
 administrative developments, 13–21
 expansion in Anatolia, 10–13, 13*f*, 29
 expansion in the Balkans, 10–13, 13*f*,
  23, 26
 legitimacy and identity, 21–24
 rise of, 8–9

Paul III, Pope, 193, 198, 207
personality, 1, 6, 102, 108–9, 119, 171, 276
piety displays, 246, 263, 273, 275
Pirî Mehmed, Grand Vizier, 110, 111, 167,
  175, 270
 background, 108, 126
 dismissal, 126–27
 during Süleyman's first campaign, 113–14
 role in Selim-Süleyman transition, 96,
  100–101
poetry, 2, 4, 39, 48, 53, 62, 247, 276
 patronage of, 165, 170
 study of, 54–57
 use in correspondence, 171–72, 262–63
Poland, Kingdom of, 71, 140*f*, 145–46,
  196, 199, 206*f*, 222, 240
 Ottoman rapprochement with, 147,
  161, 214
Portugal, Kingdom of, 24, 206
 naval rivalry with Ottomans, 30, 94,
  132, 186, 214, 216, 219
prophecy and prognostication, 7, 117,
  137–38, 157–58, 162–63, 182, 185,
  189, 226. *See also* apocalyptic beliefs;
  messianic beliefs

Quran, 15, 31, 38–40, 106, 131, 209, 263
 recitation, 101, 125, 141, 218, 245, 269
 use in education, 51–54
 as gift, 209, 241

Rareş, Petru, 196–97
rebellion
 of al-Ghazali, 110–112

of Ahmed "the Traitor," 129–31
Anatolian rebellion of 1511, 67, 74–78,
  82, 87
Anatolian rebellion of 1527, 163, 166,
  177
of Mustafa "the Impostor," 250–51
Rüstem, Grand Vizier, 176, 198, 200, 212,
  222, 224–25, 227, 237, 243, 253, 255–
  56, 262, 276
 death, 264–65
 diplomatic efforts, 206, 209
 dismissal, 236
 promotion, 206, 229
 image, 215, 220, 236
 marriage to Mihrümah, 198, 224
 origins, 220
 reforms, 215–16
 restoration as grand vizier, 249, 252
 role in Prince Mustafa's execution, 225,
  229, 233–34, 236–37
 role in Süleyman's campaigns, 202,
  204

Safavid dynasty, 1, 28, 57, 59–61, 67, 69,
  110, 112, 117, 130, 135, 155, 176
 in anti–Safavid Ottoman writings,
  179–82, 185, 210–11
 commercial blockade by Selim I, 95,
  107
 communications with Ottomans, 179
 diplomatic relations with Habsburgs,
  200–201
 peace settlement with Ottomans,
  237–43, 265
 political instability after Ismail I's
  death, 147
 religious message, 30, 60, 76, 94, 163–
  64, 177–78, 210
 rise of, 26
 rivalry with Ottomans, 90–92, 105,
  113, 120, 139, 162–63, 186, 191, 216–
  17, 224–25

Schepper, Cornelius de, 160, 162–63, 176, 190–91

Selim I (father), 30, 33–35, 38–39, 47–50, 61, 82, 87, 89, 106–8, 112, 115, 127, 134–35, 180, 241, 273
  accession struggle, 69, 71–72, 74–81, 232
  campaigns against Safavids, 59–60, 95, 107, 117
  campaigns against Mamluks, 90–92, 94, 105, 134–35
  death and funeral, 95, 99–102, 106, 110, 116
  district governorship, 36, 46, 59
  histories of reign, 105, 168–70
  household, 45, 48, 53–55, 63, 72–73
  memorial mosque complex, 125, 164, 218, 224, 244
  modern legacy, 275
  other children, 39
  relationship with Bayezid II, 60–61, 78, 91, 228
  relationship with Süleyman, 90–96
  role in Süleyman's education, 55–57
  securing Süleyman's first governorship, 63–69

Selim II (son), 171, 197, 201, 204, 222, 225, 229, 237–38, 257–59, 264
  accession, 270–71
  accession struggle with brother Bayezid, 250, 252–55, 256f, 258, 261–62, 265
  birth, 121
  on campaign with Süleyman, 195, 201, 222, 230
  circumcision, 154
  district governorships, 204, 228, 230, 237, 253, 265
  relationship with Süleyman, 254–55, 268

*Shahnama* (The Book of Kings), 37
  influence on *Sulaymannama*, 247–48

Sharia law, 14, 18, 65, 94, 119, 125, 134, 164, 187, 189, 233, 255, 260
  on *aman*, 118

on concubinage, 34
on *gaza*, 11–12
and Ottoman perception of Safavids, 177, 182
relationship with *kanun*, 215, 217–18
on slavery, 16

Shia Islam, 4, 27, 177, 184–85
  Ottoman opposition to, 94, 177, 179–80, 210–11, 213, 239
  Twelver school, 94, 177, 182, 208, 210, 212, 240–41, 258, 275

*sipahis* (cavalrymen), 18–19, 112, 180
  *timar* privileges, 14, 19, 21, 59, 76, 86, 90

Sigismund I, King of Poland, 196, 199

sisters of Süleyman, 49–50, 70, 75, 85, 124, 126, 130, 220, 253

slavery, 7, 16–18, 34, 41, 60, 71, 73, 98–99, 165. *See also* devşirme
  of Christian children, 16, 250
  during Ottoman military campaigns, 60, 112, 114, 143
  of Muslims, 117

Sokullu Mehmed, Grand Vizier, 234, 251, 255–56, 276
  appointment, 265
  crisis management, 262, 271

Spain, Kingdom of, 25, 115, 139, 158, 194, 198f, 204–5, 265

*Sulaymannama* ("The Book of Süleyman"), 2, 3f, 17f, 20f, 251
  commission by Süleyman, 245–50
  comparing Süleyman to Solomon, 40
  on Süleyman and his rule, 249–50, 272, 275
  on Süleyman's treatment of son Mustafa, 231, 232f, 235
  use of Persian in, 247–48

Süleymaniye mosque complex, 246f, 261, 263, 264, 271
  conception and construction, 242–48
  today, 276–77

Sunni Islam, 52, 62, 120, 163–64, 177–79, 210, 215, 239, 241, 246
  as part of Ottoman identity, 4, 125, 134, 182, 185, 216, 237, 242–44, 264, 275
  anti–Shiite stance of, 4, 94, 179–80, 184, 216, 272
Szapolyai, John, King of Hungary, 150–51, 160–61, 201, 205
  agreement with Ferdinand, 199–200
  claim to Hungarian throne, 144, 146, 148, 151, 156, 214
  enthronement, 144, 149, 197
  marriage and fatherhood, 199
  struggle with Ferdinand, 145, 151, 156

Tabriz, 40, 93*f*, 130, 177, 184, 185*f*, 186, 211, 239
  capture by Süleyman (1534), 182–83
  capture by Süleyman (1548), 211
  conquest by Ismail I, 26, 60, 130
Tahmasb I, Safavid Shah, 4, 179–181, 187, 189, 208, 263
  accession, 178
  action against Alqas, 209, 212
  campaigns against Ottomans, 181–86, 192
  negotiations with Ottomans, 239–41
  and Prince Bayezid, 257–58
  and Prince Mustafa, 234, 236–37
taxation, 30, 33, 86, 112, 138, 165, 238, 273
  and nomads, 83
  codification, 131, 217
  elite privileges and, 16, 31
  evolution in Ottoman history, 19
  forms of, 13–14, 58
  of non-Muslims, 18, 46
*timar* (revenue grant), 45, 86, 90, 106, 111, 163, 231, 251, 254, 259, 274
  administrative purpose, 14–16, 59, 104, 235, 250
  regulation, 19, 21, 76, 147, 164, 166, 214–15, 260

Timur, 12, 14, 22–23, 41, 135, 152, 247
titles of Süleyman
  distributor of crowns, 139, 197
  Master of the Auspicious Conjunction (*sahib-kıran*), 135–36, 148, 179, 185, 204, 226, 249
  Renewer (*müceddid*), 36, 136
  Shadow of God on Earth (*zıllullah*), 3*f*, 107, 134, 139, 207
  Solomon of the Age (*Süleyman-ı Zaman*), 39, 223, 268
Trabzon, 41*f*, 44*f*, 49–52, 58*f*, 61, 63, 68*f*, 79, 83, 124, 224
  built environment, 46–47
  commercial importance, 40–41, 48
  ecology, 41–43, 57, 61
  demography, 43–46
  Selim I's governorship, 36, 52, 59–61, 63, 74, 108
  Süleyman's childhood in, 36, 40–48
Transylvania, 140*f*, 144, 196, 201, 206*f*, 207, 214, 266–67, 269

Venice, 11, 13*f*, 95, 109, 121, 137, 140*f*, 159, 163, 181, 191, 196, 198*f*, 206*f*, 233
  anti–Habsburg position of, 144
  diplomacy between Ottomans and, 29, 106–7, 116, 119, 154, 181, 240
  as information brokers for Ottomans, 140, 146, 151–52, 162, 190
  in the Holy League, 196
  military clashes with Ottomans, 29, 195
  peace treaties with Ottomans, 116, 161, 198, 206
  trade, 41, 107, 198

Wallachia, 13*f*, 140*f*, 196–97, 206*f*, 250

Yahya (childhood friend), 48, 52, 70, 179–80, 260–61